Wedding Videography:
Start to Finish

Joanna Silber

COURSE TECHNOLOGY
CENGAGE Learning·

Australia, Brazil, Japan, Korea, Mexico, Singapore, Spain, United Kingdom, United States

COURSE TECHNOLOGY
CENGAGE Learning™

Wedding Videography: Start to Finish
Joanna Silber

**Publisher and General Manager,
Course Technology PTR:**
Stacy L. Hiquet

Associate Director of Marketing:
Sarah Panella

Manager of Editorial Services:
Heather Talbot

Marketing Manager: Jordan Castellani

Acquisitions Editors:
Jen Blaney, Megan Belanger

Project Editor: Kate Shoup

Technical Reviewers: Timothy Bakland
and Jan Ozer

Copy Editor: Kate Shoup

Interior Layout: Jill Flores

Cover Designer: Mike Tanamachi

DVD-ROM Producer: Brandon Penticuff

Indexer: Sharon Shock

Proofreader: Tonya Cupp

For product information and technology assistance, contact us at **Cengage Learning Customer & Sales Support, 1-800-354-9706.**

For permission to use material from this text or product, submit all requests online at **cengage.com/permissions.** Further permissions questions can be e-mailed to **permissionrequest@cengage.com.**

All trademarks are the property of their respective owners.

All images © Cengage Learning unless otherwise noted.

Library of Congress Control Number: 2009941742

ISBN-13: 978-1-4354-5448-4

ISBN-10: 1-4354-5448-0

Course Technology, a part of Cengage Learning
20 Channel Center Street
Boston, MA 02210
USA

Cengage Learning is a leading provider of customized learning solutions with office locations around the globe, including Singapore, the United Kingdom, Australia, Mexico, Brazil, and Japan. Locate your local office at: **international.cengage.com/region.**

Cengage Learning products are represented in Canada by Nelson Education, Ltd. For your lifelong learning solutions, visit **courseptr.com.**

Visit our corporate Web site at **cengage.com.**

Printed in the United States of America
1 2 3 4 5 6 7 12 11 10

Acknowledgments

I owe a warm and heartfelt thank you to all the wedding videographers who kindly shared their experiences with me, including Timothy Bakland, Peter Bruce, Erin Korbylo, Annyce Meiners, Eric and Heather Newland, and Steve Sparks. I feel a kinship with you for all the Saturdays we have spent in the same way—gasping for breath between the ceremony and the reception and snacking on cake of questionable deliciousness late at night—in our different corners of the country. Similarly, I am grateful to all the couples who gave me the right to use their images in this book, including Geof and Jes Eckerlin, Kevin and Olivia Lee, and Matt and Jyovanne Hawk. I appreciate that you not only allowed me to be a part of your special day, you let me share it with the world. Along those same lines, a special and loving thank you to my astoundingly awesome sister Mandy Silber Levitt and her completely delightful husband Dany Levitt, who weren't given much choice in the matter. Dany's brother Ronen Kinori also provided some images, for which I am very thankful.

Overdue and sincere gratitude to Bob Morrow, for first suggesting to me that maybe video editing would be interesting; to Eric and Heather Newland, for hiring me as a wedding video editor when I knew nothing about it; and to Peter Bruce, from whom I gained much of my wedding video experience, an arsenal of off-color jokes, and a lifelong friendship.

Kate Shoup changed my concept of what an editor is, adding tireless organization and near-constant support and kindness to masterful editing. I shudder to think what this project would look like without the immense amount of time and care she put in. Similarly, the efforts of Timothy Bakland and Jan Ozer can't be overstated: I was so lucky to have found them. I am also grateful to Jen Blaney and Megan Belanger for both getting this project off the ground and their steady support throughout.

Thank you, MAD, for providing an incomparable wealth of love and support regardless of whatever I may be doing, and for having a marriage that allows working in the wedding industry to actually make sense.

And finally, a huge thank you to Ben Long, for being my personal tech-support team, life advisor, professional role model, and dear friend. At this point, Ben, I'm nearly all your fault. I'd punch you for that if I weren't so incredibly grateful.

About the Author

Joanna Silber is a freelance video editor, producer, and writer living in San Francisco, CA. She has been in the wedding-videography business for more than 10 years, catering to clients all over the west coast. In addition to wedding videos, Joanna has produced and edited multiple award-winning documentaries, which have screened at film festivals around the world. She teaches video editing at the UC Berkeley Art Studio and at the Bay Area Video Coalition.

Photo Credits

Contents

Introduction

Welcome to *Wedding Videography: Start to Finish*, a resource to help you step confidently into the field of wedding videography. This book is designed to step the novice wedding videographer through the process of starting a wedding-videography business, filming a wedding, editing the wedding footage, and outputting the final product into a format your client can view, with a strong emphasis on the technical aspects of shooting and editing a wedding video. The book also provides tips for streamlining these processes to help you grow and sustain your business. Whether you picked up this book to learn more about a field in which you may be interested or to get some new ideas to help you with work you already do, I hope you find it to be both a practical introduction to the industry and a detailed manual for the job.

Who This Book Is For

Unlike most filmmakers, wedding videographers wear numerous—even dozens of—hats throughout the process of making a single video: business founder, marketer, salesperson, administrator, production coordinator, shooter, grip, sound technician, post-production editor, graphics designer, color corrector, audio engineer, and DVD author. Indeed, there are very few parts of the production process that won't dirty a wedding videographer's hands. Clients expect a well-produced and skillfully edited piece, and they expect you to give it to them!

Most likely, many readers will have some experience in one or two of these production tasks; this book will fill the gaps for those of you who have worked in some part of the production process but need some catch up work in the others. For example, if you are a video editor already, you might not need to read the editing tutorials in Chapters 8 and 9, but will definitely want to check out the shooting lessons in Chapters 5, 6, and 7. *Wedding Videography: Start to Finish* has much to offer even experienced production and post-production professionals. Those of you with experience in soup-to-nuts production work will learn valuable techniques for applying your skills to both the wedding-day shoot and the post-production workflow.

Wedding videography is a unique form of storytelling, and comes with its own set of complications. For one, there is only one opportunity to obtain footage of a wedding; you can't have a first kiss twice. And while some components of each will be similar, every wedding is as different as the personalities involved. Your clients will expect you to capture and showcase all the moments that are most important to them, which can be extremely difficult given the shooting circumstances. At the same time, there are a confusing multitude of options in the post-production phase, which involves crafting a story that captures the flavor of the wedding and the personalities of your clients using footage obtained in a single take. And of course, you must stay current on technology and industry trends, to constantly perform sales and marketing tasks (with almost no repeat customers!), and to handle seasonal work. This book offers insight, tips, and ideas to best manage the nuances of the wedding-videography business from the start-up phase through business development and maintenance.

How This Book Is Organized

Wedding Videography: Start to Finish is arranged chronologically to guide you from the initial business-startup phase to securing and completing your first job to successfully maintaining your business. Depending on your circumstances and experience in the industry, certain chapters may have more relevance to you than others. Following is a detailed list of what you will find in each section and chapter of the book.

Part I: The Proposal

Before you can start your first job, you must take a tremendous number of steps to establish your business, market and sell your product, and acquire the right gear to get the job done. The chapters in this part lead you from having the kernel of a business idea to being ready to take on your first client.

Chapter 1: The World of Wedding Videography

Wedding videography has undergone an immense evolution in the last few decades. This chapter offers insight into what your clients will expect from you and what you can expect out of the job.

Chapter 2: The Business of Weddings

Very few people enter the wedding-videography field so they can experience the joy of business development and maintenance. Nonetheless, routine business tasks are an incredibly important aspect of wedding videography. When you throw the industry nuances into the mix, it becomes especially important to make sure your business has solid grounding and direction. This chapter teaches some basic business startup fundamentals and how they are best applied to this sector of the wedding industry.

Chapter 3: Production Gear

This chapter provides a thorough description of the production gear you will need to get a wedding-videography business up and running, with a detailed discussion of camera selection as well as information on lights, microphones, tripods, and camera bags. Distinctions are made between production essentials and items that might be helpful if budget allows.

Chapter 4: Getting Post-Production Gear

Advances in computer speed, data storage space, and editing software over the last few decades have revolutionized the post-production process. This chapter guides you through selecting the hardware and software you need to create a wedding video, offering information on computer systems, editing software, and post-production peripherals such as monitors and speakers. As with Chapter 3, distinctions are made between essential and desirable equipment.

Part II: The Wedding

Weddings are joyful and often stressful affairs; energy, emotions, and expectations are at high levels. Time passes incredibly quickly as the day's events unfold, offering you one—and only one—opportunity to capture them. The chapters in this part teach you how to anticipate, manage, and roll with the flow of activities while obtaining the best audio and video footage possible.

Chapter 5: The Basics of Wedding Shooting

Before heading out to your first wedding shoot, you must understand some production basics. This chapter aims to teach a basic vocabulary and skill set related to the shots, moves, angles, and manual controls that you will find useful on the day of the wedding. Discussion of shots you will likely need to obtain is included.

Chapter 6: Pre-Production

A small oversight when preparing for the shoot—not enough batteries for the microphones or tape for the camera—can torpedo an otherwise successful job. This chapter highlights all the considerations and preparations you need to take to ensure a smooth and trouble-free shoot. You want to capture the wedding day drama—not create it!

Chapter 7: The Big Day

The culmination of months of preparation on the part of the couple, the wedding day is fraught with joy, tension, excitement, drama, and nerves—and it's your job to capture it all. This chapter takes you step by step through a typical wedding day, offering shooting advice for each event. Included are instructions for conducting two-camera shoots, handling difficult lighting situations, obtaining audio, and obtaining good interviews. It also lists special shots to consider for each event and information on vendor etiquette.

Part III: The Honeymoon

When the stress of the wedding day is over, the calm, methodical, and meticulous post-production process begins. These chapters guide you from bringing your footage onto the computer to outputting it for the client, with all the editing, effects, compositing, and DVD-authoring steps in between.

Chapter 8: Basic Editing

A rough cut is the first draft of a video—an unrefined version of the wedding story you are telling. This chapter provides a detailed description of building a rough cut, starting with moving your footage from the camera to the computer. Coverage of editing styles and techniques, music choices, and troubleshooting bad footage is included in this guide to the first stages of the editing process.

Chapter 9: Advanced Editing

With a rough cut in place, it's time to refine your piece to the point where you can confidently showcase it to your clients. This chapter teaches you advanced editing techniques including multi-camera editing, filters, compositing, animation, and sound editing, to transform your project from a basic story into a professionally produced piece.

Chapter 10: Output and Delivery

With the video edited and refined, it's time to put it in a usable format for your clients. Clients may want their video in the form of an authored DVD, posted online, or compressed for various media players. This chapter guides you through outputting the piece to different formats, with additional discussion of the formats and media you should use to archive your pieces for your own purposes.

Part IV: The Marriage

With a wedding video behind you, you're ready to tackle the tasks of developing your business (both from a creative and a financial standpoint) and maintaining it so that your energy and investments will continue to pay off over time. These chapters offer ideas to create new products and ensure that you can consistently produce, market, and sell your work.

Chapter 11: Add-On Business Ideas

Stocked with gear and expertise, you are well positioned to serve your wedding clientele. You aren't limited to doing traditional wedding videos, however; try thinking a little bit bigger and offering a wider variety of services. This will keep you on your creative toes, generate more income, and help you stand out in the marketplace as a superior vendor. This chapter offers ideas and specific instructions for creating additional products, such as photo montages, same-day edits, engagement videos, concept videos, and personalized Web pages.

Chapter 12: Maintaining Your Business

No business can survive without a bit of love and care. This chapter gives specific instructions for maintaining your business by caring for your equipment, pleasing your clients, and by monitoring your own place in an evolving industry.

DVD and Tutorials

Most chapters in this book feature tutorials for you to complete to practice the material discussed in the text. Several of these tutorials involve editing and outputting wedding video using footage and program files provided on the DVD that accompanies. To complete these tutorials, you must have a copy of Adobe Premiere Pro; instructions for obtaining a free trial copy via download are contained in the Chapter 4 tutorial.

Once the program is installed, you must copy each of the chapter tutorial folders (which contain all the project media) from the DVD to your hard drive. This will require approximately 2GB of space. It is recommended that you copy the files to the Premiere Pro default location: My Documents > Adobe > Premiere Pro > 4.0 (Windows) and Documents > Adobe > Premiere Pro > 4.0 (Mac).

It is possible that Premiere Pro will experience difficulties finding your media files when you open a project. If Premiere Pro displays an error message indicating that it can't find a file in the project, please navigate to the same folder as the project file, which contains all the content as well. Once you link to the first file, Premiere Pro should find all the others.

DVD-ROM Downloads

If you purchased an ebook version of this book, and the book had a companion DVD-ROM, we will mail you a copy of the disc. Please send ptrsupplements@cengage.com the title of the book, the ISBN, your name, address, and phone number. Thank you.

Part I

The Proposal

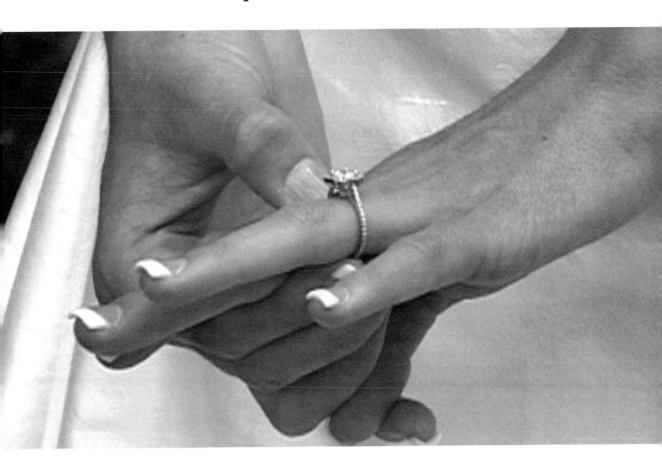

Chapter 1
The World of Wedding Videography

In this chapter:

- ▶ What does a wedding videographer do?
- ▶ Evolution of the wedding video
- ▶ Styles of wedding videos
- ▶ What makes wedding videography unique?

What Does a Wedding Videographer Do?

It is 2 p.m. You have been at work since eight o'clock this morning, and you have eight hours to go. Your feet hurt from standing in dress shoes, your shoulder hurts from carrying a tripod, and your head hurts because the bride is crying to her mother about last-minute changes to the seating arrangement. You aren't sure if you should record these stressful moments or retreat to another room. You secretly wish the bride was wearing a microphone, but you're pretty sure it would be inappropriate to ask her to put one on at this moment. Complicating things for you is the fact that the bride specified that she wanted lots of footage of the groom getting ready, but that appears to consist of him watching TV in his hotel room. Should you tell him to get dressed? Also, the ceremony starts in an hour, and you have yet to be allowed into the chapel to assess lighting; you only have one chance to get the vows, and you have to make sure you'll be standing in the right place when they happen. And of course, the florist forgot the boutonnieres, and is driving 60 miles round trip to her shop to pick them up—hopefully by show time. Stress levels are higher than anything you've ever experienced…since last Saturday's wedding, that is. You are, in short, having a typical day on the job as a wedding videographer.

The fact is, wedding videography is exhausting—with long hours, heavy gear, high stress—but it is also incredibly rewarding. As a wedding videographer, you will be regularly surrounded by people joyfully celebrating. Besides, wedding videographers thrive in a somewhat stressful environment and know that at least a small portion of the job is to advise, calm, and help the couple through the day's events. After all, the videographer has probably been "backstage" at more weddings than the bride and groom. Wedding videographers get the satisfaction of knowing that their tools, gear, and creative vision will create a tribute to the couple and their important event. A wedding videographer's artistry will shape how the bride and groom perceive and remember the day itself.

There is an immense amount of colorful material to work with in building a wedding video: leading characters in love, a supporting cast of friends and family, and a few settings almost guaranteed to be beautiful (albeit often poorly lit and with bad audio). There are also some dramatic moments already built into the script: the vows, the first kiss, the first dance, the cake cutting. Even the most jaded wedding vendor can get teary during these moments.

Our culture is somewhat defined by lifecycle events such as weddings. A wedding videographer gets to see all the humanity and emotion that goes into these milestone occasions. A good videographer treats this privilege respectfully and gratefully, as witness to the very intimate, raw, and emotional moments of their clients' lives. In the story's re-telling, the videographer re-lives this honor, and can both edit and enhance those moments to tell the exact story the clients want.

The Evolution of the Wedding Video

While shooting video of weddings is common practice today, it's a relatively new phenomenon—with today's final product differing greatly from its ancestors:

▶ In 1979, the extremely rare wedding video is a few minutes of super 8 film recorded by a determined family member or guest toting his or her hobbyist camera. The exposed film strip has to be sent out to a processor—at no small cost—and, once processed, must be viewed with a super 8 projector, most likely at the home of the same hobbyist shooter. The film itself has a grainy, jagged feel to it, with lots of dirt and vivid colors. It is possible, but very unlikely, that the film has any sound or editing.

▶ In 1989, a wedding video is almost two hours long. It's shot on a Sony camera attached to a bulky recorder with a cable. An assistant helped carry a huge light throughout the ceremony and reception, but it didn't do much to improve the poor color saturation and fuzzy shots. Nor did it ingratiate itself to the wedding guests, who danced around the production team or were scared back to the dessert table. Post-production consists of titles being added to the beginning and end and clumsily chopping the part where Aunt Gloria said the wrong name during the toast. Because of generation loss, the audio on the VHS tape that Grandma gets has degraded from the already-poor mono recording from a bad microphone to practically unintelligible noise.

▶ In 1999, a wedding video is about 45 minutes long. It's shot on a digital video camera with small, attached lights and lavaliere microphones, and is controlled by one videographer, who mingles seamlessly among guests, lowering the camera when it is inappropriate to be shooting. Though nearly five hours of mini DV footage is shot, the final product has only the best bits, cut to music chosen by the couple and delivered on a DVD that can be duplicated inexpensively and without generational loss.

▶ In 2009, a wedding video is an authored DVD with an hour plus full-length version as well as a stylistically cut highlights version. Depending on the couple's taste and budget, the video can include a time-lapse sequence showing the reception being set up, a series of interviews woven throughout the piece, and effects such as a retro super 8 look on the romantic shots and campy transitions between the groomsmen's toasts. The wedding guests are so busy shooting their own video clips on their phone cameras, they barely notice the videographer and her streamlined equipment. The final product is posted online, delivered as a DVD, and separately compressed for YouTube and the iPhone.

Recent advances in both camera technology and editing software have likewise advanced bridal couples' expectations to include an unobtrusive videographer, multiple camera coverage, heavy editing and special effects to create a far more finished and interesting final piece, all at a much lower price. This, in turn, has allowed—even demanded—the growth of the wedding-video industry. Dramatic price drops in semi-professional and consumer video equipment and post-production hardware and software have made wedding videography a line item that can now fit relatively easily into the average American wedding budget.

Almost all weddings include a professional photographer. But historically, as well as being prohibited by cost, having a videographer—not to mention both the photographer's and the videographer's respective assistants and equipment—often felt invasive. Having personal moments with an entourage and their bulky gear was understandably intimidating to many couples. But just as camera prices shrank, so too did external lights and camera size—meaning that having a crew of documentarians is significantly less burdensome than it used to be.

Indeed, although it certainly depends on the style of coverage a couple chooses, videography is increasingly a one-person operation on the day of the event. The camera operator carries, sets up, and handles his or her own gear. This is significantly less of a disturbance to the couple, and also less obtrusive to their guests—in turn increasing the popularity of wedding videos among those turned off by the perceived paparazzi effect. That being said, in today's market, there are good reasons to have two videographers available for certain types of wedding videos. For one, shooting with two cameras allows for editing between view points. So, for example, you might have one camera shooting wide and one shooting close-up for the ceremony or for the first dance, or one camera could be getting the bride while the other covers the groom during the preparations. Of course, using tripods, one camera operator might run two cameras during the ceremony or reception. But camera equipment being so much smaller and lighter means that the presence of two camera operators is significantly less invasive than it used to be.

Because digital storage is relatively inexpensive, it is easy to shoot hours and hours of footage with the intention of using only the best bits. A bride knows that hiring a videographer for eight hours doesn't mean forcing her friends to sit through an endlessly boring single take or squirming through the embarrassing shots where she screamed about her hair not being perfect. Unlike with film, the cost of obtaining more video footage is low, blank media is inexpensive, and there is less processing required. So once the videographer is on site, getting more footage is easy and cheap—leading to a better final product.

Advances in camera technology have also changed client expectations. Today's modern couple is inundated with video. Video is expected on news, entertainment, and personal Web sites; it gets carried around in handheld devices; and, most importantly, people expect more and more of their own lives to be documented on video. At the time of this writing, the average age of a bride in America was 25. Digital video was introduced at a consumer and semi-professional level in 1995. When you do the math, you'll realize that it's quite likely that a bride has been recorded on digital video by her parents since she was at least 10 years old—and probably longer.

Furthermore, nonlinear editing software, such as Adobe Premiere, allows the videographer to pile on tracks and tracks of video, cutting, slicing, and dissolving with greater ease and less cost than in the past. These advances have changed what a couple can expect out of a wedding video. Instead of an expensive, boring, single-take shot of their vows, a couple can get a stylishly edited piece that reflects their aesthetics using captions, split screens, cutaways, effects, and the music of their choice. Consequently, it is not at all surprising that wedding videography is becoming increasingly popular. Indeed, the Wedding and Event Video Association says that after their wedding, nearly 80 percent of brides regard a professional videographer as one of the top ten services. Yet, only about 20 percent of married couples obtain professional videos of their wedding. There is clearly enormous space for expansion in a marketplace getting more and more accustomed to video for all types of documentation. It is anticipated that this number will continue to increase, so now is a pretty good time to get your gear and skills ready to take advantage of this growing market!

Styles of Wedding Videos

There are numerous ways to tell a wedding story. Listed here are a few wedding-video styles. This list is not fixed; any piece may be a hybrid of some of these styles, or something completely different. However, as a beginner, this list offers you a useful way to consider your final product. If you know what style wedding video you want to create and deliver, you can be sure to budget for the right gear and market yourself correctly.

- ▶ **Documentary:** A *documentary-style* piece provides a straightforward rendition of the wedding event, typically showing the action of the day in chronological order. While any given section, such as the ceremony or the speeches, might be heavily edited, it is unlikely that any section will utilize heavy visual effects or be intercut with other scenes from the day. Even in places where natural audio isn't used, the music in a journalistic piece will be similar to the music of the actual event.

- ▶ **Cinematic:** A *cinematic-style* piece is heavily dramatized to create a certain mood. The dramatization is inherent in the shooting and enhanced through editing, effects, and graphics work. It may include slow, romantic sequences; quick-paced jump cuts to reflect the action and adventure of the day; or a vintage-style section complete with grainy effects and super 8. In any given theme, a cinematic piece will trade some integrity of the actual event storyline for the fun and visual benefit of a carefully compiled, stylized video.

- ▶ **Storytelling:** Somewhat similar to a documentary-style video, a *storytelling* video will use a fairly straightforward approach but will incorporate a lot of interviews and dialogue (not necessarily recorded on the wedding day itself) in order to both build and push the events of the storyline.

- ▶ **Highlights:** A *highlights* video will be very short and generally contains selections of the best shots from each portion of the day. It can be edited to a song—perhaps the music used for the couple's first dance—or creatively edited to the audio of the ceremony vows or speeches. Often, a couple will choose to order a highlights video as well as a longer one.

▶ **Shoot only:** Occasionally, a client will request a *shoot-only* video. In this case, the videographer provides the events captured on video for the bride and groom to either watch unedited or to cut themselves. It that situation, it's best to get a sense of what the client will be doing with the footage to best determine what types of shots to emphasize: wide angle, close-up details, Dutch angles, pans, and so on. Often, a straightforward, clean approach that encompasses as much of the action as possible is best.

Any one video or videographer's style may encompass several of the categories listed here. For example, a journalistic piece might have a retro stylized opening and a romantic sequence of shots of the couple. A highlights piece might include a fast-paced, high-energy montage or a dreamy, sepia-toned vintage section with lots of the interview audio more frequently found in a storytelling piece.

It's a good idea to be flexible enough in your storytelling to appeal to some different tastes, but also to make sure you have a defined style of your own. Potential clients may or may not like your work, but if you are clear about the things you can do (and you do those things well), you will ensure your clients' happiness.

As further discussed in Chapter 2, "The Business of Weddings," word of mouth and recommendations are incredibly important in the wedding industry. Therefore, it's better to not accept some clients if you are unlikely to please them with your work. The clients for whom your style works will reward you with recommendations and future business. That isn't to say that it's your way or the highway. Often, you need to meet your clients halfway. A talented and experienced wedding videographer will be able to combine his or her clients' input and preferences with his or her own technique and vision to deliver a piece the client will love. However, it is important to remember that smiling and nodding yes to a potential client if you don't have the gear, skills, or interest to cater to his or her preferences is a formula certain to undermine your success.

Other Video Products

Although this book mainly discusses wedding videos, it is important to realize that there is a much larger range of commonly purchased products that a savvy and capable wedding videographer can provide. Usually, these products will be in conjunction with the main service that the couple purchases from you: the video of the wedding day itself. Occasionally, however, these additional services may be standalone items. Not only are these additional products an excellent way for you to increase your revenue, but they allow you to get to know the couple better, which in turn, provides more depth, context, and footage for the main video production. Here are some examples of additional services a wedding videographer can provide:

▶ **Photo montage:** A *photo montage* is a series of photos set to music. Montages are often shown at the rehearsal dinner and/or the wedding reception, and typically include pictures of the couple before they met and during their courtship. A montage may also include pictures of family and friends and can contribute significantly to the spirit of the event.

▶ **Engagement video:** An *engagement video* depicts the "story behind the story." It may contain footage of the bride and groom explaining how they met and show scenes of them together, which may be shot for the occasion or pulled from existing footage. It can make a very funny piece to interview the couple separately about their courtship and relationship, and craftily edit their stories together, potentially pulling in other footage from family and friends. Like a montage, an engagement video is a warm and welcoming piece of entertainment for guests at the rehearsal dinner or reception, as well as something to enjoy forever.

▶ **Same-day edit:** If time and/or manpower allow, a *same-day edit* can be a wonderful addition to the reception to show footage from the morning preparations and ceremony. This involves a very basic edit, usually set to a predetermined song, to enable guests to witness what may be some funny, intimate, touching, and dramatic moments of the day.

▶ **Concept video:** A *concept video* is a piece that is created by the videographer and the couple involving footage shot before the wedding itself. The video will tell a story about the couple, but is likely fictionalized, highly stylized, or both. It may be shot in the style of their favorite movie, or a narrative may be built into the story, such as a mystery or news piece. This video is for couples who want to have a fun and creative experience together building the piece, as well as the final product.

▶ **Bridal video:** A *bridal video* is a piece highlighting the bride in her wedding dress, ready for the event. It may be shot before or on the day of the wedding and it is used to capture her beauty on the day. This video is most often an add-on service that makes a wonderful gift for the groom, parents, and grandparents.

More information about these services is provided in Chapter 11, "Add-On Business Ideas."

Why Is Wedding Videography Unique?

Wedding videography differs from other types of filmmaking and involves a distinct set of challenges and rewards. Challenges include the following:

▶ Typically, the wedding videographer plays every role in the production and post-production cycle: shooter, sound engineer, grip, editor, audio mixer, colorist, and motion graphic artist. Each one of these jobs is a specialty that can require years of experience on its own before any level of expertise is reached. Indeed, in a Hollywood setting, sound engineers and graphic artists are rarely if ever in the same room together because their skills are so refined and specialized. Nevertheless, the wedding videographer must possess the full range of skills.

▶ The wedding videographer must coordinate the expectations of the couple with the realities of the shooting day. Having put excessive hours and dollars into planning their event, it is only natural that the couple wants everything to be perfect. That translates to wanting a gorgeously produced video that looks like a staged film with choreographed shots, mood lighting, and a storyline. The fact is, although couples may want a feature film, the video must be shot documentary style: single-take shooting in loud settings, under uncontrollable light, with rapid scene changes—and no chance to redo shots. (The couple will not recite their vows twice or have a second first kiss!) With only one chance to capture most of the day's events, the videographer must constantly anticipate the next piece of action while calculating optimal light and angles for the current shots. He or she must constantly pay attention to sound quality and background noise, and must have the ideas and capacity to quickly stage shots in unfamiliar locations on the fly. Finally, to give a professional and feature-film look to poor-quality shots, a videographer must be well versed in editing and effects techniques.

► There are very few changes to the storyline in a wedding video: Boy meets girl, they fall in love, they commit to each other for life, they throw a party. A big creative exercise in wedding videography is cooking up new recipes with similar ingredients. As you'll find in Chapter 2, there are ways to approach your work that will help you think about each couple—and their event—with a fresh perspective and fresh eyes. It is important to get to know your clients, which helps you give each couple the creativity they deserve for the event they are building.

All that being said, wedding videography also offers immense rewards:

► Savvy and talented wedding videographers can do very well financially.

► A good videographer can command his or her own schedule, achieving both independence and time for other endeavors.

► Wedding work is, by definition, seasonal work, which leaves winter for other pursuits.

► There is endless room for creativity in videography; the newer and fresher the video style, the more in demand a videographer will be.

► Although the greater meaning of weddings can occasionally be lost due to stress and nerves, ultimately, weddings are celebrations of life and love. They are, for the most part, an uplifting and joyful work setting.

► Wedding videography can be quite glamorous at moments; videographers constantly find themselves in chic hotels, eating gorgeously catered food and surrounded by beautifully coiffed and fabulously dressed wedding participants. And it's not unheard of for high-end wedding videographers to get flown to exotic vacation destinations to shoot weddings for their clients or to go to conventions in Las Vegas, Orlando, and other locations.

A Day in the Life

As rewarding as being a wedding videographer can be, it would be misleading to call wedding videography a luxurious or glamorous job, even for the best-known and highest-paid vendors. It is long and tiring work. A shoot day can easily last 12 hours (before travel time), which feels even longer while wearing dress shoes. Wedding videography requires constant attention, physical labor, technical skills, and the ability to charm, comfort, and coax your subjects. Most importantly, wedding videographers must be able to think quickly and under pressure.

Those skills are just for the wedding shoot itself! A whole different skill set is involved in post-production, running a business, and gaining clientele. So before you trade in all your chips for the high energy, exciting, and often very lucrative wedding world, make sure you have a clear understanding of just how much work is involved. Here's a glimpse of the work involved on the days leading up to, during, and after a wedding.

The Day Before

The day before the event, it is imperative that everything is in place to have the smoothest wedding possible. As further detailed in Chapter 2, you will have done quite a bit of work before you even show up at the bridal dressing room to start shooting. At this point, you have had at least one—maybe several—meetings, signed a contract, and have a clear understanding of the couple's expectations for the final product both in terms of style and delivery format. Perhaps you have even put together a photo-montage video for their rehearsal dinner. And hopefully, you have communicated with some of the other vendors involved and have a written timeline of tomorrow's events.

So really, what is left to do? Well, a lot, actually. A more thorough discussion and checklist can be found in Chapter 6, "Pre-Production," but the basics of pre-production include the following:

▶ Detailed driving (or other transportation) directions to and between every location you are supposed to be

▶ A gear bag full of charged batteries and enough blank media

▶ A list of shots you need to obtain

▶ A list of contact information so you know who to find should things go wrong

Plan what to wear and pack some snack food and drinking water. You have a long day tomorrow!

The Day Of

Although every wedding has some of the same components, each one is as different as the brides and grooms involved. With your expert guidance, your clients should have outlined exactly where you need to be and which shots are most important to them. (See Chapter 6 for more information about this.) Did they specify that they wanted footage of Aunt Edna? Their first dance? The vows? The bride removing her garter belt? Make sure you have that list easily accessible so you don't miss anything. Furthermore, by this point, you should know what style video they want—as well as the styles at which you excel—so when you arrive at the first location, you should already be assessing the scene to create shots that will open the piece in the style you are looking to create. Finally, make sure you have some understanding of the setup and potential restrictions in the location(s) at which you will be shooting.

Speaking of that first location: What is it? Depending on how long you were hired to shoot and what your previously delineated responsibilities are (see Chapter 2), you may be participating in the wedding events from morning until the wee hours. Lots of brides want coverage of getting ready: the hairstyling, the make-up application, and the all-important moment when the dress is zipped up, which officially turns your client into a bride. This is a great time to capture details—her shoes waiting in the box, make-up all over the counter, close-ups of her hair and jewelry. It is likely that you will also have some responsibility to shoot the groom getting ready; this is often an opportunity to stage fun shots if time and moods allow. If the bride and groom will see each other before the ceremony, stage the meeting yourself (or in conjunction with the photographer) to best capture the moment he first sees her in white. Other shots that might occur before the ceremony even begins are shots of the bride with her bridesmaids and the groom with his groomsmen as well as family shots. See Chapter 5, "The Basics of Wedding Shooting" for lists of pre-ceremony shot ideas.

Because wedding are famous for the mishaps that occur (the bride forgets her shoes, the top tier falls off the cake), as a professional vendor, you must make sure you are prepared to record those moments—not cause them.

It is likely that by the time you reach the location of the ceremony, you will have been shooting for at least three or four hours, lugged your equipment to several locations, and made light adjustments based on the changes from morning to midday sun. Indeed, you might have already re-applied deodorant or sunscreen a few times. You hopefully have a good sense of the couple by now and may even have figured out who in the bridal party will be most likely to help you out during the day.

You should arrive at the ceremony location before the bride and groom to scope out the best angles. If you haven't already, use this time to talk to the officiant or the venue manager to discuss any shooting restrictions and coordinate with the photographer about his or her plan for the ceremony. It is likely that he or she will be moving a lot more than you are, and you want to make sure to keep the photographer out of your shot. This is also when you can gather some detail shots of the bouquets, the programs, and the guests arriving and place lavaliere microphones on the appropriate parties before standing by for the ceremony itself. There are lots more instructions, tips, and ideas for how to best shoot the ceremony in Chapter 7, "The Big Day."

The ceremony begins. Thankfully, you get good audio of the vows, some close-ups of the ring exchange, and a well-framed shot of the first kiss. The photographer walks into your shot of the candle-lighting ceremony, but that should be pretty easy to fix in post-production, so you are feeling good. You can't relax when the ceremony is over, though. Typically, the ceremony moves right into a picture session. Although it's traditionally the photographer's job to call the order of events here, you can't afford to tune out. If the photographer can't handle the crowd, you must step up. Furthermore, you must collect all these shots and then collect your gear to escort the couple to the reception venue.

It's 4:30 p.m. You have been awake since 7 a.m., on the road since 8 a.m., and lugging your gear and shooting since 9 a.m. Hopefully, you remembered to eat a sandwich, and somewhere in your bag is an energy bar. Because weddings are almost always in the hot sun, don't forget to drink water. Also: remember to use the bathroom before the ceremony starts; there are no time-outs once the processional begins!

Cocktails begin as you and the photographer shoot some romantic scenes with the couple. All of you rush to the cocktail hour so the bride and groom can have a glass of champagne and finally greet their guests. You furiously shoot the patio scenes of them mingling with drinks and hors d'oeuvres. With a few minutes to spare, you rush into the reception room to get some shots of the room and table settings before the guests come in. Guests filter in from the cocktail patio, and you capture them finding their seats and opening the party favor next to their place card. Having secured an audio feed from the band leader, and at his signal, you carefully place yourself and wait to shoot the couple's big entrance.

The bandleader announces the bride and groom's entrance. Despite your earlier location scouting, guests interfere with your shot and you don't regain focus on the couple until the welcome speech is halfway over. You will have to do something about that in post-production. That one won't be as easy as the ceremony glitch, and you grit your teeth to think of some shots you could get that might reasonably cover the error. (See Chapter 7, "The Big Day," and Chapter 8, "Basic Editing," for ideas.) Then, blissfully, dinner. You get a short break and a hot meal, but you must be on your toes again immediately after—there are speeches, the first dance, the father-daughter dance, open dancing, the bouquet toss, the removal of the garter, and the cake-cutting before your night is over. Put new media in the camera and get ready.

Table 1.1 shows a sample schedule for a wedding shoot.

TABLE 1.1 SAMPLE SCHEDULE FOR A WEDDING SHOOT

8:00 a.m.	Load gear into car and drive to first location
9:00 a.m.–11:00 a.m.	Exteriors, bride getting hair and makeup done with mom and bridesmaids (hotel room)
11:00 a.m.–12:00 p.m.	Groom and groomsmen preparing (hotel room)
12:00 p.m.–12:30 p.m.	Bride putting on dress
12:30 p.m.–1:00 p.m.	Bride with her family, bridesmaids (hotel courtyard)
1:00 p.m.–2:00 p.m.	Bride and groom see each other, couple shots, family shots (hotel lobby, hotel courtyard)
2:00 p.m.–2:30 p.m.	Drive to ceremony location (church)
2:30 p.m.–3:30 p.m.	Establishing shots, talk to coordinator, arrange audio, bride arriving in limousine
3:30 p.m.–4:30 p.m.	Ceremony
4:30 p.m.–5:00 p.m.	Formal pictures (church, outside church)
5:00 p.m.–5:30 p.m.	Drive to reception site (hotel)
5:30 p.m.–6:00 p.m.	Pictures with couple, bridal party (hotel)
6:00 p.m.–6:30 p.m.	End of cocktail hour, dining-room setup
6:30 p.m.–7:00 p.m.	Guests enter dining room, bride and groom entrance
7:00 p.m.–7:15 p.m.	Welcome speech, father-of-the-bride speech
7:15 p.m.–9:00 p.m.	Dinner, toasts
9:00 p.m.–11:00 p.m.	Cake-cutting, first dance, father-daughter dance, open dancing, bouquet toss, garter toss
11:00 p.m.	End of event

The Days After

The couple has given you their music requests and you get to work editing their wedding video. Your contract gives you four months, but because you are just starting the season, you want to get this one done quickly. There will be a post-production backlog soon enough. Luckily, you got almost all the footage you needed. However, as well as missing part of the couple's introduction at the reception, the audio is terrible at the reception and lots of the dancing shots are poorly lit.

After consulting the order form that the couple signed, you start piecing together a rough cut of their video. They requested a documentary-style video, so you are paying close attention to the audio as you go, collecting funny comments made by members of the wedding party to use throughout the piece. You err on the side of too long; more editing will be done as you refine the rough cut.

You eventually get the final piece down to about an hour, following the couple's instructions to leave the speeches and the vows intact. You use all the music they provided for you and add a few songs from your library that match their taste for the dancing sections. You add some effects to clean up the look of the dancing footage—though not many, given the style of video they chose. You design some graphic titles that employ the fonts and style of their wedding invitations and other collateral from the event. From your finished video, you cut a much shorter highlights piece that you upload to your Web site and compress for the bride to put on her iPhone. You put some DVDs in the mail, back up your hard drive, and archive the wedding video appropriately. Now all there is to do is start packing your gear bag for the wedding tomorrow!

Summary

Wedding videography is both hard work and very exciting. Before you move forward, make sure you have an understanding of the following things:

▶ The field of wedding videography is growing and changing rapidly. Dive in and don't stop swimming!

▶ Look at and play with lots of video styles. There are tons out there and more to be defined.

▶ Think about the schedule tradeoffs involved in wedding videography—the fact that it's weekend and seasonal work—in terms of how they will affect your own lifestyle.

▶ Wedding videography is much faster-paced than other fields of filmmaking. Get ready for run-and-gun shooting and fast turnover of editing.

▶ Prepare yourself for joyful, grateful clients. It's very rewarding!

Next Up

Now that you have a thorough overview of the many facets of a wedding videographer's job, it's time to look at each piece in greater detail. Before we can get to the exciting parts of the shoot and the edit, though, it's important to establish your business within the wedding industry. The next chapter provides some guidelines for thinking about your business from an organizational perspective.

Chapter 1 Tutorial: Questions to Consider about Your Potential New Career

Wedding videography can be joyful, exhausting, dramatic, dull, frustrating, exhilarating, and painful—all on the same day. Indeed, it is a very unusual field of work insofar as the tasks and skills required are quite diverse—which, frankly, most videographers regard as a huge benefit to this line of work.

As you consider launching into a new career, spend a few minutes determining whether this is a reasonable fit for your personality, lifestyle, and career interests by considering your answers to the following questions. You need not answer yes to every question to succeed as a wedding videographer; no doubt, some parts of such a diverse job will be a more natural fit than others. This list of questions, as well as what you learned in this chapter, should help you assess your potential strengths as a wedding videographer and what aspects of the job you might find particularly challenging. This analysis will help with your business planning, enabling you to best market to your strong points and budget resources (financial and emotional) for your weaker ones.

Personality

▶ Do you enjoy different types of people? Can you get along with people you may not like?

▶ Can you smile in the face of frustration?

▶ Can you remain calm in a panic?

▶ Do you have a can-do, service-oriented attitude?

Consider: Often, for wedding vendors, the customer must be right. This can be especially frustrating for those technicians and artists who possess great expertise but must defer to a client for business reasons.

▶ Is problem solving a fun challenge?

Lifestyle

▶ Are you willing to work weekends and nights?

▶ What kind of impact will seasonal work have on your lifestyle?

Consider: If wedding videography is your primary income, you will have several months of the year with very few—if any—bookings. On the flip side, if wedding videography is your second job, you will have several months of the year without a moment to yourself.

▶ Can you take on tiring physical work, as required by the production portion of the job?

▶ Can you work long hours into the night, as both the production and post-production portions of the job require?

Career and Personality Interests

▶ Do you enjoy tinkering with gear, hardware, and technical things?

▶ Are you a good storyteller?

▶ Do you have an eye for detail?

▶ Are you motivated and disciplined enough to work for yourself?

▶ Are technology trends interesting to you?

▶ Are you responsible with time schedules, dates, and calendar commitments?

▶ Do you enjoy networking and socializing *and* being alone?

Consider: A wedding videographer's job is to a) actively sell himself or herself through marketing and networking; b) meet, mingle with, and shoot near strangers; c) spend protracted amounts of time alone in front of a computer. A strange combination indeed!

Chapter 2
The Business of Weddings

In this chapter:

▶ Planning is everything
▶ Managing client relations
▶ Marketing yourself
▶ Keeping it all compliant

Nearly by definition, a wedding videographer takes some joy from the excitement, beauty, and tradition surrounding the lifecycle event in which he or she is participating. For some vendors, the job satisfaction in wedding videography lies in the celebration itself; for others, it comes from finding the perfect way to capture dramatic and emotional moments on camera or creatively rendering these moments through artistic editing and effects. In my decade of wedding videography, however, I have yet to meet the wedding vendor who got started through a love of accounting. But as with any service business, operational logistics such as budgeting, accounting, marketing and bidding jobs are integral to success.

Your arrival in the industry might change how you regard your business and your goals. For example, suppose you had a great time shooting your cousin's wedding for free and realized that becoming a weekend wedding videographer would be an excellent way to make some additional income. In that case, you'll need to learn quite a bit about both the production and post-production processes in order to remain competitive in the field. Or perhaps, having graduated from film school, you've decided to start a collective with some colleagues with the intent of supporting several videographers full-time. While your education will undoubtedly serve you in the product you are creating, managing a wedding timeline—not to mention wedding clientele—may be quite different from managing the projects with which you are familiar. Most likely, you are testing the waters somewhere in between, with some experience, small immediate goals, and larger long term ones.

Regardless of how you fell into this line of work and which aspects of it you hope to focus on, it's important, as with any business, to consider and plan the ways in which you want your business to grow. As you get further along in your business development, you must revisit your goals, revising them and extending them to match the realities you face and the vision you are striving for.

Planning Is Everything

Before you can spin off into exciting decisions such as what your Web site will look like and which magazines to advertise in (and I admit, these are both fun and important decisions), you must delve into the more basic territory of defining your videography business and your business goals. This fundamental aspect of planning your business will factor into all your other decisions, such as what types of gear to buy, how much time you will spend with your clients, the final product you will provide, and your price point.

Perhaps you are shaking your head, thinking "I want to do only a few weddings per year for some additional income. I don't need to bother with a business plan!" On the contrary, a business plan is important regardless of the projected scale of your company.

Any business owner will tell you that having a business plan is critical for building and developing your company. It is a map to guide your route into self-employment, defining the goals, or destination, of your adventure. Along the way, it will help you consider things such as taxes, accounting, and growth rates. Furthermore, a business plan will help you assess the market, your competition, the clients your style will appeal to, and the services you can and must provide. You probably won't stick to your business plan precisely, but having it in place will help you analyze the ramifications of your decision making: the jobs you choose to take (or not), the money you spend on marketing and equipment upgrades, the employees you hire or contract with.

Ideally, a map to your destination prevents you from getting lost in the first place rather than bailing you out once you are turned around. Similarly, it is important to write a business plan that addresses your goals and the associated logistics immediately and directly. That's because how you strategize and organize your business will guide your start-up decisions, such as what equipment to buy and, later, when to hire additional employees or contractors. Avoid getting lost by spending some time early on defining your business goals and the best route to achieve them as well as putting working systems in place for when your goals are realized.

A basic business plan should contain at least the following elements:

► **A description of your business.** Who are you? What services do you plan to offer? What is your mission statement?

► **Market analysis.** Who else offers similar services? How are you different? What is the market demand for your services? How much of that market can you capture?

► **Marketing plan.** What methods will you use to attract customers?

► **Operational plan.** How will you successfully complete the work?

► **Financial plan.** What are your costs, direct and indirect? Which of these costs are capital investment and which are ongoing? How much will you charge for your services? At what point will your costs and revenues allow you to break even and run profitably?

Samples of business plans can be found in books and online, and the Small Business Administration offers free courses in developing them. The following considerations will help you flesh out the details of your plan.

Consider Your Time Frame

In order to write a plan, it is important to know both what your business goals are and on what time frame you hope to achieve them. Most wedding videographers begin their business slowly, either assisting more established videographers or working for free or reduced rates for friends or couples who would otherwise not have a wedding video in their budget. This allows the inexperienced wedding videographer to gain practice in lower-pressure circumstances. For videographers entering the field with little shooting experience, this practice is invaluable. Even for established filmmakers who know their equipment well, the transition to wedding videography can be rocky, with a high learning curve with respect to dealing with the tricky and changing lighting, sound management, and recording fast-paced events in a single take. The flow of a wedding takes some time to master, even for a seasoned camera operator.

Starting Slowly

By building wedding-videography skills slowly, ideally with the assistance of a more experienced wedding videographer, you have the opportunity to try some equipment before making your own purchases as well as develop shooting techniques and editing styles. In addition, you have the chance to put together a demo video. As you'll learn later in this chapter, a demo video is key to obtaining clients. (More experienced filmmakers may be prone to dive right in but should still be aware of the differences between wedding and other videography.)

If you have never shot a wedding video, call a wedding videographer and ask if you can help him or her for free in order to learn about the pacing of the day. He or she will likely be thrilled to have someone help schlep their equipment around, and you will receive an invaluable day of training. Depending of the level of competition in your market, you might want to select a videographer with whom, for geographic (or other) reasons, you will not be directly competing. Another method to gain experience is to call a local wedding planner and offer a free video to a couple who would not otherwise purchase one. This will give you some low-pressure experience working on your own, as well as a potentially valuable business relationship with the wedding planner.

Aside from enabling you to acquire experience, another reason to start your business slowly is to allow yourself to build some start-up capital. By using initial jobs to purchase equipment and develop marketing tools (your Web site, business cards, brochures, etc.), you can build your business on revenues instead of on loans or other funding sources. That being said, building a business slowly generally requires another income source during the build-up period, which may be infeasible or undesirable to some vendors who want to get their business up and running more immediately.

Jumping In

Although it is generally regarded as the typical route, you are by no means required to build your business slowly, on your own generated revenue. Some people fund their businesses by investing their own capital by persuading friends and family to invest. Securing a business loan or a credit line for start-up costs is also an option. A major resource, both for learning and for start-up capital, is the Small Business Administration. The SBA provides online tutorials, advice, and access to loans for business start-ups.

Count Your Assets

Whether you work full time or part time, a major factor in how quickly you can move toward your revenue goals is what assets you have going into the business—and what assets you need. An experienced shooter may already have a full production setup that is workable for all of their production needs. As that shooter's business grows, he or she might want to make some gear-related adjustments—for example, purchasing lighter-weight equipment or additional microphones. But with a system ready to go, he or she may be able to make do with spending initial funds on post-production hardware and software. In contrast, I came into the business the other way around. Having started as a video editor, I had edited hundreds of weddings on my own post-production hardware and software when I began shooting; I then borrowed and subsequently bought production equipment as I slowly and steadily developed my shooting skills and preferences.

Business assets to consider include more than your gear, however. A wedding videographer needs to have production and post-production equipment, surely, but also a mode of transportation to and from wedding events, an office (see upcoming sidebar), a place to meet with potential clients, marketing materials (including but not limited to a demo DVD, a Web site, and print ad design), contracts and other legal documents, insurance policies, and an accounting system. These assets should also be accounted for when considering start-up costs and time frame.

A HOME-BASED BUSINESS?

A decision many small business owners face is whether to work from home or to rent an additional space. Not surprisingly, wedding videography comes with its own set of considerations when weighing this issue.

It is perfectly feasible to run your business out of your home. The primary advantage to a home office is the money saved on office rent. Furthermore, the flexible—and often strange—hours involved in post-production are one of the great appeals to wedding videography. If you are going to edit a wedding at 2 a.m., it might be preferable to do it from home. Even during the day, wedding videographers who operate out of their home get to wear their pajamas to work during post-production!

Keep in mind, however, that you will need a place to meet with clients as you are marketing your services and potentially screening your final version (see Chapter 10, "Output"). While bringing clients into your home can provide warmth and intimacy (an important part of the services you are selling), that is only true if you have designated an inviting, spacious, and quiet place in your house for such a meeting. While the screaming children, barking dogs, and general mess that may characterize your living room have no bearing on your talent as a videographer, such factors will flag you as unprofessional to your prospective clients and will no doubt negatively affect your sales. Also, if you opt to work from home, your home must be somewhere that is relatively easy to get to, not to mention safe. A final consideration when it comes to working from home is whether the space is conducive to your work style. Post-production in particular requires immense concentration, and working in a place that suits your work habits is imperative to completing your jobs in a timely manner.

While potentially expensive, an office may serve as a way to separate your work and home lives and provide a comfortable, professional, and easily accessible space for meeting with your clients. In either a home or office scenario, make sure your work area is secure, as you will have expensive gear stored there.

Marketing tools, which are important in any business, cannot be underestimated in the wedding industry. Further discussion of marketing is found in this chapter.

To gauge how quickly you can get our business off the ground, prepare a list of assets you will need and determine which ones you have (or have access to). Once the list is prepared, consider the pricing estimates in Chapter 3, "Production Gear," and Chapter 4, "Post-Production Gear," to help you determine some of those costs.

Understand Your Overhead

When you work in a service industry, understanding the true costs of your labor can be tricky. Weddings are notoriously budget driven and vendors can be very competitive, so it is tempting to price low in order to obtain work. While this strategy can be effective, it is important to make sure that more than just your production-day costs are covered in order to run a successful business.

For example, you might assume that between the day of the wedding and the completion of post-production, the wedding will cost you approximately 30 hours of time. If you bid a flat rate with only your direct hours in mind, ignoring the indirect costs you continually incur, your business's long-term survival will be threatened. Without additional revenue to cover the cost of a broken camera, for example, it is impossible to shoot the next wedding.

Because of the competition between vendors in the wedding industry, marketing is traditionally a very high line item in a videography business budget—but is only one of many indirect costs you will face. Although they will vary depending on the structure of the business, indirect costs will likely include such things such transportation costs to and from the weddings, disposable equipment (batteries, tape light bulbs, etc.), rent and utilities for your business location, equipment repair and maintenance, insurance, business taxes, and time spent managing accounting and meeting with clients to secure business.

Anticipating these costs up front will help you gauge both how much you need to charge for a wedding video and how long you can afford to spend on each one. There will surely be adjustments to your expenses along the way. Using a software program such as QuickBooks or Peachtree will allow you to track your spending and pinpoint how much it costs you to run your business.

Managing Client Relations

Obviously, your clients expect and deserve a professional relationship with you, their vendor. But weddings are unique in that you are providing an intimate service. It is important for you, as the service professional, to set standards that will both ensure that your clients' money is being well spent and allow them a great deal of comfort with the person who will witness, capture, and re-tell the story of a day fraught with high emotion. I have seen tears, tantrums, nudity, fights, off-key serenades, and heart-rending displays of love and loyalty. The wedding professional must remain composed, comfortable, and supportive throughout it all.

After years in the wedding industry, what becomes just another job for you is probably the most important day of your clients' lives. In all your negotiations and service provision, it is important that you honor the couple's excitement and the magnitude of their emotions. Some clients—perhaps more than I care to admit—must be treated delicately, as if their wedding were the only event you have ever cared about. While this type of client can be frustrating to all wedding vendors, the flip side of the coin is that the trust and intimacy that your clients give you can be very rewarding, both for you personally and for the quality of your video piece.

Videographers regularly cite the satisfaction they receive from a couple thrilled with their work as a highlight to the job. By spending some time learning about your clients, their family, and their event, you can become a more engaged and supportive member of their wedding team. This will increase their comfort with you and, in turn, enable you to create a better product.

While gaining your clients trust and maintaining your own enthusiasm is integral to a quality product, the friendly relationship you foster with the couple should in no way affect the level of professionalism that you offer. By clearly defining expectations prior to service engagement, you will save yourself headaches, negative marketing, and potential legal action down the road.

Defining Your Style

One aspect of satisfying your customers is being up front about the type of product you can—and are willing to—deliver. If you are a videographer who specializes in documentary-style weddings and your prospective client is looking for a music-video production, it is important that you ask yourself if you can really provide that. Do you have the effects software for the stylized look they've asked for? Do you have the equipment to get the time-lapse sequences or the birds-eye angled shots they want? Most importantly, do you have the time and desire to spend the extra hours working on a project that is unfamiliar territory? While I would strongly argue that being flexible for your clients is important for generating business and will help build your strengths, skills, and demo reel, you do not want to be mired in a project that could cost you in hours or reputation.

Clarity with your customers starts with having demo reel and a full-length video of your own work to show them as they are considering your services. Your demo reel should be short and demonstrative of the best parts of your style, whether that is slow and dreamy or fast-paced and funny. It should grab their attention and convince your prospective bride that you can capture her in a way she will be proud of. Ideally, your demo will be accessible on your Web site as something that couples can use as an initial filter in selecting your services.

A full-length wedding video should be available to potential clients to provide a sense of how you handle the longer parts of the wedding event. Do you typically edit the ceremony down to the vows and the kiss? Or do you show the whole thing from processional to recessional? Is every word of the speeches included? Is the first dance shown unedited, or with cuts of the ceremony mixed in? That allows clients to determine what aspects of your style they like or may want done differently for their own event. With their input, you will be able to assess your ability to meet their needs. For example, if you typically use two cameras but they want three-camera coverage of the ceremony, you will be able to determine whether it's worth it to you to rent an additional camera setup or shooter.

While I would caution against giving the couple too much say in every detail, clarifying for them as much of the process as possible will help you price your work effectively and maintain the client satisfaction upon which your business relies.

 The wedding off-season is a great time to experiment stylistically. Your schedule will be more open, which may afford you the opportunity to build your repertoire in time to feel comfortable showcasing it in the busier months to come.

Pricing and Bidding

Because couples plan their weddings on a budget, it is standard to present a bid with a flat rate for the entire project instead of a bid with a rate for time and materials. Couples need to know the total cost of your services up front instead of being billed later. Determining a flat rate can be tricky, however, ranging from $700 dollars to as much as $10,000. Of course, the majority fall somewhere in the middle; between $2,000 and $4,000 seems to be fairly standard in most markets. As noted earlier, videographers must stay competitive in a tough market while being wary of undercutting their own livelihoods.

There are lots of variables in pricing a wedding job. The major ones may include how many cameras and camera operators will be at the wedding, how many hours you yourself will you be at the wedding, and how long post-production will take for the style and format of video you are delivering. You should have a sense from your financial planning about what overhead costs need to be factored in; use these to come up with your total price for the job.

Packaged Pricing

Videographers often offer clients packages that specify the number of hours of video coverage, the number of cameras and the final project. For example, a menu of packages may include a version of the following:

- ▶ Six hours' coverage
  - ▶ One camera, one shooter
  - ▶ One authored DVD
- ▶ Eight hours' coverage
  - ▶ Two cameras, one shooter
  - ▶ Two authored, chaptered DVDs

- ▶ Eight hours' coverage
  - ▶ Two cameras, two shooters
  - ▶ Two authored, chaptered DVDs with highlights section
- ▶ Unlimited coverage
  - ▶ Two cameras, two shooters
  - ▶ Five authored, chaptered DVDs with photo montage and highlights section
  - ▶ Videos compressed for iPhone and hosted online

Of course, the more coverage the videographer obtains, the more likely it is that the final product will meet the couple's expectations because there will be a wider variety of shots to choose from. Being able to pick from an array of material gives couples the confidence that the final product will be something they will be proud of and enjoy.

 This does not mean the videographer needs to have the camera constantly running, however. In fact, for editing purposes (as well as hard-earned breaks during a shooting day), it is important to know when it is appropriate to turn the camera *off*. See Chapter 7, "The Big Day," for more.

Offering a basic set of packages does not prevent you from tailoring your projects to your customers' needs—often providing additional revenue to you. For example, if a couple wants basic one-camera coverage of the wedding but also wants a highlights section and coverage of bridal preparations, you can add these "à la carte" items to the basic wedding coverage.

Here are some additional services that you could consider offering to your clients:

- ▶ Rehearsal-dinner coverage
- ▶ Photo montage
- ▶ Highlights section
- ▶ Engagement video
- ▶ Projection of video (montage, engagement video, or same-day edit) at reception
- ▶ Additional hourly coverage per shooter
- ▶ Additional copies of video
- ▶ DVDs of raw footage

Customized Pricing

Some vendors prefer not to use packaged pricing. Instead, they meet with potential clients to determine their needs and preferences and then come up with a proposed price. This method of pricing offers two major advantages:

- ▶ Many couples prefer what feels like a more individualized approach to their event.

- ▶ The wedding vendor can be flexible with rates depending on his or her current needs. For example, in a heavily booked month or for a particularly difficult job, there is little motivation to bid low. But a videographer might lower his or her price if a couple is stretching their budget and the videographer really wants that particular job.

The major disadvantage to customized pricing is how labor intensive it can be to meet with and create a proposal for every client. Because price is a determining factor for many couples, having a published schedule of prices can filter out the clients who you may not be suited for before either of you invest any time.

Set Pricing

Increasingly, vendors are moving away from packaged pricing and customized pricing, instead offering one price that includes a certain set of services and deliverables. While some clients may still try to customize your services and prices to suit their interests, those clients who are exhausted by the buffet of options and decisions that accompany wedding planning will welcome your set price; deferring to your expertise may well be a relief. For the vendor, using this style of pricing ensures that you know exactly what you are in for and makes it easier to streamline your workflow. If you decide to use set pricing for your business, I suggest that you gain some experience in the field before you determine and publish your set price, as you will want to have a very firm understanding of the time and costs of your product before you are tied to a price.

 Depending on the market you are working in, out-of-season weddings are commonly priced lower than weddings in high season. You are, of course, under no obligation to provide a discount, but should remain aware of your regional market norms in order to remain competitive.

As discussed further in the next section, it is imperative that the client understands exactly what services are included with the fee they are paying. If additional costs may arise down the line, such as editorial changes or charges for additional copies, that potential should be made clear up front.

Legal Issues and Contracts

As with any business agreement, a signed contract is important to protect both you and your client. These documents can range from a few sentences to pages and pages; it's imperative that you find a balance between these. Aim for a document that is thorough yet unintimidating.

Your contract should, at the very least, include the following:

- ▶ Full contact information for both you and your clients.

- ▶ The locations, times, and events for which you are expected to provide video coverage.

- ▶ The end time of your shooting responsibilities. While the photographer and videographer are sometimes the last to leave an event, often they will leave when the dancing is underway. Whatever your endpoint, it should be specified in your contract so that the bride doesn't become angry that you won't be capturing the couple in the limo driving off when you pack up your gear to go. Your end point can be measured by time (e.g., after 10 hours) or event (e.g., after the bouquet toss). If your clients hire you for a specified period of time, such as eight hours, consider a pre-arranged hourly fee for staying longer should they request you do so on the day of the event. Be wary if the end of your workday is tied to an event; weddings rarely run according to schedule, and you may be in for a longer shooting day than you bargained for.

- ▶ The final product you will be providing. Be clear on the delivery format of the final product and the number of copies the couple will receive. For example, do they get the raw footage, or do you keep that? Are you compressing a video for them to post online, or will you post it yourself? Be sure to specify.

- ▶ The date upon which you will provide the video. In my experience, it is far better to give yourself more time than you think you will need. Couples are very understanding when you say up front that a video takes a long time to make; they're less so when you deliver later than promised.

- ▶ A defined payment schedule. Be sure to clarify when payment is due. It is typical to get 50% with a signed contract and the balance after services are rendered, but any arrangement that suits you and your clients is fine as long as it is mutually understood. Be sure to clarify which payment methods are acceptable and whether there are any applicable penalties should a personal check be returned.

- ▶ Additional fees. It is important to be up front about the possibility of additional fees. These could include additional shooting hours, extra copies of a video, DVDs made of the raw footage, etc. One line item that is especially important to clarify is editorial changes to the video once the couple has viewed it. Depending on your pricing structure, such changes may be included as part of your service—but you want to make sure that you don't fine-tune a video seven times without appropriate compensation.

▶ Disclaimers. This is the section that can take your contract from a single page to a frightening volume of legalese designed to scare off your client, complete with references to acts of God and various breaches. While I urge you to avoid that, I would recommend including a clause for both equipment failure and sound quality—two items that may be out of your control even with the best preparation.

Another thing to consider is whether you get full rights to the images captured. If you want to be able to use an image in your marketing materials or on your Web site, for example, you can obtain permission on an as-needed basis or have that clause drawn into your basic contract.

 Have a lawyer review your contract to make sure it is comprehensive enough to protect you and simple enough to be user-friendly. You may be able to obtain access to affordable legal counsel through the SBA, local professional groups, or the Wedding and Event Videographers Association (WEVA).

Marketing Yourself

Sales expertise doesn't take you far without prospective clients. All the discussion in the previous section about working with your clients hinges on them being able to find you in the first place. When brides, or their mothers, start thinking about wedding vendors, your name must come across their radar. Regardless of the scale of your business, marketing must be a continual process, as marketing opportunities tend to have a short shelf life and must be regularly refreshed. Furthermore, a busy wedding season doesn't mean the marketing can end; it just means you have more marketing material with which to work.

There are numerous methods for exposing your business, some more traditional and some based on newer Internet-related opportunities. As you develop your strategies and marketing budget, keep in mind that your marketing methods must evolve to match your clientele. Even though you might be loath to join a social-networking site, remember that the average 25-year old bride is likely to be similarly put off by the Yellow Pages phone book. That being said, traditional marketing methods still prove effective. The best marketing strategy for your business will likely combine elements of traditional and modern methods designed to suit the demographics of your prospective clientele.

Print Materials

Ideally, you will have a logo to unify all of your print materials and brand your business. If print design is not your forté, a logo can be commissioned from a designer for reasonable rates. The logo should be finalized before you, or your designer, work on your cards or other handouts. Your logo should also appear on your Web site and in the opening and closing to your video product, further branding your services for those who see it.

Business cards are a must, and should include your logo, contact information, and a link to your Web site, where sample work can be seen. Cards should be distributed frequently and gratuitously; give out several when asked for one. Larger printed materials can also be useful: 4×6-inch cards or brochures that allow room to discuss your style and even your packages and pricing, if you choose to disclose that information.

Always keep a stash of your printed materials in your camera bag for the wedding day; I once shot a wedding in which three of the four bridesmaids were planning their own weddings. Similarly, when appropriate, leave several copies of your cards or brochures on display at places where brides are likely to be in wedding-planning mode, such as bridal stores, flower shops, and wedding-cake bakeries.

Magazines: Print and Online

There are numerous print magazines devoted to helping brides plan their weddings. These publications have regional editions, allowing for local vendors to purchase advertising space. While this model has traditionally been a solid marketing approach, make sure that the magazine's clientele is appropriate for your services before making an investment. The magazine publisher should be able to provide information about their readership to help you determine whether the demographics, such as geography and budget, will match what you are looking for. There is little point in advertising to a bride that is 500 miles away if neither you nor the client can cover your transportation costs.

The Yellow Pages provide advertising space for a fee. That said, while it may be useful for prospective brides and their parents to be able to find your contact information in the phone book, it is becoming less and less likely that they will look there for referrals. I recommend being listed without paying for additional space.

Purchasing ad space on online bridal sites—either sites run by magazines (such as www.brides.com) or forums (such as www.theknot.com)—can help boost your business. As with print magazines, your digital advertisement can be placed for local viewing.

Even if you don't advertise on bridal forums, check them regularly as part of your overall marketing strategy. Such sites offer valuable tips for vendors that can directly apply to you. In addition, they give advice to brides that you should be aware of, with articles such as "What to Look For in a Wedding Videographer."

Web Site

Your Web site will be one of your key marketing tools, because it is where your work can be seen. In fact, even before you post any video, your Web site conveys your design sense and ability to transmit information. Because visual aesthetics and storytelling skills are the services you are selling in the wedding video itself, it's crucial that you use your Web site as an opportunity to put your best foot forward. Make your site easy to navigate and appealing to look at.

At the very least, your Web site must contain your contact information and some samples of your work. Ideally, it will also provide a way for you to capture the contact information of your visitors so that you can contact them yourself (see Figure 2.1). Beyond that, you (or your Web-site designer/developer) can make your site as fanciful as your imagination allows—as long as you maintain navigability and clean design, and the site loads quickly.

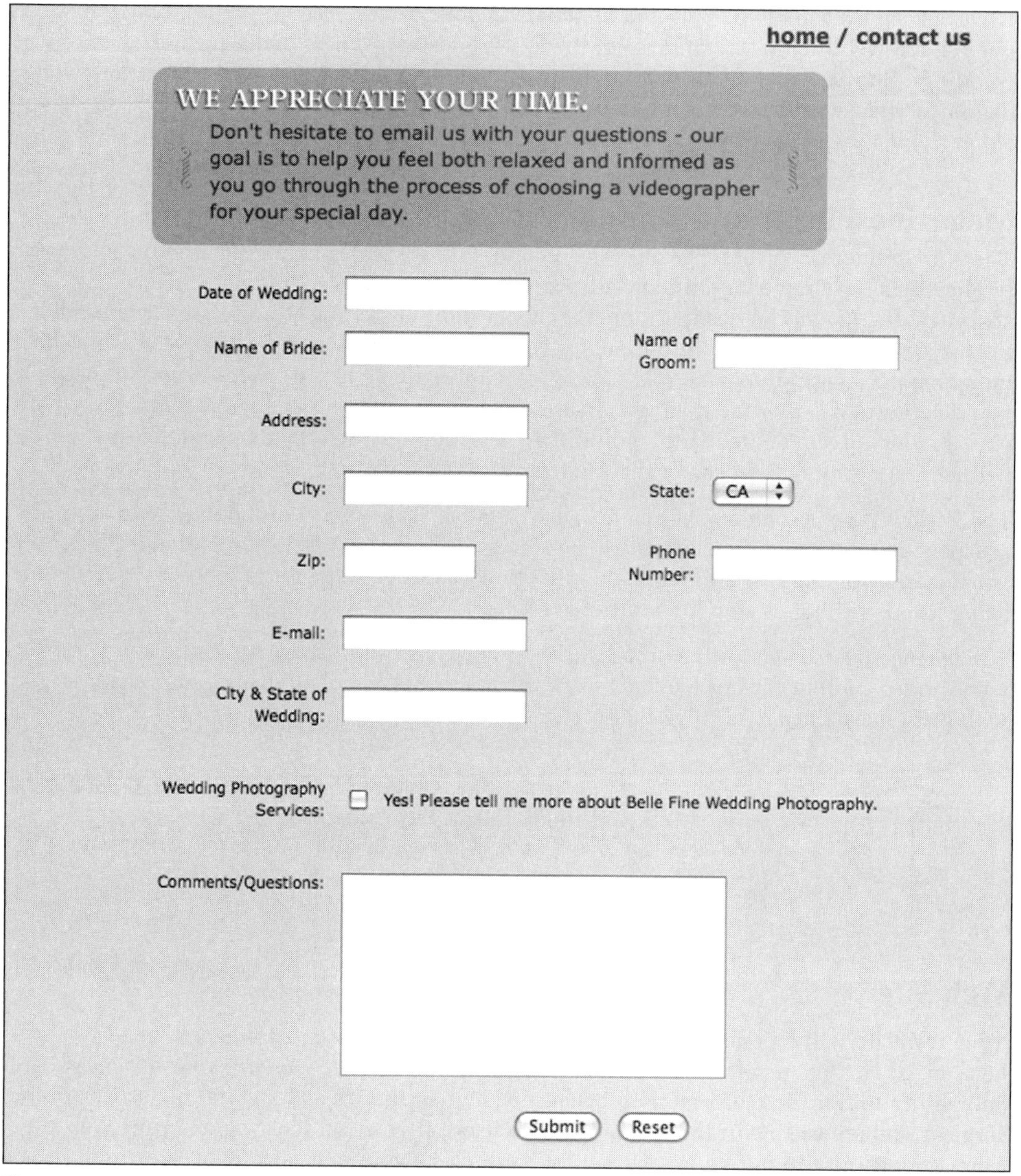

Figure 2.1
Ideally, your Web site will have a way to capture information about prospective clients. That way, you can contact them instead of hoping they contact you.

A word of caution on that last point: As a documentarian, it is natural that you will want to use the highest resolution possible for your online images and video demos. Keep in mind, however, that brides are literally inundated with information and have massive to-do lists. If your site, or your sample work, takes too long to load, it is unlikely she will notice the high quality of your images; more likely, she will give up before she has the opportunity. Make sure your site images and videos load quickly.

 One way to drive traffic to your Web site is via Google Ads, or Adsense. With this service, you can run an ad containing two or three lines of text that links to your Web page anytime someone runs a search with specific keywords, such as wedding, bridal, bridesmaids, or groom. In addition to specifying these keywords, you can set a geographical radius in which to advertise and how often links appear; in this way advertising costs are regulated carefully. For more information, visit www.google.com/adsense/login.

Your Web site, like all your marketing, should be an ongoing project, subject to both maintenance and revision. If you aren't designing it yourself, make sure that you either learn how to update your site or include site updates by a third party in your budget. You want your images and video samples to reflect recent wedding trends and your best and latest work.

One way wedding videographers update their sites regularly is by including a blog. After each wedding is completed, the videographer can post a bit about the event and even some video clips. In addition to being an easy way to keep your Web site fresh, using a blog is also a good way to bring traffic to your site, as couples are likely to forward the link to the blog entry about their own wedding to their friends and family (see Figure 2.2).

Figure 2.2
Many wedding vendors use each event as a new blog entry. Blogs are excellent marketing tools because they showcase the videographer's personality and a link to his or her work, as well as serving as a marketing tool for the venue.

« Tips from one of our brides...

Helpful and handy Wedding ideas and tips... »

Julie & Juan at the beautiful Westin St Francis on Union square

Julie & Juan at the Westin St Francis on Union Square...

After a warm and personal ceremony the day before at the great St Peter & Pauls church in North beach, Julie and Juan had a great second ceremony and party at the Westin on Union square. As the only hotel located on Union Square, The Westin St. Francis is a majestic address among San Francisco wedding sites. Julie & Juan or 'J & J" enchanted their guests with the stylish ambiance where stately marble columns, ornate balconies, and intricate woodworking of yesteryear. Even though the fog rolled in and the power went out this fun and happy couple partied on with there family and friends. Of course the professional staff of the Westin were at there best and Peter Bruce photo, along with team bELLE were able to get some great shots. Hope you enjoy,please let us know

If you decide to include a blog on your Web site, make sure to carefully proofread each entry for spelling and grammatical errors. If your blog is riddled with mistakes, you will, in turn, look unprofessional. Further-more, make sure that your posts about any given wedding, venue, client or vendor are positive. Even if intended in jest, negative or catty comments are completely inappropriate and will reflect poorly on you as a service provider.

Other Internet Marketing Tools

It is critical that you remain aware of current Internet trends as you develop your marketing strategies. Even though some of these trends might feel short-lived, annoying, and/or cumbersome, it is important to remember that in 2010, the average bridal couple had been using the Internet since grade school and may have very different expectations with respect to communication than the vendors with whom they are working.

That being said, I am not suggesting that you rush headlong into every new technology. For example, despite the current popularity of iPhones and BlackBerry devices, at the time of this publishing, I do not recommend investing in a mobile site. Wedding-planning decisions take weeks or even months, not moments; so the investment necessary to get an attractive site running on a few different mobile platforms does not currently seem worth the value of what it may bring in. A bride is still likely to plan her wedding from a computer at home or at the office as opposed to on the go.

On the other hand, having a social networking identity for your business, such as a Facebook presence or a Twitter feed, is becoming more and more popular among wedding vendors. According to Annyce Meiners of Beyond Video, social networking has created easy and free referrals (see the upcoming sidebar). While these forms of marketing communication may not be lasting trends, they come at little cost to you as a business owner and can be easily discontinued if need be. As such, they might be a reasonable, even profitable, marketing method to add to your overall plan.

Obviously, this advice is current as of the time of writing and could, of course, change in the near future. What's important here is that you remember to follow the trends in which your customers are savvy and determine which ones might be the most useful, practical and economically feasible for you to incorporate into your own marketing scheme.

ANNYCE MEINERS, BEYOND VIDEO, TUSCON AZ

"I use Facebook both for networking with clients and vendors and for advertising. Although paid advertising on Facebook worked well for one of my photographer friends, it did not generate revenue for me. On the other hand, my free Facebook presence has allowed me to reconnect with former clients who loved their videos enough to want to help promote my services, even from out of state. Furthermore, when I post trailers to my videos, I always get feedback, which is encouraging and helpful. Facebook helps me get my name out there more, even if it hasn't directly brought business in."

Word of Mouth: Brides and Other Vendors

By far the most valuable marketing tool available is good referrals. Regardless of how beautiful your Web site may be, a prospective client is much more likely to contact you if she heard from her friend that you were easy to work with and delivered a great piece than if she loved that header font you deliberated over for weeks. Referrals can come from the brides themselves, their friends, and other wedding vendors.

Keep in mind that your brides have siblings, cousins, and friends, some of whom are likely to also be planning local weddings. As mentioned earlier, do not hesitate to hand out your card at the wedding event itself (as long as your marketing doesn't get in the way of completing your tasks, of course). When you receive compliments about your work, ask the couple if you can publish their opinions on your Web site. Many videographers use a testimonial page to highlight their strengths (see Figure 2.3).

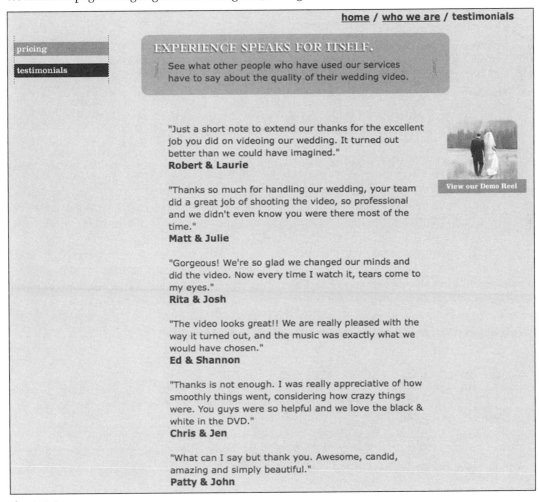

Figure 2.3
Use the testimonials from your pleased customers to highlight facets of your company that you want to show off, such as your personality on the job or your use of effects.

As best you can, maintain contact with your clients after the event by including them on e-mails that highlight Web-site updates, new blog entries, or special promotions you may be running. With memories of your good service, a DVD in their hands, and your name at their fingertips, you should be able to maximize referrals from pleased customers.

Referrals don't always come from customers, however. It is very common within the wedding industry for vendors to refer each other when they admire another service provider's product or work well with that person. While referrals from other wedding videographers will be rare in such a competitive industry, they are not unheard of. If a videographer is already booked, or can't provide the same services as you, he or she may give out your name and vice versa. More commonly, however, a different service provider such as a photographer, a wedding planner, or a reception venue will recommend you as a videographer. A referral from a photographer can be especially compelling, as the prospective client will likely understand how closely the two of you must work.

 One extremely savvy videographer I edited for made complimentary short videos for several of the venues where he had worked for the venue owners to use in their own marketing. This both endeared him to the venue owners and showed the couples booking those venues that he was skilled and familiar with the locations. Moreover, many of the venues used his videos on their Web site, amounting to targeted and free advertising!

When you find vendors with whom you work well, make sure to trade contact information and refer them. Often, you will see wedding vendors link to other preferred vendors (for other service areas) on their Web sites. This is beneficial to the couple, who might be searching for a certain aesthetic or price range that like vendors have in common. It can also be tremendously beneficial for the vendors, both in terms of marketing and because their work quality can be improved by working with familiar people. This is especially the case with videographers and photographers who, as described in Chapter 6, "Pre-Production," must perform an elaborate dance around each other throughout the day. Do not recommend a vendor or link to their site, however, just because you like the individual. Make sure you understand the quality of their work and trust their customer-service skills. Sending a bride to someone with whom she may have a bad experience will reflect poorly on your own business.

 Having contacts within the industry who want to refer you can be especially important for videographers. That's because the wedding videographer tends to be one of the last service providers contracted (usually after the venue, photographer, band/DJ, and caterer have been hired). For this reason, you should think of other vendors at the weddings you work as potential clients and treat them accordingly.

Bridal Fairs and Expos

Bridal fairs and expositions are an excellent way to both meet brides and network with other vendors. These range from small city shows to state and regional affairs. (You can find listings online.) There is no reason to snub the smaller shows; not only are they less expensive to participate in, but it is often much easier to meet local brides and vendors in shows that are constrained both in geography and floor space. Indeed, many vendors would argue that better business and customer relationships are formed in the smaller shows.

Should you decide to spend part of your marketing budget on a bridal show, make your entry fee worth it. Arm yourself with print materials to hand out, give away demo DVDs if possible, and make sure you can play some of your work at your table or booth. Consider a giveaway or other promotional item; if a bride gets a free engagement session from you, she is likely to hire you for the whole job.

Professional organizations such as the Wedding and Event Videographers Association (WEVA) may also be good marketing and educational tools. They have a yearly conference and provide member listings, information for brides, technical assistance to members, and business-related services such as group insurance rates and equipment leasing programs.

Keeping It All Compliant

In order to run a legitimate and safe operation, you will need to abide by the rules of your local and state governments as well as secure appropriate insurance coverage to protect yourself and the people you may affect in the course of your business. Because these regulations are made locally and change regularly, it is impossible to outline an exact set of rules for you to follow; a trip to your local city hall should put you on track.

License and Permits

Many city and local governments require a business registration. Fees will vary by location, but are generally fairly inexpensive. Check the requirements for your local jurisdiction at your city/county tax collector's office; it may be illegal for you to practice without being a licensed business. In many cases, you will need a license in order to obtain a business, as opposed to personal, checking account.

Depending on your state, you might also be required to charge sales tax on your services, which requires you to obtain a seller's permit. Some states allow you to charge sales tax only on the DVD or tapes that you sell as a final product (i.e., the cost of the blank media); other states include the labor that goes into the final product as the total value of the item, which means charging sales tax for the entire cost. Learn about sales tax for your state at your local tax collector's office; they will direct you to obtain a reseller's permit if needed. If you are required to get a seller's permit, it is generally an easy process. Plus, depending on the state, the permit may grant you the ability to buy supplies tax-free.

If you are being taxed by your state on the revenue of the entire video, make sure you build that cost into your pricing structure. Your competition will primarily be local and must therefore do the same thing.

Insurance

Although some venues or clients may require it, you are not obligated by law to hold insurance. That said, I strongly recommend it. Liability insurance will protect you and your business in the event a guest is injured because of you or your equipment. While this is not a particularly likely event, it is far from the realm of impossible; you will often be moving quickly, hefting heavy equipment in the air, and setting up hastily. Complicating matters, you will often be amongst a crowd.

Depending on the policy, liability insurance may or may not cover your equipment in the event of theft on the job, another unlikely but possible event. Ideally, your equipment should always be covered by insurance—through homeowner's or renter's insurance if you work from home, through car insurance when it is packed in your car, through liability insurance on the job. You will obviously have to look at the details of various policies to find the best plan for your setup, which may require a policy of its own.

Finally, some wedding vendors invest in Errors and Omissions insurance, which will cover the damages should a wedding videographer not be able to provide the service contracted, due to accident, equipment failure or other mishap.

Local professional organizations might be able to help you find group rates that may be cheaper.

Summary

From this chapter, you should have the framework to develop the following:

- ▶ Personal business goals
- ▶ A business plan
- ▶ A list of assets that you have and need
- ▶ A description of your video style
- ▶ A method to price your work
- ▶ Ideas to build your marketing plan
- ▶ The methods to keep your business compliant and legally protected

Next Up

After some plans and goals about your venture have been set, it's time to start ramping up for production. To maximize both your budget and your production quality, you will need to make careful decisions about the gear you purchase. Use the next chapter to think about the equipment you will need and what factors are crucial to a professional, high-quality production.

Chapter 2 Tutorial: Counting Your Assets and Estimating Operating Expenses

Depending on how big of a career leap you are making, starting a wedding videography business can be quite overwhelming. As discussed in Chapter 2, "The Business of Weddings," business planning is a crucial part of your development, independent of how quickly you want to start up or how much revenue you are looking to generate.

Counting Your Assets

Use the following worksheet to help you determine what assets you already have and those you will need to obtain. Keep in mind that this sheet does not reflect ongoing expenses, only startup expenses. Furthermore, there may be items unique to your business that are not included on this list.

	Quantity Needed	Quantity Owned	Quantity to Obtain
Office Equipment and Startup Business Expenses			
Desk and chair			
Phone line/voice mail			
Printer			
Computer (if separate from editing station)			
Insurance policy			
Business license fees			

	Quantity Needed	Quantity Owned	Quantity to Obtain
Production Equipment			
Camcorder			
Camcorder batteries			
Tripod			
Monopod			
Steadistick			
Wireless microphones			
External light(s)			
External light batteries/battery belt			
Camcorder bag			
Post-Production Equipment			
Computer			
Hard drive storage space			
Computer monitor			
External monitor			
Speakers			
Headphones			
Deck/spare camera			
Card reader			
Post-production software			
Scanner			
DVD burner			
DVD printer			
Blu-ray burner/player			
Service Expertise			
Legal counsel (contracts)			
Web design			
Graphic design			
Printing (cards, brochures, blank media, etc.)			

Estimating Operating Expenses

Use the following worksheet to help you determine your annual operational costs—those expenses that will reoccur. Think about whether costs occur per year (regardless of revenue) or per wedding (dependent on revenue) so that you can consider what costs you will incur no matter how many clients you serve. Customize this list as needed; chances are it contains some items that don't pertain to you. Also, there are extra lines for items unique to your business.

	Cost Per Month	Cost Per Wedding	Approximate Annual
Office and Business Expenses			
Phone line/voice mail			
Gas and electric			
Internet service			
Insurance			
Annual business registration			
Subtotal:			
Production Expenses			
Phone line/voice mail			
Gas and electric			
Internet service			
Insurance			
Annual business registration			
Subtotal:			

	Cost Per Month	Cost Per Wedding	Approximate Annual
Post-Production Expenses			
Blank media			
Media cases/labels			
Printer ink			
Royalty-free music			
Additional hard drive space			
New equipment budget			
		Subtotal:	
Marketing Expenses			
Blank media			
Media cases/labels			
Printer ink			
Royalty-free music			
Additional hard drive space			
New equipment budget			
		Subtotal:	
		Total Operating Expenses:	

Chapter 3
Production Gear

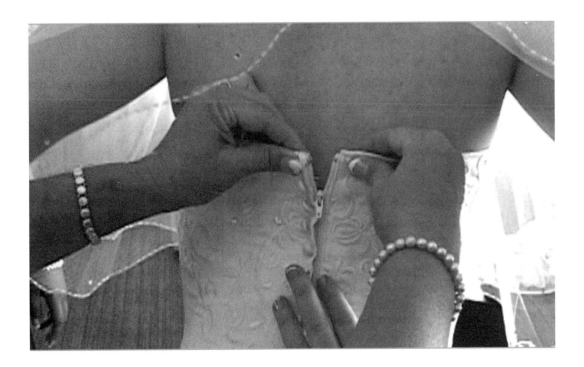

In this chapter:

▶ Choosing a camcorder
▶ Tripod
▶ Audio
▶ External lights
▶ Bags
▶ A word about multiple setups

A camcorder bag stocked with the newest and most advanced technology that money can buy won't make you a good wedding videographer. A good eye, creativity, and enthusiasm are the critical skills for the job. These talents, coupled with a willingness to understand and realize your customers' vision and the experience you bring to the event are what will make your service and your product stand out. In selling your services, these are the attributes that you must present to your clients, who probably don't know (or much care) about the difference between camcorder sensors.

That being said, as you undoubtedly have already realized, you are in a profession that relies heavily on your equipment. The right equipment is what will help make your video look professional, providing image clarity, color definition, light and sound quality that simply can't be obtained by an amateur videographer. But what might be "right" in the eyes of the filmmaking world might not be best for your needs. For example, while a light-kit might give the bride a gorgeous rim light on her hair during the ceremony, the chances of you being able to set up an extensive lighting rig is highly unlikely. Your gear must be suited to the run-and-gun style of a wedding videographer, while still offering the sophistication that a couple wants to see in a professionally made video.

The following sections on gear selection for wedding videography assume that you are starting from scratch in selecting your gear. It is more probable that in reality you already have amassed parts of your set-up, or have equipment you can borrow. Use this chapter as a guideline for selecting which pieces of gear are integral to your initial set-up and which items can be added or upgraded as you move forward. As you make purchases, be sure to think about how they fit with your current set-up and how they will work with gear upgrades you have planned.

Choosing a Camcorder

Camcorders—often referred to as cameras or video cameras—are so named because they contain a camera and a recorder in the same unit. Originally, video cameras had a separate recording unit, which may have been attached to the camera operated or located in a different room altogether. Thankfully for the modern wedding videographer, things have changed! Similarly, the advent of digital video camcorders allowed the modern wedding video industry to flourish, as described in Chapter 1, "The World of Wedding Videography." This book limits its discussion to various types of digital video and digital video camcorders.

It goes without saying that the centerpiece of your camcorder bag is your camcorder, a purchase that should be taken seriously. I can't begin to review all the options in this chapter—entire books are written on that subject alone—but I can offer some advice as to what you should look for and what factors you can ignore.

Given the amount of time you will spend with your camcorder, I encourage you to choose one that not only fits your practical needs and budget, but that you will enjoy. You should feel comfortable holding it and like its look and feel (see Figure 3.1).

Figure 3.1
Camcorders have different physiques, varying in size, shape, and weight. As well as considering the technical factors listed in this chapter when choosing your camcorder, make sure you like how it feels when you hold it.

While you might get the best deal by ordering online, make sure you have seen and handled the camcorder before you make a purchase. If you do order online, read the return and warranty policies carefully, and conduct business only with a reputable dealer.

When choosing a camcorder, you'll want to consider the following features:

▶ HD capabilities and resolution

▶ Lens

▶ Sensor

▶ LCD screen

▶ Storage

▶ Media transfer

▶ Inputs and outputs

▶ Stabilization

▶ Manual controls

HD Capabilities and Resolution

In early 2009, more than one-third of all American homes had high-definition (HD) televisions, and by the time this book is printed, all television broadcasts will be digital. Likewise, HD video downloads are increasingly popular. Viewing audiences are trained to expect clearer, crisper images; your product should comply with their aesthetics to remain competitive in the market.

If you are in a position to choose a new camcorder, there is little reason to stick with standard definition (SD) in the face of an electronics world that is aggressively moving to *high definition* (*HD*). HD provides a much clearer and detailed image through higher resolution, or more image data. Although still slightly more expensive, opt for an HD camcorder over an SD one. Previous deterrents to using HD camcorders—such as cost and the required computer strength to deal with huge files—still exist, but are significantly more manageable barriers now than in years past.

All that being said, many videographers still shoot weddings in standard definition. Besides, most delivery methods, such as the majority of DVD players and Internet streaming, do not allow for the benefits of high definition anyway—although that is rapidly changing. (See Chapter 10, "Output and Delivery," for more information.) If you own a high-quality SD camcorder, you need not rush out and immediately purchase an HD one; plenty of companies still shoot exclusively on SD. Considering, however, that the market is changing, you should probably put an HD camcorder on your list of upgrade expenses to consider in the future.

As indicated previously, the key difference between HD and SD cameras is the amount of resolution, or image data, that is recorded for each frame of video shot. Camcorders offer different *resolutions* that will change the look and image quality of your final product. When thinking about resolution, the first thing to consider is the *aspect ratio*, or ratio of width to height in a video format's image. Footage shot in SD will typically have an aspect ratio of 4:3, producing an almost square image, as seen on older TV sets. Footage shot in HD will typically have an aspect ratio of 16:9, making a relatively wider image that mimics movie screens and is becoming the new television standard (see Figure 3.2).

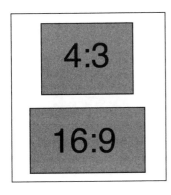

Figure 3.2
Aspect ratio defines the ratio between width and length of a video format. Although other aspect ratios are used, 4:3 is the most common aspect ratio for SD video and a widescreen 16:9 is the most common aspect ratio for HD video.

A camcorder's resolution is measured in *pixels*, or the smallest discernable units of image data. You can think of pixels as dots of a single color (although they aren't round). To determine a camcorder's resolution, multiply the number of horizontal scan lines (that is, the image height, in pixels) by the number of pixels horizontally (that is, the image width, in pixels). You derive the image width using the aspect ratio. For example, HD video with 1080 horizontal scan lines (or a height of 1080 pixels) and an aspect ratio of 16:9 is 1920 pixels wide. So the camera has a resolution of 1080×1920 and produces an image with a total of 2,073,600 pixels. Video with an aspect ratio of 16:9 but only 720 horizontal scan lines has an image width of 1280 pixels, for a total of 921,600 pixels—a lesser HD resolution. SD video tends to have an aspect ratio of 4:3 at a resolution of 720×540 pixels for a total of 388,800 pixels, obviously significantly less image data.

Many SD cameras enable you to shoot footage in a widescreen mode. One way cameras do this is to *letterbox* the image, in which case the frame is cropped at the top and bottom to change the aspect ratio. Be wary of this method, however, as you capture much less image data than when you use the standard mode. Some cameras or lens adapters enable you to shoot *anamorphically*, optically squeezing the image to fit more on the camera sensor horizontally. When you view the footage on your camera's LCD, it will appear distorted, but your editing software will unsqueeze the image to provide a true widescreen image.

 If you are shooting on SD, look into shooting in widescreen format to capture images that look more like the HD media presentation your clients are accustomed to seeing, despite lacking the HD resolution.

When manufacturers indicate the resolution of a camcorder, they follow it with either an "i" or a "p" to denote *interlaced* or *progressive*, respectively. Video is made up of two fields: odd and even. In interlaced video, each frame shows either the odd fields or the even fields; in progressive video, each frame shows both even and odd fields (see Figure 3.3). For example, in 1080i resolution, the odd 540 rows will be displayed in one frame and the even 540 rows will be shown in the next. In a 1080p resolution, every line of pixels is shown in every frame. Progressive video looks better to the eye—cleaner and smoother—than interlaced. This is particularly true when the final output is shown on a computer. 1080p resolution is considered "full HD." Many camcorders offer a range of resolution options; only higher-end camcorders offer full HD.

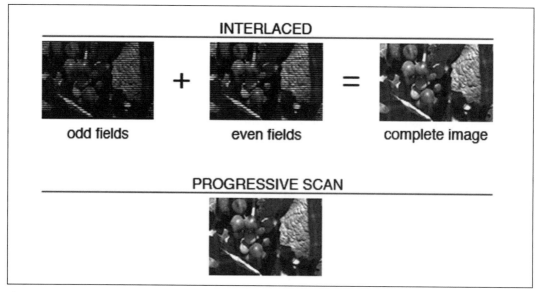

Figure 3.3
Interlaced video uses two fields to make one complete frame of video; progressive video does not.

Lens

A lens is often categorized by its zoom—that is, the ratio between the longest and shortest focal point, or the point at which light rays converge after passing through a lens (see Figure 3.4). For example, a zoom lens with focal lengths ranging from 100 mm to 800 mm may be described as an 8:1 or 8× zoom.

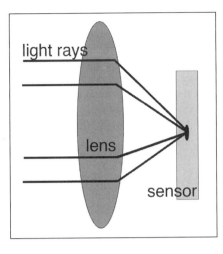

Figure 3.4
The light rays pass through the lens to focus on the sensor, at the focal point. The distance that the lens is allowed to move will change the distance of the focal point, the range of which is called the zoom.

There are two types of zooms: optical and digital. An *optical zoom* moves the lens to bring the subject closer or farther in a manner similar to that of a magnifying glass: by changing the point at which light rays are refracted, as discussed. A *digital zoom* enlarges an image that has already been captured by making the image's individual pixels larger, a process that can also be accomplished in image editing (see Figure 3.5). The optical zoom on a higher-end camcorder will typically range from 10× to 20×, while the digital zoom will likely be significantly higher—say, 150× or 300×.

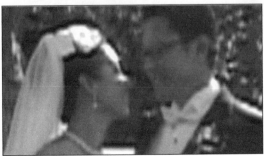

Figure 3.5
Unlike an optical zoom which moves the lens to change the magnification of an image as it hits the sensor, a digital zoom simply enlarges an image already recorded. This method of shooting gives a grainy image, as shown in the second image with 4× digital zoom.

Making individual pixels larger via digital zoom (or in post-production) leads to a grainier, less sharp image—like an impressionist painting close up. Because of this, a camcorder's digital zoom feature is not particularly relevant. You should pay closer attention to the optical zoom, which will deliver an image as crisp and clear as the lens can make it.

 Occasionally, manufacturers will try to combine the digital and optical zooms in their product descriptions; make sure you are clear on the optical zoom capabilities.

High-end professional camcorders may also have interchangeable lens mounts, enabling you to use different lenses such as one with increased zoom capabilities, a wide angle lens, a fish-eyed lens, or a telephoto lens. Even before the purchase of these additional lenses, this option may be very expensive—but can add a whole new level of professionalism and artistry to your work. Some mid-range models may have lens adaptors that allow you to record wide angle or telephoto images. Some high-end video camcorders offer compatibility with high-end still camera lenses, which can be a valuable bonus for videographers who also shoot still photography.

Sensor

An image sensor is required to convert images captured by the camcorder into digital format. There are two types of sensors: *charged coupled device* (*CCD*) and *complementary metal-oxide semiconductor* (*CMOS*). CCD technology is older and more refined, but CMOS sensors are much smaller, generate less noise and heat, and use less power.

Whichever type of sensor your camcorder uses, its size and makeup can be important with respect to your final image. A larger sensor will yield higher quality (less grain) in low-light conditions. This is particularly relevant in wedding video, as church lighting may be dim and receptions are often candlelit affairs.

The ideal way to determine whether the sensor in the camcorder you are considering buying will be adequate for your needs is to view some sample footage shot by the camcorder in low lighting. If the camcorder manufacturer or vendor you are working with cannot provide any low-light footage, consider renting the camcorder for a day or two and testing it yourself. This may cost time and money, but could provide invaluable research on low-light shooting and other features of your major purchase.

Although several factors go into a camera's low-light capabilities, and CMOS technology can be perfectly adequate, it's fairly standard for wedding videographers to use a 3-CCD camcorder (that is, a camcorder with three separate CCD sensors). In fact, many videographers will announce this feature on their Web site, and some couples will know to ask for it (despite often having no idea what it means).

LCD Screen

Your camcorder will have an *LCD* screen for viewing your video both as you shoot and during playback. It should rotate 360 degrees as well as flip outward 90 degrees to allow for better viewing in different lighting conditions. Because some wedding videography occurs outdoors in bright light, your LCD screen should not be the only viewfinder; you should opt for a camcorder that also features a traditional eyepiece viewfinder (see Figure 3.6).

Figure 3.6
A good camcorder will have a flip-out LCD option as well as an eyepiece viewfinder.

Some LCD screens have touchpad menus that serve as the camera's main—or only—control panel. This can be somewhat frustrating, as a good videographer often works controls by sensory memory while watching the video or action being recorded. Your frustration will be compounded when you are shooting outdoors, when the LCD screen is hard to see. For these reasons, you should opt for a camcorder with both a traditional viewfinder and menu control buttons that are located on the body of the camera, not on the LCD.

Storage

Tape is no longer the only storage medium for camcorders. In fact, tape appears to be on its way out. That being said, many manufacturers still make tape-based HD camcorders. These tape-based HD camcorders shoot in the *HDV* format, using MPEG-2 compression on standard MiniDV tapes.

There are a lot of conveniences associated with using tape. For one, archiving finished projects is easy; a simple shoebox does the trick. Because of that, tapes can also be a good way to store raw footage and for backing up media drives. Disadvantages, however, include limitations on shooting time (approximately one hour per tape) and the inconveniences involved with reviewing your footage and capturing your clips, both of which occur in real time and with much rewinding.

Camcorders that don't use tape instead use one of the following or combine a few of these options:

▶ A hard drive

▶ Flash memory

▶ Removable memory cards,

▶ Mini-DVD discs

These camcorders use the *Advanced Video Codec High Definition* (*AVCHD*) format—a high-definition format that uses the MPEG-4 AVC/H.264 codec. When you import AVCHD files to a Mac or a PC, the files will consume an enormous amount of space and require a fair amount of processing power. Normally, to edit AVCHD files on a Mac, you need an Intel-based Core Duo processor or better, or a Core2Quad processor or better for a PC. Only later versions of most types of editing software can handle AVCHD files. When you select your camcorder, you should make sure your hardware and software can handle these types of files.

 For a long time, DVD camcorders captured video only in MPEG-2 format, which lacks quality. Now, however, HD camcorders can store AVCHD files on DVD.

Hard-drive and *flash-memory* camcorders store files to a built-in microchip, similar to how files on your computer are saved. The primary difference between the two is that flash memory has no moving parts, and is thus more durable than a hard drive. Both allow easy access to your clips, without requiring you to rewind (as with tapes). Similarly, you don't have to worry about taping over a piece of previously shot footage; hard drives and flash drive camcorders automatically fill up free space.

Flash drives tend to be significantly smaller than hard drives. While this offers a benefit in terms of lightness and memory access, it's a detriment for both recording time and price. At the time of this writing, flash memory is almost double the price of hard-drive memory per gig and can't shoot for nearly as long. This is particularly relevant for weddings, when you want to be able to shoot as long as possible without interruption. That being said, flash drives typically offer another storage option—for example, a slot for a removable memory card or a DVD drive—whereas hard drives do not. When the hard drive gets full, you must download its contents to an external hard drive—something you *don't* want to be doing when the best man begins his speech.

Although mini-DVD discs offer the high quality and random access benefits of hard-drive and flash storage, a typical DVD holds only 22 minutes of footage. That means a typical religious ceremony will require at least two media changes. This process first requires *finalization* of the DVD, which can take between 10 seconds and 10 minutes—valuable time if the first kiss is approaching. Be wary of selecting this storage medium for your primary camcorder, although it could be useful as a secondary camera for detail shots and close-ups.

 The amount of time you can shoot without interruption is particularly relevant when using a stationary and unmanned camcorder, such as in the two-camcorder, one-operator scenario described in Chapter 7, "The Big Day." Avoid purchasing a camcorder that will force awkward media changes or prevent you from easily handling a two-camera shoot.

Media Transfer

How you transfer the data in your camcorder's storage medium onto your computer varies with the camcorder and your system. Macs have historically used *FireWire* to transfer this data but are moving toward *USB 2.0*, the current PC standard. With removable media, you can simply attach a card reader to your computer to transfer the media.

Inputs and Outputs

Your camcorder might include various ports, such as an *HDMI* port to connect the camcorder to an HDTV or an analog out to connect the camcorder to a television. This is particularly relevant if your camcorder is part of your post-production workflow, used as a deck to watch your edits on an external monitor.

Quality audio is often taken for granted—until it is missing. At least one external audio port is also crucial; it will be either a *mini jack* or an *XLR*, and will get an audio feed from your wireless microphone (see Figure 3.7). Additional ports are useful if you have more than one wireless microphone, have a directional microphone, or are hoping to pick up an audio feed from the ceremony or reception venue. When purchasing a camcorder, make sure you do not limit your audio options, even if you do not currently own external microphones. Leave yourself room to upgrade your audio equipment if you can't start out with everything you might want.

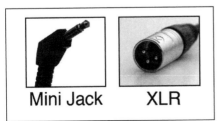

Figure 3.7
Even the built-in microphone of a high-quality camera is not up to the task when it comes to wedding videography. You will need external microphones that connect to your camera via mini jack or XLR cables and/or wireless microphones whose receivers will also connect here. *(Photo ©iStockPhoto.com/mm88.)*

Stabilization

While you'll likely film the ceremony, toasts, and possibly other parts of the wedding reception (depending on your style) using a tripod or other stabilization device, you'll likely capture a lot of footage in hand-held style. For example, you'll probably be mingling with the crowd, working hand-held, while the wedding guests dance and during the cocktail hour (if there is one). No matter how steady your arm may be, a little shake will inevitably occur when you are off tripod. Especially when you are zoomed in, tiny incidental movements will look like pans gone awry.

Quality camcorders have image stabilization built in. There are two main image-stabilization technologies:

> ▶ **Electronic image stabilization (EIS).** Sometimes called digital image stabilization, *EIS* subtly shifts an image to counteract motion by borrowing pixels from outside the border of the visible picture. This can occasionally result in slightly blurred images, as the camera is constantly moving the image around to compensate for the motion of your hands.

> ▶ **Optical image stabilization (OIS).** Instead of moving the image, *OIS* uses a motor to move the lens in response to any movement it senses. Unlike EIS, the integrity of the image will not be affected—although this technology is significantly more expensive.

While both image-stabilization technologies will mask some smaller movements, you should not count on image stabilization to save you. It won't. There will undoubtedly be lots of unusable footage in your hand-held footage. Although image stabilization can certainly be a factor when it comes to boosting the professionalism of your end product, practicing smooth and steady hand-held movements and getting comfortable with your tripod, monopod, or steadistick will be far more useful than any image-stabilization features your camcorder might offer. (More information about tripods, monopods, and steadisticks is provided later in this chapter.)

Manual Controls

A key difference between a professional-grade camcorder and a consumer model is the ability to manually control *exposure* and *focus*. Designed to produce a solid shot under average conditions, automatic mechanisms are simplistic and inhibit artistry. Camcorders with automatic focus will focus on what they determine to be the subject of a scene. But your subject can drift—and an auto-focus camcorder may have trouble keeping up. Moreover, in more stylized shots, you might want several subjects or you might want to focus on the non-obvious.

With manual focus, *you* choose what to focus on and ensure that the camcorder's focus stays locked in. You can also incorporate more artistry in your shots such as a rack or pull focus. A focus ring around the lens is the easiest way to use manual control, and is a feature to look for in a high-end camcorder (see Figure 3.8).

Figure 3.8
Manual controls, like the focus and exposure rings on this camera, allow for both a higher degree of precision and more artistry.

Similarly, the ability to manually control exposure will enable you to change the amount of light passing through the camcorder lens. This may be especially valuable in low light situations, where an automatic-only setting may not be opening up enough to give you the necessary amount of light. It could also be useful in awkward light situations, such as in front of windows or in extremely bright sunlight, when your camcorder's automatic settings aren't responding well enough or fast enough for you to get usable footage. Finally, for stylistic effect, you may want to let too much light in, or blow the shot out, to get a stark white contrast to your subject.

Using a manual setting for *gain* is another way to manipulate the brightness of your images. Unlike with exposure, changing your gain does not change the amount of light that hits the camcorder sensor. Instead, it amplifies the signal that hits the sensor, regardless of what type of sensor the camcorder has. It effectively increases the exposure without you having to think too hard about apertures and shutter speeds. In automatic mode, however, gain can quickly make the image too grainy. In manual mode, you have more control over how much gain you apply in any situation and can prevent the video noise and grain that often occur when the camera is in automatic mode.

Camcorders: A Comparison

Table 3.1 contains a comparison of some common camcorders used in the wedding videography business, highlighting some of their features and their price (as of the printing of this book). This table represents a small sample of the dozens and dozens of suitable camcorders available. The listing of a camcorder here should not be construed as an endorsement; the idea is to provide a range of manufacturers, features, and prices. While the features noted in this chart are of primary importance to wedding videography, this does not represent a comprehensive list. Once you have narrowed your list by major features, make sure to also learn whether the audio and video inputs and accessory shoes are appropriate; whether you like the look and feel of the camera body, viewfinder, and LCD; and what all the other features are.

TABLE 3.1 COMMON CAMCORDERS

Make/ Model	SD/HD	Price*	Optical Zoom	Sensor	Storage Type	Maximum Resolution	Digital Video Interface	Manual Controls
Canon XHA1	HD	$3,999	20×	$1/3$-in 3CCD	MiniDV tape	1440×1080p	IEEE-1394 (FireWire)	Yes
Canon GL2	SD	$2,799	20×	$1/4$-in 3CCD	MiniDV	720×540p	IEEE-1394 (FireWire)	Yes
Panasonic HDC-SD5BNDL	HD	$995	10×	$1/6$-in 3CCD	Memory card	1920×1080p	HDMI, USB	No
Panasonic AG-HMC150	HD	$3,995	13×	$1/3$-in 3CCD	Memory card	1920×1080p	HD/SD-SDI, USB	Yes
Panasonic AG-HPX170	HD	$5,695	13×	$1/3$-in 3CCD	P2 card and memory slot	1920×1080p	HD/SD-SDI	Yes
Sony HDR XR500V	HD	$1,199	12×	1/2.88-in CMOS	120GB hard drive	1920×1080p	HDMI, USB	No
Sony HVRA1U	HD	$2,750	10×	$1/3$-in 3CMOS	MiniDV tape	1440×1080p	IEEE-1394 (FireWire)	Yes

*Prices are listed from manufacturer's web site at time of writing and may not indicate current pricing from other retailers.

Tripod

A major difference between your video and the bride's cousin Betty's video will be the result of the *tripod* that you are lugging around. I love and hate my tripod. It is heavy and awkward and slows me down as I am scrambling to get ahead of the bride and groom walking up the garden path—but it is impossible to get a professional-looking shot without it. Your arm alone simply can't do the job required.

A professional tripod will do more than hold the camcorder still for you; it will also enable you to move your camcorder. For professional camcorder moves—say, a pan or a tilt—you need a fluid-head tripod. Fluid-head tripods literally use fluid, a viscous oil, between moving components to facilitate subtle movements, jerk-free pans, and smooth starts and stops. Even the best friction-head tripod will not give you the smooth, clean camcorder moves that a fluid-head tripod will deliver. The difference is striking.

Unlike camcorders, tripod technology does not change rapidly. You can reasonably expect to replace your camcorder more often than you upgrade your tripod. With that in mind, make sure to invest in a tripod that will enhance—not inhibit—your artistic abilities, and that will be sturdy enough for your current camcorder and any foreseeable upgrades. Well-known tripod manufacturers include Bogen, Manfrotto, Miller, and Sachtler; a good tripod can range in price from about $300 to $2,000.

In addition to carrying a tripod, wedding videographers often carry a *monopod*, also called a unipod (see Figure 3.9). A monopod is a lightweight, single-legged staff on which you can mount your camera. (Unlike with a tripod, you still must support the camera on a monopod.) Mono-pods can be handy because they are easy to carry around. Using a monopod can reduce move-ment in the vertical plane while allowing movement in the horizontal plane, giving the footage a bit of added style without being as jumpy as with a hand-held camera. By holding the base of the monopod perpendicular to your body from a height—such as a stage, hill, or balcony—you can get a great bird's-eye shot of the wedding; I carry a small monopod for that reason exclusively.

Figure 3.9
A monopod requires a steady arm to get a good shot, but significantly reduces motion in the vertical plane. The built-in level on this monopod helps you reduce movement on the horizontal plane, too. More lightweight and maneuverable than a tripod, monopods are particularly useful in crowded shooting conditions, like cocktail hours and reception dancing.

Finally, more and more wedding videographers are opting to use *steadisticks*, which are sticks or platforms on which you mount the camera and then attach to your waist. This is a particularly good option for removing shake from moving shots, such as ones that circle the bride as she gets ready or the couple as they dance. Steadisticks range from professional, heavyweight Hollywood versions that cost several thousand dollars to lightweight and easily manipulated models that will put you back about $200. Although you may hear that the cheap and lightweight sticks aren't worth the money, keep in mind that you will have to carry all your gear around with you; should you opt to purchase steadisticks, find a balance between sticks that will get the job done without burdening you all day. It's pretty easy to weigh down your budget with steadying gear; think about where and when you will use the gear to help determine how much weight to carry and how much money to spend.

Audio

Any camcorder you buy will include on-camcorder audio recording. Depending which part of the wedding you are shooting and the sound conditions, however, the on-camcorder microphone may be woefully inadequate to pick up the sound you want and eliminate the background noise. Another distinction between professional wedding videographers and their amateur counterparts is their ability to obtain various audio feeds for both sound clarity—not to mention insurance, should something go wrong.

In particular, a wireless *lavaliere microphone* (also called a *lav* or *lapel microphone*) is indispensible for the wedding ceremony, especially since your camcorder will likely be far from the couple, who are quite likely to whisper or even choke through their vows.

Lavaliere mics have three parts: the microphone, the *transmitter*, and the *receiver* (see Figure 3.10). The microphone and transmitter are worn by the subject; the receiver is connected to your camcorder, through an XLR or mini jack. During the ceremony, the groom will typically wear the lav microphone and carry the transmitter in his pocket. This allows you to obtain an audio channel that is separate from your camcorder. This is crucial because, depending on where you are standing, your on-camcorder microphone might be picking up noises like children crying or guests fanning themselves with their programs instead of the important business at hand. If time for setup allows, using a lav microphone for toasts and interviews can also dramatically improve audio quality—although if possible, it might be easier to get an audio feed from the DJ or band.

Figure 3.10
Typically, the groom wears a wireless microphone attached to his lapel, with the transmitter in his jacket pocket. The microphone and transmitter are shown in this image. The receiver for the microphone, similar in size to the transmitter, attaches to the camcorder via XLR or mini jack.

It is generally accepted that *ultra high frequency (UHF)* diversity microphones are best for weddings, although this is not universally true. (When referring to microphones, diversity means the use of two antennas to reduce the possibility of an audio dropout between the transmitter and the receiver.) UHF is regarded as a better option than *very high frequency (VHF)*, however, because despite being more expensive and chewing more batteries, UHF offers a larger frequency spectrum and therefore has less chance of interference. A UHF lavaliere system can run between about $250 and $1200. Well-known manufacturers of wireless lavaliere microphones include Shure, Sony, Sennheiser, and Audio-Technica.

A hand-held microphone (see Figure 3.11) can also be very useful—especially because they require virtually no setup. An interviewee can simply hold onto the microphone, which is connected directly to the camcorder through the same port that your lav microphone uses. This can be especially handy if you want to get comments from guests during the reception; using a hand-held mic will eliminate much (though not all) of the background talk and music without having to be set up in a hallway or other sound-protected area.

Figure 3.11
A hand-held microphone can attach right to your camera. In certain situations, such as guest interviews, it doesn't hurt the shot to have the microphone visible.

Because audio can often go wrong, many videographers invest in a non-camcorder audio backup source such as a digital audio recorder. Lightweight and relatively inexpensive, this device—most crucial during the ceremony—is usually left running throughout the entire proceedings, placed somewhere near the officiant (for example, on a podium or table). It can't be monitored, but tends to be quite stable and can be a solid option should other audio inputs fail. These recorders are also useful at the reception, placed near the people giving toasts to ensure good audio there. Also, make sure you have a set of decent-quality headphones so you can monitor your audio. These should be attached to your camcorder and worn whenever you are recording to ensure that audio levels and quality are appropriate.

 There are two ways to monitor audio: by watching the meter levels on your camera or by listening through headphones. While the moving meter levels will tell you that yes, audio is being recorded on the channels specified, you can only determine the *quality* of the audio by actually listening. Using headphones throughout will help you listen for interference, static, low volume, and other audio problems.

External Lights

For feature or commercial shoots, professional videographers tend to have lighting kits—soft boxes, rim lights, etc.—to build a particular mood. While it would be great if wedding videographers could also use these, the fact is that wedding videographers are constantly on the run and must work quickly. Even if logistics allowed, it is unlikely that the couple would want such a large and invasive setup. So instead of using a large lighting rig, wedding video shooters must learn how to best manage available light and bring as much portable light with them as possible.

Some camcorders have built-in lights attached. These lights tend to be highly directional and therefore very harsh—when they are noticeable at all. That is, in general, instead of casting a powerful glow, they cast a tiny ray. Furthermore, the light runs off the same battery as the camcorder itself, sucking it dry very quickly. For these reasons, camcorders with built-in lights have become significantly less popular.

A much better way to add light is to use an external, add-on light that fits in your camcorder's *hot shoe* (also called an *accessory shoe*), a slotted bracket designed to connect external devices to your camcorder (see Figure 3.12). If the camcorder doesn't have a hot shoe, other brackets can be customized. An add-on light will be much brighter than a built-in one and will also allow more control. Each design is different, but you should have some control over brightness and diffusion. Well-known add-on light manufacturers include Bescor and Cool-Lux; these lights can range from about $100 to $350. Another lighting option that will fit in a camera hot shoe is a small panel of *LED* lights. Litepanel LED offers a range of models. Although more expensive—they tend to start at over $600—these LED panels use far less battery power and don't burn out for thousands of hours. Check out this option for your setup; although you will pay more for the light itself, you may break even or even save money when you take into account batteries.

Figure 3.12
A hot shoe, or accessory shoe, is a slotted bracket on the top of the camcorder body that allows external devices, such as a light, to be attached.

Add-on lights attach to an external, dedicated battery that is typically worn by the shooter, often in a belt or a bag around the waist. For long shoots, a chain of batteries can be worn. Buying multiple batteries can be expensive, but having them is incredibly helpful if, say, the entire reception is in low light, requiring you to use your add-on light for hours on end. Make sure you know how long your batteries will run your light and that you have enough for any given wedding timeline.

Bags

Videographers can be as finicky about their gear bags as they are about their gear. This is not entirely unwarranted: Their bag not only houses and protects their precious equipment, it may be the thing that saves their back and shoulders from a grueling day. To paraphrase one product reviewer, a camcorder bag might never be big enough, comfortable enough, sturdy enough, or light enough, but if it is, you can't pay enough for it.

It is impossible to determine what kind of bag you need until you have all your gear. Once you have your gear accumulated, bring the major pieces with you as you shop for a bag. That way, you can actually put the pieces in each bag you're considering buying and see how the loaded bag feels. Make sure the bag will also accommodate all your smaller bits and pieces. If your workflow requires you to download media to a drive or a laptop, don't forget to include that in your estimation. Finally, consider future gear purchases when you buy your bag. Bags are not an incidental purchase; you'll save money in the long run if you give yourself some room to grow. Like tripods, it is better to grow into your bag than grow out of it.

The major considerations when picking out a bag are size, handle, material, and compartment configuration. It is possible—albeit unlikely—that you will be able to fit all your gear into a backpack. More likely, you'll be shopping for a bag with a shoulder strap and handles; having both is very helpful. Maneuvering through crowds is difficult with a big bag over your shoulder, but the shoulder strap is key for freeing up your hands—which will likely be otherwise occupied or simply exhausted.

With respect to material, you'll need to choose between a hard case and a soft one. The advantages of using a hard case are twofold: sturdiness for travel and the ability to lock it. That being said, a soft case is recommended for weddings because of how much you'll need to lug it around and dig through it on a typical shoot. Soft cases may be nylon, PVC, or leather. Some have a sturdier material on the bottom, such as rubber.

The number and allocation of compartments you'll want is highly personal. All video bags have multiple padded compartments in which to stash the camcorder, lights, and other equipment. Some bags also have pouches, zippered enclosures, and other assorted nooks and crannies. I consider these compartments a blessing and manage to fill each and every one with markers, extra batteries, media, and other miscellaneous items carefully stored to save me in an emergency. Some people, though, find the array of zippers and snaps confounding and would prefer that their items be laid out more explicitly. How you organize things is personal, as evidenced by your clothing closet or your filing system. It makes sense that the type of bag you prefer will be too.

While a tripod bag can be handy, it's often not necessary. In fact, I find that mine gets in the way since I use my tripod so often. Although carrying a tripod in a bag with a shoulder strap is significantly more comfortable than lugging it around unsheathed, it's such a pain to constantly shove the tripod into the bag and yank it back out that I usually tote the tripod around over my shoulder by using the handle while the bag sits in the car. As with how you organize your bag, whether you buy a tripod bag is a matter of personal preference. If you're on a tight budget, however, you can certainly manage without one.

A Word About Multiples

If you are shooting weddings with two cameras, you will naturally be building your gear up to two (or more) full kits. This may happen incrementally. For example, you don't necessarily need a lavaliere microphone for each camcorder, especially if you are only shooting the ceremony with dual-camcorder coverage. As you build up your equipment inventory, however, make sure that all your systems are compatible with each other. Ideally your camcorders are identical; at the very least, they should work well together. For example, they should shoot the same color tone and resolution.

Having compatible camcorders will help in several ways, including ease of shooting and smooth editing. If your camcorders are similar, you have the advantage of familiarity: Your hands get used to making the same motions, and you grow accustomed to the series of menus involved in making the selections you want. Having camcorders that function the same way will also decrease your fumbling as you look for the manual focus or the neutral density filter. Furthermore, two camcorders from the same maker will produce images that edit together more smoothly, without requiring you to do color correction; different camcorder makers tend to generate images with a slightly different color tone.

Finally, you want all your accessories to match all of your camcorders. For example, if all your lights mount on all your camcorders, you will have more options in the event of equipment failure or on weekends that are double-booked. Moreover, the same cameras will use the same batteries, which drastically eases the logistics and expense involved in ensuring you have enough power with you for the day.

STEVE SPARKS, BELLE WEDDING VIDEO, SAN FRANCISCO, CA

I was shooting the bride getting ready, and the image in the LCD viewer kept getting bluer and bluer. I checked the daylight and tungsten settings; they were correct. I replayed some of the footage hoping it was just a viewer problem, but no such luck.

I immediately called the owner of the company I was shooting for, and in one hour (which was 10 minutes after the ceremony was scheduled to start), his wife showed up at the ceremony with an identical camcorder. The audio and tripod were ready to go; I just clicked the replacement camcorder in place and we started. The congregation knew what was going on; they laughed when I snapped the camcorder on the tripod and said "Ready!"

(continued)

STEVE SPARKS, BELLE WEDDING VIDEO, SAN FRANCISCO, CA (continued)

It was a little embarrassing that the ceremony was held up on my account, but at the same time, due to how fast everyone reacted and how well matched all my equipment was, it was about as seamless as possible. In fact, a 10-minute delay is nothing in wedding time. Now when I go on one-camcorder shoots, I try to bring two camcorders. Of course, I have never needed it again, but that is because I am prepared. You only get in trouble when you aren't.

Summary

From this chapter, you should be able to determine what characteristics to look for as you obtain production gear:

- ▶ Camcorder
- ▶ Tripod
- ▶ Monopod
- ▶ Wireless lavaliere microphone
- ▶ Hand-held microphone
- ▶ On-camera lighting and associated batteries
- ▶ Gear bags

Next Up

With all your production gear in place, you are ready to shoot your first job. That is only half the battle, though. After you shoot the video, you need to turn it into the version that doesn't include the bride swearing or your accidental shots of the floor. Instead, it must tell the story with style and grace—however you want that to be. In order to do that, you have to get your footage onto (and off of) an editing system. The next chapter discusses the hardware and software requirements for your post-production workflow.

Chapter 3 Tutorial: Choosing a Camcorder and Packing Your Gear

Choosing a Camcorder

When you begin shopping for camcorders, use this worksheet to help you consider all the features of the camcorders you are considering. Note details about the specific parameters of each feature—e.g., the size of the LCD screen and whether it rotates 360 degrees, which kinds of audio inputs it has (and how many)—so you have a full picture of the benefits and trade-offs of each camcorder. Don't overlook the importance of the worksheet's last two categories: look and feel. Get a sense of whether the camcorder feels comfortable to hold and handle. You must enjoy your camcorder; you're starting a long relationship with it!

	Camcorder #1	Camcorder #2	Camcorder #3
Make/Model			
Price			
Media			
Video Interface			
Sensor			
Manual:			
Gain			
White Balance			
Focus			
Exposure			
Audio Inputs			
Video Outputs			
Lens			
LCD			
Look			
Feel			

Packing Your Gear

It is alarmingly easy to arrive at a wedding site, only to realize what you have forgotten. Have a checklist available so that every time you pack your camera bag, you can scan for each item and avoid that problem. Depending on your service, you might not need every item listed here (such as a laptop or projector); build your own list by customizing this one to your own service and gear bag(s).

- ▶ Camcorder
- ▶ Camcorder batteries
- ▶ Camcorder battery charger
- ▶ Tripod/tripod plate
- ▶ Monopod/monopod plate
- ▶ Steadistick
- ▶ External lights
- ▶ External light batteries/battery belt
- ▶ External light battery charger
- ▶ Wired microphone

▶ Wireless microphones: all parts

▶ Wireless microphone batteries (lots!)

▶ Audio cables

▶ Blank media (lots!)

▶ Headphones

▶ Lens cleaner/lens tissue

▶ White balance card

▶ Laptop

▶ Laptop power cord

▶ Laptop external drive

▶ Interface cables/card reader

▶ Overhead projector

▶ Cable converter for overhead projector

▶ Pens

▶ Tape

▶ Utility knife/scissors

▶ Business cards

▶ Paperwork

▶ Stepping stool

▶ Plastic bags

▶ Umbrella

▶ Personal items

Chapter 4
Getting Post-Production Gear

In this chapter:

▶ Post-production hardware
▶ Post-production software
▶ Effects software

Post-production lacks the drama, panic, and excitement of the wedding-day shoot—and that is not always a bad thing. For me, the post-production part of the job, which requires deep and uninterrupted concentration, is characterized by solitary, calm, and methodical work; interruptions that come in the form of my phone, client meetings, and other issues of daily business are beyond my control, of course. It is an excellent balance to the thrill, chaos, and social interactions usually required on the wedding day. And unlike on the wedding day, during which you have very little control over events, in post-production, you are completely in charge. Didn't like the bride's sister's off-handed remarks? Take them out! Think the bride's dress looks better with a slight blue tint? She will too! Editing allows you to craft a piece of your own artistic creation—and happily, current technology allows your artistic creations to be very elaborate.

In this chapter you learn ways to best equip yourself for post-production to make the technical aspects of the job go as smoothly and easily as possible. A major complication of selecting post-production equipment is ensuring it is all compatible with the various other parts of your system. To make sure all the pieces of your system—hardware and software—work seamlessly together, it is imperative to make big decisions first and let the smaller decisions follow suit.

As in the previous chapter, I will try in this one to distinguish between the elements you absolutely must have from the equipment that could benefit your workflow or your product but can be considered optional if you are on a tight budget.

Post-Production Hardware

Presumably, you will do your post-production work on either a Mac- or PC-based digital, nonlinear editing system. *Nonlinear* refers to the fact that the system has random access. That is, unlike tape-based systems, nonlinear systems can access any frame of video with equal ease. Most recent versions of nonlinear editing systems can handle both SD and HD footage and have dramatically improved in the last decade in terms of their costs and capabilities.

Besides a computer, hardware you will absolutely need includes the following:

▶ Computer file storage space (which may be inside your computer, external, or, ideally both)

▶ A computer monitor

▶ An external video monitor

▶ Speakers

You will also need a *video interface*—that is, a method for moving footage from your camera to the computer. The method you choose may depend both on your camera and your budget.

Computer Requirements

It is likely you already have a computer, but before you check that off your list of assets, make sure it's powerful enough to effectively run editing and post-production software (primarily a measure of the CPU and RAM) and can store the big files you'll be working with (a measure of storage space). If not, you will need to consider either adapting your system by upgrading some components or getting a whole new system.

The *central processing unit (CPU)* of your computer is responsible for all operations. Every software program must communicate with the CPU in order to execute functions; the CPU's speed will determine how powerful the computer is in executing these functions. The speed of the CPU is measured in *hertz (Hz)* and describes how many cycles of commands that the CPU can handle in one second. For example, a 1 megahertz (1MHz) processor can handle one million instructions per second. A gigahertz (GHz) is 1,000MHz, so a 2GHz processor can handle two billion instructions per second. Software specs identify how much processor speed is required to run the software; it is recommended that your CPU be above the minimum requirement for the software you plan to use.

Random access memory, or RAM, is the high-speed memory used inside a computer to store internal applications and data. RAM provides temporary space for your computer to read and write data to be accessed by the CPU, reducing the number of times the CPU must communicate with the hard disk. For this reason, editing programs will also have a minimum RAM requirement. The amount of RAM your computer has is critical to how fast your applications run—especially when you run several programs at once. (This is often the case in a post-production workflow, when you might have video-editing software, image-editing software, DVD-authoring software, and an e-mail application all open at once.) Take your RAM requirements seriously, and then consider adding more!

Any editing software will list all of its technical specifications on its Web site or packaging. Make sure what you are buying is compatible for your system. A few basic requirements for some of the most popular software among wedding videographers—Adobe Premiere (versions CS3 and later available for PC and Mac; earlier versions for PC only), Apple Final Cut Pro (Mac only), Avid Media Composer (PC and Mac), and Sony Vegas (PC only)—are listed in Table 4.1.

TABLE 4.1 PRIMARY REQUIREMENTS FOR FOUR POPULAR EDITING SYSTEMS*

Editing System	Processor	RAM	Drives
Adobe Premiere Pro CS4 (PC)	2GHz (DV) 3.4GHz (HDV) Dual 2.8GHz (HD)	2GB	Dedicated 7200 RPM (DV) Dedicated 7200 RPM (HDV) RAID 0 (HD)
Adobe Premiere Pro CS4 (Mac)	Multicore Intel processor 3.4GHz (HDV) Dual 2.8GHz (HD)	2GB	Dedicated 7200 RPM (DV) Dedicated 7200 RPM (HDV) RAID 0 (HD)
Apple Final Cut Pro 7	Intel processor	1GB (DV) 2GB (HDV) 4GB (HD)	
Avid Media Composer 3.5 (PC)	Intel Core Duo 2.33GHz	2GB (DV) 2GB (HDV) 4GB (HD) 4GB (Vista)	7200 RPM
Avid Media Composer 3.5 (Mac)	Intel Dual, Dual Core 2.66GHz Xeon Intel Core Duo 2.33GHz (laptops)	2GB (DV) 2GB (HDV) 4GB (HD)	7200 RPM
Sony Vegas Pro 9 (PC)	1GHz Multicore/multiprocessor (HD)	1GB	

*Other hardware requirements will be specified by the software manufacturer, and should be checked before final purchase.

Similarly, most video-editing programs will have minimum requirements for a *video card*, which is the circuit board dedicated to generating graphics. This should not be an issue in newer computers, but might be problematic if you are attempting to adapt an older computer to fit your workflow. If you plan to edit on a computer you already own, make sure that you look carefully at all your hardware specifications and upgrade options. It is not a good idea to spend a lot of money making upgrades, however; you will hit a ceiling in how much you can upgrade, and will eventually be locked out of the newest software. It is probably wiser to spend money on a newer system—perhaps even a lower-end one—to which you can add more bells, whistles, speed, and storage at a later date.

ERIN KORBYLO, CLASSIC PIXELS HIGH DEFINITION VIDEO PRODUCTIONS, LOUISVILLE, KY

"I can't help but think that Macs are for right-brained people and PCs are for left-brained people. I started on Avid Liquid Pro, but as a left-brainer, switched to Sony Vegas Pro– which was a great move for me and the company. I find the program to be flexible, and my workflow has been much simplified. Compressing files for any format is easy, and burning Blu-ray DVDs isn't much harder than the click of a button."

Some of your hardware decisions may depend on your software preferences, as certain editing programs (discussed later in this chapter) run only on either a Mac or PC platform, but not both. But deciding between a Mac and a PC is difficult to do from just an editing standpoint because you will also want to use your computer to run your business. So when deciding what computer buy, you'll want to consider both editing software and the software you want to use for daily business operations.

Here are a few other considerations when it comes to deciding between the PC and Mac platforms:

▶ The top PC will tend to be faster than the top Mac.

▶ PCs offer a wider set of choices when it comes to setting up a system. While choice is rarely a bad thing, it does tend to breed compatibility issues. As a result, setting up and maintaining a PC can be more troublesome than setting up and maintaining a Mac, where the number of options—and room for error—is smaller.

▶ Macs have a sleeker look and an easier, more user-friendly interface. Although there are people who will loudly (and justifiably) disagree, that tends to be the general sentiment (as well as my opinion).

▶ There are more PC viruses out there than Mac viruses, although viruses spread through user error can strike Mac and PC owners equally easily. (Read: Don't open unknown attachments!)

▶ Every Mac comes bundled with enough software (iMovie and iDVD) to create a basic wedding video DVD. While these are not the software applications I would recommend, if you are building your business slowly, they will get the job done until you can upgrade.

▶ Movie Maker is the PC answer to iMovie, offered as a free download. Like iMovie, it is not a good enough editing program to run your business on, but it could be used in a pinch. It does not offer a DVD-authoring solution, however.

TURNKEY SOLUTIONS

It is possible to avoid dealing with all the various editing-setup issues with both hardware and software by purchasing a *turnkey system*—that is, an editing system that is ready to go, out of the box. If you are slightly technophobic, own zero starting equipment, and/or want all the bells and whistles without having to look hard for them, this might be a viable option for you. Another advantage is the technical support that you will receive from the manufacturer or distributor. It should be noted, however, that turnkey editing systems tend to be more expensive and sometimes prohibit the functionality of the computer when being used for something other than editing. That is to say, they are often more simple to set up, but you will pay for this simplicity in dollars and/or functionality.

Storage Space

In the last decade, computer storage, once prohibitively expensive, has dropped dramatically in price, helping to facilitate the shift to an affordable, editing studio—and the increase in the wedding video market. In 1980, a 1GB hard disk cost $40,000—and weighed more than 500 pounds! Today, a 1GB flash drive is less than $10, weighs a few ounces, and can easily be lost in a purse (well, mine anyway). Of course, 1GB doesn't take you anywhere in the world of video; depending on the format, it barely stores a minute of footage.

The amount of storage space you need for any given wedding will depend on several things, including the type and amount of footage you shoot and your post-production style. You must also have enough space to accommodate working on several weddings at once, back up your data, and keep enough space free that things don't slow down too much. Ideally, to maintain optimal speed, a drive should be no more than 75 percent full.

The video format you use will help you pin down your storage requirements. Standard-definition DV consumes about 13GB of storage per hour of footage, while DVC Pro HD requires approximately four times that: 60GB per hour. Full, uncompressed HD is unusual in the wedding world—in part because it guzzles 558GB of storage per hour of video. Table 4.2 shows some of the most common video formats, along with how many gigabytes one hour of footage consumes and how many hours of footage will fit into a terabyte (TB) of storage.

TABLE 4.2 STORAGE CONSUMPTION OF VARIOUS VIDEO FORMATS

Format	GB/Hour	Hours/TB
DV	13	75
HDV 720p	11	90
HDV 1080i	13	75
DVCPro HD	60	17
Uncompressed HD, 720p, 10-bit	497	2
Uncompressed HD, 1080i, 10-bit	558	1.8

If you are using uncompressed HD video, you will also need to consider the drives you are using, which will need to be arranged in a *RAID* array. RAID stands for Redundant Array of Independent Disks (formerly Redundant Array of Inexpensive Disks). A RAID array is basically a series of drives banded together to act as a single drive. Several different RAID schemes can be employed, all of which serve to divide and replicate data. This is important for both data protection and easier retrieval of big files, such as uncompressed HD footage. Your RAID drives can be either external or internal.

Computer Monitor(s)

Even in their most basic configuration, editing programs typically have several windows. Even before additional tools are added, these programs take up quite a bit of screen real estate on the monitor. A large screen is desirable, and a setup that allows for two monitors is even better. Before you get into a two-screen situation, however, make sure that your video card can handle it, and that you will also be able to use an external video monitor in your configuration.

External Video Monitor

An external video monitor is a crucial component of your editing hardware system.

Unfortunately, DV footage tends to look better when seen on a computer monitor or the camera's LCD screen. That is, it doesn't necessarily give you an accurate sense of how it will appear to your clients when they view it using their television and DVD player. To correctly gauge any effects you apply or any color corrections you make, it's imperative to have an external monitor. If you are shooting HD, you will need an HD monitor to see the full-resolution version of your video.

Professional video monitors offer the advantages of much higher video quality, switchable aspect ratios, compatibility with NTSC and PAL, a variety of professional inputs and outputs, and, often, input switching. Unfortunately, the video monitor is also the most expensive line item in your hardware budget. Indeed, it's not unusual to see them priced at tens of thousands of dollars.

While all the features of a professional monitor are desirable, it is the first—higher video quality—that is by far the most important to the wedding videographer. You will need to know when your whites are too high, when the reds bleed and look bad, and when your sepia and tint effects are over-applied—all things that your computer monitor may not render accurately. If your budget can't handle a professional monitor, use a consumer television set, either SD or HD, depending on your video. Assuming it has the right inputs and outputs for your system, it should work just fine. You could even make the argument that if you can make your footage look good on a bad TV, it will look good on anything.

An external video monitor or television may fit into a monitor output on your video card. Alternatively, it can be attached via S-video (and a converter) to your computer, or via S-video or FireWire to your camera or deck. The number and types of monitor ports you have on your video card will help determine your configuration.

Speakers

The audio that comes out of your computer is *line-level audio*, which means it is a fairly weak signal. You must use external speakers to get amplified sound that you can edit with. Your speakers can connect via USB or minijack. Many editors find that working with a set of high-quality headphones is the best way to get clean audio. They make it easier to pinpoint audio subtleties, while blocking noise from neighboring offices or rooms—not to mention the fact that your neighbors won't have to hear Uncle Al's wedding toast on repeat!

Video Interface

Part of building your editing workstation means setting it up such that you can link your camera or deck to your computer to transfer the footage. There are several different digital video interfaces that make this transfer possible; when piecing your editing workstation together, make sure that the interface from your camcorder is compatible with your computer system.

The process of moving footage from the camera to the computer is often called *digitizing*, which is correct when used in reference to importing analog video. Digitizing analog video creates a digital video signal and saves it on a hard drive. Since we are already dealing with digital footage, however, the term digitizing is incorrect; in this case, we are simply moving digital media already collected by the camera to a hard drive, which may be called *capturing*, *transferring*, or *importing*.

FireWire

FireWire, also called IEEE 1394, was developed by Apple in 1986 and is a very common digital interface. Faster than USB, which is another common interface for connecting peripherals, FireWire is commonly found on DV, DVCAM, DVCPro, and HDV cameras. If you plan to use FireWire for video capture, you must ensure that your computer has FireWire ports on the motherboard. If not, you will need to install a FireWire interface.

There are two types of FireWire connectors, 4-pin and 6-pin. As shown in Figure 4.1, 4-pin connectors are smaller than the 6-pin connectors, which often carry power as well as data. Typically, the camera port will be 4-pin and the computer port will be 6-pin; to connect the two, a 4-pin–to–6-pin FireWire cable is required.

Figure 4.1
In a FireWire video interface, the smaller, 4-pin port will typically be on the camera and the larger 6-pin port will be on the computer or drive.

A FireWire 400 port, as found on computers and external storage drives, is so named because it moves data at up to 400 megabits per second (Mbps) using the FireWire 6-pin port. Note that although many drives and computers also employ a FireWire 800 interface (see Figure 4.2), which can transfer data at up to twice the rate, cameras don't support—or need—this speed.

Figure 4.2
The side of this drive has a port for both FireWire 400 and FireWire 800.

HDMI

Increasingly, camcorders are using a *High Definition Multimedia Interface (HDMI)*, which transfers uncompressed SD and HD audio and video. This standard offers the advantage of being all digital, high quality, and low cost, and is gaining a strong toehold in both professional and consumer electronics and computers. Currently, some PC computers have an HDMI port for easy transfer of this footage; Mac computers do not. To use a camcorder with an HDMI output with a computer that doesn't have an HDMI port, an intermediary HDMI capture card is required, such as the Intensity Card from Blackmagic Design. Figure 4.3 shows an HDMI cable.

Figure 4.3
HDMI is becoming increasingly popular as a video interface for camcorders as well for other consumer electronics.

Card Readers

Increasingly, cameras capture data to memory cards or flash drives. In that case, the data is usually moved to the computer via a reader, which connects to your computer through a USB, USB 2.0, or *PCMCIA* interface. Make sure you have both the cards and card reader appropriate for your camera and computer.

DVD Burner

It is unlikely that you would own a computer that doesn't have a DVD burner in it, but of course there are some. Because most wedding videos are still output to DVD (as opposed to online delivery), however, a DVD burner should be a part of your system, whether it's an internal device or an external one. As discussed in Chapter 10, "Output and Delivery," there are several standard DVD formats that you are likely to use. Ideally, your DVD burner will accommodate the DVD-9 standard as well as the more common DVD-5.

If you will be shooting in HD, you might consider investing in a Blu-ray burner. *Blu-ray* is the new DVD standard that allows for as much as 25GB of data on a standard disc, as opposed to the 4.7GB that a DVD currently holds. With that level of storage, you can easily house a fully uncompressed HD wedding video of well over an hour on a single disc, which is impossible with standard DVDs.

That being said, it is important to realize that to watch a Blu-ray disc, a Blu-ray player is required. Blu-ray discs do not play in standard DVD players or all computers. At the time of this writing, Blu-ray players have not penetrated the market to a degree that it makes a Blu-ray burner a necessary purchase for your wedding business. Because technology is constantly changing, improving, and getting cheaper, I suggest waiting to buy a Blu-ray burner until your business calls for it in some way: as a marketing tool, a competitive edge or to keep up. (Some videographers report that providing a Blu-ray disc is a huge marketing tool because grooms see it as an excuse to buy a Blu-ray player or a Sony PlayStation 3, which plays Blu-ray discs.) To determine whether you should buy one, carefully examine your own regional market.

Other Items to Consider

So you have the hardware you need and a workstation that is waiting only for software (and your first job, of course). If you have some money left in your budget, here are some things you may want to consider both to help you in the editing process and to add value to your products.

Deck

If your camcorder records to tape, you might want to consider purchasing a deck or a *video tape recorder* (*VTR*) to protect your camcorder from the wear and tear caused by the searching and winding inherent in the editing process. While your camcorder is capable of handling those tasks, it is a more delicate piece of equipment than a deck, and not necessarily designed to be an editing workhorse.

The things you will need to consider when you buy a deck are the tape format on which you are shooting, the video interface, and the device control—that is, the way your editing software remotely handles the deck to play, rewind, and fast forward, which happens through a cable that connects your computer to your deck. Make sure that your video interface and your deck inputs and outputs match.

If you have a FireWire-based editing system, you can control your deck easily through FireWire. Be advised, however, that FireWire doesn't offer frame accuracy, which means your edit could miss a mark by plus or minus five frames. That being said, frame accuracy is not necessarily needed for wedding videos, and it's not worth investing a lot of money into. If you expect to use your deck for other projects that you might output in pieces, however, you might want to consider a frame-accurate deck.

If you can't afford a deck but want to spare your camcorder some wear and tear, consider capturing all the footage on a tape in a single clip. Then, you can break the clip into subclips within the nonlinear editing program. This approach is easy for some editors and frustrating for others, but will no doubt save your camcorder some mileage since your reviewing and logging of footage will happen after it has been captured instead of before. Alternatively, buy a camcorder that you can use exclusively for capturing. This camera won't need any fancy features, so you can get one quite inexpensively!

Custom Keyboard

Although there are all kinds of health advisories I could issue about working in the wedding industry—brides can make you crazy, Champagne toasts can be addictively delicious, and wedding cake, while rarely as tasty as it looks, can also be addictive—the only real health advisory I would offer wedding videographers relates to the long hours of post-production. If you are lucky enough to get a booked season, you will undoubtedly get an editing backup—which translates to hours, days, and weeks spent editing on the computer.

That was an awfully long introduction to what I feel is a crucial and simple thought: Learn your editing program's keystrokes and avoid using your mouse. Any editing program worth using can be driven by mouse controls or keyboard commands (or some combination of the two). Using keyboard commands helps to protect you from the repetitive stress injuries so often associated with excessive mousing. Furthermore, using keyboard commands gives you faster and more fluid control of the program—which can help you edit more quickly and without losing your rhythm, an essential part of the editing process. If you are new to editing, you have the advantage of having no bad habits to break. If you are a seasoned editor but haven't bothered to learn your program's keyboard commands, start now. There is no time like the present to save time and, more importantly, your hands. You need them for shooting.

One way to learn your keyboard commands is to purchase a custom keyboard. These keyboards are color-coded with icons to enable you to easily see the various keyboard commands. Even experienced users might learn commands they didn't know with the features on these keyboards. Figure 4.4 shows a few keys of a custom editing keyboard.

Figure 4.4
This keyboard is color-coded and labeled with icons to help users easily identify and learn keyboard commands.

Scanner

It's a good idea to collect the ephemera associated with each wedding: a copy of the invitation, the ceremony program, and other printed materials such as directions or gift-favor tags. That way, if you have a scanner, you can scan these items for use in your introduction or elsewhere in your video. (I tend to shoot images of these items on the day of the event as well as keeping a hard copy.)

If you are providing additional services such as a photo montage, a scanner can be especially useful. While your clients are likely to provide more recent pictures for the montage in digital form, older images for the montage (such as baby pictures) will need to be digitized via a scanner. Scanners are relatively inexpensive and are often part of a printer and fax machine, both of which are also useful for running the business side of your work.

CAN YOU EDIT ON A LAPTOP?

One of the benefits of the wedding videographer's lifestyle is the freedom it allows. When it's not wedding season, you have some marketing and some sales to do—but also some vacationing. If you have a laptop, you can do all three at once! In fact, even during wedding season, you might find yourself on some Tuesday afternoon with a long list of things to do, but you don't necessarily have to be at your desk to complete it. Having a laptop in addition to your desktop computer gives you the freedom to work wherever you want.

But is editing on a laptop really viable? The short answer is yes—but with a few caveats:

▶ Your laptop must have the speed and strength to run video, which is not a major problem for SD or compressed HD but can be an issue for uncompressed HD.

(continued)

▶ Nonlinear editing programs need a lot of screen real estate. Running one of these programs on a laptop system—even a laptop with a relatively big screen—can be frustrating and difficult to look at for long periods of time.

▶ If you edit on your laptop at a remote location, chances are your speakers and external video monitor aren't with you. That means perfecting your sound and color will be difficult.

I often compromise between the benefits and frustrations of laptop editing by doing rough cuts on my laptop, and saving final edits, color corrections, effects, and audio mixing for my desktop system.

One more thing: Buying a laptop as a second computer can be a well-justified expense when you consider that there are some products and services you can offer your clients only with a portable setup. For example, if you want to offer projection services, many venues will require you bring your own laptop. Similarly, if you offer day-of editing services (to show parts of the ceremony at the reception), a portable system is required. Furthermore, there are likely to be times at the height of the season when running two computers at once is a big time saver. For example, while one computer is rendering or compressing, you can build a photo montage on another.

Post-Production Editing Software

With your hardware in place, you will need editing software to run on your computer workstation. *Nonlinear editing* (*NLE*) systems are deep, complicated, and often expensive programs. As I have mentioned, you will be spending a lot of time with the program you select; make sure to weigh all the variables and choose carefully.

 A good editing program will offer several ways of accomplishing the same task, which ensures a certain degree of flexibility and can be comforting to an experienced editor switching to a different NLE program.

It is possible that your editing-software decision came before any of your hardware decisions. Editors tend to be loyal to programs they learn on or have used the most, which is completely understandable (if not particularly advisable). But whether you are new to editing or already know how to use a particular editing program, I urge you to review the features and benefits of various editing programs so you can be sure you start your wedding-videography business with the system best suited to your needs.

 In describing the features of various editing programs, I will tend to use Adobe Premiere Pro terms, as that is the software used in the demo for this book. Keep in mind, though, that the names are generic for features that appear in most programs.

Basic Features

The basic features of editing programs are similar across the board, although they will be named and will operate somewhat differently in each program. For example, most programs have an interface composed of four components: a Project panel, a Source panel, a Program panel, and a Timeline panel. That being said, there may be some differences between programs, as well as among certain features that are particularly important to your style of working. In the latter case, you should be sure to investigate that aspect of any program you are considering using.

It is important to realize that the features offered by high-end programs will be similar; the similarities between these high-end programs and free and low-end consumer editing software, however, will be dramatically reduced. For example, Adobe Premiere Pro CS4 and Final Cut Pro 7, both high-end programs, will offer many of the same features, with users preferring one over the other based on intricate feature comparisons and depending on the types of projects involved. On the other hand, the differences between the free PC editing program Windows Movie Maker and Adobe Premiere Pro CS4, or between the free Mac editing program iMovie and Final Cut Pro 7, are gross and structural—and will completely affect your editing capabilities and control over a project.

Interface

As mentioned, the interface of an editing program usually has four main panes (see Figure 4.5):

> ▶ **Timeline.** This panel displays the timeline of the sequence you are building, using graphical icons to represent the video clips, other media and effects you use to piece the edit together

> ▶ **Project.** This is the organizational pane for your source media.

> ▶ **Source.** This panel screens source footage, allowing you to collect selections to use in your piece.

> ▶ **Program.** This panel screens the piece you are putting together. Note that the Timeline and the Program panels are simply different representations of the same thing: your edited piece.

Figure 4.5
This image shows a basic configuration of an editing interface. Starting at the top left and moving clockwise, the panels are the Project, the Source, the Program, and the Timeline; the Media panel in the bottom-left corner allows easy access to files on the computer.

In addition, many editing programs feature a logging and capturing, or transferring, panel, for logging and capturing or transferring footage on your camera. (It's called *capturing* when the video is on tape and *transferring* when the video is randomly accessed on drives.)

A good editing program will allow you to rearrange the interface, resizing and moving the panels as needed. Often, editing programs will also have preset configurations that are handy for particular editing tasks (such as color correction or sound mixing) and that accommodate a dual monitor setup (see Figure 4.6).

Figure 4.6

A good editing program will allow for a few different configurations of the interface and should allow you to customize and save interface layouts that work best for your editing style. The first image shows an interface designed especially for color correction; the second image shows an interface for audio editing.

Timeline Panel

The *Timeline panel* is where several distinctions between editing programs occur. In general, the more customizable the timeline interface, the better the program will be. Ideally, you will be able to maneuver the timeline easily; to look at tracks in different sizes and with or without waveforms; to have all—or at least most—of your Program panel editing capabilities available within the Timeline panel; to lock and unlock your audio and video; and to separate the two tracks.

The Timeline panel offers one-line editing versus two-line editing. Some systems will show effects and transitions on the timeline in a different track, while others will combine footage and effects on one track. There is no inherent advantage to either setup, but editors do tend to have a preference for one over the other in their own working style. Consumer-level editing programs, such as Windows Movie Maker and iMovie, offer only one track of video and two tracks of audio on the timeline. More professional software packages can boast anywhere from 99 (Final Cut Pro and Premiere) to infinite (Sony Vegas) tracks. While I argue that one video track is not enough for the work you will be doing, having infinite or even 99 tracks is overkill. In 10 years of editing wedding videos, I have never used more than 20 video tracks, if that.

Project Panel

Project organization is crucial to becoming a good editor. While it would be lovely if editing dealt just with storytelling and the creative application of transitions and effects, the fact is that much of a good editor's skills and time are spent ensuring that the right media is in the right format and place and labeled in the right way. Of course, "right" is somewhat subjective because there are so many different organizational styles, but within your own system of organization, it is important to be consistent and thorough to facilitate smooth editing.

The capabilities of your *Project panel* can affect your organizational style. You want to make sure you can use your Project panel to name and rename clips, to make subclips (clips from longer clips), and to track the footage's format information. This last one is particularly important if you are mixing formats in a multi-camera shoot (a procedure I don't recommend, if it is avoidable). You will also want a good labeling system for your media so you can easily access shots that you know are good. Easy access includes the ability to search through your footage by keyword and change the parameters by which it is organized (see Figure 4.7).

One noteworthy distinction between the higher-end programs and the lower-end ones is the ability to save media separately from the project. In higher-end programs, media is saved to *scratch bins*, and the program points to the media in the bins. So, for example, the files for a project titled "Rachel and Stephen's Wedding" can be saved anywhere; when the program is opened, you simply point to the media in the scratch bin regardless of which drive it lives on and everything will be linked and ready to go. Less-advanced programs sometimes save all the media with the program itself. This is not inherently bad, but offers less flexibility for using external drives with other computers; copying the entire project will take a long time.

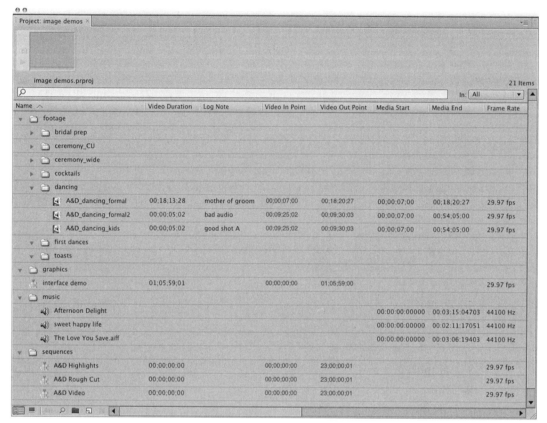

Figure 4.7
Good organization of your project media in the browser is crucial, although every editor would define "good" differently. Make sure your software allows for a flexible filing system that you are comfortable working with; you will spend enormous amounts of time working in the Project panel.

Furthermore, if you use a piece of footage in every video you produce, such as opening shots of the city where the weddings you shoot take place or your company logo, you will have to copy and save it every time, instead of just referencing it. Similarly, transferring templates that you create is much easier in applications where media is kept separate from the program file.

Source and Program Panels

The Source and Program panels, also referred to as *monitors*, are where you watch video in raw and edited footage, respectively. Learning to quickly scroll through footage in the monitors is integral to your speed as an editor. For ease and flexibility, there should be several methods to control both monitors: menu commands, mouse commands, and keyboard commands. Ideally, you will learn to work with the keyboard, usually the J-K-L system, which enables you to play footage backward (J) and forward (L) and to start/stop (K), all with small and fast hand movements. Furthermore, the J and L keys can be pressed up to four times to watch footage at increased speeds, also called *scrubbing*. Less-advanced systems such as iMovie will give you a program monitor but not a source monitor, and will not allow scrubbing.

Logging and Capturing/Transferring

An editing program's *logging* and *capturing/transferring* pane can be extremely simple or quite advanced. At its most basic, the capture/transfer interface will look like a tape recorder that starts and stops, pulling in your footage in chunks as you click Play. Other more advanced features might include the following:

▶ The ability to specify by timecode which clips to capture

▶ Support of batch captures to pull in a series of clips while your machine is unattended

▶ Support for detailed descriptions, or *logging*, of clips

A "prompt" labeling system is helpful—especially because your footage will be shot in a chronologically correct sequence—although such a system is certainly not necessary.

▶ The ability to detect when the camera starts and stops and create clips breaks at those moments

▶ Support for audio meters to enable you to see and adjust audio levels as you capture

▶ Support for waveform monitors and vectorscopes to allow for a higher quality video signal as you capture

Various external logging programs are available that, among other things, allow for more detailed logging and tagging of clips, the ability to easily break clips into new clips, and the ability to create easy-to-maneuver thumbnail versions of clips. Although I have never worked on a wedding project that required more organization options than were offered by my nonlinear editing software, some editors find external logging programs very appealing due to their flexibility and customization options.

Editing Options

Just as a good editing system will give you multiple ways to view footage, a good editing system will offer more than one way to edit it. Nonlinear editing programs can handle both *overlay* and *insert* edits, a distinction that is both important and definitive. Overlay edits place a clip on top of whatever footage was beneath it—that is, the new footage replaces the existing footage, leaving the entire sequence the same length. An insert edit places a clip between two other clips, moving the footage appearing after the inserted clip down the timeline and thereby lengthening the sequence (see Figure 4.8).

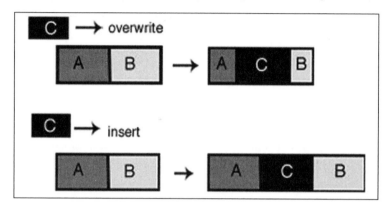

Figure 4.8
In an overlay edit, the new footage replaces the existing footage, meaning the total length of the sequence remains the same. In an insert edit, the added clip fits between existing clips, increasing the total length of the sequence.

Aside from understanding the difference between overlays and inserts, there are a few other things you need to know when it comes to editing options—namely, ways to move your inserts and overlays to and around the timeline:

▶ **Drag and drop.** With *drag-and-drop editing*, use the mouse to pull clips of footage from the viewer to the timeline or move the clips around the timeline itself, either inserting them between existing clips or overlaying the existing footage. The clip is defined by two points: an in (or first frame or start) and an out (or last frame or end point). This type of editing is rather crude; it's used for general assembly of a rough cut, but rarely for fine tuning of a piece.

▶ **Three point.** More precise than drag-and-drop editing, *three-point editing* defines the clip taken from the viewer with the in and out as well as the exact point on the timeline where you want to insert or overlay (i.e., the third point). This third point is defined on the timeline with either an in or an out point. If the third timeline point is an in, the clip from the viewer will be placed on the timeline with the in points matching and the clip starting at that point. If the third point is an out, the clip from the viewer will be placed on the timeline with the outs matching and the clip will end at that point. Matching out points in a three-point edit is also called *backtiming*.

▶ **Four point.** In a *four-point edit*, also called a *fit-to-fill edit*, a clip is defined in the viewer with an in and an out point and a space for the clip is defined on the timeline with an in and an out point. When the edit is made, the in points will be lined up, as will the out points—which means the clip will either be stretched (slowed down) or squeezed (sped up) to accommodate the time allotted. Four-point editing is particularly useful in wedding videography for a few reasons, usually as a means to slow video down. Often, you will find that there are images you want to use that weren't shot long enough; by slowing them down with four-point editing, you can get a usable image. Slowing down footage also tends to lend a dreamy and romantic look to footage, which can be enhanced with other effects. Finally, wedding sequences are often built as montages, and using four-point editing enables you to easily match the video to the audio transitions for cleaner and well-paced montage edits. It is less common to speed wedding video up than it is to slow it down, but using four-point editing to speed things up can be a fun way to show time passing—for example, with a fast-paced version of the bride getting ready or the reception room being set up or even the groom speeding down the aisle if your video has more of an MTV-stylized look to it. Not every system will offer four-point editing, but most of the better programs do in some form.

▶ **Superimpose.** In a *superimpose* edit, which is especially useful for titles and graphics, you specify an in or an out point in the viewer only; the software automatically cuts the viewer footage to match the length of the clip over which it is being superimposed on the timeline. This feature is not offered on every system—not even all higher-end ones. That being said, while it is very handy, this type of edit can be achieved through a variety of steps even without this particular editing tool.

Once a sequence is on the timeline, there are a variety of tools to help refine the edits. These tools are designed to perform a few tasks at once, such as creating a space and filling it with footage in one step. Often, these tasks will be performed in a separate panel, called the *trimming window* or *trim monitor*. Lower-end programs will not have all of these tools, although these same tasks can be performed on any interface (albeit through a more laborious process). A few of these step-saving editing-refinement tools include the following (see Figure 4.9):

▶ **Ripple.** A *ripple* tool extends or shortens a clip, moving all the other footage backward or forward, respectively, to accommodate the change. The total length of the sequence will change in a ripple edit.

▶ **Roll.** A *roll* tool changes the edit point between two clips so that the first clip will get longer or shorter and the second clip will do the opposite. The total length of the two affected clips remains constant in a roll edit.

▶ **Slip.** A *slip* tool moves the start and end frames of any one clip without changing the length of the clip itself. For example, if you slip a clip to see 15 additional frames at the beginning, 15 frames will be trimmed off the end (or vice versa).

▶ **Slide.** Suppose you have three clips, and you want to move the clip in the middle to fall a bit earlier or later in the sequence. In that case, you use a *slide* tool to move the middle clip. When you do, the first clip becomes shorter and the third clip becomes longer (or vice versa, depending on whether you moved the middle clip forward or backward) to accommodate the change, keeping the total length of the sequence constant.

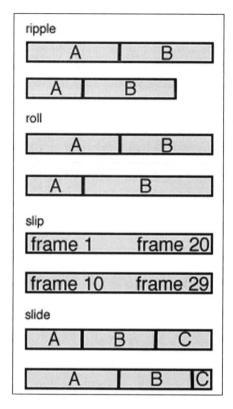

Figure 4.9
Fine-edit tools combine a few steps in one tool, allowing faster, smoother editing.

Advanced Features

You should expect some more advanced features from a higher-end editing program, all of which are useful in wedding videography. To best gauge which program and interface will work best for you, you will need to consider your own style and which of the various features available are most important to you. For example, if you know you will often be shooting with three cameras, take a good look at the multicam options of the programs you are considering. Or if you already use an external titling program that you are happy with, you can leave that out of your deliberation.

Multicamera Editing

Multicamera editing is a function that enables you to line up several camera angles by timecode or by in point and watch them all simultaneously. While watching all the angles, you can determine which is best and put that one on the timeline, in effect live-switching the angles, as in a sporting event. This can be an extremely useful timesaving tool for long sections of multiple-camera shooting such as the ceremony or even first dances (see Figure 4.10).

Figure 4.10
When looking at a synced multicamera sequence, a multicamera interface shows all the possible camera angles at once and highlights which one is currently active. In this case, the active view is on the bottom-left corner, as indicated by the both the highlight around it and the larger image on the right.

This will be discussed more in Chapter 7, "The Big Day," but keep in mind that this feature is only relevant for sections of uninterrupted video. That is, if you have to continually align or set up new sections of multicam video, much of its effectiveness is lost.

Effects

Every editing program will come with a large array of filters and transitions, both audio and video. Unfortunately, however, a program's effects package cannot be gauged by the sheer quantity of effects offered because many are awful, impractical, unattractive, and unlikely to ever be used in any type of straightforward piece trying to tell a story. Indeed, in my opinion, there is arguably a reverse correlation between the number of effects offered and the quality of a program.

The changeable parameters of the effects and whether they can be used with *keyframes* (animation) are more viable ways to measure the utility of a given effects program. For example, if you want to desaturate a shot (that is, convert it from color to black and white), a simple effect found in any editing program should take care of that easily. A slightly upgraded effects program will enable you to change the parameters to take a certain percentage of the color out of the shot—say, 50 or 75 percent.

An advanced effects package will give you keyframing capabilities, which enable you to apply an effect to an entire clip with different intensities. For example, if you want a shot of the bridal bouquet to move from completely desaturated (all black and white) to full saturation (color), you will need keyframes to indicate that the effect should change over time. Keyframing, or effect animation, adds sophistication to effects application that can't be achieved in simpler programs. Furthermore, advanced editing systems will be able to incorporate other effects packages or plug-ins, adding even more effecting capabilities.

Color Correction

Color correction is important for any editor, but it's crucial in wedding video editing for several reasons. Most importantly, the speed at which you must change locations during shooting means you regularly do not have time to white balance (although I wish I didn't have to put that in print, because of course I recommend that you always do). Furthermore, getting good colors—colors that look good next to each other throughout your piece—in a day of constantly changing scenery and light is nearly impossible. While feature shooters can set up lights and try shots at different exposures, a wedding videographer doesn't have that luxury. Finally, the amount of white you will be shooting, frequently in bright daylight, often requires toning down so as not to appear blown out. Make sure your program has good color-correction tools and a good interface to handle your inevitable color-correction needs, as shown in Figure 4.11.

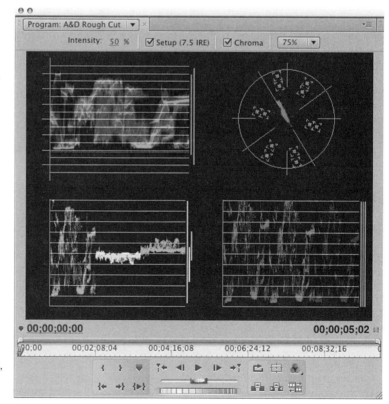

Figure 4.11
An editing program should have color-correction effects as well as tools to monitor them, such as the vectorscope, waveform monitor, and color parades shown here.

Titling

Basic titling tools come with just about all editing software and will be capable of producing simple opening and closing titles. Nicer programs can accommodate credit rolls, lower-third titling, and typewriting functions, as well as built-in templates. Should you be looking to build fancier titling sequences, like those in a feature film, you will need a more advanced titling program, or may even want to consider an additional titling or effects package (discussed later in this chapter).

Audio Tools

So often overlooked in production, good audio is unnoticeable in a final piece. Bad audio, however, represents a glaring and dramatic intrusion on viewing enjoyment. Although a good wedding videographer will use MP3 recorders to capture sound inaccessible to the camera, as with color quality, your sound options during production may be limited by the amount of gear you can carry, the time you have to set up, and the natural audio of your setting (which is often wretched).

Make sure you have some audio tools in your arsenal to clean up what might not be good original sound. Aim to get a program that accommodates an audio mixer (which enables you to change levels of different pieces of sound on your piece), equalization features, and effects and filters that can help you enhance good sound and remove bad sound (see Figure 4.12).

Figure 4.12
Get to know your audio tools so that you can effectively mix audio from different sources. Because you will often be using audio from a range of sources—camera, lavaliere, and MP3 recorder—make sure your software system has tools to mix multiple tracks in a way that is easy and comfortable, like this window that mimics an audio board.

Post-Production Effects and Output Software

Is it possible that after all that conversation on editing software, we're still not done? Is there more we need to buy and learn for post-production? Well, maybe. Most software programs come with tools for basic effects and compositing, but if you are interested in doing advanced compositing and motion—popular in opening sequences and interludes—you should look carefully at the effects programs that are compatible with your hardware and software. You might also find that some external programs have increased functionality for intricate operations such as sound editing, color correction, and output.

Bundled Packages

Most professional editing software is sold in suites with several other programs bundled in. These bundled applications often add tremendous value to the editing software. For example, just buying three applications found in the Adobe Creative Suite 4 Production Premium package—Adobe Photoshop, Adobe After Effects, and Adobe Premiere Pro—would cost $1,000 more than the whole Design Suite, which contains seven additional applications.

Although you'll find that even software from different makers can be compatible—for example, many Final Cut Pro users use Adobe After Effects in their workflow—using programs from a single suite provides advantages in terms of cost and ease of use due to the integration of the programs. For example, if you use Apple Motion, LiveType, or Soundtrack files in your Final Cut Pro project, updates in the external files will automatically be reflected in your Final Cut Pro project—without requiring you to re-import the files.

Motion Graphics

Basic compositing and motion effects can be done in a high-end video editing program; more advanced graphic looks can be achieved through dedicated motion-graphics software such as Apple Motion or Adobe After Effects, both of which are capable of 3D effects. Advanced motion graphics aren't necessary to tell a basic wedding story, but these programs do open up a level of creativity that can enable you to create a product that stands apart. They can also be very useful for creating a video logo, which you can attach to the beginning and end of your video piece or include in a DVD menu.

Audio Programs

Like motion graphics, all editing software programs feature audio-editing capabilities. Standalone audio applications, however, offer far more sophisticated audio tools and effects that give you better results with higher efficiency. In weddings, these are most useful for correcting poor sound. For example, Apple Soundtrack Pro can analyze an audio track for a recurring problem such as a click or a hum and apply your solution as a batch, saving you the trouble of finding each occurrence of the problem and applying the solution over and over by hand. Furthermore, sound programs often come with royalty-free content such as sound and Foley effects and music tracks. The music tracks can be especially useful, and I have occasionally used sound effects such as Champagne corks popping, alarm clocks sounding, and whistles blowing.

External Applications and Plug-ins

External applications and plug-ins can include filters and effects that aren't included with any image-editing program. Indeed, there are literally hundreds of these plug-ins available for most editing software. For example, Red Giant's Instant HD uses multi-vector analysis to give standard definition files a high-definition look. Likewise, there are several programs designed to give video the softer look of film, such as Digieffects Cinemotion. If you already know exactly what look or effect you want, you can usually find a plug-in to achieve it by running a simple search. If you're not sure what you're looking for, browsing what's available online will prove inspirational.

Output Options

Having a beautifully edited project in Premiere Pro, or any other program, doesn't do your client any good. They expect to see their video on DVD, on their iPhone, and online. They may want it in tape format or as an uncompressed QuickTime or AVI file.

Using any one of a variety of programs, most of which are inexpensive, you can get any file into most any format that you want—keeping in mind, of course, that you can't increase quality, only compression. Ideally, though, you won't have to use too many external applications to do that. Look at the export options of your editing program and make sure they are compatible—without requiring you to take too many steps— for the output you are looking for. Sometimes, the output options are tied to the software suites of which editing programs are one part, as discussed in the previous section. For example, to compress in one step for DVDs, Final Cut Pro uses the bundled Compressor software.

Comparison

Following are brief descriptions of some of the most common professional editing software programs, all of which include associated programs for other aspects of video production. While not comprehensive, this should give you a starting point for determining which of these—or other similar—programs you might want to research further.

Prosumer and consumer versions of these and other programs are available. While there are programs in those target markets that you can make work for your needs, make sure you have a good understanding of the functionality you are—and aren't—getting before you invest any money. The money you save in purchasing cheaper editing software will likely be spent later on in external programs and plug-ins—which will also add unneeded complexity to your workflow.

Apple Final Cut Pro

Originally released in 1999, Apple Final Cut Pro started as a prosumer software program; since then, it has quickly gained large market share. While online discussions rage about whether Final Cut Pro is really the new professional "industry standard," it is commonly agreed to be an easy-to-use program that has exceptional functionality and a smooth interface.

Complaints about Final Cut Pro tend to relate to multiple users over networked systems—not terribly relevant to wedding video editors. One complaint that may be relevant to wedding videographers, however, is that although Apple recently included support for the creation of Blu-ray discs in their suite of video products, an external burner and player are required for use of that software functionality. That is, Apple hardware has yet to accommodate Blu-ray. A further disadvantage of Final Cut Pro is that it only runs on Macs.

Final Cut Pro is sold as part of a suite called Final Cut Studio ($999 at the time of this writing), which also includes Motion 4, Soundtrack Pro 3, Color 1.5, DVD Studio Pro 4 and Compressor 3.5. Alternatively, you can purchase Final Cut Express, a standalone product with most, though not all, of the functionality of Final Cut Pro ($199 at the time of this writing).

Adobe Premiere Pro

A key advantage to Adobe Premiere Pro is that version 3 and higher can run on either Mac or PC. It has virtually all the functionality of Final Cut Pro and the added benefit of easy compatibility with Adobe After Effects, the gold standard in effects software. Also, Blu-ray disc authoring is easily incorporated into the workflow.

Complaints about Premiere tend to be in comparison with Final Cut Pro: It lacks some of the intricate options and fluidity of Final Cut Pro, especially when working with really big projects (weddings do not generally fit in that category).

Adobe Premiere Pro can be purchased as a standalone piece of software ($799 at the time of this writing) or as part of a suite of programs called Creative Suite 4 ($1,699 at the time of this writing), which also includes After Effects CS4, Photoshop CS4 Extended, Flash CS4 Professional, Illustrator CS4, Soundbooth CS4, Adobe OnLocation CS4, Encore CS4, Adobe Bridge CS4, Adobe Device Central CS4, and Dynamic Link.

Avid Media Composer

The leading designer of turnkey editing solutions and the reigning industry standard in video-editing platforms, Avid also offers software that can be purchased independently and used on PCs and Macs: Avid Media Composer.

Avid Media Composer is an excellent program that doesn't lack in functionality. It offers multi-format outputs, excellent effects, and rendering solutions that let you watch most effects in real time. The high price tag, however—$2,295 at the time of this writing—is due to the inclusion of numerous tools that aren't particularly important to a wedding video editor, including but not limited to high-end logging and metadata-management and tools for collaborative workflows.

Avid Media Composer is sold in a suite that also includes Avid DVD, Boris Continuum Complete, Sorenson Squeeze, SmartSound SonicFire Pro, and Avid FX.

Sony Vegas Pro

A PC-only program, Sony Vegas Pro has high ratings for functionality and offers lots of unique tools that are handy for the video editor—automation of many repetitive tasks and a photo-montage tool, for starters. With multi-format support and various output formats (including Blu-ray, but lacking in formats supported by various smart phones) as well as a lower price tag, Sony Vegas is a very solid option for video editors.

Complaints about Sony Vegas Pro include a clumsier interface that is harder to learn than most software programs. In addition, certain tools, such as keyframing and audio mixing, operate less smoothly.

The Vegas Pro editing software ($599 at the time of this writing) is sold with DVD Architect Pro.

CAN YOU EDIT A WEDDING VIDEO WITH FREE EDITING SOFTWARE?

As mentioned, every new Apple computer comes bundled with iMovie and iDVD, which theoretically are programs capable of putting together a video piece shot on HD. But can you make a wedding video using this software, or with Microsoft's free editing software, Windows Movie Maker? The short answer is yes. There is no reason why you can't import your footage into one of these programs and put together a good piece using the tools they include. The basics of editing are ins, outs, inserts, and overlays—all of which can be handled using iMovie and Movie Maker. After all, I would argue that it is an editor's creativity and vision that make a standout video—not his or her editing tools.

That being said, if the question were instead phrased "Can you run a wedding videography business on iMovie or Movie Maker?" I would say no. The tools that these programs lack will hurt your business in two ways. First, it will take you much longer to piece your video together using only basic editing tools without additional layers of video (much less multicamera capabilities), a viewing monitor, or fine edit tools. Secondly, without more advanced tools such as keyframing, color correction, and audio mixing, your video will lack the professional look required to keep your business thriving.

Summary

This chapter discusses the important considerations in selecting post-production hardware and software. It mentions both the items you absolutely need and the ones that might be beneficial additions. Like your production gear, you want this equipment to grow with you, leaving room for you to both upgrade and learn more.

Next Up

Several thousands of dollars later, you are now equipped for both production and post-production. Ideally, you made some wise decisions and are excited to put your new gear to use. The next chapter helps you get started using your equipment by taking a closer look at your production gear and getting a strong handle on some video basics. When you hit the rush and chaos of your first wedding shoot, that chapter should prepare you for smooth handling of your camera so you can at least *appear* calm—even if you don't feel that way!

Chapter 4 Tutorial: Getting to Know Your Editing Software

To complete the projects featured on this book's DVD, you need Adobe Premiere. To download a free trial version, follow these steps.

1. Direct your Web browser to http://www.adobe.com/downloads.
2. Place your mouse pointer over the Adobe Premiere Pro option and click Try.
3. If you don't have an account, create one. Otherwise, sign in.
4. Select your language and operating system.
5. Click Download to begin the download and installation process.

After you have installed the trial version of Adobe Premiere:

1. Insert the DVD that accompanies this book into your computer's DVD drive.
2. Copy the entire main file on the DVD (called "Wedding Videography_Start to Finish") to a designated location on your hard drive. That way, you can work from files on your computer, not files stored on the DVD.

Once the DVD files have been copied to your hard drive, follow these steps:

1. Open the Wedding Videography_Start to Finish folder.
2. Open the Chapter 4 Tutorial folder.
3. Double-click the 4_Getting to Know Your Editing Software project to open it.
4. When prompted, allow the scratch disks (this is where some media will be kept) to be set to your Documents folder.

Exploring the Panel Configuration

With the project open in Adobe Premiere, open the Window menu, choose Workspace, and choose Editing. This ensures the panels described in this section are in the same configuration as the ones on your screen. There are four primary panels associated with the editing interface:

▶ **Project.** This is an organizational viewing window for your media.
▶ **Source.** This is a viewing window for raw footage.
▶ **Timeline.** This is a graphical representation of the sequence being built.
▶ **Program.** This is a viewing window for the sequence being built.

In addition, there is a fifth panel, called the Media Browser, which is not relevant to the current exercises.

To perform a task in a given panel, that panel must be selected, as indicated by a light blue line. Practice selecting each panel by clicking the center of each one. Each panel has a drop-down menu in the top-right corner that allows customization of the panel.

In addition to these five panels, there is a toolbar (as well as an audio meter) on the right side of the program window. Like the panels, the toolbar can be customized.

Working with Media Files

We are ready to start working with the media in this project. Before we begin, however, I'd like to say a word about how the Project panel, which is where your media is organized in Premiere Pro, operates. The Project panel contains pointers to all your media. As discussed in the text, these pointers link to files on the hard drive. So if you move media files around in the Project panel—or onto the timeline—you aren't moving the actual video files, just the pointers to them. That means moving media around in the Project panel is quick and easy. By creating and using bins, which are akin to folders, you can develop organized systems to manage your media in a potentially complex project. To create a new bin, choose File > New > Bin. To open a bin, click the triangle next to the bin name instead of double-clicking the bin triangle or bin name. Clicking the triangle displays the contents of the bin within the panel you already have visible instead of cluttering your screen by opening a separate, new panel.

Follow these steps to familiarize yourself with the program.

1. In the Project panel, click the triangle next to the video clips folder to open the Video Clips bin.

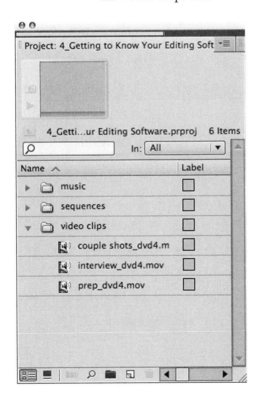

2. Double-click the coupleshots_dvd4 clip to open it in the Source panel, which is then activated by default.

When opening media files or sequences in the Project panel, be sure to click the file icon, not the name. Clicking the name simply enables you to rename the file.

3. To play the coupleshots_dvd4 clip in the Source panel, do one of the following:

    ▶ Press the spacebar.

    ▶ Press the L key on your keyboard.

    ▶ Click the Play button along the bottom of the Program panel.

4. To stop playing the clip, do one of the following:

    ▶ Press the spacebar.

    ▶ Press the K key on your keyboard.

    ▶ Click the Stop button along the bottom of the Program panel.

5. To speed up the footage as it plays, press the L key twice, three times, or four times.

6. To watch the footage backward, press the J key.

7. To watch the footage backward and at faster speed, press the J key twice, three times, or four times.

8. Watch the next clip, interview_dvd4. To do so, double-click the clip you want to view. The new clip automatically replaces the old footage in the Source panel.

9. Watch the next clip, prep_dvd4.

In Premiere Pro, a sequence is where you insert raw audio/video clips and craft them into a finished video. Premiere Pro stores sequences in the Project panel. Like your raw clips, you open them in the timeline by double-clicking them. A Premiere Pro project can have multiple sequences, which is useful if you build your wedding one scene at a time. For example, you might have a sequence for the rehearsal dinner, another for the ceremony, another for the reception, and so on; then you combine them all into one conglomerate sequence before rendering your final project.

1. Click the triangle next to the sequence clips folder to open the Video Clips bin.

2. Double-click the Selects_finished sequence to open it in both the Program and Timeline panels. Notice that the Program panel now contains an image and the Timeline panel contains icons representing the clips. If there is no image in the program panel, your playhead maybe at the end of the sequence; press the Home key on your keyboard to bring the playhead to the beginning of the sequence.

 As discussed in the chapter text, the Program panel and the Timeline panel display different visual representations of the same sequence, and as such always show the same image. Though it's technically called the Program panel, it might help to think of it as the preview window where you view the video that you're creating in the timeline.

3. Play back the footage in the Timeline and Program panels, using the same operators (spacebar, J key, K key, and L key) as the Source panel.

As you play back the footage, notice that the playhead in all three panels shows you where you are within the footage or sequence. The playhead for the Program and Timeline panels always move together; again, they are different visual representations of the same sequence. Notice, too, the time-code indicators on the left side of the Source, Timeline, and Program panels. These display the time code of the frame on which the playhead is currently sitting, which will be the same for the Program and Timeline panels. If you click this time-code display, enter a time-code number, and press Enter, your playhead will move to that point in the clip. The time-code indicator on the right side of the Source and Program panels displays the duration of a selected clip.

Selecting Clips

Building a video piece involves selecting clips (raw footage) from the Source panel and placing them on the Timeline panel. When you are comfortable watching footage in the Source, Timeline, and Program panels, you're ready to do just that. First, double-click the Selects_start sequence to open it in the Timeline panel. Notice that the sequence file currently contains no clips. In order to add clips to the sequence, you specify the clips, by using *in* and *out* points on the source footage the Source panel. To begin, follow these steps:

1. Double-click the couple shots_dvd4.mov clip to open it in the Source panel.

2. Navigate to time code 00;49;37;25. To navigate time code, either enter the time code you want in the time code indicator in the bottom-left portion of the Source panel or drag the playhead to the right until the time code in the bottom-left indicator is the time code you need (here, approximately 49;37;25). After you get close to the desired time code by dragging, you can use the arrow keys on your keyboard or the playback controls in the Source panel to navigate very precisely frame by frame.

3. Press the I key on your keyboard to set an in.

4. Navigate to time code 00;49;40;20.

5. Press the O key on your keyboard to set an out.

By selecting in and out points, you effectively tell Premiere Pro that you care only about the video frames between these two points. When you add this raw video to your timeline, only the information between the two points will be added—nothing before or after.

Press the D key on your keyboard to delete an in; delete an out by pressing the F key on your keyboard. To delete both the in and the out, press the G key on your keyboard. Alternatively, simply set a new in or out to automatically replace the old one.

Editing in the Timeline Panel

Now that you have selected a clip and set the in and out points, it's time to move the selection to the Timeline panel. To do so, it is important to specify the audio and video tracks of the Timeline panel on which the media will fall (i.e., the destination tracks) and where the clip will begin. In this instance, we will put our video on Video Track 1 and our audio on Audio Track 1 and Audio Track 2. This is already set up, as indicated by the source-track indicators (V, A1, and A2) on the left side of the Timeline panel. Later, when we use more tracks, we will move the source-track indicators.

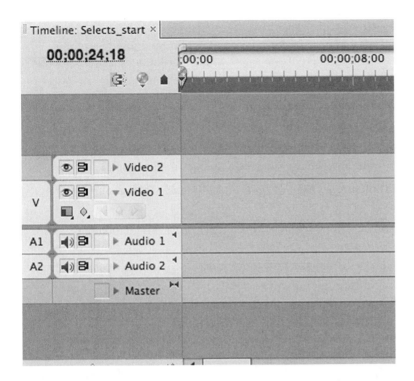

Place the playhead at the point at which you want the clip to begin. In this case, put the timeline in point, or playhead, at the first frame of the sequence, time code 00;00;00;00. This will serve as the frame at which we will place a clip onto the timeline. If you place an in point at the current position of the playhead, the in point will serve as the desired start point, overriding the playhead location even if you move the playhead.

 The in and out in the Source panel and the in (or playhead position) in the Timeline panel constitute the three points of a three-point edit.

Once you have made the selection from the Source panel that you want to add to the Timeline (and Program) panel, you can edit it into the sequence a number of ways.

Performing an Overlay Edit

Making sure the Source panel is activated, perform an overlay edit by doing one of the following:

▶ Press the . (period) key.

▶ Open the Clip menu and choose Overlay.

▶ Press the Clip Overlay button at the bottom of the Source panel.

▶ Drag the clip (from the center of the image) to the Program panel and release it.

▶ Drag the clip (from the center of the image) to the Timeline panel and release it.

To practice, overlay two additional clips from the couple shots_dvd4 footage immediately after the first clip:

▶ Clip 2: 00;49;02;04 (in)/00;49;06;00 (out); place at time code 00;00;02;26 on the timeline

▶ Clip 3: 00;49;37;25 (in)/00;49;40;22 (out); place at time code 00;00;06;23 on the timeline

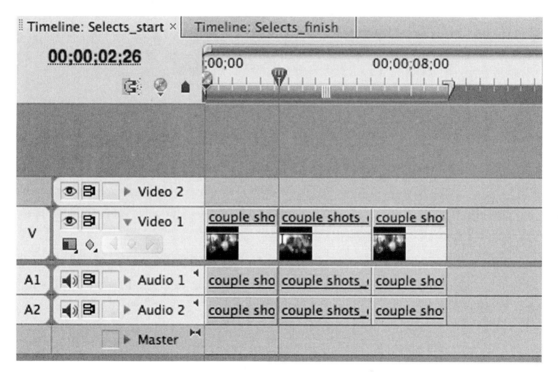

Use the playback controls in the Program or Timeline panel to review your work.

Insert Edit

Now we are going to insert some new interview footage between some of the clips that we have already placed on the timeline. We will insert our clips on new audio and video tracks to separate them visually from the ones already laid down. There is already a second video track, but we must add two audio tracks using the following steps:

1. Choose Sequence > Add Tracks. An Add Tracks dialog box opens.

2. Enter 0 as the number of video tracks to add.

3. Enter 2 as the number of audio tracks to add.

4. For Placement, choose After Audio 2.

5. For Track Type, choose Mono.

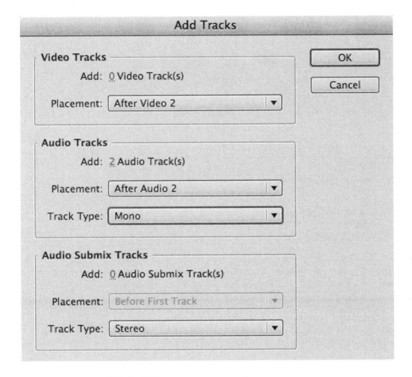

6. Click OK.

Designate Video 2 and our new Audio Tracks 3 and 4 as the destination tracks by following these steps:

1. Set the video destination track by dragging the box marked "V" on the left side of the video tracks to the track called Video 2.

2. Click the Video 2 track near the track name to enable it. (It will appear highlighted.)

3. Set the audio destination tracks by dragging the boxes marked "a1" and "a2" to the tracks called Audio 3 and Audio 4.

4. Click the Audio 3 and Audio 4 tracks near the track names to enable them. (They will appear highlighted.)

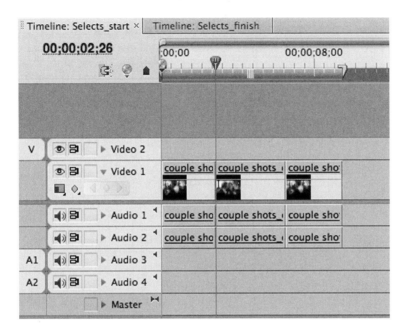

To perform the insert edit, follow these steps:

1. Double-click the interview_dvd4 clip in the Project panel to open it in the Source panel.

2. Select the following clip to put on the timeline by setting the in and out points to 00;03;57;17 (in)/00;04;01;00 (out).

3. Click the Timeline panel.

4. In the Timeline panel, place the playhead between the first two clips from couple shots_dvd4, already placed on the timeline.

 You can easily navigate between edit points in a clip with the Page Up and Page Down keys.

5. Click the Source panel to activate it and then insert the first interview clip between the first two couple shot clips by doing one of the following:

    ▶ Press the , (comma) key.

    ▶ Open the Clip menu and choose Insert.

    ▶ Press the Clip Insert button at the bottom of the Source panel.

    ▶ Hold down the Ctrl (Windows) or Command (Mac) key and drag the clip (from the center of the image) to the Timeline panel.

6. In the interview_dvd4.move clip, mark new in and out points at 04:03:20 (in)/04:13:19 (out), and insert that clip at time code 00;00;06;08.

7. In the interview_dvd4.move clip, mark new in and out points at 00;04;21;13 (in)/00;04;28;04 (out) and insert that clip at time code 00;00;23;03. Note that since you're adding footage at the end of the sequence, you can use either an insert or overlay edit.

This sequence should now match the Select_finish sequence. Use the playback controls in the Program or Timeline panel to review the work you just completed.

Part II

The Wedding

Chapter 5
The Basics of Wedding Shooting

In this chapter:

▶ A video vocabulary
▶ Manual controls
▶ Building your shot lists

Ideally, what you see in your mind's eye and what you capture on video are the same. In reality, though, it takes a lot of practice to get to that level of proficiency. Because I started as a video editor, only learning how to shoot later, I found this monumentally frustrating. I knew exactly what I wanted the shot to look like, but my hands couldn't make the camera follow my vision.

Well before your first wedding, you want to be practicing with your gear. You can't be reading your camcorder manual while under the pressure of the wedding schedule and coping with the stress levels of the various personalities involved. Practice assembling your gear: Make sure you can smoothly hook up your wireless microphone and adjust audio levels, and attach your light to see what effects it creates in various conditions. Most importantly, handle and use your camera as much as possible: Try angles, moves, and all the manual controls. Teach your hands to find the controls you want and to make smooth camera motions both on the tripod and off of it. Be able to switch settings quickly, as you will make rapid scenery—and therefore lighting—changes throughout the wedding day. Don't just use your camera; watch your practice footage to learn how your manipulations look and how to best control them.

A Video Vocabulary

Having a basic video vocabulary will help you practice your techniques as well as help you communicate to clients, co-workers, and other vendors while you work. If you say, "Excuse me, I'm going wide," the photographer will know to get out of your shot. If you ask your assistant to "Get a pedestal of the cake," you should have a pretty clear idea of the footage you'll receive. Following are some basic techniques to think about and practice.

Work the Angles

A familiarity with camera angles is more than helpful; knowing which angles are especially flattering is crucial for the wedding videographer, who doesn't want to be caught making the bride look bad. Mixing camera angles will lend excitement and style to all your work and can be particularly useful in sequences set to music. Following is a list of common angles, examples of which are shown in Figure 5.1.

▶ **Eye level.** This generally neutral shot appears to the viewer as a real-world angle. It is what we are accustomed to seeing.

▶ **High angle.** This shot shows the subject from above, with the camera pointed down, emphasizing a downward gaze. This is often a flattering angle for brides, because it tends to reduce, not enlarge, features. Stylistically, a high angle can lend a pensive, reflective or demure air to the subject.

▶ **Low angle.** This shot shows the subject from below, with the camera pointed up. This tends to be less flattering for brides as it tends to enlarge or distort features. A low angle may work better for grooms, as it can have the tendency to make the subject appear powerful—larger and dominant. It also can work well for large group shots from afar or to create an interesting look for an establishing shot.

▶ **Bird's eye.** This angle shows the scene from directly above. If space and equipment permits, this can be an excellent shot to use at the ceremony, the receiving line, and during the dancing. Some videographers carry a small step ladder to help facilitate this angle; others use their natural surroundings to help them out.

▶ **Dutch tilt.** This angle has the camera tilted to one side so that the horizon is on an angle. This can be fun and dramatic, and plays well with close-up shots of the wedding details such as jewelry and flowers. It can also be used to enliven the dancing scenes.

Some angles can be combined for especially cinematic effects. A low-angled Dutch tilt is an excellent way to capture the wedding aisle with rose petals strewn on it in the foreground and the altar or wedding arch in the background.

Eye level

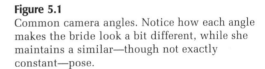

Figure 5.1
Common camera angles. Notice how each angle makes the bride look a bit different, while she maintains a similar—though not exactly constant—pose.

High angle

Low angle

Bird's eye

Dutch title

Know Your Moves

Before I cover the specific wedding shots you will want to obtain, you'll want to become familiar with a few basic shooting skills so you can pinpoint the best techniques, or combinations of techniques, for your style. If you are new to shooting, practice these moves on your own camera before you go to a wedding; your cat, the neighbor's kid, or even a vase of flowers can all be excellent models. You want to make sure you can smoothly execute these camera moves before you attempt them while also trying to wrangle bridesmaids and fight the light at the same time.

Basic Moves

▶ **Follow.** In this move, the camera follows the subject at a roughly constant distance.

▶ **Pan.** This refers to horizontal camera movement, either left or right.

▶ **Pedestal.** This refers to moving the whole camera vertically, with respect to the subject, while maintaining a constant angle.

▶ **Tilt.** In this move, the camera's angle changes vertically while the camera itself maintains a constant vertical position.

▶ **Zoom.** Technically, this is not a camera move; rather, it is a change in focal length that makes the subject appear closer (zoom in) or farther away (zoom out).

Advanced Moves

▶ **Dolly.** Here, the camera is mounted on a cart for smooth movement. In the wedding setting, this can be simulated by placing a tripod on a cart or even in a car for establishing shots.

▶ **Dolly zoom.** In this case, the camera moves closer to or farther from the subject with the lens zooming out or in, respectively, to keep the subject the same size within the frame.

▶ **Track.** Similar to a dolly, a track is any shot that moves while maintaining constant distance from the subject. It may also be called a truck.

Call the Shots

It's helpful to know the names of different types of shots, especially if you are working with a partner. For example, you might agree that one of you will shoot a section wide while the other goes tight for close-ups. If you are shooting by yourself, you want to make sure you gather lots of each type of shot so you can have dynamic edits that cut well together. Following is a list of the shots most commonly used in wedding videography, which are shown in Figure 5.2.

Within a scene, you should vary your shots for more dynamic editing, particularly in montage sections that will be set to music. In a montage scene, cutting from one medium shot to another looks dull; cutting from medium shots to extreme close-ups or point-of-view shots will liven up the visuals.

▶ **Master shot.** Also called a safety shot, the master shot is a wide, static shot. Although it may appear dull, it is extremely handy for establishing a scene or for when a more dynamic, planned shot doesn't work. Often, in a two-camera shoot of a wedding ceremony, one camera will be set up for a master shot the entire time while the other camera tries for more interesting coverage.

▶ **Two-shot.** This shot has two people as its subject and is usually, but not necessarily, from the torso up. This shot is common during posed shots with the bride and her attendants and the groom with his groomsmen.

▶ **Point of view (POV).** A POV shows the view from the subject's perspective. This can be very fun to use in bridal preparations as well as with the bouquet and garter toss.

▶ **Extreme wide shot (EWS).** Often, this shot is so wide it might not have an obvious subject. It is extremely helpful for establishing context; indeed, it is often referred to as an establishing shot. Wedding videographers use it to give an overview of the setting—that is, to indicate to the viewer where the video takes place, such as a vineyard, a hotel, or a church.

▶ **Wide shot (WS).** A wide shot shows a person from head to toe. Make sure to get lots of wide shots of your bride in her dress. You will also need wide shots to get formal pictures with lots of family members.

▶ **Medium shot (MS).** A medium shot of a person will generally be from the waist up. It is handy to mix in medium shots to give visual variety.

▶ **Medium close-up (MCU).** A medium close-up will be tighter than a medium shot, generally showing a person from the shoulders up.

▶ **Close-up (CU).** In a close-up, the subject fills the entire frame. You will want to get lots of CU shots of the pretty particulars that go into the wedding: place cards, jewelry, bouquets and boutonnieres, shoes, and dress detailing.

▶ **Extreme close-up.** An extreme close-up will be even tighter than a CU, showing perhaps only a portion of the subject's face. Like a CU, they are good shots for details and are also effective for depicting bridal preparations such as the bride applying makeup and putting on jewelry.

(a) Master

(b) Two-shot

(c) Extreme wide shot

(d) Wide shot

(e) Medium shot

(f) Medium close-up

(g) Close-up

(h) Extreme close-up

(i) Point of view

Figure 5.2
Common shots.

Maintaining Your Composition

Composition, also called framing, refers to how elements are arranged within the frame of your shot. There are some simple composition guidelines of which you should be aware. Knowing the basics of composition will help you define your own personal style, both in the ways that you follow traditional rules and in the ways that you break them.

What's the Story?

We are used to seeing the elements of the story presented in ways that are visually appealing and effectively tell a story. In terms of storytelling, composition can be used in several ways.

At its most basic level, composition should be used to convey to the viewing audience the subject of the scene. While this may sound obvious, it is a very common mistake for a videographer to assume that everyone who watches the video will look at what he or she (the videographer) is looking at. In reality, a videographer must force viewers to see what he or she wants them to see. For example, the highlight of the scene shown in Figure 5.3 is the child going crazy on the dance floor. While that may be obvious to everyone present on the dance floor, it is less clear when presented to the viewing audience as shown in the first image. When presented as the subject of the frame, however, it is obvious what the videographer wants to showcase.

Figure 5.3
Don't assume that because something is visually compelling in person, it will jump out of the frame without your help. In the first image, the flower girl is dancing up a storm, but she is lost in the scene. By centering her in the shot, as in the second image, all her movements are highlighted. The videographer can then zoom out to show her in context.

Finer understanding of composition can enable you to change the entire mood or feel of a shot or a scene, which can be particularly useful in wedding videos that are particularly stylized or themed as opposed to a more straightforward documentary style. For example, constantly framing the subject in the center of an image will give the piece a very straightforward and practical look. This doesn't mean boring; it can be quite useful if you are planning to make a succession of cuts to get a lot of information out quickly—for example, to show off the cocktail-hour scenery. Lots of off-center shots (even more off center than the rule of thirds, described in the next section) lends itself to slower, dreamier styles or to sections with MTV-style quick, disjointed cuts.

The Rule of Thirds

Typically, a viewer's eye prefers to work its way across an image—which means key elements of an image do not need to be centered. In fact, often, if you center an image, the viewer's eye will be prohibited from moving around or across the frame. In contrast, good framing, with the subject located off-center, will gently direct the viewer's eyes across the image.

Derived from classical painting, the rule of thirds provides some basic guidelines that allow filmmakers and photographers to set up images that are naturally compelling and pleasing to the eye by indicating places on a frame that the eye will naturally flow across. To apply the rule of thirds, divide your frame into thirds, both horizontally and vertically; then place key elements of the subject on those horizontal and vertical lines or where the two lines intersect.

Look at the establishing shot in Figure 5.4. The boats are along the top vertical and the tree trunk is on the left horizontal. The viewer's eye is naturally drawn to the two places where the vertical lines intersect the top horizontal. Even when shooting a single subject, such as the bride, the rule of thirds will still apply to a degree. Note that in the photo of the bride in Figure 5.4, the bride's eyes fall on the top horizontal, with her figure on the left vertical.

Figure 5.4
Both these images show the rule of thirds in action.

In truth, the rule of thirds should actually be called the guideline of thirds. While this and other such rules are useful for strong starting points and solid, usable footage, occasionally breaking the rules can make for innovative, creative work. On the other hand, breaking rules can also make for messy, amateurish shots. Be prepared to use trial and error to practice different looks. Break rules with intention and style, not haphazardly.

Natural light can represent a compelling reason to break the rule of thirds. If speckled light on the lawn or the couple's shadow provides an interesting visual balance to the subject, go with it. Don't try to compact a pretty scene into the rule of thirds.

Headroom

For a clean shot of your subject that is visually appealing without too much distraction, make sure there is the right amount of *headroom*, or space, between the top of your subject and the top of the frame. Too little headroom, as in the left-most image in Figure 5.5, can make the viewer uncomfortable, especially if the subject is cut in an awkward place such as mid forehead. Too much space above the subject will reduce its importance, as in the top-right image in Figure 5.5. Even if the shot is usable, too much headroom can make it boring. A compelling image will have the right amount of space above the subject, as in the bottom image in Figure 5.5. In the case of a close-up of a person, this often means the subject's eyes will fall on the top horizontal line of your canvas divided into thirds.

Figure 5.5
While cutting someone across the forehead can work in a close-up or an extreme close-up, there is not enough headroom in the image on the left, which cuts the bride's forehead awkwardly for a medium shot. In contrast, the middle image has too much headroom: The bride is lost in the shot. Finding the right amount of headroom, as shown in the bottom image, may not be completely natural at first, but will become so with a bit of practice and attention.

As best you can, try and figure out how much headroom is right before you start shooting. The best way to do so is to zoom the camera until your eye feels relaxed looking at the frame while incorporating as little dead, or useless, imagery in the background as possible. For example, you might focus and frame the best man as the DJ is introducing him, before his toast actually begins, to avoid awkward camera movements as he introduces himself. That being said, you will need to make adjustments on the fly, as your subject will likely be moving as you are shooting. Even if your best man isn't pacing the dance floor as he speaks (frustratingly common), it is very unlikely he will stay in frame the whole time—especially if you are shooting medium to close-up. Furthermore, a guest or vendor may suddenly walk into your shot, forcing you to readjust. Constantly paying attention to framing will help you make smooth adjustments as you shoot.

Close-ups

Yes, I just stated that framing with the right amount of headroom is important, but the extreme close-up can be extremely compelling and dramatic. So don't shy away from occasionally cutting the top of a subject's head from the frame. Extreme close-ups, like the one shown in Figure 5.6, mix well with more traditionally balanced shots and lend themselves to capturing the emotions of the day.

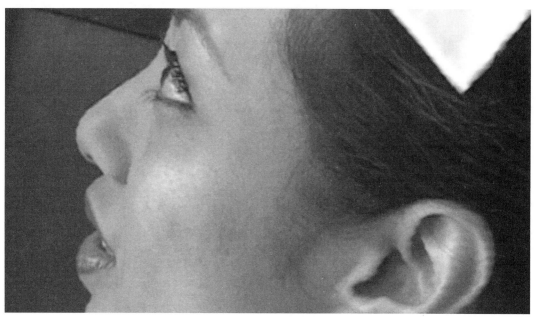

Figure 5.6
Extreme close-ups work very well in preparation scenes. There tends to be action around the bride's face as her hair is done and make-up is applied, and she will typically be emotional, whether happy, frustrated, excited, or nervous, as this shot captures.

When framing an extreme close-up, don't go too low on the forehead or it will look awkward. Similarly, make sure the shot remains balanced: Crop evenly from the top and bottom. I use extreme close-ups as the bride is getting ready and, assuming I have two cameras, during the vows and ring exchange, the first dance, and any other time a particular emotion is being shown. Be warned: It's easy to go overboard on extreme close-ups, especially since they do not tend to cut well together. But using a few well-balanced and well-composed ones will add emotion and humanity to your storytelling.

Following Action

It would be wonderful if you could block your wedding participants, the way a narrative film director can direct his or her actors. If you could plan ahead of time which direction the dip at the end of the first dance would face, the shots you could set up would be amazing. While you can take a few moments with your bride and groom to stage some of these shots (as discussed later in this chapter and in Chapter 7, "The Big Day"), usually you will be desperately trying to keep up with the action in an attempt to make sure it stays in the frame.

In situations where the camera is moving to follow the action, such as when the bridal couple enters the reception or during the father-daughter dance, it is very tempting to anticipate the movements of your subjects and place the camera where you will "find" them. In doing this, however, you lead the viewer's eye to unknown areas, which can be awkward, disorienting, and downright sloppy. Instead, take a deep breath and follow the action rather than leading it. This makes for footage that is significantly more smooth and natural for the viewer. Furthermore, following the action will give you a much better chance of landing on a well-framed shot. That means you will also generate fewer awkward corrective camera moves that you must either edit out or try to gracefully incorporate.

Clearing the Frame

Following the action is better than anticipating it. But for storytelling purposes and for visual aesthetics, sometimes you might want to clear your frame entirely by allowing your subjects to walk in or out of the frame without following them. This allows you to maintain a well-framed, static shot, as well as capture what might be an excellent opening or closing to a scene. Even if you don't wind up using the entrance or exit, having the footage will allow you the option and can provide more variance in your visuals.

I use this technique quite a bit in weddings because it provides a natural opener or closer for scenes. For example, between shots of the bride getting ready and the ceremony, I might get a shot of her walking out of frame with her train and veil behind her. Similarly, a carefully set up shot of the reception room that starts empty and then has guests—or the bridal couple—walking in can be useful to establish the reception scenes in a way that is most flattering to the room (which undoubtedly cost the couple enormous amounts of time, planning, and money to decorate).

Watching the Edges

The first time I shot anything (a music video), a more experienced shooter told me "The musicians are always compelling, so watch the edges for everything that isn't." This advice has proved invaluable for everything I have shot since—most particularly weddings. Nothing is more distracting than unrelated items at the edges of your frame: a fire extinguisher, a tripod, pedestrians passing by, a parked car.

When you have as little control over the location of your shooting as in a wedding, there are innumerable things to interrupt your shot. While one might think that if these distractions don't interrupt the subject or the action, they don't matter—but they do. A huge distinction between professional and amateur video lies in how cleanly the shots are framed—that is, how much the viewer is allowed and encouraged to comfortably watch the subject without the dirt and noise at the periphery of the frame. For example, Figure 5.7 shows two shots of the groom being photographed. In the first image, the photographer's assistant is visible in the top-right corner, as is the camera bag in the bottom-left corner. The second image is much cleaner: only the subjects of the shot are in frame. There are no distractions at the edges.

Figure 5.7
Often, a small adjustment makes a big difference. By ignoring the edge of the frame, the videographer has allowed additional elements—an assistant and a camera bag—into the first image. Notice that the cleaner version, which is the slightly zoomed-in and reframed image on the right, looks much sharper and more professional.

When you are busy watching your subject, it is amazing how easily these items will creep into the frame without your noticing. As often as possible, sweep your eyes around the edge of the frame and crop out any distractions that pull attention from your subject. At first, I found this very hard to do; somehow, I couldn't believe the subject would still be there if I removed my gaze. But trust me: It will be.

Manual Controls

The advantage of having a camera with manual controls is the way you can play with images, adding your own style to the pictures. This is particularly popular in wedding videos, where the softness of a slightly out-of-focus image—or portion of an image—can lend a quality of romance or force the viewer to look at a detail such as a ring or flower. Exposure can be tricky in both low light and bright daylight; manual controls allow for more flexibility in getting the light you want. Other controls, such as zoom and white balancing, lend control over how your image is presented. Figure 5.8 shows some of the manual controls of a Canon XL2 video camera. Of course yours will differ.

Figure 5.8
The manual controls of the Canon XL2 video camera include focus, white balance, gain, exposure, iris, in-lens neutral density filter use, and automatic exposure shift. Although certain features, such as the manual focus ring and manual zoom ring, tend to have a standard placement on the video camera, you will need to spend some time getting to know the features of your own camera and how to access them easily.

Zoom

All video cameras come with an optical zoom lens, which is not unlike a magnifying glass. The convenience and flexibility of a zoom lens can't be understated; it would be near impossible to shoot a wedding without one. Without changing your position, you can zoom and reframe to get well-composed close-up and wide shots. In a one-camera ceremony, for example, your zoom allows you to get a wide shot of the couple standing with the officiant and the scenery behind them, as well as an image of just their hands as they exchange rings—without ever getting off your tripod.

That being said, it is important to note that elements of your image will change when you zoom in and out. Although you may not always have the option to move your person and camera (such as in many ceremony sites, where you are required to remain in one position), it is important to know what your position and zoom can do to an image so that when you *do* have a choice, you can build the image you want.

Focal length is the distance from the camera lens to the sensor. Zooming in increases the focal length, while zooming out decreases it. As you zoom out (decreased focal length), objects that are closer to the lens get magnified more than objects farther from the lens. This is relevant if you are close to the bride and shooting wide; her features will be slightly distorted—nose larger, ears smaller.

An image shot from far away but zoomed in may contain the same elements as an image shot from close in but zoomed out. It is important to note, though, that the two images will have significant differences (see Figure 5.9). For example, the background in the second shot will appear smaller and farther away. The point is, you must realize that your choice of camera position and associated focal length will change the mood of the image. A close-up camera shooting wide will produce an image oddly distant and voyeuristic; pulling the camera away from the subject will warm up the image. Again, as a wedding shooter, you often have to make do with the shots you can get under tight conditions. But the relationship between camera distance and focal length can add humanity and style to your images.

Figure 5.9
Although the bride is shown at the same size in these two images (her necklace is at the bottom of the frame), she was shot from 1 foot away in the image on the left and 10 feet away in the image on the right, with the optical zoom moved accordingly. Notice the difference in the shape of her features and the depth in the background that results.

Focus

Manually focusing with a digital camera is typically easy: You simply adjust the focus ring until the image appears correctly in your viewfinder or on the LCD screen. In addition, digital video typically provides a wide depth of field in which you can achieve good focus. In fact, one of the complaints about video, as opposed to film, is how sharp and ultra focused it appears. Film has a much shallower depth of focus and is therefore harder to focus, but maintains a softer look about it because of that.

Low-light conditions can prove more difficult to focus in, because the depth of field becomes narrower and actually seeing the subject on your LCD display may be hard. In these situations, it is especially important to use manual focus (as opposed to any auto-focus features your camera may support), as your eye has a much better chance than the camera of reading the scene correctly. If you use auto-focus, as the camera searches for a subject on which to focus, it may lump lots of objects together or may move quickly in and out of focus trying to get a correct read.

Using manual focus also allows for fancier shots such as ones using *racked focus*. A racked focus shot has two subjects in frame, one in the foreground and one in the background, and switches focus from one to the other. This shot can take some time to prepare and is usually best when doing posed shots of the couple or details of their day, such as place cards or floral arrangements.

To achieve a racked focus, do the following

1. Arrange your two subjects with one in the foreground and one in the background.

2. Find the correct spot on your focus ring for the subject that will be in focus at the *end* of your shot and mark it with a piece of tape.

3. Readjust the focus ring so that the subject that will be in focus at the *beginning* of your shot is in focus.

4. Start shooting, and move the focus ring from its current position to the one marked with tape.

Another, simpler way to use manual focus to add style to your shots is to intentionally shoot a subject out of focus in manual mode and then turn on automatic-focus mode. The camera will immediately focus, creating a shot that guides your viewer's eye to the subject, as shown in Figure 5.10.

Figure 5.10
Use manual and automatic focus to add some style and movement to an otherwise static shot of flowers.

Exposure

Exposure refers to the amount of light that is allowed onto the camera sensor in order to record the image. In a video camera, exposure is controlled by *shutter speed* and the size of the opening on the rear of a lens, called the aperture. In still photography, shutter speed refers to the amount of time that a mechanical door, or shutter, is opened to expose the film or digital sensor. In video, it is a bit different, although the effects are similar: Shutter speed refers to the amount of time that the sensor will be allowed to build a charge, or record the image. Shutter speed is measured in fractions of seconds per frame; if the shutter speed is $1/60$, the image will be exposed to the sensor for $1/60$ of a second per frame; $1/120$ is faster, and $1/500$ is faster still. Remember: NTSC has 29.97 frames per second; we're looking at tiny segments here!

Aperture size is determined by the expansion and contraction of the iris, which is a series of interlocking metal leaves. When in automatic mode, a camera's iris will contract in bright light to limit overexposure and widen in dim light to get as much available light as possible, much like your eye. The opening of the iris is measured in *f-stops*. A high f-stop results in a smaller aperture, meaning it will stop more light. A lower f-stop results in a larger aperture, allowing more light through.

In automatic-exposure mode, video cameras select the aperture size that will yield the best exposure for most of the shot. This can be useful in certain settings, such as an evenly lit, indoor ceremony. But what happens if, say, you're shooting an outdoor ceremony with the couple under a shaded canopy on a bright, sunny day? In that case, because the vast majority of the scene will be well—if not over—lit, the camera's aperture will close to a higher f-stop. As a result, it won't pick up the features of the couple in the shade, who represent only a small portion of the wide shot. In this situation, you must manually control the iris to allow enough light through to the camera's sensor to capture the subjects—even though this will allow too much of the light background through, somewhat blowing it out. With the exception of low-end cameras, every video camera should allow for manual adjustment of the lens aperture (although not all will list the f-stops).

 Your camera will likely also have a neutral density filter, which will help in especially bright situations. Remember to turn it off when you move indoors again!

Similarly, if you attempt to shoot scenes where both you and the subjects are active—for example, when everyone is dancing or during cocktail hours—using auto-focus, the camera will continually adjust to compensate for your and your subject's positions. While the camera is doing its job correctly, the effect can look awful because of the continual adjustment that is unlikely to match your pace.

Comfort with manual exposure is key for shooting weddings, as awkward lighting is more standard than not. Any given wedding may have a lighting range that includes a dim church ceremony, sunny outdoor portraits, a cocktail hour that spans the sunset, and nighttime dancing in semi-dark rooms. Yes, managing the light yourself is yet another thing to think about, but will ultimately provide a much better image.

Manual exposure can also help control your depth of field—that is, the part of the image that is clearest in focus. When the subject is more focused than the background, it appears to stand out; this is called a *shallow* depth of field. A *deep* depth of field will have more detail and focus on the entire shot. Using a shallow depth of field is a good way to highlight the bride during portraits or to give a soft romantic mood to detailed shots such as images of the bride's jewelry, shoes, and flowers. To create a shallow depth of field, position your camera far away from the subject, zoom in, and open the iris as much as possible. This can be tricky, as you will be letting in more—sometimes too much—light. Automatic adjustments in shutter speed will compensate, but these techniques require some practice.

White Balance

It is important to white balance your camera every time you change lighting, whether it be moving from one room to the next or moving from indoors to outdoors or vice versa. White balancing is a way of ensuring that the colors your camera records are as accurate as possible. Because white is the sum of all colors, if the camera sensor records white correctly, the entire spectrum will be relatively correct. It is easy for a camera to fall out of white balance, the result being images cast with another color, such as yellow or blue.

To set the white balance, point your camera at something that is pure white, filling about 75 percent of your viewfinder with it. Set the focus and exposure, and then press the camera's white balance button. The camera will adjust; afterward, it should display some kind of marker, such as an icon on the LCD, that a new white balance has been set. It will remain in that white balance until the next balance is read.

Ideally, you will carry a professional white card in your camera bag to use as a balance, but if you need to move quickly or you are separated from your bag, you can almost always find something white at a wedding—like, for example, the bride. Do be careful of ivory-colored gowns, though—they are quite common and can be very deceiving! If you are even a bit confused, ask the bride what color her dress is before you white balance on it.

 Because outdoor light tends to be a bit more blue and indoor light tends to be a bit more yellow, many cameras come with presets for white balancing. Although I recommend a manual white balance when possible, the presets can be extremely handy when you are going back and forth between locations quickly, such as in and out of a church.

Building Your Shot List

Once you have mastered some of the aforementioned skills, you're ready to incorporate into your repertoire various essential shots as well as some fun shots. For a successful shoot, aim for a solid library of shots that you are comfortable with and a shorter list of experimental shots for extra flavor and style. The ideas for many of these experimental shots are likely to come to you when you are actually on site with your subjects, but it doesn't hurt to come up with ideas for new shots you want to try beforehand, too. The successful experiments will wind up in your library of basics!

As you develop your style, you will find that certain moves work well at certain moments. For example, I usually do a tilt when the bride and her father are walking up the aisle, and during the reception I try to find decorations that will allow for a good rack-focus shot. Some further suggestions for specific shots can be found in Chapter 7.

 Don't be constrained by my suggestions or especially by your own habits. A good videographer constantly tries to capture images in new ways!

Essential Shots

The list of essential shots will change slightly depending on the wedding as well as the video coverage purchased and preferences provided. There are some basic shots, however, that you should be prepared to capture. Add and revise this list depending on your style, the couple, and the event, but make sure you keep a version of this essential shot list available!

Most of these shots will need to be captured as they happen; there is no second opportunity for a first kiss. Indeed, getting all these shots is part of what makes wedding videography so stressful. There may be times, however, when you have the opportunity to re-create an important shot from your essential list, such as the image in Figure 5.11.

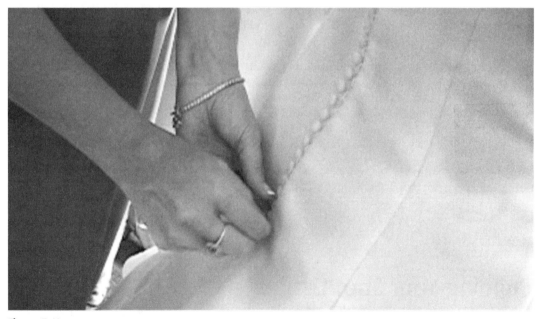

Figure 5.11
It is not uncommon for a bride to want privacy while she is putting on her dress. Ideally, she will allow you back in the room once she is fully clothed but before she has fully zipped or buttoned her dress, so you can capture those moments. If necessary, however, these shots can be quickly re-created.

Pre-Ceremony Prep

- ▶ Wedding dress
- ▶ Zipping or buttoning the dress
- ▶ Close-up of bride's rings, other jewelry, shoes
- ▶ Bride putting on the veil
- ▶ Putting on boutonnieres
- ▶ Groom tying tie
- ▶ Bride and groom with respective parents

Ceremony Shots

- ▶ Exterior of ceremony site
- ▶ Guests walking in
- ▶ Flowers, musicians, altar at ceremony site
- ▶ Families and bridesmaids entering
- ▶ Flower girl and ring bearer entering
- ▶ Groom waiting for bride
- ▶ Bride's entrance and walk down aisle
- ▶ Groom seeing bride for the first time
- ▶ Father shaking groom's hand, hugging bride
- ▶ Any readings or performances by guests
- ▶ Shots of guests seated and watching, for use in editing
- ▶ Vows
- ▶ Ring exchange
- ▶ Unity ceremony
- ▶ First kiss and introduction as couple
- ▶ Bride and groom walking up aisle
- ▶ Receiving line/guests throwing petals, rice, birdseed, etc.
- ▶ Bride and groom in car to reception site

 As discussed further in Chapter 7, services of various cultures or religions will have specific important elements. Make sure you know about any such moments ahead of time.

Formal Shots

- ▶ Bride, full length
- ▶ Bride and groom
- ▶ Bride with maid of honor, bridesmaids
- ▶ Groom with best man, groomsmen
- ▶ Bride with groomsmen
- ▶ Groom with bridesmaids
- ▶ Bride and groom with wedding party
- ▶ Bride with parents
- ▶ Bride with family
- ▶ Groom with parents
- ▶ Groom with family
- ▶ Bride and groom with all family
- ▶ Bride and groom with flower girl and ring bearer

During the Reception

- ▶ Exterior of reception site
- ▶ Bride and groom arriving
- ▶ Table centerpieces
- ▶ Table setting
- ▶ Placecards table
- ▶ Close-up of bride and groom placecard, menu, guestbook
- ▶ Wedding cake/groom's cake
- ▶ Guests arriving at reception
- ▶ Band/DJ
- ▶ Bride and groom's first dance
- ▶ Father and daughter's dance
- ▶ Mother and son's dance
- ▶ Toasts (all)
- ▶ Bouquet toss
- ▶ Garter toss
- ▶ Guests dancing
- ▶ Cake cutting
- ▶ Bride and groom toasting each other
- ▶ Getaway car
- ▶ Bride and groom leaving

Fun Shots

While the preceding section details the moments that your clients will expect you to catch on video, there is lots of room for you to be creative with your shots. This is where you can shine as a wedding videographer: The joy you can bring both during the shoot and when the couple sees the images on video can be tremendous and very gratifying.

Shots will be unique and stylized when you use a fun technique to shoot an ordinary wedding shot or when you set up a situation that might not otherwise happen. Creatively mixing the previously discussed shooting techniques with the aforementioned essential shots can lend unusual looks to regular shots. Here are some shots to try (more can be found in Chapter 7):

- ▶ Try using a tilt as the bride walks down the aisle, shooting her from behind. Not only will this give you all the detail of her dress, but allowing the train to walk out of frame can be dramatic.

- ▶ A pedestal shot is a good way to capture items close-up that won't fit in the frame without zooming out, such as a multi-tiered cake or a tall centerpiece.

- ▶ A high-angle medium or close-up shot of the bride tends to be very flattering. Start with her looking down at her bouquet and then moving her head to look up at the camera.

- ▶ Practice using rack focus on the details of the reception decorations. Typically, couples spend ages designing centerpieces, placecards, menus, favors, and the guestbook; they will appreciate you showcasing their attention to these details.

- ▶ As discussed earlier, a bird's eye shot of dancing gives a sense of how the event feels. Other fun places to use a bird's eye shot include (but are certainly not limited to) the moment that everyone clinks glasses in a toast, the head table at the reception, and the bartender preparing and delivering a drink to a guest.

- ▶ Use a POV shot of the couple in the car that brings them to or from the reception. To do this, you will have to ride in the front seat with the driver (or in your own car driving the same path) and shoot what the couple is seeing as they pull up or drive away.

Of course, these are just some ideas intended for you to use as a springboard for the execution of your own style.

When you have time, such as during the getting-ready period or when the couple and bridal party are taking pictures together, building some shots can be very fun. Not every couple will be game for staged shots, but some couples will love the creativity and humor. Whether you create staged shots, or even a whole a narrative about your couple, will depend on what the couple is like and the style of the wedding video that you are putting together. It is part of your preparation work to get to know your couple well enough to determine what they will enjoy.

Here are a few ideas for fun staged shots.

▶ Is your groom notorious for being late? Stage a shot of his alarm clock going off and show him jumping out of bed, fully dressed and ready for the ceremony (see Figure 5.12).

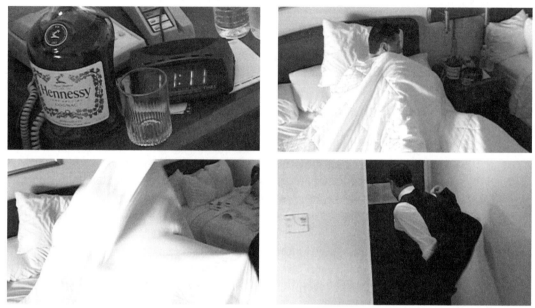

Figure 5.12
The first image sets the scene before the alarm goes off and the groom is out of bed and out the door. Even though the whole shot lasts only about 30 seconds, it adds lots of personality, flavor, and customization to your finished product.

▶ Is your bride known for loving sweets? Shoot her sneaking in to "test" the cake before the wedding starts.

▶ Often, the groomsmen and bridesmaids will be drinking alcohol as they get ready for the event. It's fun to show them handing a bottle or flask down the line, ending with the bride or groom.

▶ There are lots of romantic shots to stage involving shadows and walking. Try to get a shot of your couple walking in and out of frame; you can use this as an opening or closing.

▶ Have all the bridesmaids toss their bouquets, with the groomsmen lined up ready to catch them.

▶ A popular shot is to have your groomsmen walking past the camera in a slightly uneven but predetermined array, which you can set to slow motion in post-production. This has come to be known in and out of weddings as the *Reservoir Dogs* shot, an example of which can be seen in Figure 5.13.

Figure 5.13
This shot is easy to set up. As the guys walk toward the camera and out of the frame, you will get a fun image to add effects to in post-production.

Ask your clients what their favorite movie is. You might find a way to incorporate a shot or style that is reminiscent of it. If not, there may be room to use some of the soundtrack music in your piece.

Getting to know your couple and building enough time into your schedule to ensure that the shoot is not rushed are key to coming up with fun and unusual shots that will reflect their personalities and the tone of the event they have built.

Summary

This chapter provides some basic wedding video skills. Having read it, you should have an understanding of video angles, camera moves, types of shots, and framing fundamentals. Managing the manual controls will help you get the best footage possible, even in tough situations. Put all these skills together, and there is nothing on the shot list that you won't be able to handle. It will require practice, though; make sure to start playing with your camera before your first gig!

Next Up

Congratulations! You are geared up, and you know how to use your camera. Spend some time playing with your equipment and coming up with ideas for capturing fun, compelling images—and get ready to refine them for the specifics of each wedding you are hired to film. The next chapter talks about those specifics and how to best prepare for them, including managing your clients' expectations, exploring your location, the specific gear you need, managing a timeline, coordinating with other vendors, and etiquette on the job.

Chapter 5 Tutorial: Angles, Moves, and Lighting

The tutorial associated with this chapter allows you to see examples of the different shots, camera angles, and moves that you will use while shooting weddings. There is also a demonstration on using sunlight to your own advantage. To view these tutorials, navigate to Wedding Videography_Start to Finish > Chapter 5 Tutorial in the DVD files that you copied to your hard drive. (Refer to the tutorial in Chapter 4 if you have not yet copied these files to your drive.) If you don't have QuickTime to view these files, you can download it from http://www.apple.com/quicktime.

Chapter 6
Pre-Production

In this chapter:

▶ The rehearsal
▶ Client preferences and expectations
▶ Location limitations
▶ Packing your gear
▶ Timeline
▶ Coordination with other vendors

I used to think that only performers got nervous before a production, but boy, was I wrong. Regardless of your level of experience, even when you are behind the camera, you will be under significant pressure on the day of the event. You only have one chance to capture the big moments, and your product and your reputation as a vendor rely on your ability to do just that. While it is safe to assume that your bridal couple will be more anxious than you are, a bit of nerves on your part is natural and will help you get organized and prepare for the shoot.

Regardless of how you feel, it is imperative that you appear calm, collected, and supportive. Frantic videographers (and photographers) translate their nervous frenzy to the couple, which will affect the images you capture—not to mention their enjoyment of the day! You are in the position of making the couple feel at ease and therefore look comfortable, relaxed, and happy on camera. Remember: By the time you are shooting your second wedding, you will likely have more experience with weddings than the couple getting married does!

Heading into the day having prepared as much as possible will ensure that you have every opportunity to obtain the images and audio you need, with the cooperation of the other participants and vendors.

The Rehearsal

Most couples rehearse the wedding ceremony, usually followed by a rehearsal dinner for the bridal party and guests who have come from afar or who are especially close to the couple. Rehearsal and/or rehearsal-dinner shooting may be a service your clients request. Even if they don't, it might be a good idea to simply attend rehearsals (no shooting) for your first few weddings. Indeed, if feasible, going to the rehearsal is probably the best way to prepare yourself to shoot the ceremony for the first few weddings you cover. You will have an opportunity to survey the layout of the room and determine where best to position yourself relative to where the participants will be standing and the relevant restrictions. Figuring out ahead of time where you, your cameras, and your audio recorders will be can make the day of the event much calmer and smoother.

With some experience under your belt, attending rehearsals is probably unnecessary for the most part unless the ceremony is taking place in a venue that is especially difficult to shoot, such as a theater or music venue. (These might have stage lighting or require you to shoot from different angles than most religious or outdoor venues.)

Sometimes, you will be hired to shoot the rehearsal-dinner toasts or to show a photo montage during the event. If so, use this opportunity to prepare for the next day as well. Ask questions about the couple, learn the names of the key guests, find out which participants you should get footage of, and get a sense of the couple's comfort and ease with the camera. You might even be able to use this time to get some interview footage that will blend in with the wedding video.

Client Preferences and Expectations

It is imperative that you go into the shoot knowing what your client wants out of the final product. Ideally, you will gather this information during your marketing meeting and contract negotiations, but often, it happens significantly later. Try to reach a point of understanding with your couple before the week of the event, when they are entertaining family from out of town, frantically re-writing their vows, and fighting over the seating arrangement. Ideally, you will have clear instructions well before that chaos ensues.

What do I mean by clear instructions? You will need logistical instructions, obviously, as discussed in upcoming sections, but artistic direction is also imperative before you begin shooting. Some artistic direction is inherent in the type of package or service agreement that your client chose (discussed in Chapter 2, "The Business of Weddings"). You will obviously know how many cameras and how many shooters are coming and for how long camera coverage is expected. There are a lot of smaller issues to cover, however—many of which will differ significantly from couple to couple. For example, do they want you to interview their guests? Is there a particular shot they want set up (see Figure 6.1)? Do they want the ceremony edited or left uncut? Do they want natural audio for their first dance or would they rather you edited in a cleaner version of the song? Often, a couple will request that special attention be paid to certain family members who might be elderly or have traveled far for the event.

Figure 6.1
This image was shot from all the way across a courtyard, from another balcony. It was part of a series requested by the couple, who picked the venue in part because they liked the look of the balconies.

These preferences may change the way you shoot. For example, if a couple specifies that they want natural audio of the band during their first dance in a one-camera shoot, you want to make sure that you have a decent, medium to wide shot of the whole thing. If you try to obtain too many close-ups or crowd reaction shots to edit in, you will likely have too many instances when the camera is moving to adequately cover the whole song. If you are re-cutting their dance to dubbed-in audio, however, you have more freedom to get close-ups of the groom's hands on the bride's back or the bride's mom crying as she watches.

Knowing the musical preferences of the couple before you start shooting is especially helpful, as their musical taste may influence your style of shooting. For example, if they choose lots of slow and romantic songs, you might consider setting up framing to reflect a dreamy mood and hold your shots a little longer. If they choose mostly fast-paced music, make sure to get lots of dance footage! Getting their music choices ahead of time will also help you avoid a backlog of work as your post-production pile builds up.

While it would be exhausting for clients and artistically restrictive for you to get detailed instructions on every moment (though I have certainly had brides try), understanding their most important priorities, like shots of Grandma or the candle-lighting ceremony, is key to giving them the personalized product that they want.

I provide clients with a "video intake sheet" to help organize some of their preferences, for both shooting and editing, an abbreviated version of which can be found in Figure 6.2. Should you choose to do the same, the information you obtain will obviously be tailored to your style and setup. Note the reference to music on this sheet; you'll learn more about music rights in Chapter 8, "Basic Editing."

SO & SO'S WEDDING VIDEO PRODUCTIONS
VIDEO INTAKE FORM

Thank you for choosing SO & SO Wedding Video Productions
Please answer the following questions to help our videographers and editors customize your video

Wedding Date: _____   Wedding Locations:_____

Bride's Full Name: _____   Groom's Full Name: _____

Bride's Family Members: _____

Groom's Family Members: _____

Maid of Honor: _____   Best Man: _____

Please indicate the approximate length you would like your finished video:

15-30 min _____   30-60 min _____   60-90 min _____   As long as poss. _____

Please indicate any sections of the video you would prefer unedited:

_____

Please indicate any particular music you would like us to use (note: copyright law may not allow for all of your preferences):

_____

Please indicate any other preferences you might have about your wedding video:

_____

Figure 6.2
Customized to the information most useful to you, a video intake sheet—or customer-preference list—will help you during both shooting and editing.

Location Limitations

There are often limitations associated with shooting the ceremony, particularly in religious settings. If you are lucky, you will be given full range to set up wherever you want, but it is not unusual to find yourself in the position of shooting from a less-than-ideal vantage point such as a balcony, the edge of the pulpit, the back of the room, and so on. In the case of a Mormon wedding, it is unlikely you will be allowed in the church at all, but will instead be hired to shoot the couple leaving the church and the reception. In contrast, at a Hindu wedding ceremony, you may be expected to be right on top of the action. Make sure that you are either aware of expectations and shooting limitations prior to setting up or have a contact person affiliated with the facility who will be able to direct you when you arrive.

When faced with a shooting limitation, here are some ideas to ensure you get adequate coverage:

▶ Often, you'll be farther back than you would like, which means you will likely be shooting tighter. Make sure you are on tripod for this, as camera shake is especially noticeable when shooting zoomed in from a distance.

▶ You may have to pick a side to stand on rather than getting a straight-on shot. If so, choose the side that will offer the clearest view of the bride's face as she says her vows.

▶ It is often hard to get compelling guest shots from a balcony, as you will likely be shooting the tops of everyone's heads. If so, try to get some guest shots before the event begins, along with lots of other details shots of the room. You'll need these shots for cutaways.

Occasionally, the building's facilities will help instead of hinder your work; make sure to ask if there is an available audio feed that you can pick up or a place that videographers in this setting traditionally stand to get the best angle and light.

 After the wedding is over, make some notes about what the location was like to shoot in. Include information on restrictions, lighting, and audio conditions. This will help you in the future should you have another event in the same place.

Packing Your Gear

It would be hard to forget your camera, although not impossible—I have heard such nightmare stories. It's almost a given, however, that at some point you'll be digging through your camera bag for *something* that just can't be found anywhere.

To avoid this, write out a checklist of items required for all events. This checklist should live in your bag, which should be ready to go at all times. The day before your shoot, run down your checklist to make sure you have everything. For replenishible items, such as batteries and blank media, always bring far more than you think you need. Keeping a surplus of these items is inexpensive—but can cost the job, should you run out.

Here's my checklist. Your own list will look a bit different, but you can use this one as a starting point to build your own:

- ▶ Camera
- ▶ Charged camera batteries
- ▶ Battery charger
- ▶ Lens tissue
- ▶ Lens cleaning fluid
- ▶ Tripod
- ▶ Monopod
- ▶ Blank media
- ▶ Wireless microphones
- ▶ Batteries for wireless microphones
- ▶ Hand-held microphone
- ▶ Microphone cables
- ▶ Headphones
- ▶ Lights
- ▶ Battery pack for lights
- ▶ Bulbs for lights
- ▶ Filters/diffusers for lights
- ▶ Any tools associated with equipment
- ▶ Sharpie pens
- ▶ Business cards
- ▶ Tape
- ▶ Paperwork (copy of contract, list of essential shots, directions, timeline, and emergency-contact phone numbers)

Keep a stash of personal items in your camera bag also. You might be going a long time in the sun without eating. I always bring deodorant, sunscreen, bottled water, and a snack.

Timeline

The organization required to pull off what may be a weekend full of events for hundreds of people is nothing to sniff at. The running joke at my sister's wedding was that it was sponsored by Microsoft Excel. Although there are certainly different levels of preparation, it is safe to assume that most every bride has a timeline (see Figure 6.3); this is your map to the event. Hang on to it tightly, and make sure it's accessible during the event itself.

Wedding Day Timeline – November 7, 2010			
Start Time	**End Time**	**Total Time**	**Notes**
8:30 AM	8:45 AM	15 minutes	Hair stylist arrives in bridal suite; set-up
8:45 AM	9:30 AM	45 minutes	Hair: Mother of Groom
9:15 AM			Bridesmaids arrive at bridal suite; coffee and bagels arrive (Inna)
9:30 AM	10:30 AM	60 minutes	Hair: Sonya
9:30 AM	9:45 AM	15 minutes	Make-up stylist arrives; set-up
9:45 AM	10:25 AM	40 minutes	Makeup: Clem
10:00 AM	10:15 AM	15 minutes	Bride's hairdresser arrives; set-up
10:15 AM	11:45 AM	90 minutes	Hair: Bride
10:25 AM	11:05 AM	40 minutes	Makeup: Mother of Groom
10:30 AM	11:30 AM	60 minutes	Hair: Lisa
11:05 AM	11:45 AM	40 minutes	Makeup: Sonya
11:15 AM			Groomsmen arrive at apartment; watch game and lunch (Groom to order)
11:30 AM	12:15 PM	45 minutes	Hair: Jen
11:45 AM			Lunch arrives (Bride to order)
11:45 AM	12:25 PM	40 minutes	Makeup: Bride
12:15 PM	1:15 PM	60 minutes	Hair: Clem
12:25 AM	1:05 PM	40 minutes	Makeup: Lisa
1:00 PM			Photographer #1 and Videographer arrive at bridal suite. Photographer #2 arrives at Groom's apartment.
1:05 PM	1:35pm	30 minutes	Makeup touch-ups as needed; make-up stylist leaves.
1:15 PM			Shuttle arrives at apartment
1:15 PM	1:45 PM	30 minutes	Hair touch-ups as needed; hair stylist leaves
1:30 PM			Florist arrives at bridal suite with bouquets
1:25 PM	1:45 PM	20 minutes	Shuttle leaves apartment for hotel; Groomsmen to bring cooler, snack bag
1:45 PM			Bridesmaids head to hotel lobby to wait for shuttle
			Jen to take ring pillow and flower girl baskets
1:45 PM	1:55 PM	10 minutes	Groomsmen head to hotel to wait for shuttle
			Groom goes to bridal suite
1:55 PM	2:10 PM	15 minutes	Photos of Bride and Groom only (first look) in bridal suite; exchange cards; put on boutonniere
2:15 PM	2:45 PM	30 minutes	All bridal party leave hotel in shuttle to photo location #1; Sonya in charge of keeping photo schedule
2:45 PM	3:05 PM	20 minutes	Photo/Video at location #1 (Shakespeare Garden/Botanical Gardens or Legion of Honor if it rains)
3:00 PM			Tim to meet Tom (AV) in ballroom with laptop for slideshow testing
3:05 PM	3:35 PM	30 minutes	Wedding party group leave location #1 in shuttle, travel to location #2
3:35 PM	3:55 PM	20 minutes	Photo/Video at location #2 (Bentley Reserve/Financial District or back to hotel if it rains)
3:55 PM	4:15 PM	20 minutes	Wedding party group leaves location #2, travel to hotel
4:15 PM	4:40 PM	25 minutes	Wedding party freshen up before ceremony
			Clem to set up programs, vases and candles for ceremony.
			Officiant arrives.
			Videographer to set up camera microphone and camera for ceremony; Greg (AV) to set up other microphones; officiant and groom to wear microphones.

Figure 6.3
This is the timeline of an organized bride. Some schedules will have less detail, some will have more; they might even be broken down to minute increments. Don't be fooled by this level of organization, though; the real event is unlikely to match up exactly!

4:30 PM			Groom, groomsmen and ushers meet upstairs welcome guests and distribute programs; Groom to give rings to ringbearers.
			String trio arrives; set-up for ceremony.
4:40 PM	5:00 PM	20 minutes	Bride, bridesmaids, flower girl, ring bearer and parents meet at VIP Club Lounge for ceremony.
4:50 PM	5:00 PM	10 minutes	Groomsmen meet outside VIP Club Lounge for ceremony.
			String trio begins music as guests are arriving.
5:00 PM	5:30 PM	30 minutes	Ceremony (Skyline BC)
5:30 PM	6:30 PM	60 minutes	Cocktail hour (Skyline A); string trio plays during cocktail hour
5:30 PM	5:45 PM	15 minutes	Extended family pictures in VIP Club Lounge
6:20 PM			String trio ends.
6:30 PM	6:50 PM	20 minutes	Cocktail hour ends; guests escorted downstairs via elevators
			Wedding party stays upstairs while guests being escorted down elevators
6:50 PM	7:00 PM	10 minutes	Grand entrance of wedding party
7:00 PM	7:03 PM	3 minutes	Bride and Groom first dance:
7:03 PM	7:05 PM	2 minutes	Bride's parents welcome
7:05 PM	7:30 PM	25 minutes	First course served
7:15 PM	7:20 PM	5 minutes	Maid of Honor speech
7:30 PM	8:10 PM	40 minutes	Second course served
7:45 PM	7:50 PM	5 minutes	Best Man #1 speech
7:50 PM	7:55 PM	5 minutes	Best Man #2 speech
7:55 PM	8:10 PM	15 minutes	Slide show
8:10 PM	8:20 PM	10 minutes	Father/Daughter dance, Mother/Son dance
8:20 PM	8:40 PM	20 minutes	Dancing begins
8:40 PM	8:45 PM	5 minutes	Cake cutting
8:45 PM	8:50 PM	5 minutes	Bride and Groom speech and toast
8:50 PM	11:00 PM	130 minutes	Dancing resumes
9:00 PM			Photographer and Videographer leave
11:00 PM			Reception ends; Florist arrives for tear-down

Review your timeline carefully prior to the event. There may be points during the day where you have to make decisions: Do you go to the cocktail hour or capture the picture session with the couple? Do you shoot the bride getting dressed or the groomsmen posing together? Since the answer is often "both," use the timeline to decide how to best maximize the amount of footage you can get.

Keep in mind that no matter how stern the wedding planner may sound, the timeline is only an estimate. Events are rarely skipped in the name of saving time. Instead, the entire timeline will be pushed back. And it practically goes without saying that I have never seen a wedding run ahead of schedule. This is particularly relevant if you are contracted to work for a certain amount of time but still expected to stay through certain events. As discussed in Chapter 2, make sure you have an understanding of what to do in this extremely common situation.

Coordination with Other Vendors

While the bride and groom are the stars of the show, the wedding party and family are the supporting cast, and the guests are the audience, you and the other vendors are the production crew. Just as a theater curtain wouldn't rise before the stage manager had talked to the lighting director, the major events of the wedding shouldn't happen without the coordination of the vendors. During the reception, the people with whom you will be in closest communication are the DJ or band leader and the photographer. If there is a wedding coordinator, some of your communications with the other vendors may go through him or her.

The band leader is your stage manager and will be calling the cues for you: introducing the couple for their entrance, calling up guests to give toasts, inviting the first dances, and announcing such events as the cake cutting, bouquet toss, and garter-belt toss. Make sure to introduce yourself and request that he or she give you a warning before each event is announced so that you aren't interviewing Uncle Al when the bride and groom cut the cake. If you are trying to gauge time—do you have long enough to run to the bathroom before the first dance? Will the bouquet toss be before 10 p.m.?—The bandleader or DJ is the one to turn to. It is unlikely—although certainly not unheard of—that you will need to speak to the DJ before the actual event, but make sure to find him or her as soon as possible once you arrive at the venue to request that you be kept in the loop about the timeline.

It is much more likely that you will talk to the photographer before the event; your relationship with him or her is slightly more nuanced. With similar goals, you can either step on each other's toes or help each other in the process of capturing the day. Make sure you have a similar idea of the timeline and what might happen during times designated for pictures with the couple, especially if a location hasn't been determined.

Most often, it'll be the photographer who calls the shots—literally—setting up the bridal session, posing the formal pictures, lining up the bridal party for both fun and serious shots. If the photographer isn't doing this, it's your job to step in. And don't be shy about asking participants to hold the shots a little longer or to set up some shots of your own. In fact, if you know you have a few shots to stage with the couple, let the photographer know ahead of time how much time you will need. You need to leave the day with enough footage that you can style your own piece; if the photographer's setup won't give you that, it's up to you to make sure you get it on your own.

For the ceremony itself, be sure you know exactly where you will stand for the processional and discuss ahead of time where the photographer will be. Both of you are trying to get the best shot possible without including each other in it. If you are granted access to the aisle itself, it is common for the photographer and videographer to each take one side at approximately the same distance from the front of the room. That way, you can communicate as needed, which often occurs through hand signals, shoulder taps, and in some cases, glares. For posed images, such as formal shots in the church or with the bridal party outside, let the photographer know that you will set up your tripod slightly behind his or her workspace. You will need to be far enough away to encompass everyone in large shots, zooming in for close shots. For the reception events, such as the cake cutting and dances, talk to the photographer before each one begins as you are likely to want to be on the same side of the room to keep each other out of frame.

Etiquette

Your reputation as a vendor will in part rely on how professional and easy to work with you are the day of the event, when you are in extremely close proximity to your clients and mingling among their family and friends. There are no hard and fast rules about how to approach this, but you will want to make sure that at no time does your presence make anyone uncomfortable. Mingling with guests is part of your job, so if you befriend some guests, you are probably doing your job well. Always keep in mind, though, that you are there in a professional capacity, and you must concentrate primarily on your videography tasks.

Because you want to mingle somewhat easily in the crowd, make sure you are dressed appropriately. That doesn't mean that you should wear a tuxedo to a black tie wedding, but Bermuda shorts are certainly out. Many vendors opt for slacks and a collared shirt or all-black clothing. Avoid overly bright colors and loud patterns that will draw attention to you. Tank tops, logoed t-shirts, and hats are inappropriate; comfortable shoes are imperative.

It is typical, though not mandatory, for clients to provide a meal for you when the guests are dining; check on this with your couple beforehand. Depending on how the couple sets up their reception, the vendors may have a table of their own or they may be in a separate room. It is common for vendors to be offered a different (and less expensive) meal than the guests. If you are invited to join a buffet line, ask the caterer if you may go through the line early in order to finish your meal before the guests, allowing setup time for the events that will follow dinner. Keep in mind that drinking alcohol is inappropriate while you are on the job. Eating wedding cake, on the other hand, is generally appropriate—if you are certain there is more than enough for the guests.

Wedding vendors are often paid the night of the event. If that is how you have set up your payment schedule with your client, agree on who should pay you by the end of the night—and make it someone other than the bride or groom. You will not want to be pestering the bridal couple while they are dancing or saying goodbye to their guests! Make sure to get your payment before you leave, though, as your couple will likely be on a honeymoon in the coming days. Note that although wedding videographers often receive cash gratuities, they are not necessarily expected as they are for some other service professionals.

Summary

To do your best work, preparation is essential. This chapter gives you some idea of things you need to think about before you arrive at the wedding venue, such as artistic and logistical expectations, shooting limitations, what to bring, who to communicate with, and what to wear. As you get more experienced, the preparation process will become much faster, but as a beginner make sure to spend adequate—even excessive—time getting ready. That time will be well worth it when you have a smooth and successful shoot.

Next Up

The big day has finally arrived. All your planning, shopping, training, and event preparation will culminate in the wedding-day shoot. The next chapter gives you step-by-step advice on getting through each event of the day, as well as more generalized information about dealing with lighting, camera movement, interviews, and audio throughout.

Chapter 6 Tutorial: Building Your Master Shot List

Shots are suggested throughout this book, including shots that are typically—though not necessarily—expected. In some places, I went so far as to suggest styles to use with various shots. Following is a master list of shots you should obtain from every part of the day. To complete this tutorial, use this master list as a starting point to create your own shot list for a specific wedding. Your list will undoubtedly reflect your style and your client's preferences. If you are creating a list for a specific wedding you are shooting, make sure to include any shots of religious or cultural customs or traditions particular to that event.

 Many of the shots listed here are further discussed in Chapter 7, "The Big Day." Because preparing your shot list is most definitely a pre-production activity, however, I have included them here.

A shot list can be incredibly useful for making shooting decisions and keeping you organized and on track throughout the day, but don't get so hung up on your list that you miss what's going on. Remember: As the days unfolds, an awful lot will happen in front of you, regardless of whether it is included in your list. Be flexible and watch for what makes each event different. Often, that is where you will find the proverbial "gold" in wedding video.

Event	Shot Description
Prep	
	Establishing
	Wedding dress hanging up
	Close-up of bride's rings, other jewelry, shoes
	Final touches of make-up
	Zipping or buttoning the dress
	Bride putting on the veil, shoes
	Bride with parents
	Bridesmaids getting ready, toasting, with bride

(continued)

Event	Shot Description
Prep (continued)	Staged shots with bride and bridesmaids
	Bride interview
	Bride fully ready
	Groom tying tie, putting on boutonniere
	Groom with parents
	Groomsmen getting ready, toasting, with groom
	Staged shots with groom and groomsmen
	Groom interview
	Bride and groom seeing each other
Ceremony	
	Establishing
	Exterior of ceremony site
	Guests walking in
	Ushers handing out programs
	Flowers, musicians, altar at ceremony site
	Families and bridesmaids entering
	Flower girl and ring bearer entering
	Groom waiting for bride
	Bride's entrance and walk down aisle
	Groom seeing bride walk down aisle
	Father shaking groom's hand, hugging bride
	Welcome from officiant
	Any readings or performances by guests
	Shots of guests seated and watching, for use in editing
	Vows
	Ring exchange
	Unity ceremony
	Declaration of husband and wife
	First kiss

(continued)

Event	Shot Description
Ceremony (continued)	
	Bride and groom walking up aisle
	Receiving line/guests throwing petals, rice, birdseed, etc.
	Bride and groom in car to reception site
Formal shots	
	Bride and groom with wedding party
	Bride with parents
	Bride with family
	Groom with parents
	Groom with family
	Bride and groom with bride's family
	Bride and groom with groom's family
	Bride and groom with all family
	Bride and groom with flower girl and ring bearer
	Bride, full length
	Groom, full length
	Bride and groom
	Bride with maid of honor, bridesmaids
	Groom with best man, groomsmen
	Bride with groomsmen
	Groom with bridesmaids
Couple shots	
	Full length
	Close-up
	Close-up of wedding rings
	Kissing
	Walking toward the camera
	Bride and groom under bride's veil
	Groom kissing bride's neck/shoulder

(continued)

Event	Shot Description
Couple shots (continued)	
	Bride sitting on groom's lap
	Groom holding bridal bouquet
	Bride and groom walking away from the camera (from behind)
Cocktail hour	
	Bird's-eye view of whole scene
	Bartender pouring drinks
	Appetizers being offered
	Guests chatting
	Guests toasting
	Guest book
	Place-card table
	Other details such as lights, candles, flowers
	Musicians
	Guest interviews
Reception details	
	Exterior of reception site
	Whole room
	Tables
	Centerpieces
	Menus
	Bride and groom place cards
	Favors
	Candles
	Wedding cake/groom's cake
Reception	
	Guests arriving at reception
	Bridal-party entrance
	Bride and groom entrance
	First dance

(continued)

Event	Shot Description
Reception (continued)	
	Band/DJ
	Welcome toast
	Food being served/wine being poured
	Father/daughter dance
	Mother/son dance
	Toasts (all)
	Guest performances
	Open dancing
	Cake cutting
	Bouquet toss
	Garter throw
	Getaway car
	Bride and groom leaving

Chapter 7
The Big Day

In this chapter:

- ▶ Lighting
- ▶ Camera movement
- ▶ Two-camera shoots
- ▶ Interviews
- ▶ Audio
- ▶ Specific points in the day

Congratulations! You are officially a wedding videographer, complete with a business entity, production and post-production equipment, and, most importantly, your first clients. All the rest has been preparation; now it's time to let the fun begin.

Okay, "fun" might not be the word that comes to mind as you frantically search your bag to make sure you brought the right audio-input cable, but remember: This event is all about emotion. As a member of the day's production team, lead by example by taking some joy in both the celebration of the couple and the fruits of your labor. Your business is officially off the ground!

That being said, it is far easier to have fun during the wedding when you aren't panicking because you don't know what you're doing. This chapter steps you through a typical wedding-day agenda, providing a glimpse of what's going on, an idea of the mood, pacing, and atmosphere of the various events of the day, and specific audio and video tips for each one.

Of course, every wedding is different, but they all contain some of the same elements. Even if the wedding you are recording does not include all the events detailed in this chapter, or if it does but they are conducted in a unique manner, this chapter will provide valuable tips about what to expect and how to obtain great footage—often under trying circumstances.

Before I get into the day's first event, there are a few points that you will want to keep in mind throughout the day:

▶ At what points during the day will your style and your couple's preferences require that you obtain continuous footage?

▶ How much natural audio will you try to incorporate?

▶ How many stylistic shots require some setup time? How many would you like?

▶ Do you have an optimum amount of footage you want to obtain throughout the day?

If you know, for example, that you want to obtain some establishing shots that might take some time, build that into your schedule. If you know you want to leave with minimal footage to ensure a fast edit, be extremely careful about when you turn your camera on; make sure you're shooting footage you want and that the shot is set up. If you know that your style employs lots of natural audio, you make sure you have your MP3 recorders ready to go at all times, or that you shoot even when the visuals aren't terrific. (But be careful—consider your editing here!) With an idea of what you are looking for overall, you can move into making specific shooting decisions throughout the day.

Lighting

One of the main difficulties in shooting weddings is how dramatic—and dramatically bad—the light can be. It is not uncommon to have an overexposed ceremony and a poorly lit reception—or the reverse—only minutes away from each other in time. This section is designed to provide tips to help you understand your lighting options. Later on, this chapter discusses how these tips will apply to specific events during the wedding day.

Although a lighting kit would rarely if ever be used for a wedding shoot, understanding the goals of studio lighting can help you try to mimic the techniques using what you have available. A basic lighting kit includes three types of light:

▶ **Key light.** The *key light*, usually a bright light placed in front of the subject and slightly off center, casts the main light on the subject.

▶ **Fill light.** A *fill light*, while still placed in front of the subject, illuminates the subject from the opposite angle to fill in the shadows cast by the key light. A fill light is typically a slightly softer light.

▶ **Back light.** A *back light* is placed behind the subject, creating some depth between the subject and the background.

Again, it is rare that you will set up lights during a wedding shoot. Even if time permitted this (and it doesn't), most couples would consider the lighting setup invasive. Being adept at using natural light to take the place of a key, fill, and back light is helpful to getting good shots of your subjects. To achieve this, you'll want to consider a few general guidelines for all your shots, whether indoors or outdoors:

▶ Ideally, you will want to shoot in even light. Bright sunlight hitting the bride on her right will leave her left entirely in shadow. If you are shooting outdoors with bright overhead sunlight, be wary of the harsh shadows it will cause; consider moving into the shade for more even levels.

▶ Aim for a light source, natural or not, to hit your subjects from the front or gently from the side.

▶ Unless you are intentionally looking for a silhouette effect, as in Figure 7.1, never shoot with the main light source, especially the sun, directly behind your subject.

Figure 7.1
Although sunset imagery can be very compelling, avoid using the sun behind the subjects as your only light source unless you are shooting for a silhouette instead of a detailed image.

▶ Set your camera exposure for the subject, not the background. A blown-out background is more acceptable than a blown out subject—and easier to manipulate during editing.

▶ The ideal time to shoot outdoors is when the sun is up, but low in the sky—about an hour before sunset. This provides a soft, golden, warm, and even light. If you have any influence over the schedule of events, talk to your couple about doing outdoor portrait shooting during this time of day.

▶ While worrying about a back light is often a luxury for which you won't have time, there are certain points during the day when you will be able to set up such shots. Take advantage of them when they occur.

Shooting in Low Light

Here are some of the problems—and remedies—for shooting video in low light, a situation that can arise at any point in a wedding, but will most often occur at the ceremony and/or reception. Notice that most of these problems are solved with good understanding of and dexterity with your camcorder's manual controls.

▶ **Focus.** If your camera doesn't receive enough light to find the subject, it will auto-focus on various elements in the scene—or nothing—and will result in a blurry mess (see Figure 7.2). In low-light settings, make sure to use manual focus; the human eye is much faster and more adept than the camera lens. This is pretty important; you will open your aperture quite a bit either manually or automatically, which shortens the depth of field, or the amount of margin you have in which to focus. You have a much better chance than your camcorder of focusing correctly with these bounds.

Figure 7.2
This poorly lit dancing scene in shows the camera's inability to focus in automatic mode, leaving the subjects nearly unrecognizable.

▶ **Noise.** Often, adding gain will help with shooting in low-light conditions by amplifying the signal that is sent to the sensor. Adjusting the *gain* +3dB is roughly equivalent to opening the lens about one f-stop. That being said, the electronic amplification that occurs when gain is added can lead to *noisy* or grainy images (see Figure 7.3). A general rule of thumb is that even though it may be tempting in low light, don't change the gain by more than +6dB.

Figure 7.3
While it's tempting to boost gain to combat low-lighting situations, be careful; if you boost too much, the resulting noise can make your image grainy.

> ▶ **Streaking.** Small areas of bright light in an otherwise low-light scene, such as candles, can cause streaking in a camera movements like pans or zooms. Using manual focus will help combat streaking; if you use your camera's auto-focus, it will continually attempt to focus on the light.

> ▶ **Blurred motion.** As with gain, it is tempting to dramatically reduce shutter speed to allow more light into a dimly lit scene (on those camcorders that allow manual shutter speed adjustment, that is). That works to a certain extent, but be wary: Your footage will blur if you reduce shutter speed too much. A rule of thumb is to avoid shutter speeds slower than 1/30 of a second to reduce the chances of blurred images and to be very steady under these conditions. Make sure you use a tripod (or monopod or steadistick) to lessen the motion blur likely to occur.

Shooting in Bright Light

Like low-lighting conditions, bright light can occur at any point in the wedding, but is most likely troublesome during the ceremony and formal pictures. Shooting in bright light is difficult, as your camera will adjust for the light source rather than your subjects, which may be underexposed—possibly even silhouetted. Other elements to think about in bright light include shadows and overexposure. Consider the following:

▶ **Backlighting.** If you use your manual controls to increase the exposure so that the background is blown out, you will have a better chance of properly lighting your subjects. While this is not ideal, it is far better than the opposite: a perfectly exposed background and underlit subjects.

 It is possible that your camera has a backlighting mode that will help you manage this exposure adjustment. Check your camera's manual for details.

▶ **Neutral density filters.** Many cameras include neutral density filters, which reduce the amount of light allowed into the camera without changing the color levels. They can be very helpful; often, your camera will tell you when one should be applied. Don't forget about it when you go back inside though; that is embarrassingly easy to do.

▶ **Shadows.** Be aware of the shadows that you, your camera, and your subjects are casting in bright-light situations. You must position yourself carefully to avoid ruining your own shots.

▶ **Zebra stripes.** Most professional camcorders feature *zebra stripes*, or zebras (see Figure 7.4). These enable you to see on the LCD screen which parts of a brightly lit image are overexposed (usually indicated by red lines) or are approaching overexposure (usually indicated by green lines). Overexposed images are at 100 IRE, which is a composite video-signal measurement; the settings for approaching overexposure should be adjustable and usually range from 70–90 IRE. A well-contrasted image may include some parts that approach over exposure; it is when your whole image has zebra stripes or when parts of it are overexposed that you should be concerned. Zebra stripes are distracting to some videographers, but others use them on a regular basis to determine when an exposure adjustment is needed.

Figure 7.4
The zebra stripes on this bride's dress indicate where the image is blown out or overexposed. When dealing with the amount of sun and white subject matter commonly found in a wedding, a small bit of overexposed image is not much to worry about; when these stripes take over the whole image, however, it is time to change your exposure.

SHOOTING IN THE RAIN

Alanis Morissette says that rain on your wedding day is "ironic." While I disagree with her definition of irony, I would concede that it can be disappointing—in part because rain makes it harder to get good images from the event. Incidentally, while your bride might be disappointed, gray skies or a light mist can provide a even, soft light, free from harsh shadows, that makes shooting easy. It is when you get to real rain—rain that makes you, your subjects, and your camcorder wet—when the difficulties occur.

There are a few things to consider when shooting in the rain:

> ▶ **The protection of your clients.** If you have an indoor place to shoot, it may be more comfortable for your clients—who are unlikely to want to mess up their outfits, make-up, and hair. If, however, they prefer to shoot outdoors, do your best to make them comfortable by making decisions about shots *before* you go outdoors, and work as quickly as possible. Also, maintain a cheery, upbeat mood; if you are complaining, you will bring their day down. If rain is a regular occurrence in your part of the world, consider investing in a high-quality, large umbrella to bring along. A bright-colored umbrella will be a great prop for a cute shot (see Figure 7.5) as well as a comfort to your clients.

(continued)

Figure 7.5
There is very little that is convenient about shooting in the rain, but with some creativity and preparation, you can still get great-looking footage.

▶ **The protection of your gear.** The outer parts of your camera can deal with a little water; the inner parts can't. If the rain is a light drizzle, you shouldn't have much to worry about; the camera's casing will be enough to protect the sensitive camcorder parts—especially if you use a jacket or other light cover to protect it. Be sure to wipe the camera dry with a lint-free cloth after using it even in light rain.

(continued)

SHOOTING IN THE RAIN (continued)

▶ The protection of your person. I regret to inform you that you rank low on the list of priorities here. Be sure to bring a rain jacket and whatever other rain gear you would normally use. If you have an assistant, part of his or her job should be shielding you and your gear from the weather. If you face inclement weather regularly, you might want to consider an umbrella hat, unless the goofiness of it is, understandably, too much for you to deal with.

If you are shooting in a heavy rain, you will want a layer of camera protection that is sturdier but doesn't inhibit camera function. The usual solution in this situation is to cover the camera in a clear plastic bag (a garbage bag, a Ziploc bag, or a vinyl garment bag) with a hole cut for the lens. Use a rubber band or tape to tightly secure the bag around the lens, being careful not to rub against the focus ring, which will prevent it from working. The bag's opening should be at the back of the camera, allowing your hands to access the controls. This is far from a perfect system; continually check the integrity of the bag and its positioning around the lens.

Alternatively, you can purchase waterproof gear for your camera, available from camera-bag makers such as PortaBrace. These offer more security than the plastic-bag option and may be a good investment if you live in an area where the wedding season regularly gets a lot of rain. (Hawaii and Florida, I'm looking at you!) For us dry western states, the amount of time spent shooting in the rain is unlikely to warrant such an expense.

Shooting without lights will underemphasize the rain; the even, grayish natural light will make it less noticeable. In contrast, bright beams or back lights will reflect off the raindrops, making them stand out more. To avoid that, follow the normal rule of having the sun (if there is one) face your subject. If highlighting the raindrops is an effect you are after, try shooting facing the sun's position. With enough cloud coverage, you don't have much to worry about in terms of harsh light and shadows, although if the sun is managing to do its job despite the rain, you still may have the issue of silhouetted subjects. Then again, that might be a very compelling image on a stormy day. If you expect to regularly shoot in the rain, conduct some camera experiments on your own time so that you can get artistic shots and still work quickly while your clients are out in the elements.

Camera Movement

Camera movements—zooms, pans, and tilts—add style and charisma to your video style; I encourage their use. Remember, however, that although these shots add flavor, they should not be used all the time. Constant movement may work in a short highlight or MTV-style piece, but won't work for a full-length wedding video; too much movement is tiring on the viewer's eye. Be particularly careful of moving the camera too much when you are looking to document an event in a straightforward style, such as with a toast or the ceremony. There is room for some motion here, but a well-framed, still shot allows the action or dialogue of the scene to speak for itself. Make sure to hold some shots for at least 10 or 15 seconds, if not minutes at a time.

Similarly, while a handheld section might add some character, for the most part you should be on tripod as often as possible. A steady shot will always look more professional; besides, a piece's warmth and personality is most often felt through the quality of the content you are shooting, not the style. When you must go handheld—and there will certainly be times when you must—concentrate on using a steady arm. When possible, brace yourself against a wall, pillar, or table to get the steadiest shot you can.

Two-Camera Shoots

The various times throughout the wedding when you are likely to be using two cameras are noted in the section titled "Specific Points in the Day," but there are a few general things to note about using two cameras.

As you shoot, remember that you will want the footage from both cameras to sync up easily during editing. The easiest way to do this is to run both cameras continuously; that way, you only have to find one sync point. This will be intuitive for the camera operator shooting a wide safety shot, but might be less natural for a roving shooter, who must remember to leave the camera on while changing position. (Chapter 9, "Advanced Editing," discusses the mechanics of multi-camera editing.)

Also, discuss with your fellow camera operator the techniques you want to use to ensure that you are getting ample coverage of the event, without redundancy. Some tactics might be to have one shooter follow the couple while the other shoots scenery, or to have both shooters in the same place, shooting wide and close up, respectively.

Make sure to turn on your *tally light* so your co-videographer knows when you are shooting and can avoid disturbing your shot. Toggled on in your camcorder menu, a tally light is a small red light that lets other people know when you are recording.

Audio

Audio is unique in that it has the power to invite the listener inside, often much more than imagery can allow the viewer in. (If you don't believe me, consider the helicopters in *Apocalypse Now*.) Capturing good audio distinguishes professional video from amateur video—and being able to weave natural audio into the images that you capture from the day will make the event more real.

A few things to remember about capturing sound:

> ▶ Sound files are small and MP3 recorders are cheap—meaning there's practically no limit to the amount of audio you can capture. The drawback? It takes a lot of time to go through all those audio files. But if these audio files primarily serve as backup to your on-camera microphones and lavalieres, there is no reason to scrimp.

► Use lavaliere microphones as often as possible. The audio quality they afford is vastly superior compared to the audio you'll record using your on-camera mic. That said, they can be a pain to set up—meaning you may miss capturing important footage in the time it takes to set one up. When deciding when a lavaliere mic should be used, weigh what you may be missing in the time it takes to set one up against the "intrusiveness" of your general presence with the on-camera mic (taking into account the lavaliere's superior audio quality, of course).

► If a participant is wearing a microphone, you may or not want to warn that person that you can hear him or her at all times, even if you aren't recording. You might opt not to warn them if you're concerned about them becoming self conscious. On the other hand, a quick word of warning might not be a bad idea for less shy individuals. I have heard countless grooms swearing, complaining, and urinating while they are waiting for the ceremony to begin! Regardless of whether you inform the person ahead of time, use the audio you capture (or the information you hear) outside the ceremony or toasts judiciously, professionally, and appropriately; err on the side of conservative unless you have a very clear understanding of the couple's preferences in that regard. A general rule of thumb is to use lavaliere audio for the ceremony and toasts only. (See Figure 7.6.)

Figure 7.6
I won't tell you what my brother-in-law said to my sister as they left the sanctuary as newlyweds, but I will say that using a lavaliere microphone on the groom can provide some great sound bites. Remember, though: Professional etiquette dictates that you not use anything that could possibly make the clients uncomfortable. If your client is also your sister—well, maybe the rules change a bit!

► Put fresh batteries in all your audio equipment on the morning of the event. Even if the old ones have a bit of life left, new batteries are extremely cheap insurance and one less thing to worry about throughout the day. And carry extras, just in case!

► When you rearrange your audio inputs as you change microphones or go to or from the church or DJ audio feed, make sure to check that all your connections and levels are appropriate. Like a fresh battery, a quick sound check is very cheap insurance.

Interviews

Chances are, there will be lots of opportunities to conduct interviews throughout the day (assuming interviews are part of your services at all). For example, you might conduct interviews during wedding preparations, the cocktail hour, and the reception—really, any time but the ceremony. For all your interviews, here are a few tips:

▶ Make sure your clients want you to conduct interviews. This should be a point you clarify in your pre-production planning. Couples who want a hands-off documentation of their event might prefer that you not approach their guests.

▶ If you have time, use a microphone with your interviewees. You don't need to set up a wireless mic for each person; a handheld microphone attached to your camera will work.

▶ If you frame your interview request as a favor for the couple, participants tend to be much more willing to engage. Don't force a guest to conduct an interview against his or her will, however.

▶ Ask open-ended questions that invite long answers, but keep it reasonable. The alcohol at weddings has a tendency to enhance long-winded and excitable storytelling later in the evening, so don't be afraid to interrupt someone or turn off the camera if it gets out of control.

▶ Request that interviewees respond to questions in complete sentences that incorporate the question itself. That way, you can edit the question out of the video, and the interview will still be cohesive and make sense. For example, if you ask a groomsman what he likes best about the bride, the response "I love Jenny because she drinks beer and goes fishing!" will work better than "That she drinks beer and goes fishing!"

Interviewing is a great way to personalize your final product. Although interviewing can add quite a bit of work to both the production and post-production phases, sprinkling just a few sentences here and there throughout your video can help convey a familiar, warm, and funny tone, particularly if you develop your own style for it.

TIM BAKLAND, TIMOTHY BAKLAND VIDEOGRAPHY, BEVERLY, MA

"I've found it very difficult to get quality interviews. Most people don't want to talk to a stranger, much less a stranger with a camera pointing a microphone in their face. One way I have obtained much better interviews is to have one of the bridal party—usually the best man or maid of honor—conduct the interviews while I shoot. This makes the interviewee more comfortable and often elicits funnier footage, since the guests are more likely to have a history with one another. The interview footage winds up being warm, funny, and conversational, instead of awkward and stilted."

Specific Points in the Day

In addition to keeping in mind the general advice presented in the preceding sections of this chapter, there are specific things you should know about shooting each portion of the wedding day. While every wedding will be different, certain elements tend to be similar—for example, formal shots are often shot outside, churches typically have low lighting, and shooting at dinner rarely makes for good video. The following sections cover what you can expect in terms of atmosphere, etiquette, and shooting conditions for each of the day's events.

 Don't forget to white balance as you move between wedding events, every single time.

Establishing Shots

Most likely, you will want at least one solid establishing shot for your video. You may or may not choose to open with it, but the shot will provide some context for the day, letting viewers know where they are. Between preparations, the ceremony, and the reception, weddings often have several locations; some videographers opt for an establishing shot of each one.

Ideally, establishing shots will be both informative and visually compelling. If you lack the time, space, or inspiration to produce a unique shot, the shot should at the very least be well framed and pretty. Because an establishing shot does not necessarily require natural audio, you will ideally be able to take some time to set up this visual shot carefully, planning the framing of your elements and potential camera movements.

Some ideas for establishing shots include the following (see Figure 7.7):

▶ A dolly or tracking shot depicting the approach to the grounds to the site

▶ An extreme wide shot of the building

▶ A tilt of the building

▶ A pan of the building's signage

▶ A creative still of the building's signage or of a distinguishing detail of the building

▶ A shot of the wedding invitation, artfully placed

▶ A shot of signage related to the wedding couple

▶ A pan of the building grounds

▶ A wide shot of the bride or groom walking into the building, either dressed up or in street clothes

Figure 7.7
A good establishing shot will be visually compelling and tell the viewer where the action is taking place, such as the exact location (images A and B) or the city (image C). An establishing shot may also include signage specific to the couple (image D). Try combining some of these elements to give the viewer even more information. For example, as the cable car in image E goes by, the shot tilts up and zooms out to end on image F, showing the viewer that we are in San Francisco at the church where the wedding ceremony will take place.

To give yourself time to set up good establishing shots, try to take care of them before even going in to meet the bride at the start of the day. Arrive at your first location at least 30 minutes early (or more if, like me, you are nervous about being late!) to look around and set up an establishing shot. This may require crossing streets, climbing ladders, or lying on the ground; give yourself time and permission to be creative here. You can also use this time to inspect the grounds for scenic areas and nice lighting in which to shoot the bride and groom, either together or separately, once they are all dressed up.

Wedding Preparations

Depending on the type of video coverage you have agreed to provide to your couple, you may or may not be shooting the wedding preparations (i.e., shooting the participants as they get dressed for the day), which may or may not include both the bride and the groom—who, by the way, might be in separate locations. Often, the bride will get ready at the same venue as the ceremony or the reception—for example, in the church or at the hotel where the reception will take place. The bride, especially, is likely to be surrounded by family members and bridesmaids, and often by stylists for her hair and make-up. This tends to be a somewhat chaotic time, as there are florists making deliveries, children of the bridal party present, and high tension. It is not unusual to be in a cramped hotel room or a giant—and ugly—recreation room

If there are two cameras involved, one should be on the bride and one should be on the groom—with two separate operators. Male and female shooting teams often have a competitive edge here, because often a bride or groom will prefer to work with a videographer of the same gender when they are getting ready. This is obviously not always true, and it is the duty of the videographer to make the client feel at ease regardless. That starts in the marketing session, but continues throughout the day of shooting, beginning with the preparation shots.

There's a good chance you will see the photographer for the first time during the wedding preparations—although hopefully, you will have spoken to him or her beforehand as recommended in Chapter 6, "Pre-Production." Make sure you take a moment at this time to get a sense of each other's work plan for the day to foster a cooperative relationship. Ideally, you will also talk to the photographer about both of your shooting styles, especially for the ceremony, and ways to keep out of each other's shots. Often, a simple request to the photographer at this time to watch your tally light can save you an entire day of irritation as he or she accidentally walks through your shots.

Footage to Obtain

Shooting preparations is a way to set up the story, both literally and figuratively. This is a very good opportunity to get the personalities of the couple on camera because the action is slower; there is more time to chat and set up shots. That being said, be careful of overshooting the preparation. You don't need minutes of the make-up case or the lipstick being applied; one shot of each will do. Often, during wedding preparations, you can carefully set up shots and record only what you need—which makes editing easier.

Audio

While I caution against overshooting during wedding prep, it is often a time when great natural audio occurs. A group of family and friends in a happy (albeit somewhat tense) setting—often drinking alcohol—can make for great snippets of conversation that you might want to include in your coverage to build to the excitement of the wedding in your storytelling. Consider your own style and the wedding videos you like. If using natural audio and conversation is important, run the camera more during this portion of the day.

 To help with editing, jot down the timecode of moments that you know will work well in your video as they happen.

Interviews

I often use wedding preparations as a time to interview the bride and groom, asking such questions as "How did you meet?" "Are you nervous?" and "What part of the day are you most excited about?" Their replies give context to your storytelling—showing their personalities, the inevitable quirks of their romance and courtship—and to the unfolding of the day. The work you have done getting to know your couple in your marketing and preparation communications, as well as your own social skills, will be invaluable at this point; you want to draw the couple out as much as possible, getting their emotions and opinions on tape, without making them feel uncomfortable or overexposed.

 Although I often interview the bride before she is fully dressed in her gown, I always wait until she applies her make-up. The make-up, especially if applied professionally, will make a huge difference in how she looks on camera, reducing shine, improving her complexion, and highlighting her eyes and cheekbones. Most people find it hard to watch themselves on camera; do everything you can to set up your shots in the most flattering way possible.

This is also a time to get comments from the parents and friends of the couple. Simple statements such as "It's about time they tied the knot!" or "We loved our new son-in-law from day one" can add a lot of warmth and personality to your video when woven into a montage of preparation images. It also helps to introduce the principal cast of characters that will be seen throughout the day, again giving context to your storytelling. Refer to the "Interview" section in this chapter for additional advice on getting interviews on camera.

Extreme Close-Ups

Because coverage of the wedding preparations is often shown in montage form—images set to music (again, natural audio works very well when carefully mixed in)—it's important to get a great deal of variety in your shots. You want to have some wide shots as well as some close-ups. I find that preparation shooting is also the best time to include extreme close-ups

(ECUs). Why? Because wedding preparations are about details: the boutonniere being pinned on, the charm hanging off the bouquet, the eye shadow just so. These details are painstakingly planned by the couple; capturing them on video both validates their efforts and enables them to see their work up close-up, which they might not otherwise have the time for (see Figure 7.8).

Figure 7.8
Avoiding the traditional eye-level, mid range shot, extreme close-ups offer the opportunity to show pretty features and details in creative ways.

Additionally, shooting ECUs can be very visually compelling—and you might not have as many opportunities when the action of the day speeds up. Take all the pretty images you can during wedding preparations; you might even be able to work them into later parts of the video. That being said, you don't need 12 different shots of any one detail; the bouquet isn't going to change much. Spending a few minutes setting up a couple of perfect shots is much more beneficial—and this is one of the only times during the wedding day that you will have that luxury of time.

Finally, capturing ECUs during wedding preparations is often a good idea because often, the room in which these preparations take place will be very un-photogenic; shooting ECUs will help you avoid the chaos of the setting.

Some ideas for extreme close-ups include the following:

▶ Final touches of make-up being applied
▶ The make-up box
▶ Hair styling

▶ Dress detailing

▶ The bride's accessories, such as her shoes, jewelry, garter belt, gloves, and veil

▶ Flowers

▶ The groom's cufflinks and boutonniere

▶ Gifts to the bridesmaids and groomsmen

▶ Room details (hotel number or signage, Champagne, and snacks)

Remember that while ECUs are compelling—the eye gets exhausted watching a montage that doesn't have shot variety. While the wedding preparations offer a unique opportunity to grab ECUs, make sure to also get a good mix of close-ups, medium shots, and wide shots in your preparation shooting.

Specific Shots

Ideally, you will arrive on the shoot with a shot list that is customized both to your style and to this particular couple and their stated preferences. Some moments that you will want to consider in your basic coverage include the following (see Figure 7.9):

▶ Hair being done and lipstick being applied

▶ Flowers being taken from their boxes or vases

▶ The dress being zipped or buttoned up

Some brides are perfectly comfortable having photographers and videographers in the room as they get in their dress. Indeed, I have had brides request nearly naked lingerie shots in the final video. Other brides, however, brides are understandably more modest. You can accommodate both types of brides—and still get footage you need—by asking the bride if she would like you there as she puts on her dress. If she says no, ask her to refrain from the final zipping or buttoning until you are there to get the shot.

▶ Shoes being put on

▶ The veil being put on

▶ Rings ready and waiting

▶ Ties being tied

▶ Toasts, interviews, or comments from bridesmaids or groomsmen

▶ Toasts, interviews, or comments from parents and other family members

▶ Children getting dressed and ready

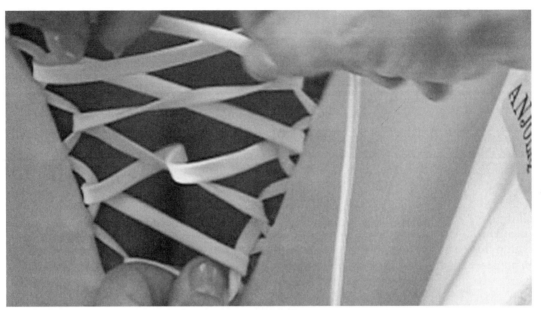

Figure 7.9
After the amount of time she has undoubtedly spent readying her outfit, even the most modest bride will appreciate some attention being paid to the process of getting dressed. Fasteners and shoes as well as jewelry, hair accessories, and the veil are all photogenic.

Wedding preparations are also a time for setting up some fun shots. Using your own creativity and the personalities of your couple, utilize this time to create some sequences that are visually inspired or revolve around the personalities of the couple. Some ideas for visually compelling shots include using a steady-cam or dolly to capture the bride getting ready as you move slowly around or past her or using a ladder to get a bird's-eye shot of the bride being styled or of the entire preparation room. If you have the ability to do a time-lapse sequence, the preparations can be a great setting. Set up a camera with a wide shot for about 20 minutes of what would otherwise be somewhat dull footage. When viewed as a 30-second time-lapse sequence, you will see a stirring interlude of bridesmaids buzzing around the bride, building excitement for the event. Alternatively, if (and only if) your subjects are game, you might shoot sequences that revolve around the story and personalities of the couple. For example, I once shot one groom, a bicycle fanatic, performing a series of bike tricks for his wife-to-be while decked out in a tuxedo.

Don't be afraid to propose fun ideas for shots like these to your couple; your creativity is part of the reason they hired you. At the risk of sounding like a broken record, talking to the couple will help you determine their likes and dislikes, which will help you come up with fun ideas. For example, if, through talking to the couple, you learn that the groom memorized a poem to propose to his bride, you might have him recite it on camera. Or if you learn that the bride loves country music, you might show her deciding whether to wear cowboy boots or high heels with her dress. You can also use the bridesmaids and groomsmen to help you create these personalized shots; ask them questions and solicit their participation. More often than not, they will be eager to foster a fun and joyful atmosphere for their friends, and will help you come up with appropriate and creative ideas.

Keep in mind, though, that not everyone is comfortable being on camera. Don't pressure your subjects into any situations that will feel forced or awkward to them. This is their day, not yours. You must carefully read their cues about what is fun and what might be pushing them out of their comfort zone. You will be able to determine how they are feeling about the shoot by whether they suggest ideas and play to the camera or they seem unenthusiastic, uncomfortable, or simply more concerned with other issues.

Although wedding preparations are usually less harried than other parts of the day, that does not mean you can take your eyes off the clock. Most weddings are well-orchestrated, highly scheduled events—and you don't want to be what slows everyone down. Keep the schedule on hand, wear a watch, and use it to ensure that your creativity doesn't fall outside the confines of their agenda.

Complicating Matters

There are several things to watch out for as you shoot the wedding preparations:

▶ Often, the rooms in which these preparations take place are cramped and chock-full of people and their personal items. It is not unusual to see a bed and floor literally covered in personal effects: hairspray, purses, T-shirts, underwear. As you set up shots in the room, take the additional few seconds to move these items out of frame; it will make a big difference later. A bottle of hairspray in the corner of your shot of the flower girl will compete for the viewer's attention, detracting from the professionalism of your video.

▶ While I typically try to get some audio clips during this time, it is often complicated by the chatter of friends, the crying of babies, and background music. If there is something you really want to shoot—bridesmaids delivering special messages or an interview with the groom—make sure to use a lavaliere microphone or an MP3 recorder. Also, don't feel like you can't ask people to be quiet for a minute or two or turn down the music—but as with all parts of the day, make sure you do so as unobtrusively as possible.

▶ The lighting in the preparations room may be problematic. This is, however, one of the few points in the day when you know you will be indoors and when you might have time to make adjustments. Keep these points in mind:

  ▶ Be careful mixing outdoor light from windows or doors with the indoor light in the room. While it may be helpful, it might introduce a great deal of unevenness. Survey the room carefully and consider whether it is best to shoot in an area that is mostly lit by natural light through the window or to draw shades or blinds to level out the light in the room.

  ▶ If there are lamps in the room, consider moving them to put more light in front of your subject—ideally coming from both directions so that the light is fairly even.

  ▶ The small hot shoe light that you have in your camera bag can be set up as a backlight to give some additional depth or highlight to your subject. This works particularly well on the bride, as it can be used as a rim light to separate her from her background and add a flattering and romantic glow around her.

Etiquette

At this point, you should know your couple well enough through your marketing meetings and their discussion of what they want from their video to know how to avoid stepping on their toes during the wedding preparations. Remember: Some couples prefer no interference or staging from their videographer; they just want a documentation of what is already going on. If this is the case, don't stage any narratives, no matter how good your idea may be. If the bride and groom *do* want to have some fun staging a few shots, don't push them out of their comfort zone. Odds are, nerves will be on edge and timing will be tight; make sure to read the mood of the room before you let your directorial side take over. Very often, you will need to be a calm, steadying presence—or no noticeable presence at all—not creating more action in an already tense setting.

The Ceremony

If you are hired for only one part of the day, it is likely to be the ceremony. Although more of the couple's energy is typically spent planning the reception, the ceremony is the heart of the event. Often, it is for the ceremony—specifically the vows—that couples hire a wedding videographer. They know that a photographer can't do this part of the wedding justice the way a videographer—i.e., you—will.

Formulating Your Shooting Strategy

Because of the importance of the ceremony, it is critical that you get this part of the day right. You can stage some extra romantic shots or shoot a bridesmaid interview anywhere, but you only have one opportunity to capture the ceremony. To obtain the best coverage of the ceremony possible, formulate a strategy ahead of time. Use the number of cameras (and camera operators), the type of coverage you need to obtain (continuous coverage, an edited coverage, or both, as dictated by your own videography style and/or by the couple), and the setup of the room as the variables for determining your shooting strategy (as well as your strategy for placing sound gear to obtain audio).

 Be sure to discuss your strategy with the photographer so that your paths don't cross too much.

The level of editing desired is particularly relevant with a one-camera shoot because if you plan to include an unedited version of the ceremony in your final product, it is generally good practice to get safer shots that will allow for a continuous flow of the action unfolding. That means capturing lots of mid-range to wide shots, going in for some close-ups and moving the camera only when you can do so safely. Because most (if not all) of what you shoot will actually be in the final version, you may find it hard to work around too many camera moves, which can be visually jarring. If, on the other hand, your style and the client's expectations involve an edited piece, you have more freedom to make camera moves and go for close-ups. You can remove a lot of the incongruous and awkward camera movements in editing.

Whether your final product will include an edited or full version of the ceremony, you want to make sure that with a one-camera shoot, you will be able to obtain a clear shot of all the proceedings. Positioning your tripod on the edge of the aisle until the processional is complete and then moving into the aisle as the ceremony begins is often the best way to achieve this (assuming this is within the guidelines of the venue). Another good place to position yourself is behind and slightly to one side of the officiant, so that you are facing the guests and the couple. Depending on the venue, however, you may be forced to shoot from a balcony or from one side of the central area.

Regardless of the number of cameras, if you are forced to choose a side, always pick the side that will allow you a clear view of the bride's face as the couple face each other for their vows.

Although it is certainly possible to get great coverage of the ceremony using only one camera, there are very compelling reasons to use two. When working with two cameras, you can use one camera can obtain a wide shot and the other to get stylistic shots and close-ups—for example, capturing the couple's faces and hands while they exchange vows and rings.

If you have only one camera operator for two cameras, set up one unmanned camera on a tripod—we'll call this Camera One—to obtain a wide, static shot of the entire ceremony. This probably won't be a very compelling shot, but it will be useful for the times when the footage obtained by the manned camera—Camera Two—is unusable, such as when it is moving between close-ups or changing locations. (For this reason, Camera One's wide shot is often called the safety shot.) Be aware that the range of movement of Camera Two's operator will depend on the rules of the venue and the preferences of the couple, who may prefer that the videographers maintain a low-key, still presence. Note, too, that you, as the operator of Camera Two, will want to stay out of Camera One's shot as much as possible. With no operator feedback, this can be quite difficult; before the ceremony begins, you must figure out the exact boundaries of Camera One's view range and find the best place (or places) to shoot from outside those boundaries. To maximize the shot obtained from Camera One and from Camera Two's range of motion, make sure Camera One is capturing as tight a shot as possible while still capturing all the action of the ceremony. In making this determination, keep in mind that speakers, candle-lighting ceremonies, and other rituals may not occur front and center; they are often off to one side.

A final—and of course more expensive—option is to have two manned cameras. This will provide the best opportunity for full coverage because one camera, strategically placed to get a wider shot than the second camera, can still follow the action somewhat, moving to get mid-range shots and keeping the second camera operator out of view.

To sum up, there are a number of positions from which you can capture a good view of the ceremony. Many churches have balconies, and often require that videographers remain on them (see camera position A in Figure 7.10); this is also a good spot for a safety shot in a two-camera shoot. Camera position B can be effective for getting a clean shot of all the proceedings, especially on a one-camera shoot. If you choose this position, shoot from inside the seating area (or just behind and to one side of the last row of guests) for the processional, and move into the aisle after the bride has walked by. Camera positions C and D are similar; the one you choose will depend on which offers an unobstructed view and whether you have a second camera to get a safety shot. Camera position C affords you a more angled view of the bride.

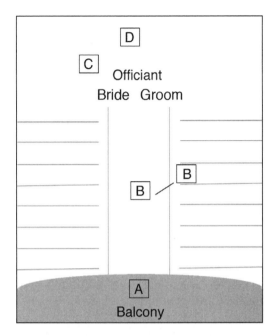

Figure 7.10
A ceremony venue may offer other good shooting places; these are just a few common ones.

 When using two cameras, regardless of the number of operators, remember to shoot both without interruption to make syncing easier in post-production.

Footage to Obtain

Regardless of whether the ceremony will be edited, you will want to be sure to capture certain elements common to many ceremonies. These include the following:

▶ Processional
▶ Bride meeting groom at top of aisle
▶ Bride being given away
▶ Welcome from officiant
▶ Speakers
▶ Exchange of vows
▶ Exchange of rings
▶ Unity candle or other service
▶ Declaration of husband and wife
▶ First kiss
▶ Recessional

In addition to covering the events of the ceremony, try to get coverage of the venue itself. These shots—both wide and close-ups—will be useful either as an introductory shot or as cutaways during your editing of the ceremony. Similarly, obtain some coverage of the venue filling with guests and some of their reactions throughout the ceremony. These, too, can serve as introductory shots as well as B-roll. Obtaining venue and guest B-roll shots is especially important in a one-camera shoot, in which movements might cause unusable moments of footage that you need to smooth over. While it is best to arrive at the ceremony location early to set up and obtain these shots, there are several points in the ceremony itself that you might be able to get them (if the ceremony is going to be edited in length) such as during communion of a Catholic mass or during the third verse of a song.

Audio

Never skimp on audio at the ceremony. No matter how harried you might feel, it is worth spending the time to set things up correctly. Don't forget to use your lavaliere microphones; be sure to get one channel of sound on your camera per lavaliere microphone as well as getting a channel of sound from the on-camera microphone.

Place a lavaliere mic on either the officiant or the groom (or both, if you have multiple lavaliere mics), both of whom are likely to be wearing outfits that will accommodate the microphone and wireless transmitter quite easily. (I never us a microphone on the bride, as her outfit is unlikely to hide it well.) One advantage to miking the officiant is evenness of sound; he or she will typically be standing midway between the bride and groom. Also, the officiant speaks more frequently than the couple. On the other hand, if the groom is wearing the lavaliere microphone, you will get a better recording of him talking before the ceremony, his reactions as the bride walks up the aisle, and the comments the couple makes throughout the ceremony and at its conclusion, which can be very fun. For these reasons, when working with only one lavaliere microphone, I tend to mic the groom; it's easy to clip the microphone to the dress shirt or jacket lapel and put the transmitter in a suit pocket or clip it to the back of his pants. If you are using MP3 recorders to gather alternative channels of sound, place one (or more) as close to the action of the ceremony as possible—on table at an altar, on a podium, or lodged in a wedding arch. If possible, stash an audio recorder at the podium from which readings or sermons are delivered. This position may be a significant distance from the position of your lavaliere microphones in larger churches, synagogues, or other venues.

 If the wedding venue runs a sound board, ask if you can get an audio feed to your camera. The audio you get from this feed will mix the audio from any microphones or amplifying systems that the venue has set up. This would likely be an XLR connection, but not necessarily. (Make sure you have looked into this ahead of time or have all the audio cables you might need.) And of course, keep all your audio feeds coming into separate channels on your cameras.

Complicating Matters

Setting up for the ceremony can be quite tense. You want everything to be in place before you start, but often you are running late from shooting the preparations beforehand. Do your best to get to the ceremony location early, especially if it is a venue you haven't shot before, so that you can formulate your shooting strategy or confirm that the one you have already formulated will work. You can also use this time to shoot cutaways.

If you haven't already, immediately determine whether your venue has shooting restrictions. Are you allowed to move around? Are you allowed to be in the aisle? Behind the officiant and the couple? Religious venues tend to be more restrictive than non-religious venues, such as wineries, hotels, parks, and stages, but often offer balconies to shoot from when access to the main sanctuary floor is prohibited.

Be aware that even the best-laid plans can go astray. For example, you might find that a floral arrangement or candelabra blocks the angle you planned on, or that the side you wanted to shoot from will give you more shots of the room and officiant but not the bride. If this happens, you must quickly develop a new strategy. Often, you will have to make some trade-offs, especially in a one-camera shoot.

As shown in Figure 7.11, lighting can be a complicating factor when shooting a ceremony. Some churches are underlit—even dark. Others have skylights that create pockets of overexposure. In an outdoor wedding, you may find yourself shooting into the sun, with your couple backlit, causing shadows if not silhouettes. What will save you in these situations is a flexible, no-panic attitude and an adeptness with your camera that will allow you to get the most from it given the conditions. You should know how to maneuver exposure, gain, and density filters to best accommodate light that is hard to work with, using some of the tips and ideas at the beginning of this chapter.

The wedding photographer can also be a complicating factor during the ceremony. With lightweight gear that doesn't require a tripod or continuous coverage, it is likely that he or she will be moving about the room to the extent that the venue and the wishes of the couple allow. This of course means the photographer may wander in and out of your shot—especially if he or she is moving up toward the couple and the officiant or behind them to get facial expressions. When that happens, you have two choices: Look for a shot—a close-up or a reaction—that will eliminate the photographer from frame or incorporate the photographer in the shot. Your choice here will depend on your style of video and your options during editing. For example, if you are on a one-camera shoot trying to obtain continuous coverage, you might be safer allowing the photographer into your documentary-style piece. If you are building something more stylistic and have lots of room to edit, getting a cool close-up might work better. As mentioned, you will want to talk about strategy and styles with the photographer beforehand; while a few shots that include him or her might be fun, you don't want too many overrunning your piece.

Figure 7.11
If you are indoors, try to get a shot of the doors opening to reveal the bride ready to walk down the aisle. In a church setting, there will be often be two sets of doors—one to the leading to the sanctuary, one leading outside. Try to make sure the doors leading outside are closed or your image will get backlit by a flood of bright daylight that will silhouette your bride, as is the case in the image on the top. In the image on the bottom, the doors leading outside are closed, providing more even light.

Etiquette

The ceremony is not a time to be an overt presence. You should fade into the scenery as much as possible. This is rarely a time to interview or play around with guests; simply let the event unfold and capture it in such a way that you achieve the highest quality of image and sound that you can.

While I would recommend always dressing conservatively and subtly as a wedding vendor, make sure to know if there are specific clothing or etiquette requirements for the type of service you will be shooting. While you are not obligated to follow the customs of the couple or their guests—for example, wearing a yarmulke at a Jewish wedding—you don't want to be flagrantly disrespectful either.

Formal Pictures and Couple Shots

After the ceremony, families will typically gather for formal pictures (although this sometimes occurs in full or in part between the wedding preparations and the ceremony itself). This is a time when the photographer is likely to reign, calling for different groups of family and friends with whom the couple has specified that they want shots—for example, the bride's extended family, the groom and his siblings, and so on. These formal pictures are often shot at the site of the ceremony itself, though they may be at the reception or at a scenic, alternate site.

After the larger group shots, the bridal party and the couple will typically take additional photos while the guests head toward the reception, usually arriving for appetizers or cocktails well before the couple. (Of course, not every wedding has the same flow of events, but this is an extremely common one.)

The number of camera operators you have at the wedding and proximity of events will determine what type of coverage you get during formal pictures and couple shots. One strategy is to follow the bride, which means you will capture all the portraits being taken and a fun session with the bridal party, arriving at the reception (hopefully) in time to capture some shots of the cocktails and some details of the reception room before it is full. A second strategy would be to capture more of the guests at the cocktail hour and obtain more setup shots of the reception, missing the formal shots. If you have two camera operators (and two cars), you can do both.

Some videographers are willing to miss the formals shots because typically, they are carefully set up for still photography, which doesn't give videographers the opportunity to best use their medium. (Feel free to take that statement as a challenge!) In contrast, the cocktail party and the beginning of the reception allow lots of room for video creativity: time-lapse sequences, guest interviews, stylized shots of details, and bird's-eye establishing shots are only a few of the possibilities, given enough time on location.

Sticking with the couple, however, is also a good—and probably safer—strategy for several reasons. First, if your goal is to retell their version of the day, then their actions throughout the day are important. To use an extreme example, if a couple's limousine breaks down and they wind up hitching a ride to their own reception, having footage of that would be priceless. (That, sadly, has never happened to me; I use it only as an example of a good reason to stick with the couple.) Another compelling—and significantly more probable— reason to spend more time with the couple is to get some shots of them and their closest friends to use throughout the video. This may be the only time you have on the wedding day to shoot just the couple alone, especially if the couple chose not to see each other before the bride walked down the aisle.

Footage to Obtain

Luckily, formal pictures are likely to be in the same place as the ceremony, so managing light will be the same. There are a few other considerations specific to formal shots, however, with which to concern yourself:

▶ Maintain a wide enough angle that you can shoot large groups, zooming in for close-ups. The photographer is likely to be shooting even wider. Since he or she will be moving quite a bit, you will probably be better off setting your tripod up behind his or her work area.

▶ Vary your shots and incorporate some camera movement. The photographer will already be capturing these images in still, so you want to make sure the video camera is adding value.

▶ Work quickly and set up your shot before you start recording. Remembering to turn off your camcorder as the photographer arranges the groups and as you frame your own shots will save you valuable editing time later on.

▶ Make sure to get a sense from your clients who the key guests are: perhaps an elderly grandparent or a friend who traveled far. Extra shots of these guests will add to the personalization of your final product.

▶ Be very aware that the real events might not be what is in front of the photographer's camera. The compelling footage might actually be the groomsmen horsing around while waiting for their turn or the flower girl falling asleep on the church pew. Constantly scan the room. Since the couple will have the still shots of the family and friends from the photographer, use your eye and your video camera to look for the action and stories of the day that might not otherwise be told.

Often, immediately following the formal photography session, the bridal party and couple will go for an additional photo and video session. The grounds of the ceremony or reception site (ideally, pre-scouted) will almost always offer a scenic location for these shots. If you are in charge of finding the spot, make sure to consider the advice offered in the beginning of the chapter: Look for an outdoor location with even light that is facing the subjects, not behind them. Speckled light (light mixed with shadows) can be fun for a few shots, but often requires extremely delicate placement of the subjects and can get dull to look at for too long.

Knowing your couple will be tremendously important in this shooting time. Some video- graphers base their business around having an unobtrusive, fly-on-the-wall style. Some videographers tout their playful, fun approach to storytelling, which often requires the cooperation and input of the subjects. If you are opting for the former, use this time to capture the action going on—the posed shots of the couple and the attending bridesmaids and groomsmen. It is likely that these shots will go into your video in montage form, so be sure to get very well framed, pretty, and flattering shots that use a variety of camera moves and angles. If you are given some license to "play" with your couple, use what time you have here to set up some shots that will be fun and show off their personalities (see Figure 7.12). Use the suggestions from Chapter 6 and from the "Wedding Preparations" section in this chapter to get some ideas for fun ways to incorporate action-driven shots that showcase the couple's personality.

Figure 7.12
Get as many fun and romantic shots as possible. There will always be use for them in your video. A relaxed attitude on your part will produce the same in your subjects.

Cocktails

Not every reception will have an appetizer and cocktail hour, although it is very common. Usually during this time, guests arrive at the reception site (if it is different from the ceremony site) and enjoy hors d'oeuvres and drinks while the couple shoots video and pictures and enjoys a few minutes to themselves. The cocktail hour creates a relaxing interlude for guests to mingle between the formal ceremony and a seated reception.

Footage to Obtain

The cocktail hour is a fun time to shoot, allowing room for creativity and usually a scenic canvas to work with. There are very few "required" shots here; what you need to do is capture the mood and joy of the event—and there are lots of ways to do that. Here are just a few suggestions for shots that help establish the mood of a cocktail hour to kick-start your own creativity.

- ▶ Bird's-eye shot of the whole event
- ▶ Guests drinking, talking
- ▶ Guests making comments to the bridal couple
- ▶ Food and drink being served
- ▶ Pan of placecard table
- ▶ Close-up of guestbook being signed
- ▶ Dutch angles of musicians playing, CU of their sheet music
- ▶ Time-lapse sequence of a wide shot of the whole event (see the upcoming sidebar), of the bartender serving drinks, or of guests signing the guestbook

The cocktail hour is a time of movement. Take advantage of that by incorporating movement into your shots (see Figure 7.13). For example, instead of a close-up of the tray of appetizers, show the server offering a guest an appetizer; or instead of showing the guest book, show a close-up of a guest actually signing the book.

Figure 7.13
The cocktail hour is full of merriment and movement, as captured by these shots of guests walking toward the party, a guest toasting the couple and a bird's-eye view of the whole room.

SHOOTING TIME-LAPSE SEQUENCES: LOTS OF FUN, LITTLE WORK

Time-lapse sequences tend to convey time passing; they play back a scene at a speed much faster than the one at which the images were captured. In other words, you can watch a few minutes in a matter of seconds. Time lapse is not a matter of speeding images up, however; the technique involves showing only certain video frames at regular intervals but omitting others. For example, a time-lapse could capture one frame per second or one frame per minute; played back at 29.97 frames per second, these would result in 10 minutes of total elapsed time shown in 20 seconds or 10 hours of elapsed time in 20 seconds, respectively!

For a time-lapse sequence to work well, there needs to be some action or movement that will be reflected over time. Also, the camera must be still. Time-lapse sequences are really just a series of jump cuts that are so close that the result appears to be continual (albeit somewhat jerky) action. If the camera angle or position changes, the continuity of the time-lapse sequence is lost; it stops making sense.

There are several ways to accomplish a time-lapse sequence:

▶ Your camera might have an interval setting, enabling you to record images in pre-determined intervals onto your media.

▶ With some editing software, such as iMovie, you can attach a camera to your computer and record images at intervals directly onto the hard drive instead of onto blank media in the camera. In other words, even though the camera is collecting 29.97 frames per second, the computer will record only some of them, at defined intervals.

▶ The most complicated method involves collecting all the images onto your blank media, exporting them as an image sequence (a series of still files in which each file is a frame), and then reassembling a sequence using certain still images at regular intervals.

Time-lapse sequences work well in faster-paced sections. They imply energy and movement. In a wedding video, they work well to show the reception room being set up, the caterers cooking, a bird's-eye view of the cocktail hour, or a buffet line at dinner.

Getting a good time-lapse sequence and folding it into your video might take some a few tries, but it's a really fun thing to practice. Have some fun with it; it can really liven up your work!

Complicating Matters

Depending on when you arrive at the cocktail hour, it can be quite hectic. The main problem you are likely to face during this time is getting enough shots without running around and forcing them. (See the upcoming sidebar.) Having made this mistake myself (an embarrassing number of times), I will remind you that is far better to get a few shots that are well set up than to rush around gathering bad footage that you can't use. If you are working under pressure, don't panic; instead, be discerning and calculating. Find a few things that will convey the mood of the festivities without trying to show everyone and everything.

ERIC NEWLAND, HYBRID MOON VIDEO PRODUCTIONS, PORTLAND, OR

My whole approach to wedding video requires patience. I am always watching and waiting. There is nothing worse that a shooter running around frantically and then missing the real action. On the contrary, I move slowly and methodically. I know that if I am watching, a great shot will come to my camera; they have been for well over 10 years now. It's a matter of separating yourself from the camera to really watch what is going on, looking at the scene from different angles, and watching the guests and seeing how they behave. The goods present themselves, and you need be ready for them.

One time, my style at the ceremony and reception was so calm and unobtrusive that the bride called me the next day, furious that I missed her wedding. It was one of the funniest conversations I have ever had, as I told her all about the wedding to prove I was there. She came to my office a few days later to view the raw footage and was overwhelmed and overjoyed with the images I got. They were different from her photographer's and different from those found in a usual wedding video. She saw parts of the wedding she had missed herself. That's what wedding videography can do at its best. It has taken me a long time and a lot of practice in the business to be able to work this way—but like I said, I am patient.

While difficult lighting can plague any portion of a wedding, the cocktail hour is usually easier in this respect. In an outdoor setting, the sun is usually lower by this time of the day. Sometimes, cocktail hour coincides with the golden hour, approximately one hour before sunset, in which a warm, flattering glow is cast on everything. If that is when you are shooting an outdoor cocktail hour, yell "Bingo!" to yourself, pump your fist in the air, and remember to shoot with the light on your subjects, not behind them. In an indoor setting, cocktail hour still tends to be a bit easier, because it is unlikely (although not unheard of) that the lights will be at the low levels often used for the dinner and dancing that will follow. In fact, cocktail hours tend to be festively well lit, even indoors. Should you run into lighting difficulties, the same tips and tricks already discussed will apply.

Etiquette

Aside from maintaining the same generally polite, well-dressed, and non-intrusive demeanor that you have exhibited throughout the day, the only cocktail hour–specific etiquette rule is to remember that the cocktails being served are for the guests, not the vendors. If you are thirsty—a safe assumption at this point—bring some water of your own or ask the bartender or caterer for a non-alcoholic beverage.

Reception

A wedding reception is personal to the couple and, as such, won't ever be the same twice. That being said, no matter how often a bride insists that "My wedding will be totally different," there are certain elements that will be similar throughout all of them—especially when you consider that your video style and price points will filter your potential clients.

In a moment, I will briefly touch on the basic elements of a wedding reception, pointing out some relevant shooting tricks and tips. Prior to that, though, there are a few general things to note about shooting a reception that will apply to the whole evening:

▶ Place your gear bag in a spot that is easily accessible, secure (weddings are an unlikely place for thievery, but it is certainly not unheard of), and out of the way of both the guests and your shots. I have ruined numerous shots by including my own tripod in the frame (see Figure 7.14). As soon as you arrive, spend a few moments finding the right spot for your gear.

Figure 7.14
An otherwise fun shot of guests dancing is ruined by the videographer's own tripod in the background. This should serve as a reminder to put your gear in a secure spot, out of the way of guests and your own work!

▶ Be aware of the timeline. Know which event will be happening next and what gear you need to have ready for it. As discussed in Chapter 6, "Pre-Production," close communication with the bandleader or DJ will help ensure you are always in the right place at the right time. With that mind, be prepared to be flexible and move quickly; timelines are prone to change, and the DJ may or may not remember to notify you!

▶ Don't chase or create the action. Be ready to shoot it when it happens.

▶ Don't be afraid to turn your camera off. Very rarely are images of people eating attractive. Similarly, people milling about don't tend to be particularly photogenic. Wedding receptions have a lot of eating and milling about; don't worry that you are not capturing every moment. Save your energy and eye for the important events.

▶ Never be far away from the action. Even though I just said turning off your camera is expected, always be ready to turn it back on again. Someone might spontaneously propose a toast or give a surprise serenade. (Yes! That really happens!) Don't get caught on the phone in the next room or fumbling about looking for your gear while the groom is showing his love for his new bride by break dancing on center stage.

▶ If you have two camera operators at the reception, divide responsibilities by designating certain elements for each videographer to cover or discussing who will get wide safe shots and who will get close-ups. And be sure to come up with ways to stay out of each other's shots—particularly important for the camera operator shooting wide, who will be more likely to get the close-up operator in frame. As mentioned earlier, using a tally light can be very helpful in this situation.

▶ The light is likely to get progressively darker throughout the reception; at some point, you will have to attach your on-camera light and wear the batteries—usually on your belt or waistband. Although I typically don't need the on-camera light until the dancing portion of the evening, that is highly variable, and will depend on the room's lighting scheme. Once you start using the light, keep in mind it can be quite irritating to guests; so make sure you point it just slightly upward (above eye-level) when you are shooting, and turn it off when you aren't.

The sections that follow are intended to provide background information on what happens during the different portions of the evening, things to be aware of, and ideas on how to get good coverage. Unlike the ceremony and other parts of the day, there are very few specific shots or images that the couple might expect. Instead, the reception is usually a series of events to cover in the way you feel best. Use the suggestions in these sections as starting points for your own ideas, which will develop as you become increasingly comfortable shooting weddings. As you read about each part of the reception, keep in mind that your style is exactly that: yours.

Details

It is very helpful to shoot the details of the reception before the room fills up with guests. The couple will want to remember the centerpieces, placecards, and favors that they spent so long designing. Get in the room early and shoot the tables, flowers, centerpieces, and any other room details that will look visually compelling or that the couple will want a reminder of (see Figure 7.15). Often, the cake will already be on display; this is a great time to shoot a wide shot of it, as well as a close-up of the frosting decorations.

If time allows, this could also be a good time to set up a fun shot for your piece. One idea is to get a wide shot of the empty room, carefully marking the tripod position with masking tape and noting your camera's settings. Then, when the room is full, go back and get the exact same shot. Blending them together through compositing in post-production can produce a fun effect; compositing is discussed further in Chapter 9, "Advanced Editing." Or, if you have an extra camera available, set up a time-lapse shot showing the staff putting the final touches on the room and extending into the guests filling the space. Compressing this down to 30 seconds or so of time lapse could create an upbeat, fun transition into the reception footage. If the couple is available, have them come check out the room before everyone else gets there; there are lots of beautiful images to be had with one couple in an empty hall!

Figure 7.15
Reception details are an
excuse for fun, visually
innovative shots, as well as
an opportunity to showcase
the characteristics of your
clients, such as this
bicycle-loving couple.

Introductions

Often, the DJ or bandleader will announce the arrival of the bridal party and bridal couple
as they enter the reception room. If this is the case, learn where the participants will be
walking from and to. Place yourself so that the majority of their walk is toward the camera,
not away from it. Don't spend too much time following the individuals to their seat or you
will miss the next entrance.

If possible, place an audio recorder near the announcer so that you can be certain to get
their introductions clearly, regardless of where you are standing. You might even be able to
get a direct audio feed from the DJ's soundboard. The introductions are often set to music,
which can make for tricky editing later; leave the camera running from start to finish so that
you have a complete audio track. To fill some holes, try to also get some shots of guests
watching and applauding the entrance.

One more thing: Guests will likely be standing when the bridal couple is announced. Make
sure your tripod height will accommodate the couple in frame over the standing crowd.

First Dance/Parent Dances

The first dance can occur at any number of points during the reception. For example, it
might be a continuation of the bridal introductions, or it could come after dinner. Whenever
it happens, make sure you are ready for it. Ideally, you will have a sense of what the couple
will be doing for their first dance, because it is actually relevant to your shooting. For
example, if the couple has a choreographed number and you have one camera, you'll want
to be sure to get a safe shot that will allow you to use most of the footage unedited, like the
wide shot in the top image in Figure 7.16. If they'll be doing an unchoreographed slow
dance, you will have a little more leniency in shooting close-ups, such as in the bottom
image in Figure 7.16, because it is much easier to cut slow-dancing shots that don't
necessarily need to match the music perfectly.

Figure 7.16

You'll want to obtain an uninterrupted safe shot if the couple has a choreographed number, as in the image above. For an unchoreographed slow dance, you have a little more leniency, as in the image below.

If the music is not live, you can obtain a copy of the music the couple used and dub it over (see the discussion of music rights in Chapter 8, "Basic Editing"). But as often as you can, aim for natural audio, which will include the guests reacting to and applauding their spins and dips. Even if you move the camera, don't turn it off during the first dance so that you'll have the natural audio to work with.

If you have two cameras, make sure to use one grab some close-ups, such as of the bride's hands on the groom's neck or shoulders, the groom's hands on the bride's back, details of the back of her dress, the couple's mouths as they sing along to the music, their feet moving. Also use the second camera to get some guest-reaction shots. You can aim for some close-ups and reaction shots with a single camera shoot, also; just do so very cautiously. You want to have plenty of mid-range to wide shots, held long enough to see the couple dancing; just keep in mind that you will likely lose some footage as you move the camera between shots.

Make sure to also shoot at the margins of the dancing. Get the couple both entering and exiting the dance floor. Aside from being helpful footage for editing transitions, you might catch a fun high five or romantic kiss when you keep the camera running an extra minute.

In terms of shooting techniques, there is no difference between the couple's first dance and the father-daughter or mother-son dance. Be aware, however, that sometimes, the parent dances open up into open dancing for everyone, and prepare accordingly.

A WORD ON SHOOTING DANCING

Although shooting dancing can be tricky, there is a large margin for error, which relieves the pressure somewhat. What you are looking for will depend on your style. Keep in mind, however, that it is difficult (although not impossible) to shoot long sections of compelling dance footage; most likely, this section of your video will be in a highly edited montage style.

Although I try to avoid a lot of camera movement when shooting dancing (after all, the movement is built into the shoot), I aim for lots of variation in the shot angles: wide, medium, and close-ups; eye-level, foot-level, and Dutch angles; and so on. Make sure to hold each shot for an amount of time that will allow you edit smoothly (i.e., more than five seconds). If possible, get a bird's-eye view of the dance floor, using a monopod or from a balcony or stairway. As with formal pictures (and most parts of the day, really), setting up your shot before you start shooting will save you a lot of time in the editing room.

Toasts

Hopefully, the toasts by the best man, maid of honor, and others will make for easy shooting. Just set up the camera on tripod, mic the speaker (or get an audio feed from the DJ or put an MP3 recorder nearby), and go. Okay—in reality, they may be a *bit* more challenging, although they are usually much easier than other parts of the day.

Remember that the "action" of the toasts is what's being said aloud. There is no need to do anything tricky or fun; usually the best approach is to pick a well-framed shot and hang tight. Sometimes, however, it just isn't that easy to get a well-framed shot. The speaker might pace (see Figure 7.17), an ugly and unavoidable fire extinguisher might ruin your framing, there might be a light directly behind the speaker, and so on. Ideally, you'll get a sense from the layout of the room and from talking with the DJ or bandleader where the speakers will stand. (Don't be afraid to make recommendations yourself about their position!) If the speakers will be toasting from their own seats, make sure to determine the best place for you to put your tripod, and be prepared to move very quickly between speeches. Also, have blank media available and ready to go. Toasts are often longer than expected; that shy maid of honor might bust out into a 15-minute speech, complete with music and props. Don't miss her punch line because you're fumbling to remove the plastic wrap on a new tape!

Figure 7.17
This maid of honor is a pacer. Notice her changing position relative to the DJ set up behind her. In this situation, it is easier to have a medium-to-wide shot that your speaker can comfortably walk through than to try to follow with a tight shot.

In addition to obtaining a fairly steady shot of the person delivering the toast, you might want to get some reaction shots in this section—particularly from the bridal couple but also from guests. These make for great cutaways, both when you need to cover something and when your main shot feels too long and boring. Often, a guest will be called out and will stand for applause; at that point, if you feel comfortable and confident, you can whip the camera around to get a shot of him or her and then whip it back for the continuation of the toast. Make sure to get at least a few seconds of steady shot of the guest; with some editing tricks, discussed in Chapter 9, "Advanced Editing," you can cut out the camera movement. Of course, if you have two camera operators, such movement is unnecessary; designate one camera operator for close-ups and reaction shots.

Cake Cutting

Funnily, almost every couple is baffled by how to do the cake cutting. In short order, a wedding videographer will have more cake-cutting know-how than their subjects. That means you may be able to position the bride and groom as best you can for the available lighting and show them how to cut the cake (a triangle from the bottom tier, unless otherwise instructed by the baker or caterer) and feed each other a small bite.

Since cutting a triangle of cake takes two slices and the couple tends to work slowly, in a one-camera shoot, I aim for a wide shot on the first slice and a close up on the second, leaving my camera in place to capture the cake being served onto a plate close-up. This consideration is unnecessary with two manned cameras. Nor is it remotely a rule, just one method to get thorough coverage. Your style will dictate how to obtain these shots.

The cake cutting is another place to add creativity (see Figure 7.18). Is there is a balcony for a bird's-eye shot? Maybe you want to shoot the couple from the point of view of the cake? Whatever you decide, there will inevitably be laughter, kissing, and occasionally a big mess (for the cake-smashing couples). Have a good time with it!

A   B

C   D

Figure 7.18
Image A was shot when the videographer got the detail shots of the reception room, prior to the guests entering. The mirror provides a more interesting visual than the cake alone. Images B, C, and D offer a few different looks to the cake footage, although all were shot without moving the camera or tripod. Be ready to go off tripod quickly if the mild frosting face-painting depicted in image D turns into a full-scale food fight.

Bouquet and Garter Toss

The bouquet and garter toss usually take place on the dance floor. While I generally recommend tripod shooting, I find capturing the tosses on tripod very difficult, so I often go handheld for this event. Make sure to get some wide shots of the available bachelors and bachelorettes waiting to catch the flying prizes, a mid-range or close-up as the bride and groom are preparing their respective throws, and as much of the object in the air as possible (see Figure 7.19). There is lots of room for fun effects treatment for these sections, which we will discuss in Chapters 8 and 9.

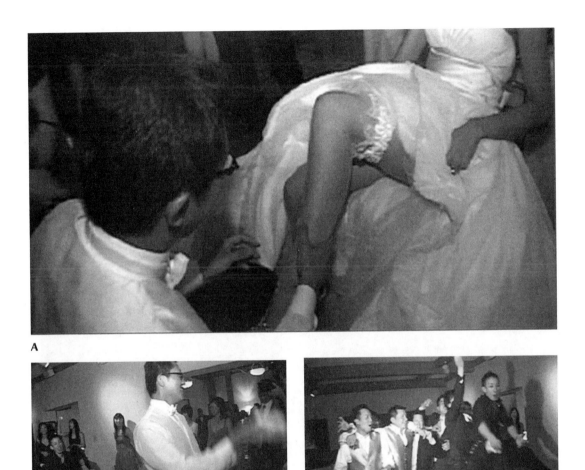

Figure 7.19
It can be difficult to get one angle that allows you a view of the garter being removed (image A), thrown (image B), and caught (image C). Don't be afraid to request that the subjects reposition slightly for you, but also be prepared to move quickly yourself.

Like the dancing, make sure to shoot at the margins during the bouquet and garter toss. The winning shot might not be the throw at all, but the groom's expression as he realizes he is going to pull the bride's garter off with his teeth or the bride and her cousin hugging after the cousin catches the bouquet toss.

A WORD ABOUT WEDDINGS IN DIFFERENT CULTURES

Different cultures have different customs associated with their weddings. For example, as shown in Figure 7.20, Chinese weddings often include tea ceremonies, which you may be expected to shoot. Jewish weddings often have a ketubah signing, and the groom breaks a glass at the end of a ceremony; you don't want to miss that. Persian weddings typically have a ritual table filled with symbolic foods, as well as endless, gorgeous dancing that usually involves lifting the bride and groom up to shoulder level.

Figure 7.20
Different cultures have different wedding-related events that you may be expected to capture, such as the Chinese tea ceremony shown in the image on the left and the Jewish tradition of breaking of a glass shown in the image on the right.

Make sure to ask your clients about any cultural traditions they plan to incorporate in their wedding, read up on them, and understand them before you shoot so that you don't miss key parts that you weren't prepared for. In addition, look at wedding videos done by other videographers for ideas of how to best capture images of traditions you have not yet witnessed.

Closure

Your contract should specify how much coverage you need to provide at the end of the evening. Will the couple be leaving in a limo and expecting you to shoot it? As discussed in Chapter 2, "The Business of Weddings," make sure to have this information. Often, there is no specified ending event; instead, you will leave when you feel you have captured enough footage to complete your job. In that case, make sure you have a shot or two that can end the video before you leave. There is a huge range of potential ending shots (which do not necessarily come at the end of the evening). Here are just a few:

- The couple dancing or kissing on the dance floor with their friends around them
- The couple dancing or kissing somewhere else at the reception
- A posed or candid shot of the couple together at some point in the day
- The couple holding hands and walking away in a nice setting
- An appropriate interview or comment from a guest or the couple themselves
- A candle burning low at one of the reception tables
- The moon
- A shot of the dance floor through an exterior window or taken bird's eye
- An exterior shot of the venue, taken in dim light as the party goes on inside
- The bride jumping in the swimming pool (Really! I'm serious! Check out Figure 7.21!)

Turning the Camera Off

There will be lots of moments throughout the reception when you will be scrambling to make sure that you and your gear are in the right place. (Clients clearly do not have videography in mind when they create their timeline.) Don't let the scramble of getting the events on video affect your judgment about shooting the more casual shots of the guests and mood of the evening. It's very easy to get panicky, where you shoot, shoot, shoot, and run around looking for more to shoot. While you of course want to leave the event with lots of footage, a calm and relaxed approach will bring the good images to you. Hunting them down will result in poorly shot images that appear forced.

Remember: Your clients hired you for your eye. So although you should have your camera ready, you should also turn it off and relax a bit. Give your eye the chance to wander and see, waiting for good shots to present themselves. When they do, your expertise and dexterity with the camera will take over, and you will find yourself getting better, more natural images. This might take some time and practice, but make sure to turn your camera off long enough to develop this skill.

Figure 7.21
If you aren't lucky enough to obtain an obvious ending shot for your piece, like the couple driving away in image A or the bride jumping into the pool in image B, make sure you have a few shots that could serve as an ending, such as the couple together on the dance floor (image C) or a scenic shot (image D) as the party is winding down.

Etiquette

During the reception, as in the rest of the event, you will be expected to dress appropriately and at all times be polite to the guests. And while most vendor contracts will provide for dinner and non-alcoholic beverages, you should be sure to check with your clients about that. If dinner is provided, there should be a designated area for you to sit down and take a dinner break. If dinner is served buffet style, ask the caterers if you can go through the line early; that way, you can be done eating and ready to work by the time the after-dinner events—toasts or dancing or cake cutting—begin.

When you are shooting guests, keep in mind that some will be shy on camera. Do not make anyone feel uncomfortable for the sake of your video; there will be plenty of guests who enjoy or feel neutral about being on camera. As you move through the crowd, especially on the dance floor, you will have to be purposeful and determined, but make sure to be also be gracious, polite, and constantly aware of your gear so as not to hurt anyone.

And don't forget: Weddings are fun. You might not feel that way if this is your 20th wedding of the season—or if it's your first wedding ever and you are nervous about what to expect. But this is the most important day in your client's lives—a day of celebration and joy—and you are part of the production team. Lead by example: Have some fun.

Summary

Every bride thinks her wedding is completely unique. But while every video shoot will have its quirks, there are certain common elements to every wedding event. Knowing the commonalities, having some shooting goals, and learning strategies to deal with the challenges of various shooting conditions will enable you to easily capture the wedding and free you up to find the shots that are different, personal, and artistic. This chapter provides an idea of what to expect, recommendations for what to shoot, and common problems to avoid for each part of the day. Don't expect to get it all on your first try, though. There is a lot to learn in one day of shooting packed with so many settings. Use this chapter as a guide until you get the hang of the flow of events on your own.

Next Up

Phew! You made it through your first wedding. Now that you have a better sense of what to expect and some practice behind you, your shooting days will become easier. Now it's time to take all that footage you shot and turn it into the product you promised your clients—a piece you are proud of. The next chapter goes over how to get your footage into an editable form and how to put a basic wedding video together.

Part III

The Honeymoon

Chapter 8
Basic Editing

In this chapter:

▶ Preparing to edit
▶ Getting a rough cut

Editing is a silent art. Done well, it is unnoticeable. When performed poorly, however, it can be painful for the viewer. Inappropriate cuts, awkward transitions, unbalanced sound—there are numerous ways in which editing can ruin even beautifully shot footage. And although bad editing can ruin even the best-shot footage, great editing cannot magically make bad footage good. That said, there are certainly tricks that can help. That is one part of an editor's artistry.

Before the magic of editing can occur, a lot of grunt work needs to happen just to get you to get to the point where you can build a *rough cut*, or first draft, of the video. First, you need to decide which footage (and other media) to bring onto your computer. Then you must label it appropriately and organize it within your project. Finally, you can assemble a rough cut using clips pulled from your media.

This chapter will start you off on the editing process and step you through the basics of completing your rough cut. After that, you can apply the bells and whistles, found in Chapter 9, "Advanced Editing."

Preparing to Edit

For many wedding videographers, creative freedom is the appeal of the job. I started as an editor myself, and I love the creativity involved in shaping the events in a way I find compelling and pretty.

While it would be wonderful if editing were an entirely free-form creative process—after all, there are literally hundreds of tools you can use to actualize even the craziest ideas—the editing process is far from free form. In fact, the best and most creative editors must be extremely organized. Organization is critical through every step of the process, beginning with the way you bring the footage into your system and ending with the way the project is output and archived.

Experimentation, trial and error, and playfulness are integral to being a creative and innovative editor. To achieve that, however, you must be able to easily place clips on the timeline to determine whether they will work for the sequence you have visualized—and you must be able to scrap the sequence and start over if they won't. It's impractical to spend days looking for the right clips to experiment with; they must be at your fingertips to allow for your arranging and rearranging. Quickly identifying good clips and developing organizational systems to keep track of them will allow you to quickly and easily find the media you need. Furthermore, if you have a logical method for organizing your media, another editor can step in and help, should you find yourself swamped during wedding season.

All editing programs share an important characteristic, which helps explain why project organization is so crucial. The clips that an editor places and moves along the timeline within a project are in fact pointers to specific media files that live in designated locations on a hard drive. As the editor moves these clips, the media itself (usually very large files) never changes its location. In order for the links between the pointers and the actual media to function, the media must not be moved or renamed. (Okay, it's *possible* to relink the media files with the pointers in the event the media files are renamed or moved mid-project, but doing so can lead to serious—and annoying—complications in putting your project back together.) All this is to say that correctly naming and placing your files at the outset will save you enormous amounts of time and frustration in the event of mistakes or problems with your hardware later.

Two important aspects of keeping organized are *logging* your footage and *capturing* it—that is importing, or *transferring*, it to your computer. It's critical that you develop systems for handling each of these tasks. The following sections on logging and capturing your footage will teach you how to effectively organize a project to minimize your time fighting your files and maximize your time working with the footage.

Logging Footage

When you log footage, you create a reference system in order to easily identify the pieces you want to use (or discard) as you build your wedding video. Although logging is frequently confused with capturing or transferring (especially because they often—although not always—happen at the same time), they are in fact different. *Logging* refers to naming or labeling clips, while *capturing* and *transferring* refer to the process of importing clips into the computer.

On a small project such as a wedding, logging systems can be as personal and haphazard as how you arrange your desk drawers or closet or computer desktop. On larger projects, such as feature films or stories shot for news stations, there will be strict protocols to enable logging of massive amounts of media that different people will have to access. Logging differs by editor, too. A documentary filmmaker might listen to and transcribe every tape before bringing a single piece of footage onto the computer, while a feature filmmaker may have an incredibly detailed, systematic way of referencing scenes, angles, and cameras as they log their footage for capture.

Although you will likely work by yourself when editing your wedding footage and thus can probably get away with a bit of chaos, developing a logical logging system that can be replicated for every project provides lots of advantages. For one, an organized and consistent naming system—for example, always labeling your clips with identifiers such as "good sound bite" or "reception cutaways"—will enable you to locate the footage you need more quickly. Also, if you ever need to redo a project or if you get stuck in a holding pattern, you will want a clear system that makes sense even after a significant amount of time has passed. This is a relatively common occurrence; sometimes, you'll start a project but have to wait for music selections from the couple, or they'll want some changes made after the project is completed. (In one fairly dramatic example, one of my brides had me re-cut her wedding video a year after the wedding to eliminate any shots of her mother-in-law, with whom she had a falling out. Needless to say, I was grateful to have a well-organized Project panel!)

There are two basic approaches to logging. The simplest is to use a numbering system; alternatively, you can use time code. You'll learn about both approaches next.

Using a Numbering System

All your source media should be well organized under one project within your editing application. The simplest way to accomplish this is to create a numbered system for your tapes, or your raw files. A numbering system can include other data as well, such as the name of the couple, the date, etc., but make sure to keep your naming system simple. Every piece of media that comes in—CDs with music or photos, DVDs with old footage to incorporate, and so on—should be named in the system you use before you begin working with the data.

 Your media should be labeled on the tape, CD, or DVD itself, not just the packaging or case.

One efficient numbering system is to include a name for the project and number the media sequentially after that. For example, the first tape of a wedding that took place on April 12, 2009 could be labeled 041209_001, where 041209 represents the project name and 001 represents the tape number. There is nothing inherently correct about this label except its simplicity and the fact that it allows room to accumulate—and keep organized—a huge amount of media under one project. You could also use the groom's last name (e.g., Silvio_001, Silvio_002), the bride's and groom's first names (e.g., Carlo_Kaley_001, Carlo_Kaley_002), the location (e.g., HolmanRanch_001, HolmanRanch_002), etc. When you begin logging the media on the tapes, the tape name will be the first data you include; that way, you can find the original footage indicated in the logging notes and time code in the event it is needed.

Using Time Code

Like a page number for writers, *time codes*, which follow standards set by the Society of Motion Picture and Television Engineers (SMPTE), are the markers that editors use to determine where they are within a given piece of video. Every frame of video is given a time-code stamp, indicating sequentially where it fits within a piece. Time code is written using a format that includes hours, minutes, seconds, and frames, separated by colons. For example, the image shown at 9 minutes, 26 seconds, and 7 frames would be represented by 00:09:26:07. That can be confusing, as we tend to expect seconds to occupy the digits furthest on the right.

Compounding this confusion is the fact that there are a few different time-code standards (to accommodate the fact that different film and video formats use different frame rates). For example, NTSC digital video shoots 27.97 frames per second, which means that if all the time code appeared sequentially, the amount of footage would run slightly short of its label by a rate of 3.59 seconds an hour because of that missing .03 frames per second. To make up for this discrepancy, *drop frame time code* was invented, which literally drops some of the time code labels (not the frames themselves) so that drop frame time code will match clock time. To distinguish drop frame time code from non-drop frame code, semicolons are used instead of colons (see Figure 8.1). For example, the image shown at 1 hour, 10 minutes, 23 seconds, and 3 frames in drop frame time code would be represented by 01;10;23;03.

Figure 8.1
Both the Source and Program panels have two time-code counters. The counter on the left shows that the play head and image represent the frame located at 00;25;32;24. The time-code counter on the right indicates that the duration of the selected clip (determined by the in and out points) is 14 seconds and 12 frames long.

Because wedding videos do not tend to be time sensitive down to the frame, it should not matter which time code you are working in. For fine edits, however, it will be helpful to understand the difference and know why you might occasionally not have a certain frame in sequence.

Time code is marked on your source footage, or master tapes, by the camera, which marks each frame sequentially. Once you bring it into your project and start a project sequence, you will have another set of time code to work with, designated by the timeline. For example, your opening montage might begin with a clip taken from the middle of your first tape (00;31;20;00–00;32;00;00). That approximately 40-second clip will now occupy the time code 00;00;00;00–00;00;40;00 in your new sequence, although the source time code will still be accessible to you should you need it (see Figure 8.2).

Figure 8.2
Although the time code for this frame in the source footage is 00;25;32;24, the frame is assigned a new time code when it becomes part of a new sequence, as shown by the play head on the timeline at 1;00;14;11.

Logging: How Much Detail?

As a busy wedding video editor, you will want to come up with a system that enables you to record enough detail that you can easily find and use media in an organized manner, but not so much that you spend precious hours or even days on the task. The most basic way to log footage is to watch it on a player or on your camera, jotting down notes about what is happening at any given point and whether it is usable (or even good). Theoretically, this can be accomplished with paper and a pencil, although your editing system will provide you with more sophisticated tools to help this process move more efficiently.

Typically, the more footage you collect, the more detail you will want to log to help manage a large amount of media within your project.

Your logging process will dictate how you capture your clips—that is, bring clips into your computer—meaning you can log very generally and capture long clips or you can log very specifically and capture short clips. The advantage of the former method is that you don't spend very much time on this part of the process. You can literally name a clip the same thing as the tape itself (for example, 041209_001), set your computer to capture the entire tape as one clip, and then go to a marketing meeting with a potential client as your tape is captured in real time. (This process is slightly different for files that are captured on drives or memory cards, but the principal is the same.) After booking your next gig, you will return to find that your first clip is ready to look at in the Source panel and be cut into useable bits to put in your Program panel.

This method of logging can be quite useful. The benefits are that you don't have to scrub much footage, which takes time and wears your camera or deck (if you are using tape). You can break apart the long clips into *subclips* within your editing application and label them within the program. This method becomes easier to handle as you shoot more and more weddings because you will tend to gain an understanding of what's on each tape.

That being said, there are a few downsides to capturing hour-long clips. For starters, the primary goal of logging is to make some initial editorial decisions that will ease your workload when you are working on the rough cut. In other words, if you don't break your clips up into usable, named pieces, you'll wind up with an hour-long clip in your Source panel and no idea what's on it. Furthermore, if storage space is tight on your system, you will have wasted some of it by indiscriminately capturing everything on the tape, including the part when you accidentally shot footage of the reception-room floor for 20 minutes after forgetting to turn the camera off.

The other side of the spectrum is to log very specific clips and capture them as nearly usable pieces on your timeline, labeled appropriately so you know where they will fit. This approach is advantageous because by the time you actually put your piece together, you are well familiar with the good takes, the pretty images, and the funny sound bites. Ideally, you may be able to start building your piece in your head as you log, enabling you to organize things in such a way that you can quickly assemble the piece. Additionally, you can determine which bits to discard before you capture, meaning you will use significantly less storage space on your computer. The downside to laborious logging is, of course, the amount of time it takes. Also, it's much easier to scrub your clips once they are captured than to watch them using the wind and rewind buttons on your camera or deck. (If your camera collects media to a drive, the consideration about scrubbing is not relevant, as you can randomly access all your footage on the drive-stored clips.)

Somewhere in between these two extremes might be a more appropriate logging method for your editorial style. The intended organization of the final piece should provide some clues on how to organize your clip collection. For example, if you are telling a chronological piece that will move through the day's events, you might want to log by event, labeling clips as "Preparation," "Ceremony," etc., which you may further subdivide as you move pieces to the timeline.

If you are inclined to log before you capture, here are a few other points to keep in mind:

▶ **Log more than you need.** As you move through your media sequentially, log everything, good and bad. You can decide later in the capture process whether you actually want the clip. For example, if you find a better shot of the flowers later in the media, you'll find it much easier to review your footage and decide which clip to use on a second pass if everything is labeled.

▶ **Avoid logging over a time-code break.** Time-code breaks are the bane of an editor's workflow, if not their very existence. Any frame that displays no time code on your deck or camera's counter is a break. Some systems refuse to capture over a break; others will capture over them with specific capture settings. If tape is allowed to move beyond the last frame shot (for example, if the camera is used in VCR mode during the shooting day), your time code might start over, creating a very obvious time-code break. Sometimes, the camera will just drop a frame or two, which will be very hard to spot in footage that progresses at the rate of nearly 30 frames per second. Because of this, allow your settings to capture breaks, but avoid logging ones that you can see.

▶ **Log with handles.** A *handle* is a bit of footage—just a few seconds—at the before and after the portion of a clip you think is usable. Logging with handles helps in the editing process with dissolves, fades, and making your footage match the timing of your audio. Many programs enable you to automatically add a handle of a pre-determined length to your clips (see Figure 8.3), a good idea if your footage is mostly free of time-code breaks. If you have reason to suspect that your footage has time-code breaks, add the handles yourself to ensure that you don't unintentionally capture footage with breaks.

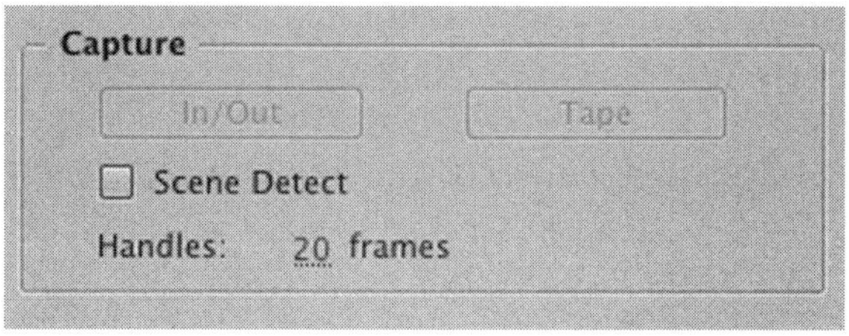

Figure 8.3
Many capture utilities will automatically add handles at user-specified lengths, as indicated by this preference in the Premiere Pro capture utility.

Logging: The Process

In any editing application, you will have some version of a capture utility. Regardless of the software you are using, there are some basic logging steps that must be followed. Here are the basic steps for logging from a tape or from a drive.

1. Connect your capture source (deck or camera) to your computer using the appropriate method for your system.

2. Launch your editing software, open a new project, and save it.

3. Make sure the capture settings are correct for the type of video you will be importing and determine where on your hard drive the footage will go.

4. Navigate to the log and capture utility. In a tape-based system, you should be able to use the tape transport controls to view the footage from the deck or camera. If you are viewing footage from a drive, open the folder to view the footage.

5. Select the clips you will be capturing by setting in and out points in the program's window. In most programs, you can set in and out points by pressing the I and O keys, respectively.

6. Check that the time code on the clip you have created matches the time code that you wanted from your source footage. Consider adding handles or, if your software allows it, enable the function that adds handles automatically.

7. Click the Log (or similarly named) button. A dialog box should appear, asking for naming information (see Figure 8.4); add the relevant data and click OK.

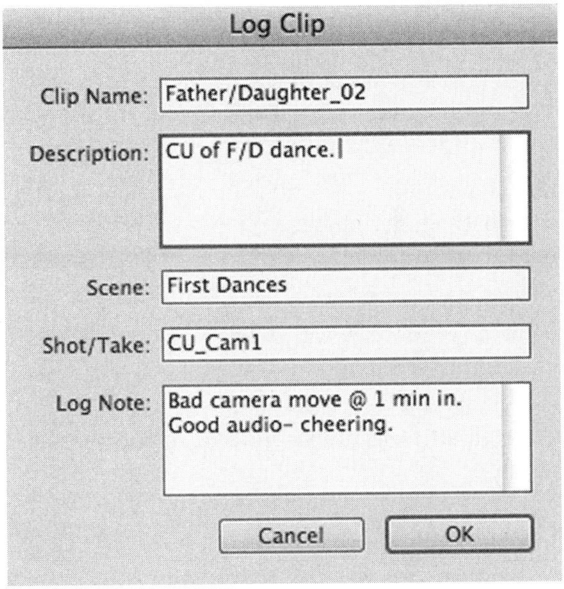

Log Clip	
Clip Name:	Father/Daughter_02
Description:	CU of F/D dance.
Scene:	First Dances
Shot/Take:	CU_Cam1
Log Note:	Bad camera move @ 1 min in. Good audio– cheering.
Cancel	OK

Figure 8.4
Good editing software will allow you to include a lot of information in the logging process, which will be available as you look at media files in the Project panel.

Just because you have logged the clip doesn't mean you can now view it in your viewer or edit with it. At this point, the clip is still *offline* and must be captured, as described in the next section.

Capturing

Once you have your clips logged, you can decide which ones you will actually capture, or bring into your computer system. The capture process creates files on your hard drive that store the media and automatically brings the files (or representations thereof) into the software Project panel for your use in editing, as shown in Figure 8.5. Most editing programs' capture utility (or transfer utility, if you are working with footage from a drive or card) will be in the same window as the logging utility.

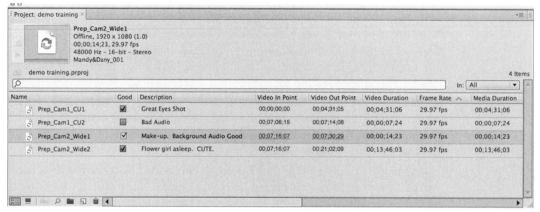

Figure 8.5
Logged files show up in the Project panel, marked as offline. When the clips are captured, a thumbnail will appear and the clips will be able to be viewed in the Source panel. Note that the Project panel allows you to see the notes that you collected in the logging process.

Before you begin, it is very important to make sure that your capture settings are correct. Every system will be different, so you will have to reference your hardware and software manuals for the specifics, but in general, you'll want to do the following:

▶ Make sure your footage will be placed in the correct location on your hard drive. Designate a folder for each project, and make sure that when you capture, all footage lands in the intended folder.

▶ Check that your device control settings are correct. They should match the method you are using to control your video deck or camera, such as FireWire.

▶ Match your input settings to the format of the media you shot, such as HDV or DV NTSC.

▶ Ensure that you are capturing both audio and video—unless, of course, you are just capturing an audio source.

If you are using a capture card or an analog system, your editing software might have the option to alter the video quality as it is being captured. Most likely, your input device will not accommodate that. See Chapter 9 for more information about using color- and contrast-correction tools that may be applicable here.

Most higher-end editing programs will allow you to do a batch capture, collecting all the clips you have logged at one time (changing tapes when necessary). That is often the easiest way to capture, especially if you have spent a lot of time logging. While the specific steps for performing a batch capture will differ depending on your software, in general, you will select the clips you want to capture, and then click the Capture (or similarly named) button in your log and capture utility.

Most programs will indicate the space requirements for the clips you have selected for capture. Make sure you have enough hard-drive space to accommodate the clips before you initiate the capture process; you will waste valuable time starting an incomplete capture if you do not have enough room. Furthermore, you will max out your drive space as the editing software crams in as many files in as it can. To maintain the speed and strength of your drives, you want to prevent them from becoming too full. Advice differs, but a general rule of thumb is that at least 25 percent of your drive space should remain unused.

Most software systems offer two other capture modes. The first is continuous capture, which starts and stops at your command instead of being defined by time code. A continuous capture dialog box is shown in Figure 8.6. A more precise method is to capture clips one at a time, either as they are logged or after all logging is complete. Some software applications offer an option called Scene Detect, where long pieces of captured footage are automatically broken into clips when the software detects that the camera has been turned off and on again.

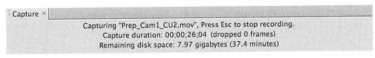

Figure 8.6
Higher-end editing programs offer several modes for capturing clips. Adobe Premiere Pro allows capturing for a single logged clip (Capture In/Out), capturing a batch of logged clips (Capture Batch), and the capture-on-the-fly mode (Capture Tape), which does not require logging but will capture continuously until the user indicates otherwise by pressing the Esc key.

Troubleshooting Capturing

Capturing can be the source of great frustration, and is often a point in the workflow in which editors throw their hands up in the air in frustration and daydream about becoming painters instead. Here is a list of things to consider if you are having trouble capturing:

> ▶ Are all your software settings and preferences set correctly? Once they are, relaunch the program and try again.

▶ Are your computer technical specifications enough to handle the job? Refer to the software documentation to ensure that your processor, RAM, and video card are able to run the program.

▶ With your system off, check all your cables. A loose wire, cord, or port connection can wreak havoc.

▶ If capturing through time-code breaks is an option, make sure to enable that preference.

▶ Many software programs require five or so seconds of footage before being able to capture, which means you might not be able to capture the first few seconds of footage. Make sure to learn the limits of your software program and ensure that your clip, including the handles, allows enough pre-roll room for the software.

▶ Clean the heads on your camera or deck using a tape cleaner. Head cleaning, a maintenance task that you should perform on a regular basis, can be an immediate fix to problems viewing video. Tape cleaner is inexpensive, and can save you a lot of time and money. (You'll learn more about head cleaning in Chapter 12, "Maintaining Your Business.")

▶ Using the same brand of tapes as your camera or deck can make all the difference in a capture gone awry. If your tape stock is of a different make from your camera or deck and you are having problems, try to borrow a camera of the same make as the tape.

Importing Other Media

You may need to import non-video files for your final piece, such as photos, music, and scanned print materials (the invitation, the program, and so on). Although these items can be added as you edit, it's a good practice to collect all your media before you begin so that everything is ready in your Project panel as you start the rough cut (see Figure 8.7). Here are a few important considerations for the other media you collect:

▶ Make sure you know what file formats your software supports for the types of media you want to import. For example, Final Cut Pro accepts AIF and WAV music files but not MP3 files. Change the file formats appropriately.

▶ Name all your media files using the same naming system you use for your video footage. This will help you stay organized, especially when archiving your projects.

▶ Copy media files from DVDs, CDs, and other drives into the same place that you keep your video files, and then import them into the program from there. If you import files to your software program directly from the DVD or CD, you will need that DVD or CD every time you open the program.

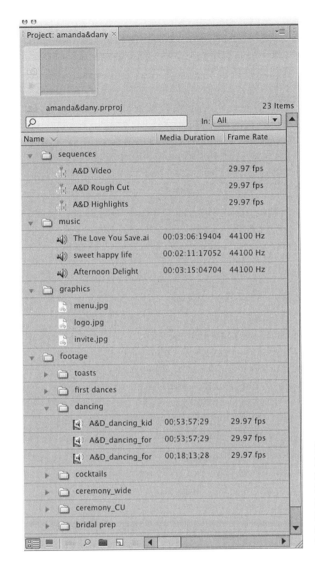

Figure 8.7
Different types of files are represented with different icons in the Project panel. In this figure, the icons for a sequence, video footage (a strip of film with associated audio), graphics (a picture), and music (megaphone) files are shown. The icon for a sequence represents a timeline with a playhead on it.

Basic Editing

Editing is both an art and a skill. Although getting the mechanics down won't give you an eye for images and storytelling, it will give you the dexterity and flexibility to experiment with styles and to skillfully build what you imagine. This section, in conjunction with some of the information in Chapter 4, "Getting Post-Production Gear," and the tutorials on the accompanying DVD, will give you the basic tools to put together a rough cut of your wedding video.

While this chapter will provide skills, lessons, and tutorials for editing a wedding video, it is not a replacement for learning the methods and tools of your own software. This and the following two chapters will be easier to understand if you have some familiarity with your own editing program. Study your software's user guide and tutorials to learn.

Before you begin working on your piece, make sure that any work you do from here on out is backed up somewhere different from your normal save location. Advanced programs have a function called autosave, which creates a vault of saved versions of your project. That means if your system crashes or you lose the file that you regularly save to, you will have another cache of files that will restore your project. Although a somewhat clumsy method, you can also use the autosave vault to return to an earlier version that you liked better. The application user settings will enable you to specify how often your project should be autosaved and how many versions of the project are allowed. It is not uncommon for a fast editor to autosave every 15 minutes or so and keep dozens of copies; after all, the project files (without the media) are very small.

Approaches to the Rough Cut

By the time you start putting shots on the timeline, you should have some idea in your head of what the piece will look like. After all, at this point, you have defined your style (and sold it to a client), shot the wedding event, and logged the footage. That being said, translating between the images on the raw footage and the images in your head can be overwhelming—especially if you have a lot of footage. The first step is to get a *rough cut*— that is, an early version of the piece that contains the footage you want to include but lacks the details, effects, transitions, and smoothness of the final version.

If you have some cool scenes or effects in your mind, it is tempting to spend a lot of time perfecting a few shots before you've got the whole story laid out. I strongly recommend against this; the way you use a particular shot might change depending on how you need it to fit into a larger story.

The realities of your footage may not match up with the picture in your mind. Although a good editor will have the skills and vision to manipulate around any discrepancies, it's best to find these holes early on and save the detailed work for those shots that will actually make it to the final cut.

There are several approaches to putting together your rough cut. Two of the more common approaches—master shot style coverage and radio cut—are described next. You might find that the approach that works best for you is a hybrid version of these, or even completely different. Note, too, that if you break your wedding video into sections, you might use a different approach for each section.

Master Shot–Style Coverage

As you know, a master shot, often called a *safety shot*, is a wide shot that captures a good deal of the action. Because master shots can be quite dull, they are best used when synced with other camera angles, cutaways, and reactions. When you edit using *master shot style coverage*, you first lay down the master shot; then you add shots from different camera angles (if available) on the next track before finally adding cutaways and reaction shots to give the whole piece more character and flavor.

Master shot–style coverage is most commonly used for editing video from two-camera shoots, but even with footage from a one-camera shoot, I tend to use a master shot to lay down the rough cut for the wedding ceremony. That doesn't mean the master shot itself must be unedited; the master shot can be trimmed to the vital parts as it is laid down.

This style of editing expands outward from the first line of video. To create a master shot–style rough cut, you assign the first video and audio tracks to the master track, the next video track(s) to additional camera angles, and the top tracks to cutaways and reaction shots, as shown in Figure 8.8. (For more information about working with multiple tracks, see the upcoming sections.)

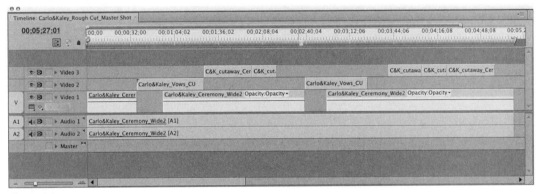

Figure 8.8
The timeline of a rough cut that uses a master shot will have one video track that is the basis for the rough cut. The second and third tracks are close-ups and B-roll shots, respectively. These shots are used to fill holes and add a range of visuals to the master-shot coverage.

Radio Cut

A *radio cut* is an edit that lays down the sound first. Usually, this means the natural audio, such as participants and guests talking, but will also include music, such as the band playing the first dance. This can be a very efficient way to edit, as the sound often drives the story, and there are a number of visuals that can appropriately accompany the sound.

Radio cuts are especially useful in pieces or sections with a lot of dialogue; see Figure 8.9. I often use radio cuts for roughing out a wedding-preparations scene that includes bridesmaid chatter, a first dance (or father/daughter dance) that is cut to the natural audio of the band, or the toasts. A radio cut might also be useful in editing the vows during the ceremony or using a continuous piece of music from the band while showing images of the guests enjoying cocktails or dancing.

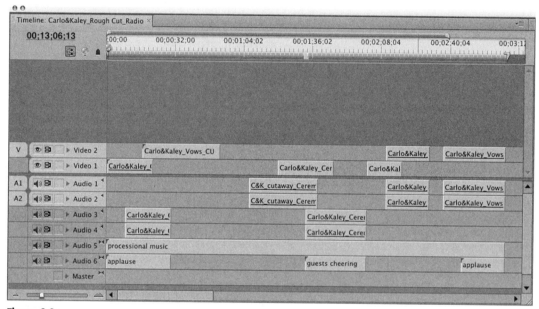

Figure 8.9
The timeline of a radio cut will start with more audio laid down than video. Once the audio is a *lock*, or complete, more video will be added.

WHOSE SONG IS THAT, ANYWAY?

The issue of using music in your video can be a very thorny one indeed, as it raises that not-so-small question of music rights—and boy oh boy, that's one way to heat up a discussion quickly. Here's the rub: You cannot legally use any recorded music with a copyright in a product for which you are charging money. End of story. That being said, lots of couples ask for it, and lots of wedding videographers do it. So far, the Recording Industry Association of America has not cracked down on wedding videographers—most likely because the commercial audience for any one video is so small and because it could be argued that using a given song in a wedding video is ultimately beneficial to the artist. That being said, allow me to repeat myself: *Using copyrighted music in a wedding video is not legal.*

(continued)

Here are some ways to legally obtain music for your wedding videos:

▶ Royalty-free music can be purchased quite inexpensively—as low as a few dollars per song. A monthly subscription fee to a royalty-free music library will make it even cheaper if you regularly need royalty-free music. These vast music libraries are available for sampling online. The music tends to be categorized, making it easier to pick the music you need for the scene you are working on. Some even have sections of wedding music.

▶ Often, wedding bands will be thrilled to give you permission to use their music in your video. Make sure to grab a copy of their CD and get their permission in writing. Get specific instructions as to whether you can use their music only in the video for the wedding at which they performed or if you can use it for all the wedding videos you edit. Most likely, they will love the free advertising and will let you use their work in all your videos.

▶ An increasing number of Web sites, such as www.zoomlicense.com, enable you to purchase music rights for videography at extremely reasonable rates. While the selection is not nearly what you might find in, say iTunes, these libraries are growing, and can help you keep your clients happy, keep your video compliant, and make sure the artists get their share. I encourage the use of these sites; their growth will support and aid our business in the future.

One more thing: While under no circumstances would I recommend it, should you choose to ignore the copyright law and use music in your videos illegally, you will not be alone among wedding videographers. But do be sure to avoid using music illegally on any demos or on your Web site; the audience is significantly wider and your violation will be considered more flagrant.

A sound-driven editing style expands outward from the first line of audio. To create a radio-cut edit, assign the first audio track(s) to the main set of natural audio, as shown in Figure 8.9. (Leave the associated synced video intact in the accompanying video line, even if you don't plan to use it.) Build out from there, adding audio tracks, such as music, sound effects, or other natural audio from the event. Once the audio is in place, the synced video or other video can be laid on top.

Processes

As discussed in Chapter 4, any high-end video-editing program will offer multiple ways to accomplish the same tasks, such as getting footage from the Project panel (where it is represented as a file), to the Source panel (where the video file can be seen in raw form), to the timeline or Program panel (where the raw footage is pieced together into a sequence and represented graphically and in video form, respectively). The following sections discuss a few common methods employed by lots of different programs. (Keep in mind that your editing software will likely have other options as well.) In addition to covering some editing mechanics, these sections discuss the best way to use these mechanics in piecing together your video.

Of course, the best way to become adept at the mechanics of the editing process is to practice. Use the tutorials provided in this book, by your software publisher, and with footage you shoot on your own to practice.

Getting Clips on the Timeline

The basic method for getting footage on the timeline is called *drag and drop*. In a drag-and-drop edit, you select the clip in the Source panel by indicating an in point (that is, the starting point) and an out point (the ending point). Most programs enable you to set the in point and out point using one of several methods, the easiest of which is generally pressing the I key and the O key, respectively. Once the selection is made, use your mouse to click the image, or an icon of the image, in the Source panel and drag it to the timeline, releasing the mouse button where you want the clip to fall. To move a clip that is already in the timeline from one point in the timeline to another, simply click it and drag it to the new location.

A slightly more precise way of editing is called *three-point editing*. With three-point editing, you set the in and out as before. You then set a third point, either an in or an out, on the timeline. If the point on the timeline is an in, the clip selection will start at that point; if the third point is an out, the clip selection will end at that point. A three-point edit can also be made by selecting an in and out on the timeline and an in or an out in the Source panel; the software will then determine how much footage is needed to cover the space on the timeline.

A three-point edit can be one of several types, the most common being overlay edits and insert edits. An *overlay edit* covers up everything beneath it, which may be nothing (if the clip is placed at the end of a sequence), or may be other footage that will no longer be seen. An *insert edit* pushes everything after the new clip backward (that is, later in the chronological sequence) to accommodate the new clip. In Premiere Pro, if you drag the clip selection with your mouse from the Source panel either to the Program panel or the timeline, you can choose whether you want an insert edit or an overlay edit by pressing modifier keys while releasing the mouse button (see Figure 8.10). There are also keystrokes for accomplishing this quickly. Other edit options are discussed later in this section and in Chapter 9.

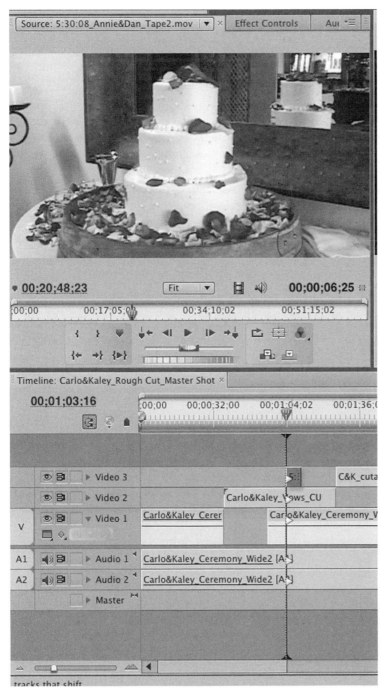

Figure 8.10
Most editing programs will offer a variety of types of edits that can be accessed through menus or keystrokes, or by bringing a clip to the Program panel. Here, a drag-and-drop edit is being applied from the Source panel to the timeline. The arrows and slashed lines indicate that the edit is an insert, not an overlay.

Using Multiple Tracks

Whether you use master shot–style coverage, the radio-cut technique, a hybrid of the two, or a totally different approach to assembling the rough cut, you will use multiple tracks to get all your clips on the timeline. In most programs, the timeline makes layering tracks quite intuitive, but there are still a few things to know and a few tricks to help make multi-track editing easier:

▶ In drag-and-drop editing, you can specify the track on which the selected clip will be placed by dragging the clip and releasing the mouse button on the desired track. In three-point editing, you must indicate beforehand the track on which you want the clip to be placed as you insert or overlay.

▶ New tracks are typically created in a sequence settings menu. Some programs, such as Final Cut Pro and Adobe Premiere, will create a new track for you if you click and drag the selected clip and hover over the top track.

▶ Video tracks are always placed above audio tracks. Most interfaces enable you to adjust how much screen space is designated to audio and video, which can be helpful as advanced edit work typically occurs on one or the other.

▶ By default, when video tracks are layered, or *composited*, only the top track—that is, the highest track on the timeline, not necessarily the one you've added most recently—will show (see Figure 8.11). Compositing, or the visible layering of more than one track, can be achieved using techniques discussed in Chapter 9.

▶ Unlike with video, when audio tracks are layered, they do not cancel each other out. Instead, they work additively. That is, all are audible—often increasing the sound level to the point that they need to be lowered or carefully mixed. See Chapter 9 for more discussion of audio mixing.

▶ Because audio tracks are additive, the track in which audio clips are placed in the timeline has no relevance in the final playback. It will sound the same whether music is on the top track or the bottom track. That being said, having some consistency with the placement of types of audio within a project is very helpful—for example, simplifying matters if you want to turn off the music and listen to only the dialogue or to adjust all the levels on a single track. I recommend establishing a system that will work for all your projects. Most editors place dialogue or other natural audio on the upper tracks and added music and sound effects on the lower tracks, as shown in Figure 8.12.

▶ Often, you may want to bring either the audio or the video from a particular clip to the timeline, but not both—for example, with video cutaways or with audio comments that will be laid over video of the action. To bring only audio or video onto the timeline, disable the destination track and then perform a regular drag-and-drop or three-point edit. In Premiere Pro, disable tracks by clicking near the track name so that it is deselected (see Figure 8.13).

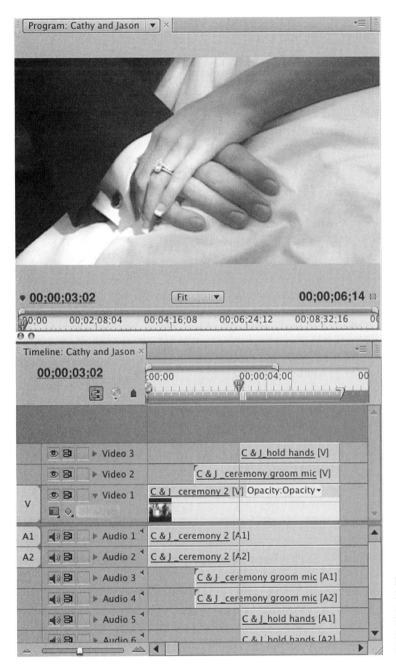

Figure 8.11
By default, only the top line of video will appear in the Program panel—in this case, the shot of the couple holding hands.

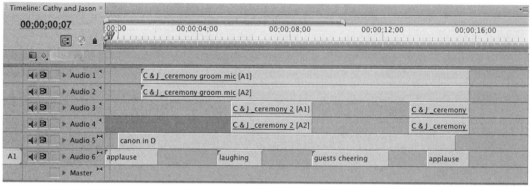

Figure 8.12
A common audio-editing protocol is to assign the first four tracks to two stereo tracks of natural audio, followed by two tracks of music and two tracks of audio effects. Having a consistent method, however, is more important than which tracks you designate for which type of audio.

▶ Locking tracks enables you to work on certain tracks without disturbing ones that you want to leave intact. For example, in a radio edit, you might lock the audio tracks so that as you shift video images around, the audio will remain untouched. Locking is another way to disable tracks, as described in the preceding bullet. A word of caution: If you have locked tracks and you perform an insert edit, everything will move backward to accommodate the added clip except the tracks that are locked (see Figure 8.13). This might be exactly your intention—for example, in a montage in which you want to move the images around while leaving the music constant. But if the locked track also contains synced audio after the montage music, that audio will stay in place as its associated video moves backward. (Some systems issue a warning when moving tracks will cause a sync problem.) For this reason, you should use insert edits with locked tracks very carefully. Also, this scenario is less likely to occur if you designate certain tracks for distinct types of audio, as discussed previously.

▶ If audio and video are linked (a setting preference or a modification that can be made to a single clip), the changes made to either the audio or the video will affect the other. For example, in a linked clip, extending the length of the audio will also extend the length of the video. To work on the audio or video separately, you can unlink the clip, manually override the link, or lock one track.

▶ When working with unlinked clips, the audio and video can fall out of sync quite easily on the timeline. This can happen when a track is locked and other tracks are manipulated or simply when small adjustments are made to either the audio or the video. Sometimes, audio and video are intentionally out of sync; more often than not, however, it is something to be corrected.

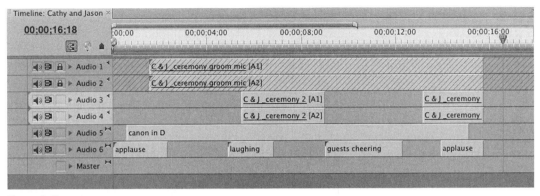

Figure 8.13
Locking and disabling tracks have similar but slightly different functions. Neither locked nor disabled tracks accept clips from an insert or overlay edit, but locked tracks remain intact as things move around them. In this figure, tracks A1 and A2 are locked and disabled, and tracks A5 and A6 are disabled, but not locked. Tracks A3 and A4 are enabled, as indicated by the fact they are highlighted.

▶ To correct a sync problem, you must determine how far forward or backward the audio or video needs to move. Some programs will show you this with a highlight on the timeline (see Figure 8.14). Select either the audio or the video (you might need to unlink the clip, manually override the link, or lock a track first) and drag the highlighted portion into the correct place. If you need more precision than a drag affords, you can also move the clip using the time code, as described in the section "Finer Editing Tools" later in this chapter.

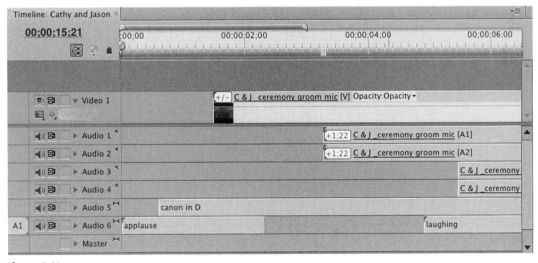

Figure 8.14
When the audio and video from a linked master clip are separated, most editing programs indicate how far the sync is off in time code. In this case, the video is 1 second and 22 frames behind the audio, as indicated by +01;22 on the first and second audio tracks.

Types of Edits

A rough edit consists of putting clips on the track, and a key component to that is determining which shots go best next to each other to tell a cohesive story that is visually engaging and pleasant to watch. A key aspect of this is creating seamless cuts—that is, cuts that don't draw attention to themselves, but instead flow naturally without being noticeable.

One trick to creating seamless cuts is to have *motivated*, or *cued*, edits—for example, a glance, a piece of dialogue, a sound effect, or a music cue. Sometimes, edits lacking motivation, such as jump cuts (discussed in more detail momentarily), can be used for stylistic effect; they tend to be jarring and can add energy. Although that can be creative and compelling at times, avoid using such edits too often; they can be visually exhausting. For the most part, your edits should merely be an understated method to showcase the clips, not vice versa.

Overlapping Edits

An *overlapping edit*, often called an *L-cut*, is an edit in which the audio moves before or after the video instead of at the exact same time (see Figure 8.15). For example, suppose you are showing the bride and groom reciting their vows. In a traditional cut, you would show the audio and video groom reciting his vows and then switch to the audio and video of the bride reciting her vows. In an overlapping edit, however, you might extend the video of the groom as the audio of the bride begins, waiting a beat before switching to the video of the bride. This overlapping edit softens the transition, making it less noticeable; by first presenting the bride's voice, you prime the viewer to see her. In longer scenes of dialogue shot with two cameras—mainly the ceremony, but also toasts, interviews with the couple or guests, and the cake cutting—overlapping edits create natural, unnoticeable transitions by cueing, or motivating, the video with the audio, avoiding a ping pong–style back and forth.

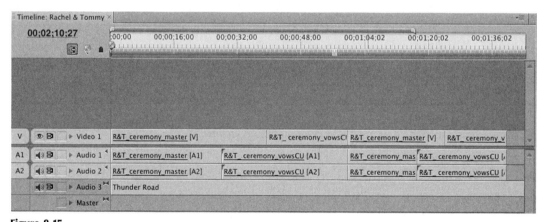

Figure 8.15
Here, two overlapping cuts are shown on the timeline. In both, the audio changes before the video, giving the viewer a sound cue that a visual change is coming.

Cutaways

One way to smooth out a rough cut out is to impose a *cutaway* shot on top of it. A cutaway is a shot of something that is not the direct action but will still make sense in the scene. For example, to cover a jump cut in the toasts, use a close up of the speaker's hand holding the Champagne glass, or a shot of the room.

Reaction shots are a specific type of cutaway that not only can be used to smooth over rough points but also can add to the story. A shot of the mother of the bride crying during a toast can serve the dual purpose of covering a bad camera move and heightening the emotion of the moment. Similarly, a boring first dance can be spiced up by the reaction shots of guests cheering and laughing. Most importantly, cutaway shots are invaluable for covering your own footage flaws—jerky camera movements or the guest who walked in front of your shot.

Jump Cuts

According to its true definition, a *jump cut* connects two shots of the same subject taken from slightly different angles, causing the subject to "jump" in the viewer's eye in a way that does not reflect continual space and time. In video language, "jump cut" has come to mean the placement of any two shots next to each other resulting in a gap in continuity, which, due to its lack of realism, is jarring to look at.

In wedding videography, jump cuts are particularly problematic when you have one camera capturing a long shot, such as the ceremony or a toast. If you want to edit out a piece of a toast but there is only a slight movement on the part of the speaker, the result will be awkward. It is generally recommended to smooth over such cuts over with a cutaway, such as a shot of the couple listening, a shot of guests' reactions, a pan of the room, or a close-up of the Champagne (see Figure 8.16).

A

B

C

Figure 8.16
Moving directly from image A to image B would create a jump cut in the middle of this father-of-the-bride speech. Without a compelling pay-off for such a jarring visual, this jump cut should be avoided. Instead, use a reaction shot to smooth over the seam, like the one of the couple listening in image C.

Although jump cuts are generally jarring, that doesn't necessarily mean they're all bad. They can convey excitement, tension, and energy, and can flow nicely in a montage where logical storytelling rules are more forgiving. Jump cuts can even work in a toast, especially if the jump leads to something funny or punchy being said. But you should use jump cuts sparingly to avoid fatiguing the viewer. Frequent use of jump cuts will prevent the construction of a cohesive and sensical piece.

Transitions

In a feature movie, typically transitions are used only between scenes. In a wedding video, which typically contains lots of montages and often focuses on conveying a mood (as opposed to storyline), transitions are often used within a section, a scene, and between scenes. Transitions can do a lot to define the mood and character of a piece; the style of video will determine the types of transitions to use.

Transitions between sections are important because they pace your piece, giving viewers time to digest what they've seen and to prepare themselves for the next place, time, character, or mood. Be sure to build some kind of transition between every section. This could be as simple as a second of time passing or a carefully selected hard cut, or might be something significantly more elaborate such as a fade to white with titles.

Transitions within sections are stylistic and less about giving information to the viewer. A brief discussion of various types of transitions, and where they are commonly found in wedding videos, follows. As with everything else, your style is your own, but knowing what tools are available to you and where they are typically used will give you a base from which to establish your own methods.

Establishing Shots

Establishing shots act as a transition between scenes or sections, announcing to the viewer where he or she is literally and figuratively. Literally, an establishing shot can function as a transition between places or can signal a jump in time by showing where the action is about to take place and what the action is. For example, after the ceremony, a shot of the reception venue lit up can tell the viewer that the action that is about to occur will be at a restaurant during the evening.

Figuratively, establishing shots can be used as a transition in mood. For example, a shot of the church not only tells the viewer that we have arrived at the ceremony, but the style of the establishing shot can convey to the viewer a mood or context. If the shot of the church is a long, slow pan, it might introduce a slow and elegant processional, whereas a series of quick cuts of the church's exterior and signage could lead into the dressing room, where the nervous bride and her bridesmaids frantically attend to her finishing touches.

Hard Cuts

A hard cut is one used without an effect to soften the transition. Although hard cuts are very common within a scene or section, they should still be carefully selected to ensure good flow. Things to select for include motivators and clean starting and ending points, as discussed further in the section "Finer Editing Tools" later in this chapter.

In addition to using hard cuts within scenes, you can use them *between* scenes—although using them that way is more of a stylistic statement as, true to their name, they can be quite hard. This is a tricky thing to do; make sure you have a strong motivator to use a hard cut between scenes, such as the last note of the father-daughter dance leading to the father's speech, or the bridesmaids clinking Champagne glasses during the preparation time cutting to the first bridesmaid beginning the processional.

If you use hard cuts between sections, make sure the music supports your editorial decisions.

Dissolves, Fades, and Other Transitions

Editing software will include a package of transitions, typically found in the Effects bin or the Effects menu. Usually, applying these transitions is very simple: Just drag the selected transition effect to the timeline and drop it on the edit point between two clips. More advanced programs have adjustable parameters for each transition, such as the length, color, rotation, axis, and so on (see Figure 8.17).

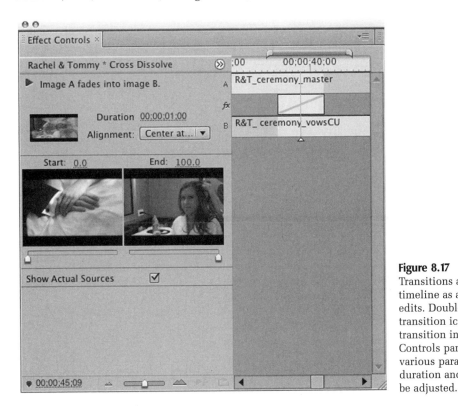

Figure 8.17
Transitions appear on the timeline as an icon between edits. Double-clicking the transition icon opens the transition in the Effect Controls panel, where various parameters, such as duration and alignment, can be adjusted.

Many of these transitions, such as page wipes and box spins, may be considered campy, but wedding videos can be stylized enough that some of them can be made to work in a fun and playful manner. If your style allows, experiment with the various options in your editing software; you may find it sparks your creativity. Be careful of using these transitions indiscriminately, however. They can be tiring when used too often, and inappropriate if used in the wrong context.

Dissolves and fades, often used between scenes in feature films to provide smoothness, are more traditional transitions. Often, a dissolve will create a dreamy mood, while a fade to black might indicate time passing. In a wedding video, in addition to being used in the same way as in feature films, these common transitions may also be used between sections of a scene. It's the nature of wedding video to feature long sections containing images only, romantic sections, or scenes with fast-paced cutting, all of which lend themselves to the use of dissolves and fades.

Although transitions are more frequent in wedding video than documentary or feature film, I still caution against overusing them. To prevent your video from looking amateurish or tacky, make sure all your transitions add something to the overall look and feel of the piece and aren't just being applied haphazardly.

 A very fast fade to white, such as four frames, can mimic a flash bulb going off. This transition can be useful for formal pictures or if the footage contains an actual camera flash (such as during the dancing clips). It works particularly well with faster paced cuts.

Natural Transitions

As discussed in Chapter 7, "The Big Day," sometimes you can shoot footage that provides a natural transition, such as the limousine passing by or the train of the wedding dress crossing the entire frame (natural wipes) or someone walking out of frame in one shot and into frame in the next. Other natural scene closers could include a candle being blown out in one place (such as the ceremony) and another one lit in the next location (such as the reception), or a one door closing (such as the limo) and another opening (such as the hotel entrance doors). It's unlikely that you'll have too many natural transitions, as it takes some patience and practice to set them up during shooting. By playing with these natural transitions in the editing process, though, you will learn what to look for and how to shoot them the next time you are in the field (see Figure 8.18).

Figure 8.18
An example of a natural transition is the bridal car leaving the church in the image on the left and driving up to the reception in the image on the right.

Finer Editing Tools

Once you have a rough cut on your timeline, it's time to begin refining your cuts. Basic refinement of your rough cut involves taking a second pass at the whole sequence, deciding what does and doesn't work, and making the appropriate changes. Such changes, most of which will occur on the timeline, might include extending or trimming clips, eliminating clips, changing the order of clips, and so on. When these refinements are finished, you still won't quite have a final piece; rather, you'll a less-rough rough cut. Advanced editing software will have lots of tools to help this process along; let's look at some of the tools for editing your clips on the timeline.

Zooming In and Out

While working on the timeline, it's very important to be able to quickly move between a comprehensive view of your piece and a detailed view. A comprehensive, or zoomed-out, view shows the whole piece and where you are working within it; you use this view when moving major sections around. A detailed, or zoomed-in, view shows just a few clips or even frames. This view is useful for looking at edit points, making fine adjustments to the edges of clips, and applying transitions. Figure 8.19 shows two views of the same timeline.

A good program offers numerous tools to allow you to change the view of the timeline. These include the zoom in/out tool, the timeline display controls, and a keystroke command that will allow you to see the entire timeline at once. Working in the view that provides the correct level of detail for the task at hand is key to speed and precision as an editor. Become adept at manipulating the different zoom tools to facilitate this.

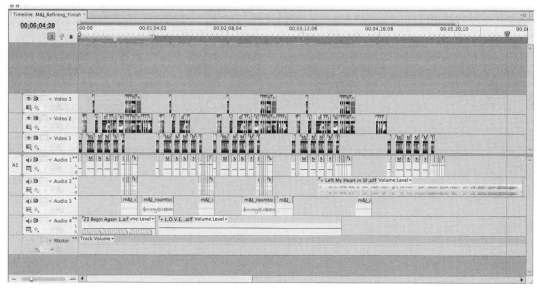

Figure 8.19
The image above shows the whole highlights piece, approximately six minutes, in one view. The image below shows approximately the first six seconds. It is common to frequently change the scale at which you look at the timeline.

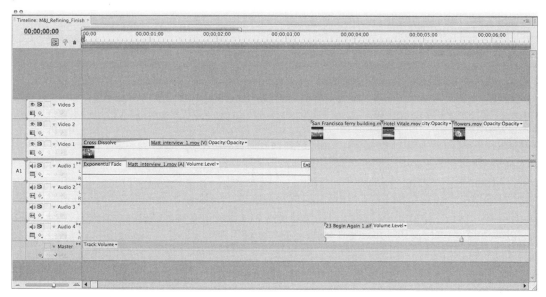

Snapping

Snapping is a handy feature that is very useful for ensuring that there are no gaps or accidental overlaps while moving clips to or around the timeline. When enabled, snapping gives clips a magnetic property that causes them to jump, or "snap," into place, sitting precisely next to other clips on the timeline. Most of the time, snapping is very useful for quickly putting things in the right place. Occasionally, however, you will want to turn snapping off—for example, if you are intentionally offsetting clips and need to be able to move clips incrementally over each other without having them jump into alignment.

Moving and Eliminating Clips

To move a clip or group of clips around on the timeline, use the drag-and-drop method. Simply click a clip on the timeline (or draw a marquee around several clips), drag the selection to a new location, and let go. Most programs offer a keystroke option to drag and drop a clip as an insert edit, but typically it will be an overlay edit by default. Another way to move clips on the timeline is to use relative time code—that is to move a clip a certain distance, measured in time code. For example, to create a 10-second space, select a clip and move it 10 seconds of time code, or 00;00;10;00, forward. This method won't work if there is another clip on the timeline blocking the movement, but is a useful technique for precisely timed sections.

As you go through your rough cut, there will undoubtedly be clips that shouldn't make the final piece. Getting rid of such clips in almost all programs is a matter of selecting the clip and pressing the Del key on your keyboard. This removes the clip, but leaves a space that must also be deleted. Performing a *ripple delete* enables you to remove the clip and the space behind it in one step—a big time-saver. In Premiere Pro, perform a ripple delete by selecting the clip and pressing the Shift and Del keys at the same time. As with performing insert edits, you must use ripple delete carefully when one or more tracks are locked; otherwise, you may accidentally unsync the audio and video within a clip or move an entire clip to the wrong place on the timeline.

Trimming Clips

An important part of clip refinement involves adding frames to or shaving frames off the beginning (head) or end (tail) of a clip. A good video editor will make sure that every clip is as clean and precise as possible. This entails looking not just at the gist of the clip, but at every frame, and starting and ending at the best possible moment. In addition to selecting the portion of the clip that is the cleanest—with no stray activities and distracting clutter in the background—you should look at the image itself and make sure the starting and ending points are clean.

Yes, this fine editing at the edges of your clips is laborious and time consuming. But it is such an important part of editing that just about every editing program offers tools designed for just this process, often called *trim tools* (or something similar), as well as a special mode for trimming, generally called the *trim monitor* (see Figure 8.20). These tools, which are applied either on the timeline or in Trim mode, are timesavers because they often combine two or three common steps into one simple action. They're also useful because they allow very precise adjustments with automation of certain error-prone steps, such as moving a series of clips backward on the timeline.

Figure 8.20
Trim mode enables you to look at the last frame of the outgoing clip and the first frame of the incoming clip, adjusting the two until they are right.

As described in Chapter 4, these tools include the following:

▶ **Ripple.** Extend or shorten a clip, moving everything else forward or backward to accommodate the change.

▶ **Roll.** Move an edit point forward or backward by lengthening one clip and shortening another.

▶ **Slip.** Move the start and end point of a single clip forward or backward, leaving the clip length intact.

▶ **Slide.** Move the middle of three clips forward or backward, simultaneously lengthening and shortening the surrounding clips.

Spend some time learning how to efficiently trim your clips to get the cleanest possible footage in your final piece. Familiarity with the fine edit tools will improve both your speed as an editor and the look and precision of your cuts (see Figure 8.21). As discussed earlier, learning the keystrokes for these tools will improve your editing speed as well as reduce your risk of repetitive stress injury.

Figure 8.21
Choosing exactly the right frame on which to start and stop can change the look of your whole piece. The image on the left, just 11 frames past the image on the right, is a much cleaner start to the clip. Over the length of your piece, this type of frame-by-frame tightening will add professionalism to your work.

Using Basic Editing Tools to Fix Shooting Errors

The expression "Fix it in post"—the assumption that no matter what shortcuts are taken during production, the magic of post-production will deliver the desired final look—makes editors cringe. Forgot to white balance? Fix it in post. Have an ugly fire extinguisher in the shot? Fix it in post. Want an image of doves flying around the room but don't have any doves to shoot? Fix it in post. Bride's dress ripped and stained? Fix it in post.

Some of these fixes are possible—and some aren't. Most of the possible fixes fall under the category of effects and motion graphics, which are discussed in Chapter 9. There are, however, a few basic editing tools that can be used to fix some basic shooting errors.

Fit-to-Fill Edit

Earlier, you learned about a three-point edits, in which the selected clip is defined with two points (in and out) and where it falls on the timeline is defined by a third point (in or out). Another type of edit, the *four-point edit*—also called a *fit-to-fill edit*—is very handy one for covering up a small hole in your timeline. For example, suppose you have a continuous clip with a small section of unusable footage, such as someone walking through the frame; you need to maintain continual audio but remove the offending piece of video, leaving a small spot that needs to be covered. In a four-point edit, the clip is defined by two points (in and out), and its intended position on the timeline is defined by another two points (in and out). The clip's in selection is placed at the in point on the timeline, and the clip's out selection is placed at the out point on the timeline.

Because the duration from in to out might be different for the selected clip and its intended position on the timeline, this type of edit will scale the clip to fit the determined position. If the clip is longer than its place on the timeline, the clip will be sped up. If the clip is shorter than its place on the timeline, the clip will be slowed down. For example, suppose you have footage of the best man giving a toast. Near the end of the toast, the camera does a quick and sloppy pan to the couple raising their glasses and kissing. You can cut the messy pan and use a four-point edit to slightly slow down the footage of the couple kissing to fill the gap.

The four-point, or fit-to-fill, edit is extremely useful for errors by slightly slowing down a video clip while keeping the audio intact. Remember, though, that this trick will not work if the video includes someone talking; in that case, the edited video will appear out of sync. In the previous example, slightly slowing down the best man would not work. Fit to fills are best used with cutaways, but can also be used with most establishing, dancing, scenery, montage, and wide-angle shots.

Basic Resize

Editing programs have a basic motion tab that enables you to change the size and rotation of a clip. Slightly enlarging a clip will allow you to reposition it by creating additional real estate on the visible portion of the images (see Figure 8.22). This can be very handy for cropping, recentering, or rotating an image slightly to compensate for a non-level tripod. There are definite limitations to resizing, however: enlarging an image too much will make it grainy and poorly defined. A general rule of thumb is that an image should not be enlarged more than 10 percent of its original size, although this can vary from image to image. Experimenting with the image itself will show you what works.

Figure 8.22
These two images are the same shot; the image on the right has been slightly magnified and moved to the right. In this case, the adjustment edits out an ugly building in the background and nicely frames the subject using the rule of thirds. It is important to remember that these adjustments come at the cost of potential graininess to the image.

There are certain errors that you will undoubtedly come across as a video editor. Here are some common problems and solutions:

> ▶ **You started shooting too late.** If you missed the beginning of a toast or a dance because you were adjusting your camera position, but you still have usable audio, use an overlapping edit to hide the portion of the video that is missing.

> ▶ **The camera moves abruptly or someone walks past.** Use a cutaway to smooth over a moment when the tripod is accidentally kicked or a wedding guest ruins the shot by walking past the camera.

> ▶ **There's a jagged camera move.** If you have a camera move that simply doesn't work, cut it out. Either use a cutaway to cover the hole or fit to fill the clips on either side so that they are unnoticeably different in length.

▶ **There's a distraction on the edge of frame.** If there is an ugly or distracting visual on an edge of the frame, try enlarging and then cropping the image slightly to get rid of it. You can also re-center the image after enlarging it to give yourself more room to cut something out. Be careful of enlarging too much, however, as you don't want to ruin your image by making it too grainy or washed out.

▶ **The tripod wasn't level.** If you shot a section, say a toast or even part of the ceremony, with your tripod unlevel, try enlarging the frame and then rotating the image until it lines up correctly with the horizontal axis. Again, don't enlarge an image too much; there are limits on how far this trick can take you.

Summary

Learning the basics of video editing is no small feat. This chapter goes all the way from moving footage to the computer to completing a partially polished rough cut. It talks about basic editing skills as well as some more advanced tools that can complete a few steps at once. It covers layering audio and video and a few different methods to build your piece. The tips for covering shooting errors will undoubtedly be helpful at some point in your editing career; even the best shooter needs to hide a few things. Finally, while I encourage you to follow your own aesthetic, knowing some of the basics described in this chapter should give a strong foundation to build from. Remember that ironing out so much material will take time and practice; have fun playing with your options!

Next Up

Completing a rough cut is a major accomplishment. You have successfully moved your footage into the computer and have arranged (and undoubtedly rearranged) the media to build a story. Now that you have the basics of your video down, it's time to have some fun with it. The next chapter covers some of the more advanced aspects of editing, such as effects, color correction, sound editing, titles, and animation.

Chapter 8 Tutorial: Build a Rough Cut

This tutorial teaches you specific editing skills to begin building a wedding video. To complete this tutorial, you will need a copy of Adobe Premiere Pro and to copy the files from the DVD accompanying this book to your computer hard drive. Instructions for downloading a trial version of Adobe Premiere Pro and copying files to the DVD are found in the tutorial for Chapter 4.

To begin this tutorial, navigate to Wedding Video_Start to Finish > Chapter 8 Tutorial and launch Adobe Premiere by double-clicking the 8_Building a Rough Cut project file in the Chapter 8 folder. When prompted, allow the scratch disks to be set to your Documents folder.

Open the Sequence bin in your Project panel and notice that it has three finished sequences (M&J_Radio Cut_Finished, M&J_Rough Cut_Finished, and M&J_Rough_Polish_Finished) and three started sequences (M&J_Radio Cut_Start, M&J_Rough Cut_Start, and M&J_Rough_Polish_Start). In this tutorial, we will use the started sequences to build to the finished ones, which you can review as reference.

As well as the Sequence bin, the Project panel contains five bins of video clips and one bin of audio. Open the clips, play them, and put them on the timeline using the techniques you learned in the Chapter 4 tutorial. In this tutorial, the clips have been preselected: You will place the clips on the timeline in their entirety.

Make a Radio Cut

To begin, double-click the empty M&J_Radio_Cut_Start sequence. You can also open the M&J_Radio_Cut_Finished sequence if you would like to use it as a reference.

Mark the Music

After you open the Radio_Cut_Start sequence, follow these steps:

1. Open the Audio bin in your project file.

2. Double-click the 23 Begin Again_Unmarked icon to open that piece of music in the Source panel.

3. Play the audio clip in the Source panel from the beginning from the clip. As you listen to the music, add unnumbered clip markers on the beat, starting with time code 00:00. To add a clip marker, do one of the following:

   ▶ Click the Clip Marker button along the bottom of the Source panel.

   ▶ Select Marker > Clip Marker > Unnumbered.

   When you are finished, your markers should fall at the following approximate time-code points in the music clip:

00;00	02;00	04;06	06;08	08;08	10;10	12;14	14;10	17;23	19;24
21;24	23;26	26;00	27;26	29;25	31;21	33;24	35;24	37;24	39;25
41;29	43;29	46;02	48;02	50;07	52;11	54;07	56;09	58;07	

 You can also navigate directly to these points and add the markers.

4. Move to the Timeline panel and move the A1 (source-track indicator) next to the Audio 3 track to set it as your destination track.

5. Click the Audio 3 track header to enable the track. (When it is enabled, it will appear highlighted.)

6. Place the playhead at the beginning of the empty sequence. You can do this by dragging the playhead in the timeline or pressing the Home key on your keyboard.

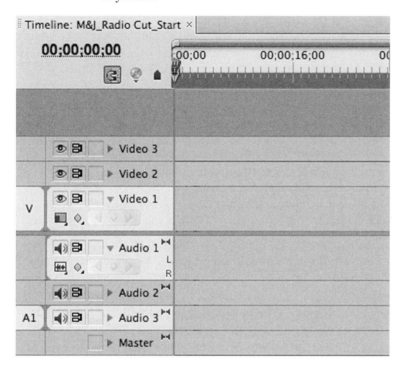

7. Move the music clip from the Source panel to the Timeline panel using an overlay or an insert edit. The music should start at the beginning of the sequence (time code 00;00). To perform an overlay edit, do one of the following:

   ▶ Press the . (period) key.

   ▶ Select Clip > Overlay.

   ▶ Click the Clip Overlay button along the bottom of the Source panel.

   To insert the clip, do one of the following:

   ▶ Press the , (comma) key.

   ▶ Select Clip > Insert.

   ▶ Click the Clip Insert button along the bottom of the Source panel.

Rather than using steps 4, 5, and 7 to move the audio clip to the timeline, you could just click and drag the clip. However, to drag an audio clip into the Program or Timeline panel, you must *grab*, or click, the audio icon underneath the Program panel monitor. Unlike with video, you cannot grab the audio from the center of the audio waveform images.

Add Matt_Interview and M&J_Vows Clips

Follow these steps to add clips to your piece:

1. Open the Interview bin in the Project panel.

2. Double-click the icon next to the Matt_interview_1 clip to open it.

3. In the Timeline panel, move the A1 (source-track indicator) next to the Audio 1 track to set it as your destination track.

4. Click the Audio 1 track header to enable the track. (When it is enabled, it will appear highlighted.)

5. Place the playhead at the beginning of the sequence, at time code 00;00. You can do this by dragging the playhead in the timeline or clicking the Home key on your keyboard.

6. Using an insert edit (as described previously), insert the Matt_interview_1 clip at time code 00;00, pushing the music back in the timeline. The music should start immediately after the clip ends, at time code 03;11.

7. The remaining radio-cut clips will be overlaid instead of inserted to keep the music track intact. To avoid inadvertently affecting the music track, lock it by selecting the checkbox to the left of the track name in the track header of the Timeline panel. Once clicked, the checkbox will appear as a small lock, and a striped zebra pattern will appear over the track itself.

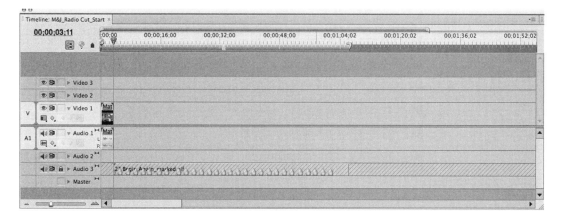

8. In the Project panel, double-click the Matt_Interview_2 clip to open it.

9. In the Timeline panel, place the playhead at time code 07;00.

10. Perform an overlay edit (as described previously).

11. Repeat steps 8–10 for the following clips (all found in the Interview bin), placing them at the specified starting points on the timeline:

Clip	Starting Point Time Code
Matt_interview_3	15;22
Matt_interview_4	22;02
Matt_interview_5	29;29

12. In the Project panel, open the Ceremony bin.

13. Repeat steps 8–10 for the following clips, placing them at the specified starting points on the timeline. (Notice that many of the cuts have been placed on the markers to coincide with beats in the music.)

Clip	Starting Point Time Code
M&J_vows_1	37;05
M&J_vows_2	40;11
M&J_vows_3	42;04
M&J_vows_4	43;18
M&J_vows_5	45;04
M&J_vows_6	46;21

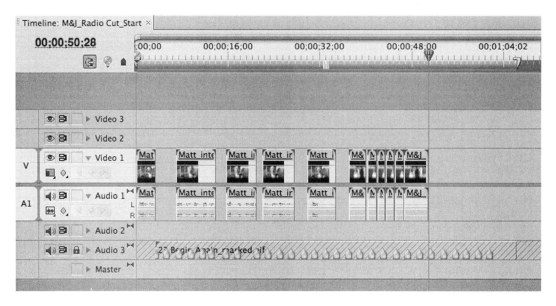

Adjust Sound Levels

The Audio Meter tool, which is found on the right side of the screen, indicates the output level of all the tracks being played. (If the tool is not visible, display it by selecting Window > Audio Meter.) You use this tool to ensure that no level surpasses 0dB, which can cause distortion. When audio levels peak, or go above 0dB, red markers light up at the top of the meter and stay lit as you play the clip. To adjust sound levels, follow these steps:

1. While watching the Audio Meter tool, play the entire clip. Note that the audio goes over 0dB in the first few interview clips and that the dialogue is nearly impossible to hear over the music in the ceremony clips.

> Chapter 9 discusses audio editing in more detail; for now, let's just bring the music level down and increase the vow audio so we can hear the dialogue a little better. We will make further adjustments later.

2. Unlock Audio Track 3 by clicking the lock in the track header.
3. Click the triangle next to the Audio 3 track to expand it. This displays the audio meter line; to better see it, click the Set Display Style icon in the lower-left part of the Video 3 track label box (just below the speaker icon) and choose Show Name Only. Do the same for Audio Track 1.

4. Select the Pen tool by pressing the P key on your keyboard or clicking the Pen tool icon in the toolbox, found on the right side of the screen. (If the toolbox is not visible, display it by selecting Window > Tools.)

5. Use the Pen tool to drag the audio level line down to approximately −18dB.

6. Use the Pen tool to drag the audio level line up to approximately 6dB for all of the M&J_Vows clips.

7. Press V to switch from the Pen tool to the default Selection tool or click the Selection tool icon in the toolbox.

8. Save your work.

You have now finished the radio cut! Let's move on to making a full rough cut.

Adding Cutaways

Let's turn our completed radio cut into a full rough cut by adding more video to the sequence you just finished; alternatively, open the M&J_Rough Cut_Start sequence in the Sequence bin in the Project panel.

Add a Cutaway Track

To provide more compelling visuals and to cover some spaces and sloppy edits, we are going to add some cutaway shots to our timeline. To add a cutaway track, follow these steps:

1. Open the Establishing bin in the Project panel and double-click the San Francisco ferry building clip to open it in the Source panel.

2. In the Timeline panel, lock audio tracks 1 and 3 by selecting the checkbox to the left of the track name in the Timeline panel. This will prevent audio clips from moving around as your video shifts.

3. Move the V (source-track indicator) on the left to the Video 2 track to set it as your destination.

4. Click the Video 2 track header to enable the track. (When it is enabled, it will appear highlighted.)

5. Lock the Video 1 track by selecting the checkbox to the left of the track name. This will prevent accidental shifts in the video track beneath the one you are working on.

6. In the Timeline panel, place the playhead at time code 03;11.

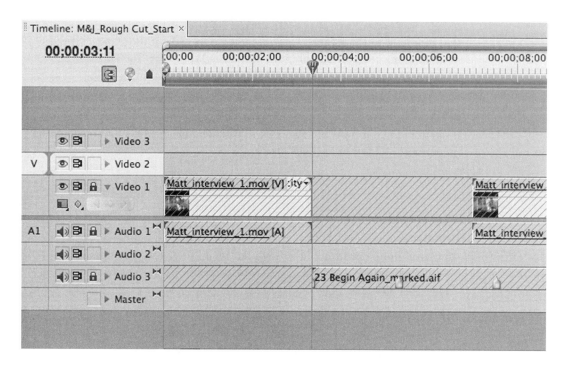

Timeline: M&J_Rough Cut_Start ×

00:00:03:11

00:00　　00:00:02:00　　00:00:04:00　　00:00:06:00　　00:00:08:00

Video 3

V　Video 2

Video 1　Matt_interview_1.mov [V] :ity ▾　　　　　　　Matt_interview

A1　Audio 1　Matt_interview_1.mov [A]　　　　　　Matt_interview

Audio 2

Audio 3　　　　　23 Begin Again_marked.aif

Master

7. Using an overlay edit, insert the San Francisco ferry building clip at time code 03;11. To perform an overlay edit, do one of the following:

   ▶ Press the . (period) key.

   ▶ Select Clip > Overlay.

   ▶ Press the Clip Overlay button along the bottom of the Source panel.

8. Open the following clip in the Establishing bin in the Project panel and repeat steps 6 and 7, placing it at the specified starting point on the timeline using an overlay edit on Video Track 2:

Clip	Starting Point Time Code
Hotel Vitale	04;12

Although the San Francisco ferry building clip has audio, Premiere Pro doesn't add it to the project because the designated target track—Audio 1—is locked. If you wanted both audio and video from this clip (which we don't want here) you would designate Audio 2 as the target by dragging the A1 source track indicator to the left of Audio 2.

9. Open the following clips in the Prep bin in the Project panel and repeat steps 6 and 7 for each one, placing them at the specified starting points on the timeline using an overlay edit on Video Track 2:

Clip	Starting Point Time Code
Flowers	05;13
Groom_2	13;23
Dress	18;14
Shoes	25;16
Zip dress	27;19
Garter	29;11
Bride	33;06

10. Open the following clips in the Couple Shots bin in the Project panel and repeat steps 6 and 7 for each one, placing them at the specified starting points on the timeline using an overlay edit on Video Track 2:

Clip	Starting Point Time Code
M&J_Couple _1	40;05
M&J_Couple _2	42;04
M&J_Couple _3	43;18
M&J_Couple _4	53;21
M&J_Couple _5	55;24
M&J_Couple _6	57;18
M&J_Couple _7	59;22

11. Open the following clip in the Ceremony bin in the Project panel and repeat steps 6 and 7, placing it at the specified starting point on the timeline using an overlay edit on Video Track 2:

Clip	Starting Point Time Code
First Kiss	45;04

12. Save your work.

Four-Point Edits Using Fit-to-Fill

Our next step will be to make a four-point edit—that is, an edit in which the in and out points are specified in both the Source panel and on the timeline. The footage in this type of edit will either be slowed down or sped up to match the duration selected on the timeline. In this tutorial, the four-point cutaway edits will use Video 3 as their destination. To begin, follow these steps:

1. Open the Prep bin in the Project panel and double-click the Groom_1 clip to open it in the Source panel.

2. In the Source panel, select an in on the first frame (press the I key on the keyboard) and an out on the last frame (press the O key on the keyboard).

Discussion of selecting edits from source footage using in and out points can be found in the Chapter 4 tutorial.

3. Move the V (source-track indicator) on the left side of the Timeline panel to the Video 3 track.

4. Click the Video 3 track header to enable the track. (When it is enabled, it will appear highlighted.)

5. You should have Video Track 1 locked; go ahead and lock Video Track 2 as well. Make sure that Audio 1 and Audio 3 are still also locked. Locking the audio tracks prevents audio from being placed on the timeline, which is what we want for these cutaway shots.

Because these clips have been pre-trimmed, you need not select the ins and outs; the default in and out points will be the first and last frame. But it's good practice to select the in and out points. Also, it's important to make sure there are no stray in or out points, which a new in and/or out will eliminate.

6. Drag the playhead to 11;19 on the timeline and then press the I key on the keyboard to place an in point there.

7. Drag the playhead to 13;23 on the timeline; then press the O key on the keyboard to place an out point there.

8. Return to the Source panel and do one of the following to insert the clip as a fit-to-fill edit:

   ▶ Press the , (comma) key.

   ▶ Select Clip > Insert.

   ▶ Press the Clip Insert button along the bottom of the Source panel.

9. A dialog box appears, asking whether you want to change an in/out point or change the clip speed (fit to fill). Choose Fit to Fill and click OK.

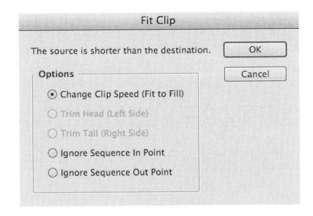

 Notice that on the timeline, the clip appears with a percentage next to its name. This percentage reflects the percentage of full speed at which the clip is being shown—in this case, 67.69%.

10. Perform another fit-to-fill edit, this time with the Recessional clip as the source (found in the Ceremony bin in the Project panel), placing it on the timeline between time codes 49;06 (in point) and 53;21 (out point).

11. Click the timeline to make sure it's selected, click the Home key to move the playhead to the start of the video, and click the spacebar to preview your video.

12. Save your work.

Polishing the Rough Cut

Before we move on to more advanced editing techniques, there is just a bit of spit and polish to be done on the rough cut. Let's polish the rough cut by trimming and adding some transitions to the sequence you just finished; alternatively, open the M&J_Rough Polish_Start sequence located in the Sequence bin in the Project panel.

Trimming Clips

The beginning of the Dress clip is messy, so let's trim it. Do the following:

1. In the Timeline panel, go to the Dress clip, which starts at time code 18;14.

2. Place the playhead at time code 20;00. This will be the point to which we trim.

3. With the default Selection tool selected (press the V key on the keyboard), position the mouse pointer over the front edge of the clip until the arrow changes into a bracket-shaped tool.

4. Drag the left edge of the clip back to meet the playhead. Notice that as you make this movement, the amount that you are trimming is reflected in the left time-code indicator (location) on the Program panel.

5. Repeat steps 1–4 to trim frames from the final clip (M&J_couple_7) except drag the edge on the right so that the last frame is on time code 1;03;16.

You trim audio the same way you trim video. Practice trimming audio by taking the first three frames off of two clips in the sequence: Matt_Interview_3 and Matt_Interview_4. This will clean up the clips by eliminating an "um" and an "and," respectively. Since the audio is linked to the video files here, you'll be deleting the first three frames of the video as well, which is okay.

 To edit audio without video (or vice versa), right-click the clip on the timeline and choose Unlink.

Moving Clips

To move a clip that is already on the timeline, simply select it and drag it to the desired location. When you are ready to overlay the clip, release the mouse. Alternatively, hold down the Command (Mac) or Ctrl (PC) key when you drag and release to create an insert edit. Let's practice:

1. Put the playhead at time code 34;27.

2. Drag the bride clip that currently starts at time code 33;06 so that its first frame is at the current playhead location (34;27).

3. Holding the Command (Mac) or Ctrl (PC), release the bride clip to create an insert edit. Notice that the cursor changes while you hold the Command/Ctrl key, indicating an insert instead of an overlay edit. Notice, too, that when you release, the footage behind the inserted clip moves backward.

4. Undo the insert edit by choosing Edit > Undo or by pressing Command+Z (Mac) or Ctrl+Z (PC).

5. Drag the bride clip that currently starts at time code 33;06 so that its first frame is at the current playhead location (34;27) and release to create an overlay edit.

6. Watch the changes you have created in the timeline.

Notice that with the bride clip at this new location, the bride's eyes are looking up to match the music; these small touches can add a lot to the overall cleanliness and tightness of your piece.

Performing a Basic Resize

Play the recessional clip that starts at time code 49:13. Notice that although the slowing of the footage (the fit-to-fill edit) helps some, that is not particularly steady shooting. Near the end of the frame, a gentleman comes into view, distracting the viewer from the action. To minimize his presence, let's enlarge and reposition the clip:

1. In the Timeline panel, double-click the recessional clip to open it in the Source panel. This view of the clip is different than if we had opened the recessional clip from the Project panel because it reflects the clip on the timeline rather than the raw footage.

2. Click the Effect Controls tab in the Source panel.

3. Click the Motion triangle.

4. Find the Scale setting and click its value (100).

5. Replace the 100 with 120 to scale the image at 120%.

6. Change the values for the Position from 360 to 300 (x axis) and from 240 to 230 (y axis). The image is now moved slightly to the left to eliminate the guest on the left side of the shot.

 If you prefer, you can make changes visually instead of using numbers. To do so, make sure the clip is selected in the timeline and then click the clip in the Program panel. Then, in the Program panel, grab the image by the handle in the middle of the frame and drag the image around with your mouse. If your Effect Controls panel is open, notice that the values for the position setting change as you drag, reflecting the image position. You can also resize the clip visually by dragging any of the handles (small boxes) on the edges in or out.

For additional practice, scale the bride clip that starts at time code 33;06 to 110%. Follow these steps:

1. Double-click the bride clip in the Timeline panel to open it in the Source panel.

2. Click the Effects tab in the Source panel.

3. Click the Motion triangle.

4. Change the Scale value to 110.

5. Save your work.

Adding Transitions

Transitions will help keep your piece clean—if they are applied discriminately. Here, we will add video transitions. (You will learn how to add audio transitions after you have done more advanced audio editing.)

1. In the Media panel in the bottom-left part of the screen, click the Effects tab. Alternatively, press Shift+7.

2. Open the Video Transitions bin to reveal several more bins. Each bin contains lots of transitions, all with customizable parameters. Click the Dissolve bin's triangle.

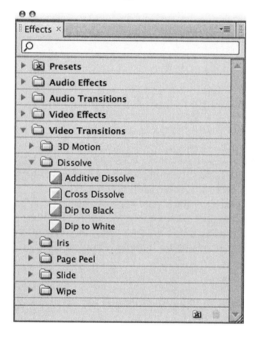

3. In the timeline, navigate to the beginning of the sequence.

4. Drag a Dip to Black transition from the Dissolve bin to the beginning of the first clip and release the mouse. This applies the transition, as indicated by the purple box at the beginning of the clip on the timeline.

5. To view the parameters of the transition, double-click the transition on the timeline (the purple box). The Effect Controls panel opens, displaying information about the transition, including its name, length, alignment (where the transition is placed), how much of the transition appears on the outgoing clip, and how much appears on the incoming clip. In this instance, the transition is entirely on the incoming clip.

If you have trouble clicking the transition in the timeline, enlarge your view of the timeline by pressing the = (equal) key on your keyboard while the timeline is selected or using the scale slider in the bottom-left part of the Timeline panel. Press the − (minus) key to zoom your view back out.

6. Make sure the Duration setting is 1:00. If it isn't, type 100 and press Enter.

7. Repeat steps 4–6 to add another Dip to Black transition to the last clip of the sequence (M&J_couple_7), making sure the transition duration is one second long (1:00).

8. Navigate to time code 20:00 on the timeline.

9. Drag a Cross Dissolve transition to the beginning of the dress clip.

10. Navigate to time code 33:06 on the time line.

11. Drag a Cross Dissolve transition to the end of the garter clip.

 Some transitions require additional frames on either side of the clip in order to create the effect. Much of the media on this particular sequence has no handles, or additional frames. If you attempt to add other transitions and find that they can't be applied, try trimming some frames from the clips on the sequence to have additional frames from which to build transitions.

12. Drag the playhead to the beginning of the sequence in the timeline or press the Home key on your keyboard and watch your rough cut from the beginning.

13. Save your work.

Congratulations! You have built a rough cut. In the next chapter, you will learn and practice advanced editing techniques to make this a finished piece.

Chapter 9
Advanced Editing

In this chapter:

- ▶ Multi-camera editing
- ▶ Filters
- ▶ Basic compositing
- ▶ Motion and animation
- ▶ Audio editing
- ▶ External plug-ins and programs

Finishing a rough cut is like completing the first draft of a term paper or manuscript. The hard part is done. Although there is some relief in that, you still have a ways to go—polishing, refining, and cleaning—before completion. Some editors prefer to take a short break after completing the rough cut to be ready—emotionally and artistically—to dive back in. Others are more likely to eat, sleep, and breathe the project until it's out the door. You'll develop your own working style naturally. Regardless of which method you choose, do take a step back and look at your project as critically and with as much detachment as possible as you begin to refine the rough cut.

This chapter looks at some of the advanced features of non-linear editing programs that will help you turn your rough cut into a professionally edited piece to proudly give your clients. A few of the techniques covered in this chapter are advanced methods for getting source media on the timeline, but most deal with adjusting the footage that is already there. Because professional editing software is so deep, and because the various programs differ in their capabilities, this chapter cannot serve as a replacement for your software's manual, but does highlight the features that will be most commonly used and are effective for wedding videos.

Before you begin refining your sequence, duplicate it. (Click it to select it, right-click it, and choose Duplicate.) Then, as you progress, make regular duplicates of the various sequences. You'll often find that experiments don't turn out as planned; these backups make it simple to return to a previous point in the process. Label your copies systematically so you can easily return to the desired point.

Multi-Camera Editing

For two-camera shooting, *multi-camera editing* can be both a time-saving tool and a way to easily ensure that every shot you select is the best option available. By lining up, or syncing, all the cameras that were operating at a given point, multi-camera editing shows a simultaneous display of every angle captured, often allowing the editor to "live" switch between tracks to create a sequence almost as if the edit were a live cut for a sports or news broadcast.

In wedding video, multi-camera editing is most useful for long stretches of continuous footage where more than one camera is being used, typically the ceremony or the toasts.

If you regularly turn off either camera during shooting, the functionality of the multi-camera tool decreases significantly, as you will have to re-sync the cameras each time a camera is turned off.

Creating a Multiclip

The first step to multi-camera editing is to create a *multiclip*—that is, a sequence that contains the videos from each operating camera. The key to creating a multiclip is finding the correct sync point, which is set manually. If the sync point is off, the multiclip will not be a useful multi-camera editing tool because one of the angles will not match the other at any given moment in time.

Although it's possible to sync by time code, multiple clips will rarely (if ever) have the same time code, which would require all cameras to start at the same 30th of a second. Instead, you must determine the sync point by locating the frame on each camera's footage that represents the same moment in time. Here are a few techniques for doing this:

▶ **Camera flash.** Usually, a photographer's flash offers the easiest way to sync tracks. Often (though not always) visible regardless of the camera angle, a flash will last at most a few frames, and it's easy to find the first frame of white and mark it. The only hitch to using camera flash to sync is to make sure you're using the right one; you'll find that camera flashes shower most of the footage. Use audio clues to ensure you're working with the same flash on each clip you are syncing.

▶ **Audio cues.** Audio cues are helpful for finding frames to sync from because even if the cameras are positioned differently, a sudden or loud noise will be audible on all the camera recordings. Finding the first frame of the audio should be easy; just play the audio frame by frame, particularly if the noise occurs in an otherwise relatively quiet moment. Turning on the audio waveform overlays and zooming in on them will give a visual reference point to the audio occurrences.

▶ **Visual cues.** Visual cues are often the most difficult to sync to because cameras don't often include the same visuals at the same time. Occasionally, however, you will get lucky, and a sudden movement event such as a door opening or a candle being lit will be visible in all of the clips, providing a frame-specific reference point with which to sync all the clips.

Once you locate the sync point, define it by inserting a marker, or *in point*, on all the clips designated for use in the multiclip. Then select said clips in the browser and convert them into a multiclip. The precise steps to make a multiclip sequence will differ depending on the program you are using, but will always involve syncing clips, creating a sequence with all of the clips aligned, and enabling a multi-camera mode to view several camera angles at once.

In Adobe Premiere Pro, you'll create two sequences for each multi-camera sequence that you produce. The first sequence is where you sync your clips. Then, you drag the first sequence into another sequence—a technique called *nesting*. You choose the camera angles in the second sequence using a multi-camera interface.

It's a good idea to designate your sequences as normal (multiclip) or nested (multiclip nested) so you can tell them apart.

Follow these steps to create a multiclip (see Figures 9.1 and 9.2):

1. Drag all clips to be synced into a sequence, putting one on top of another on the respective tracks. So, camera A might be on the Video 1 track, camera B on the Video 2 track, and so on.

2. Add a numbered clip marker (not a sequence marker) to the sync point of each clip. To do so, place your playhead at the sync point on the timeline, highlight the clip, and choose Marker > Set Clip Marker > Next Available Number (or Other Number).

3. Synchronize the clips. To do so, select them on the timeline and select Clip > Synchronize. You'll be using numbered markers to synchronize, so click the Numbered Clip Marker radio button, identify the clip marker in the drop-down list, and choose OK.

4. Check whether the clips are synchronized by previewing the sequence. To do so, click the spacebar on your keyboard. If you only hear one instance of the audio file, you're probably in great shape. If you hear three or four instances, your markers obviously weren't in the right spot.

5. Create a new sequence (right-click in the Project window and choose New Item > Sequence) to contain the multi-camera sequence you just created; then double-click the empty sequence to open it in the timeline. This will be your nested sequence.

6. Drag the sequence that contains all the camera angles into the new nested sequence.

7. Click the nested sequence and choose Clip > Multi-Camera > Enable to enable the multi-camera function of the new clip.

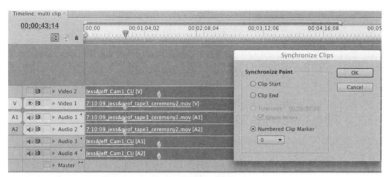

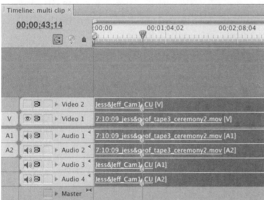

Figure 9.1
Aligning clips in the multiclip sequence. Initially, the Video 2 track lags behind the Video 1 track; this is evident from the clip markers appearing on different frames of the timeline in the first image. After you synchronize the clips using the options in the Synchronize Clips dialog box, the clips align, as illustrated by the lined-up markers in the second image.

Figure 9.2
When a multiclip is displayed in the Multi-Camera viewer, all the camera angles of a given synced moment are shown. Although more than two angles (as shown in this figure) is unusual for wedding videography, some high-end editing programs can accommodate up to 16 camera angles in customizable viewer displays (although Adobe Premiere Pro can accommodate only four).

Editing a Multiclip

The first pass of editing a multiclip is different from editing a regular clip. Instead of selecting clips to remain in the sequence, the decision points revolve around which clip will be shown at any given point in time. To enable you to edit the multiclip—or decide which angle will be used—an editing program will typically offer an interface showing all the angles at once, allowing you to click the angle to be shown at any particular instance. Clicking different angles switches the view being shown.

To edit a multiclip in Adobe Premiere Pro, follow these steps (see Figure 9.3):

1. With the nested sequence selected, choose Window > Multi-Camera Monitor. As you saw in Figure 9.2, the left side of the Multi-Camera monitor displays all videos synced in your first sequence, while the right side of the monitor offers a larger view of the camera angle currently selected.

2. In the Multi-Camera monitor, click the red Record button to record the camera angle switches performed.

3. Play the sequence in the Multi-Camera monitor using the controls beneath the timeline. As the sequence plays, click the desired camera angle on the left side of the monitor; it will appear in the larger window on the right. When you stop playing the sequence in the Multi-Camera monitor, angle selections will show up as edits in the Timeline panel.

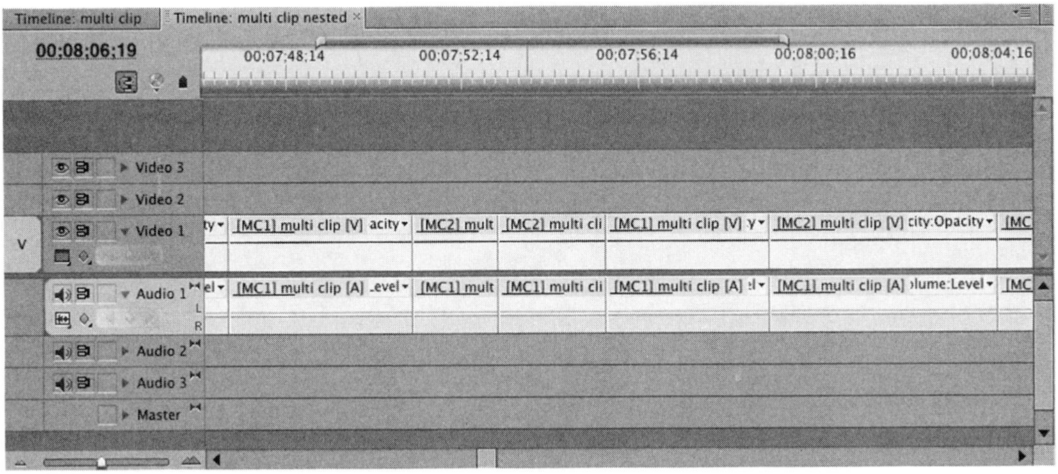

Figure 9.3

While "live" switching between camera views, Adobe Premiere Pro puts the cuts on the timeline, indicating where angles were changed. (Notice that the clips indicate whether the footage came from angle one [MC1] or angle two [MC2].) The cuts can then be further edited on the timeline using the fine edit tools.

Don't get too hung up on switching angles on the exact frame; you can either delete them with a single undo operation or refine them with the fine editing tools described in Chapter 8, "Basic Editing."

Filters

A *filter* is an effect applied to enhance the look of a video clip. Most editing software applications come with more filters than you will ever use; many will be inappropriate for even the most outlandish and wild wedding video. That being said, it's worth familiarizing yourself with all the effects at your disposal. Some, like color-collection filters and motion-steadying tools, will noticeably change the quality of your footage, while others, such as blurs, tints, and desaturation tools, will change the aesthetic and mood of the images.

Understanding and experimenting with your effects will be useful for improving poor-quality footage and inspiring new looks and feels for your images. But be warned: It's very easy to overuse filters; indeed, an effects-laden piece is the hallmark of a new or lazy editor. Over-application of filters creates a piece of negligible structure and questionable style. Instead of applying every filter that looks compelling, use visual effects carefully to accentuate the mood you are already creating with your content and your cutting style. If effects become the story or the message itself, the piece will look campy and tacky. Used judiciously, however, filters will enhance the structure of the story being told.

Common Aesthetic Filters

Certain filters tend to work well with the types of footage and moods created in wedding video, and are commonly used throughout the industry for their romantic visual characteristics. Several are listed here (see Figure 9.4):

► **Desaturate.** A Desaturate, or Black & White, filter strips color from the image, making footage appear in black and white. This is especially useful to show clips that are chronologically incorrect and also works well with clips that have been slowed down. It's frequently used with other color-related filters such as sepia or highlight. Using a mask, you can desaturate just part of an image, which serves the purpose of highlighting the portion of the image left in color. For example, desaturating everything in the image except the flowers is a common way to show off the bridal bouquet.

► **Gaussian Blur.** A Gaussian Blur filter softens or blurs an image, reducing the level of noise and detail. (It's called "Gaussian" because of the name of the function upon which the blur algorithm is based.) The soft look created by a Gaussian Blur filter is especially useful for enhancing shots of the bride, the bridal couple, and the church and reception settings. Like all filters, it's easy to get too heavy-handed with blurs. Avoid applying too many Gaussian blurs or any one filter with settings that are too high, which will render your piece overdone or too soft or muddy, respectively.

► **Vignette.** A Vignette filter softens and darkens the perimeter of an image to focus the eye on the center portion. The radius and position of the area in focus is usually adjustable in the filter parameters. Like other filters, this filter works best when applied subtly.

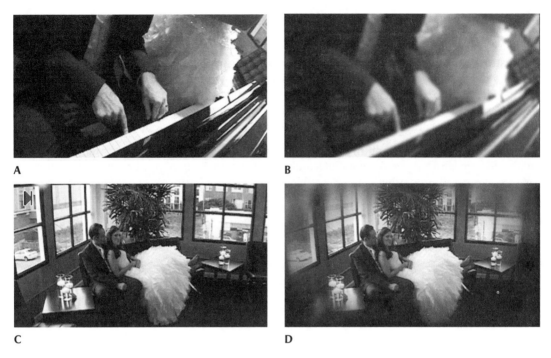

A   B

C   D

Figure 9.4
Images A and B provide an example of footage without and with a Gaussian Blur; images C and D provide an example of footage without and with a Vignette filter.

Different sections and styles of the video will call for different filters. For example, a highly edited, fast-cut piece might use filters such as Posterize, Bad TV, or Kaleidoscope—just three examples of dozens of dramatic and fun filters that come with editing software.

Common Corrective Filters

In addition to filters that provide noticeable changes to the video, such as the ones discussed in the preceding section, there are numerous filters that do exactly the opposite: change video clips so that irregularities or imperfections in shooting are *less* noticeable. Applied well, these corrective filters enhance the footage by allowing a more seamless fit with other shots and eliminating common errors. The most common corrective filters for wedding videos are color-correction tools and tools for smoothing motion to lessen jerky camera movements.

A good editing application will offer numerous corrective tools—enough to correct almost any problems you come across. That being said, external applications dedicated to effects—including but not limited to color correction and motion smoothing—are also commonly used. These external applications are discussed briefly at the end of this chapter; the tools covered here are ones included in most editing applications.

Color Correction

Whereas a big-budget Hollywood film might employ numerous people dedicated strictly to the art of color correction, it's just one of the many of the hats worn by a wedding videographer. The color tools covered here are used mostly to correct footage that is poorly colored due to user error or to low light or other poor shooting conditions, but can also be used for artistic effect. For example, casting a light across a sequence or amping up the colors in a certain shot or series of shots can enhance the mood and change the style of your piece. Good knowledge of these tools affords you more visual creativity, as well as the ability to clean up your own poor footage. Remember, however, that no matter how good you become at correcting or altering your footage, the best way to get good color is to start with a clean, accurate color slate. Shoot with the right white balance!

Video Scopes

The editing program you use should have a color-correction mode or toolbar that provides *video scopes*—that is, image-measurement tools—for the footage you are looking at. Ideally, the program includes a preset editing interface that accommodates these scopes, allowing you to constantly monitor color during your regular editing. In some programs, however, you must bring up these scopes on an as-needed basis.

There are several scopes that can help define whether your colors are in the right ranges and when they need tweaking (see Figure 9.5):

► **Vectorscope.** A *vectorscope* measures and displays the hue and saturation of colors in an image using a color wheel with the main colors (red, green, and blue) and the secondary colors (yellow, cyan, and magenta). An image's colors will be represented in white on the vectorscope; the more saturated a color is, the farther out it will extend from the center of the target.

► **Histogram.** A *histogram* measures and displays the strength of the luminance values in an image. The X axis of this graph goes from 0 to 100, where 0 is black and 100 is white. This is a good tool for showing contrast, as the peaks and valleys displayed in the monitor indicate the number of pixels in the image at that luminance level. A graph with a clump in the middle will have low contrast, while a graph with high and low points will have high contrast.

► **Waveform monitor.** A *Waveform monitor* measures and displays the brightness of an image. The Y axis of this graph goes from 0 to 100, where 0 is black and 100 is white. The monitor displays information from left to right, approximating the rectangle of video. This shows which parts of an image are bright and dark—and sometimes, too bright or too dark.

► **RGB parade.** The *RGB parade* scope is similar to the Waveform monitor, but shows the red, green, and blue images side by side and does not consider secondary colors. If an image has a reddish cast to it, it will be easy to see on the RGB parade, as the red values will be higher than the green and blue values.

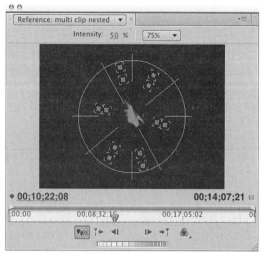

A

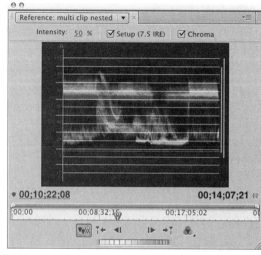

B

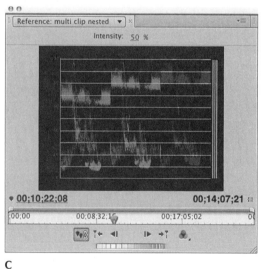

C

Figure 9.5
Most editing programs include a vectorscope (A),
Waveform monitor (B), and parade scopes (C), and
offer a custom interface layout to facilitate the
color-correction process.

In Premiere Pro, it is useful to enter the color-correction interface by choosing Window >
Workspace > Color Correction. This will give you a Reference monitor as well as your
Program panel, allowing you to look at an image and its associated scope at the same time,
as shown in Figure 9.6.

Figure 9.6
The color-correction workspace includes a Reference monitor, which allows you to see the scope (or scopes) of an image while looking at the image itself in the Program panel.

Safe Colors

Television sets have a smaller range of acceptable colors than computer monitors do. This can be dangerous for a video editor because colors that look fine on a computer screen might not display well when viewed on a client's TV screen playing from the DVD. Specifically, whites may be too bright, and oversaturated bright colors, such as red, tend to bleed. Unfortunately, most applications' internal titling tools allow the use of colors that are not color-safe for NTSC, which can result in messy-looking titles.

Your program's video scopes can help you determine when an image goes beyond acceptable limits. If an image is too white or too black, it will extend beyond the boundaries of the Waveform monitor (see Figure 9.7). If a color is oversaturated and likely to look bad, the lines in the vectorscope will extend beyond the outer circle of the graph.

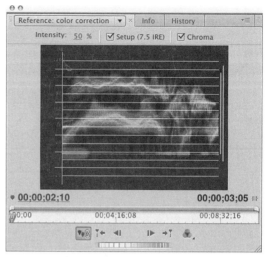

Figure 9.7
The Waveform monitors reflect the brightness of each image. Notice in the first image that the whites extend above the 100 line and the blacks are crushed at the bottom (below 7.5), indicating unsafe color. In the second image, effects have been applied to change the contrast, bringing the whites down and the blacks up, making for a safe image, with less contrast.

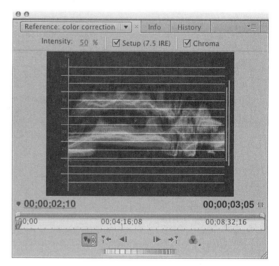

When luminance is too high, a filter designed to bring luminance down to broadcast-safe levels can be applied. Often, a series of clips shot at the same place and time will require the filter, which can be applied to many clips at once. Not surprisingly, the filter is often called "Broadcast Safe" or "Broadcast Colors," although various editing applications may name it differently.

As well as glancing at the video scopes to monitor the color and luminance values of your images, it's important that to continually watch footage on an external video monitor—*not* on the computer monitor. An external monitor will help you glean information about color and luminance and keep an eye on changes that might not work on your client's TV screen.

White Balancing

As discussed in Chapter 7, "The Big Day," it's important to white-balance every time you change shooting conditions—moving from room to room, indoors to outdoors, etc. This is because video is an additive color system; all the colors add to white. If the definition of white is off, all the colors that comprise it will be off as well.

Often, if an image has a tinge of color across its entirety, it's because the white balance was not done while shooting. In that case, you can use a white balance filter to fix the footage. White balancing during color correction involves setting the white after the fact, telling the program what color *should* be true white and adjusting the rest of the colors accordingly.

In Adobe Premiere Pro, one effective but highly usable tool for white balancing is the Fast Color Corrector filter (located in the Color Correction subfolder of the Video Effects folder), which permits a look at the color wheel as well as tools to reset the white balance of an image. To rebalance white, click the eyedropper next to the white color chip to select it, and then click a region in the video frame that's supposed to be white. Press the Ctrl key (Command key on the Mac) while you click, and Premiere Pro will average the color values of multiple pixels around the pixel that you clicked, which should improve the accuracy of the correction.

Notice that when you click the frame to select the color, the dot found in the center of the wheel moves; if the image started out with a blue cast, the dot will reference white at a point closer to red or yellow (directly across the color wheel) to compensate (see Figure 9.8). If the image started with a green cast, the dot will move toward magenta. A more advanced interface can be found in the Three-Way Color-Corrector filter (also in the Color Correction subfolder of the Video Effects folder), which allows for separate correction of blacks, grays and whites (see Figure 9.9).

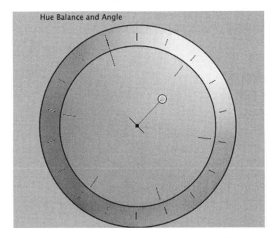

Figure 9.8
This figure shows the Fast Color-Correction filter with some corrective changes made. As indicated by the dot in the center of the color wheel, white has been shifted toward magenta and blue to compensate for an image with a greenish cast (directly across the color wheel).

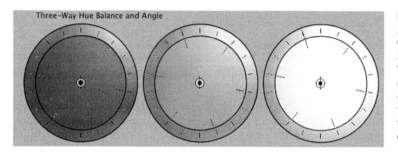

Figure 9.9
In this view of a Three-Way Color-Corrector filter, the settings are all at default: The dots are in the centers of the color wheels. That doesn't mean the frame has the correct colors; it's just the starting point for making color changes.

Luckily, in wedding videos, there is almost always something white to use as a reference point. That doesn't mean you can pick haphazardly, though. Be sure to enlarge the picture in the canvas so that you can see individual pixels before you select a white. Also, avoid choosing a white that is the result of an image being blown out rather than a white that is intentionally so; a blown-out white will not serve as a reference.

Luminance

If an image has whites that are too bright or darks that are too dark, adjust the contrast using the saturation sliders, found in the color-correction filters. In Adobe Premiere Pro, the saturation sliders are found beneath the color wheels in the Fast Color Corrector and the Three-Way Color-Corrector filters; every program's color correction tool will have some version of the same. Pull the white slider down (to the left) to make whites legal, pull the black slider up (to the right) to make blacks legal. Adjusting the gray level will help level out the contrast so that your image doesn't appear too dark or too washed out.

If, on the other hand, an image looks flat—or the Waveform monitor indicates an image with all the luminance values in the middle—increasing the whites, decreasing the blacks, and appropriately adjusting the grays will create an image that offers more contrast. Higher-contrast images are more defined and thus more engaging, but avoid overdoing it; you can overcorrect an image and wind up with a muddy or grainy picture.

Another way to brighten dark video is to use a gamma-correction filter (see Figure 9.10). A *gamma point* is the midpoint between an image's whites and blacks. By raising the gamma point using a dedicated gamma-correction filter, you can brighten your image's mid tones without lightening or washing out the blacks—an ideal fix for images that are too dark because they are shot in low light.

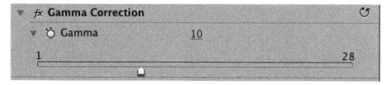

Figure 9.10
Offering a more simplified interface, a gamma-correction filter is good for certain types of corrections, such as for dark images that need the mid-tone ranges raised while leaving the blacks intact. Because weddings are often shot in low light, adjusting gamma using a slider like the one shown is an easy fix, and is regularly used with dark footage.

Color

As indicated previously, all the colors readjust when a white balance is manually applied. You can also move colors around to stylistically change hues by dragging the central dot in the direction of one color. Saturation of any given color will increase near the perimeter of the color wheel; a visible color cast will appear and become brighter as you drag the dot outward along any color vector.

Matching Footage

Although there is some standardization, different camera manufacturers consistently produce cameras that are different from their counterparts in terms of color and sharpness. When using multiple types of cameras on a shoot, take care to notice the differences between the two and account for them using available color-correction and sharpening effects.

To correct for these discrepancies, first choose the camera with the preferred footage and make all the necessary adjustments and changes. Then attempt to match the second camera's footage to that of the first camera. This can be a tiring, time-consuming process, full of trial and error, but the Reference monitor will help you closely compare different shots. After you have adjusted one clip from the second camera, batch-apply all the filters you used to all the second-camera footage.

Steadying Filters

Several high-end programs and third-party software developers offer plug-in filters for smoothing out jagged camera movement. Final Cut Pro's version is called SmoothCam; Magic Bullet Steady 1.0 integrates well with Premiere Pro. Although they operate slightly differently, all these plug-ins analyze the footage, determine how the image's pixels are moving frame by frame, and then offer compensatory smoothing techniques.

These types of filters are usually applied slightly differently than other filters because they must first go through an analysis process. It's worth noting that the analysis process can be enormously long—measured in days, in fact. Yes, they're often background processes—which means you can edit while the analysis occurs—but it might not be your most useful tool if it takes 36 hours to do its job. Of course, the length of the clip affects processing time, as does the speed of your computer. But if you have the time, patience, and need, these filters can give stunning results by removing unwanted shakes from your video clips.

Applying Filters

Advanced editing programs provide various options for applying filters: via a menu or with a separate tab (see Figure 9.11). With a tab, applying the effect is as simple as dragging a filter onto the clip on the timeline. Once the filter is applied, double-click the clip to display it in the Source panel, and then click the Effect Controls tab to see which filters you've applied to the clip and their customizable parameters. Try experimenting with these parameters to get the right look.

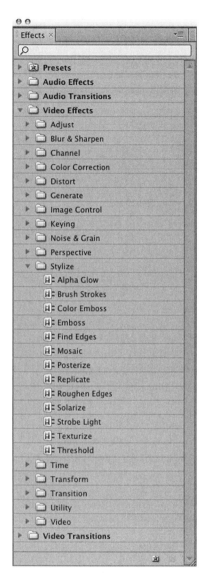

Figure 9.11
The Effects tab contains dozens of stylizing and corrective filters, organized by category in bins or subfolders. Although all filters are applied to the footage the same way, experimentation is the only way to learn how a given filter will look and if you can incorporate it into your style.

It's common to apply several filters to a single clip. When you do, be aware that the filters will affect the clip in the order applied. That is, the order in which you add filters can change the resulting effect. For example, if you want to create a clip that's black and white with pink highlights, you must first apply a Black & White filter to the clip to remove any existing color and then apply a pink highlight effect to the black-and-white clip. If the filters are applied in the opposite order, the desaturation filter will remove the pink highlights, leaving a black-and-white clip.

It's also common to apply one filter to several clips. In this case, you should first set the parameters of the filter. Next, use the default Selection tool to select all the clips in the timeline to which you want to apply the effect. Finally, drag or paste the filter onto one of the selected clips to apply the effect to all of them.

Setting the parameters of a filter that isn't already applied to a clip (preparing a filter to be applied to many clips) will differ depending on the editing application, but may include a preset or "favorites" bins (a folder to store commonly used effects with modified parameters), a paste attributes function (a paste option that allows the copying and pasting of certain characteristics of a clip without copying and pasting the content itself), or the capability to open a filter in a source window before applying it to a clip. To remove a filter, double-click the clip in the timeline to display it in the viewer (the same method used to modify a filter's parameters), select the filter, and press the Del key on your keyboard.

Favorites and preset bins are useful because they make batch application of a filter particularly easy. They are also useful because, in addition to making commonly used filters more accessible, they make these filters part of your user preferences, which you can access even if you change projects or computers.

Analyzing Effects

As you apply filters, it's important to be able to compare an affected clip with both its original, raw form and any surrounding clips. This is to ensure that the clip looks better with the effect than without, and to perform any necessary parameter adjustments to make sure the clip fits comfortably into the sequence without being visibly jarring. This is helpful for all affected clips, particularly color-corrected ones.

There are several ways to analyze your effects. In Premiere Pro, one is to select the clip in the timeline, double-click it to display it in the Source panel, and select the Effect Controls tab to see the filters you have applied. To the left of each filter title is a small *fx*; clicking this causes the *fx* to disappear and disables the effect. Clicking it again causes the *fx* to reappear and enable the effect. Toggling the effect on and off in this way allows you to easily view the clip with and without the effect to assess its effectiveness.

Another useful tool for making decisions and adjustments for effects is Adobe Premiere Pro's Reference monitor, which provides a view of two clips at once. That way, if you're color-correcting clip A to make it match clip B, you can have clip B open while you're adjusting clip A. To open Premiere Pro's Reference monitor, choose Window > Reference Monitor. It will open as a floating window that you can drag anywhere in the interface.

Normally, the Reference monitor shows the same frame as the Program panel, which is no help if you're trying to match clip A with clip B. In editor-ese, the two monitors are synced or *ganged*. If you disable ganging by clicking the Gang to Program Monitor icon in the Reference monitor (last icon on the bottom left) to deselect it, you can drag the playhead on the Reference monitor to any frame in the sequence. This lets you look at any two frames of the video at the same time, allowing for delicate comparisons of footage, with and without filters (see Figure 9.12). Other editing programs such as Final Cut Pro also offer different interfaces, such as a Frame Viewer tool, to allow such comparisons.

Figure 9.12
When taken out of gang mode, the Reference monitor allows comparison of two clips in separate locations on the timeline. This is helpful for creating consistent color effects throughout your footage, such as when intercutting interview footage with dancing footage, as shown here.

A final tool for comparing a clip with an effect applied with the original is Match Frame, which determines a clip's source footage and time code on the timeline and displays it in the Source panel, providing a handy reference to the original (see Figure 9.13). Using the Match Frame tool is easy: With your playhead on the frame you are trying to match in the timeline, press the M key on the keyboard to show the clip in the Source panel, displaying that exact frame. Applying and tweaking filters is just one use for the very handy Match Frame tool, which is also useful for reassessing original audio, looking at the options for clip adjustments, and simply finding a master clip that may be hiding in the files of a particularly large project.

Figure 9.13
Using the Match Frame function enables you to easily bring up a specific frame in the Source panel, which can then be compared to the affected version in the Program panel. Here, a frame is shown without and with the Posterize filter applied.

Filter Rendering

When you apply a filter to a clip, Premiere Pro lets you immediately preview the effect in the Program panel, but that's really only a simulation of what the effect will actually look like in your final rendered video. Sometimes, this preview is accurate enough for editing, but sometimes you have to actually render the effect to feel comfortable that the look is right.

To render an effect, press the Enter key on your keyboard or choose Sequence > Render Effects in Work Area. During rendering, Premiere Pro applies the effects to the source footage and creates a new clip, which it stores in the location designated in your preferences. While rendering takes place, all editing must stop.

Rendering used to be a massively time-consuming affair—one that often occurred over long lunches or even overnight. As computers and graphics cards have become more powerful, Premiere Pro's unrendered previews have become more accurate, and rendering has become quicker (see Figure 9.14). Often, with light effects applied, affected clips can be viewed in real time, without rendering. With heavier effects, you'll still have to preview to get an accurate feel for final appearance.

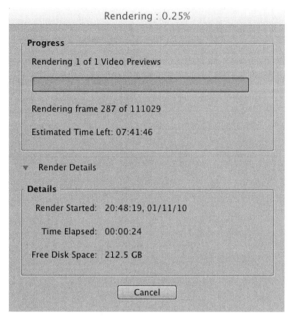

Figure 9.14
Rendering times have decreased tremendously with improved computer speeds. Heavily applied effects can still take awhile, though, so it's still worthwhile to plan the timing of longer renders carefully, as you cannot edit and render at the same time. Adobe Premiere Pro's Render window provides useful information about how long the render will take and how much space will be required.

Editing programs offer different real-time viewing settings for unrendered files and offer different speeds for creating rendered files—both of which are also hardware dependent. Find a compromise that enables you to see effects quickly at a decent image quality so that you can easily experiment to find image effects you like.

Some programs offer auto rendering at designated intervals. This can be a fun feature when you leave your computer for lunch and are surprised to return to a fully rendered piece, but can be a time and space suck when you are working continuously. Turn auto render off if you plan to spend large chunks of time editing.

When your piece is complete, with effects, graphics, and animation, you will have to render the whole thing—even though parts will already be rendered. More information about rendering for final output can be found in Chapter 10, "Output and Delivery."

Basic Compositing

As discussed in Chapter 8, when video layers are stacked on top of each other, only the top layer will show by default. The art of *compositing*, however, allows for several tracks of video to be shown in layers, creating a collage-like effect. Compositing is used in creating special effects, often using green-screen techniques that allow for the blending of tracks to insert a subject into a background entirely different from the one on which he or she was shot.

Wedding videos rarely offer the opportunity for advanced compositing; such effects typically require a lot of planning and time to shoot. Furthermore, couples tend to prefer a realistic rendition of their event. But some simpler compositing techniques regularly come into play when editing a wedding video. Your ability to comfortably manipulate multiple layers of video will give the wedding piece a higher level of sophistication.

In its simplest form, compositing involves stacking two clips top of each other on the timeline. At full opacity (no transparency), only the top line of video will be seen, as shown in Figure 9.15. If, however, the opacity of the top clip is lowered, making it partially transparent, the image underneath will be visible, as shown in Figure 9.16. With two pieces of moving footage, there is seldom a use for this simplistic compositing effect, which tends to look messy. But understanding the basic concept of opacity will enable you to appreciate other compositing tools.

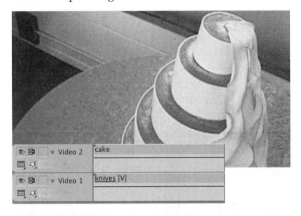

Figure 9.15
This image is the result of two clips stacked on the timeline at full opacity. Only the top clip, the cake, is visible.

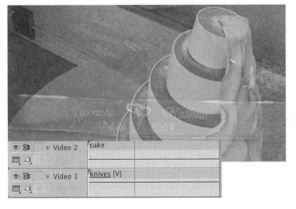

Figure 9.16
This shows the same two clips stacked on the timeline, with the top clip brought down to 50-percent opacity, as indicated by the Opacity line being lowered on Video Track 1. As a result, the clip underneath, showing the cake knives, is visible.

You can change a clip's opacity by dragging the Opacity handles on the timeline, which appear as lines in the middle of the video track. Place your pointer over the Opacity handle; then, when the handle turns into a two-headed arrow, click and drag the Opacity handle down or up to adjust opacity. (You may have to toggle on your timeline handles to see this feature). Opacity will always default to 100 percent, but can be brought to any level.

Split Screen

You can manipulate the size and position (centering) of one track of video to make room for a second track of video on the screen. Simply stack another re-sized, re-centered image on top of the first in the timeline to see them both at once, splitting the screen. You aren't limited to sharing the screen between two video layers to equal size; you can stack infinite layers at customized sizes.

To change the size and position of a video clip, double-click the clip in the Timeline panel to open it in the Source panel and click the Effect Controls tab. Open the Motion control and you'll find settings for scaling, rotating, and centering the video layer. Cropping is also useful for creating split screen composites by allowing more of the visual real estate space to be dedicated to the important parts of the image. Some programs, such as Final Cut Pro, include options for cropping an image under the Motions tab; others, such as Adobe Premiere Pro, have a separate effect for cropping.

There are numerous scenarios in which a split-screen effect can help your storytelling. For example, using one in interview sequences—showing a guest talking on one side while images of people dancing are shown on the other—enables you to move the story along more quickly, without spending too long on a boring head shot. If you interview the bride and groom, intercutting them jointly as they tell their courtship story can be amusing—especially if there are discrepancies in their versions of the story (see Figure 9.17).

Figure 9.17
This split-screen image shows Matt and Jovie each telling their sides of their courtship story. In this carefully cut sequence, they are finishing each other sentences—a fun trick when content allows.

Split-screen imagery can also be good for getting a lot of visual information out quickly. If your clients want a short video but you have a lot of good images of a particular section, showing three or four images at once can effectively compact a lot of data. As when you are working with one layer of video, the speed, size, and transitions in your split-screen segment will help create a mood (see Figure 9.18).

Figure 9.18
This is a complicated example of split-screen imagery, built using the tools described in this section. In this interview, shot during the morning of the event, Jovie is talking about how excited she is for the reception later in the day. Reception images shown simultaneously liven up her dialogue, provide a visual reference to what she is saying, and allow a lot of information to be presented at once, making for a fast-paced and fun video.

Mattes

Akin to a stencil, a *matte* is a layer that masks, or covers, part of a video layer. Covering part of a layer is an important part of compositing because it enables you to show or apply an effect to only part of an image. There are different types of mattes, which can block out luminance (light), chrominance (color), or even a portion of the image. In Premiere Pro, you can find a number of matte-related filters in the Channel and Keying folders in the Video Effects tab.

Using mattes allows you to mix video with and without effects—for example, a shot of the bride that is black and white except for her bouquet, which is in color. To create that image, you'd take these steps:

1. Select and duplicate the video you want to work with.

2. Stack the duplicate clips on top of each other on the timeline.

3. Apply a garbage matte to the top layer. A garbage matte enables you to define an area of the image to appear in the final rendered video, with all else excluded. Premiere Pro has four-point, eight-point and 16-point garbage matte

effects; I'm using the four-point garbage matte effect here. After applying the effect, move the points of the matte to create a contiguous zone encompassing the part of the image that you want to keep (in this case, the bouquet).

4. Apply the Black & White filter (in the Image Control subfolder of the Video Effects folder) to the bottom clip.

Following these steps produces a composite video in which the garbage matte hides everything in the top, color video except the part of the image that you want to keep, allowing the bottom, desaturated image to show through (see Figure 9.19). In this case, the fully colored bouquet would appear over the black-and-white background.

Figure 9.19
Two identical images are stacked, or composited, in this figure. The top image, which is sharpened, has a garbage matte, "throwing away" everything outside the four adjustable points which surround the bouquet. The bottom image was converted to black and white and softened with a Gaussian blur, and fills the area "discarded" by the garbage matte on the top image. Eight-point and 16-point garbage mattes can be used for finer precision, as can various other mattes that come with any editing program.

Titles

Whether layered on a piece of video or on a solid background, titles are a basic form of compositing. Some wedding videos use only a logo or the couple's names; others go to great length to give credit to every member of the bridal party and all the vendors. Regardless of how many titles you use, understanding how they work and some basic style techniques will help you make your video look sharp.

Your creativity will dictate the look of your titles, but here are a few stylistic considerations:

▶ Create your titles to reflect your company. That way, you can build a template that you can reuse that will reinforce the branding of your videography business.

▶ Create titles that reflect themes of the couple's wedding—for example, using the colors and fonts they chose for their invitations (assuming those colors and fonts are visually appealing and legible in video). Maintaining the visual themes selected by the couple is one detail your clients will notice and appreciate.

▶ Consider whether you want your titles to go over video images or on a plain colored slate. If titles are to be superimposed, be sure to select images in your rough cut that will accommodate composited titles. Typically, these would be close-ups or images that don't have too much action.

Types of Titles

There are many types of titles (see Figure 9.20). Familiarity with the names of these will help you use your editing program's titling function to its fullest potential:

▶ **Title card.** An unmoving title.

▶ **Opening/closing credits.** A series of credits that starts or finishes a movie. For a feature, opening credits might include the names of the studio, director, producer, lead actors, and so on, with closing credits being more extensive. In the case of a wedding video, such credits may include the couple's names, the date, the locations, parents' names, the names of members of the bridal party, the videography company, other vendors, and so on. Some video editors build elaborate opening title sequences similar to those found in feature films; others prefer a simple title or two.

▶ **Title roll.** Credits that scroll from the bottom of the screen to the top. These are usually used for opening and closing credits, as they are an efficient way to pack in a lot of information.

▶ **Title crawl.** A line of titles that moves horizontally across the screen, usually along the bottom. A crawl is often used to describe or editorialize video content.

▶ **Superimposed.** Titles placed, or superimposed, over other video or graphics.

▶ **Lower thirds.** Titles that fit in the lower third of the frame, usually used to identify a speaker.

▶ **Pad.** A box or stripe behind a title to make it more visible and legible.

Figure 9.20
The size, placement, color, font, and type of titles used will lend various feels to your video. In this figure, all the images use the same straightforward font but create a different tone due to the type of title built. Image A is a title card, image B is a title crawl (in progress), image C is superimposed, and image D is a title roll (in progress).

Generating Titles

All editing programs give you an option for creating titles. Indeed, as editing software has matured, titling options have dramatically improved; most editing programs enable you to build very complex sequences. That being said, you may find it easier to create your title sequences using the more refined tools of an external titling or effects program. Titles built using your software program (as opposed to being imported from another program) are called *generated video*. Generated video operates just as source video does (although it might require rendering with greater frequency).

To build a generated video title, select the type of title you want to build (your program will have a list similar to the one in the preceding section) and use the Title tool in the viewer to change the text, font, colors, drop shadows, and other parameters to suit your style. The resulting text in the Project panel operates exactly as if it were a piece of video; use in points and out points, drag and drop, inserts, and overwrite edits to move text to the timeline (see Figure 9.21). Once the text is on the timeline, all the fine editing tools are available. As with audio, it's best to place all your titles on a single, otherwise uninhabited track of video. If your title is already on the timeline but requires changes to the words or design, double-click the title clip in the timeline to reopen the title and make the necessary changes.

Figure 9.21
Adobe Premiere Pro's Titler enables you to look at the title you are creating with and without the footage underneath it. This feature is a big timesaver, since the alternative is to repeatedly open the Title tool to inspect for the inevitable, minute adjustments.

 If you have a lot of titles, write them in a word processing program first so that you can more easily proofread them for spelling and grammar. Then cut and paste the error-free titles into the titling utility of your editing software.

Some editing programs include the option for title rolls and typewriter text (text that appears one letter at a time). Instead of specifying how quickly these titles move, most programs have you specify when the title should begin and end and then determine an even pace automatically. Stretching a timed title will slow down the movement; shortening it will speed it up.

Title Style

When designing your titles, make sure to consider legibility. Remember that the TV screen on which the video may be viewed may have less resolution than your computer, so it's important both to style your titles with care and to preview all titles carefully on your external monitor. Factors that contribute to a title's legibility (or lack thereof) include the following:

▶ **Typeface.** Choose a style that is clear and solid. A typeface with delicate swirls or very thin lines can be difficult to read, and may flicker on a TV screen.

▶ **Size.** The typeface you use will help determine how small a font can be and still be legible, but a general rule of thumb is to use a font size larger than 20 points.

▶ **Color.** Because your titling utility may allow colors that aren't color safe for TV, make sure to check video scopes and an external monitor to ensure the color is color safe and looks clean.

▶ **Superimposition.** Superimposing a title over video can look great and be an efficient presentation of a lot of information, but be careful that the video underneath the titles isn't too busy to accommodate a graphic. Fast-moving images with a lot of action or clutter can make the title text hard to read.

▶ **Position.** To accommodate differences in television sets, a video signal will contain more information than can be displayed. This is called the *overscan area*. Because the overscan area cannot be precisely determined, lowest common denominators have been calculated as guidelines, usually called the *title safe* area. As long as your titles stay within the title safe lines, they will be visible on any TV screen. Your software will provide a toggle for displaying these guidelines; make sure it's on while you position your titles (see Figure 9.22). If you're producing video solely for the Web, you don't have to worry about these guidelines because there is no overscan; the entire video frame is seen.

Figure 9.22
When applying titles, be sure to turn on your safety overlays, which will show where on your screen you can place titles and have them visible on any monitor. Plot-driving action should also be kept within these guidelines so that the viewer doesn't miss valuable information. Notice that in this image, the groom's eyes are outside the action safe region, indicating that perhaps a wider shot would be a better choice.

Importing Other Graphics

Some titles require more precision or detail than can be accommodated by an internal titling utility. In addition, there is often a need to import a graphic, such as a logo or a scanned image, such as a wedding invitation, that was built in another program. Your editing program will be able import various types of graphics, including JPEGs, TIFs, and Photoshop files. Note that you may have to reformat or resize a file in order to use it in your sequence. Make sure you are familiar with your sequence settings so you can appropriately size the images to match.

Motion and Animation

Animation is the process of creating the effect of movement with a video clip or graphic. It does not refer to the movement that may be occurring within the footage—for example, a bride and groom dancing—but instead to the movement of the entire layer of video across the screen (see Figure 9.23).

Figure 9.23
Animating a clip does not make elements within the clip move; rather, it makes the entire image, or piece of footage, move around the screen. In this figure, the clip is animated to move from the top-left corner to the bottom-right corner, as indicated by the dotted line tracing the clip movement.

Animation relies on a process called *keyframing*. In traditional cel animation, an artist draws the character as it appears at various points of time, usually at regular intervals. These cels are called keyframes. Once keyframe images are defined, artists fill in, or *interpolate*, the images required to get from one keyframe to the next. Computer animation operates in the same way: You specify the keyframes, or points where motion should start and stop; and your video editor then generates the intervening, or interpolated, frames.

Animation can be used to change many properties of a clip, including size, shape, position, cropping, and rotation. This is particularly handy for livening up photo-montage sequences and opening-title sequences. Furthermore, most editing programs enable you to animate filters so the effect appears (or disappears) over time instead of all at once. For example, you might apply an animated desaturation effect with the image starting in black and white and returning to full color by the end of the clip.

 You will learn to move and rotate images in the Chapter 11 tutorial.

Audio Editing

Audio is often ignored in the production and post-production process—which is a huge mistake. Good sound will contribute to the feel of a story, inviting viewers into the wedding as guests at the event and making them feel as if the celebration were happening around them. Bad sound will be a constant reminder that the video they are watching is a two-dimensional representation of some things that happened one night. For a compelling and inviting story, having good audio is imperative.

Wedding-video sound is particularly difficult because these videos often contain sections that are very visually driven. That is to say, details of the reception room or of the bride's dress often don't come with a compelling soundtrack. It's your job, both in the basic edit and the sound edit, to make sure that the audio doesn't alienate these images but helps bring them to life.

Another complicating factor to wedding video sound is that, as with most of the video images, you have only one opportunity to capture audio. Unlike a feature film, you aren't afforded multiple takes; the bride says her vows once. Plus, she might have a huge sniffle in the middle, or you might wind up with some interference on your microphone. Either way, you are stuck with what you've got. The trick to creating inviting sound for a wedding video is to get audio that is true to the event and to mix your natural and added sound well.

It's likely that you will have enough tools within your software program to edit and mix your sound. If you find you need more capabilities and filters, dedicated sound programs will be compatible with any editing program you have.

Assessing Your Tracks on the Timeline

Having completed a rough cut, your basic audio should be on the timeline, ready for you to begin refining and correcting. As a reminder, it's good practice to dedicate certain tracks to natural audio, music, and sound effects. Among other things, this separation will help you easily make a systemic change to audio that comes from one source, such as the reception sound; it will be sitting on one track, ready for you.

Before starting the sound edit, take the time to listen to the whole thing. It goes without saying that you will need a decent set of speakers for a critical audio analysis. Leave the output audio at a constant volume as you listen; if you find yourself constantly needing to adjust the sound levels of the output, it's an indication that you have some work to do on your sound levels. As you listen to your audio, take note of the following:

▶ **Sound content.** Is the content inviting, or does it feel flat? Are there long sections with no natural audio? Does the content match the music well?

▶ **Sound levels.** Can you hear the dialogue over the music? Does the music change volume levels over the course of the video? Are the effects loud enough?

▶ **Sound problems.** Listen and take note of hums, dropouts, clicks, and other noises so that you can go back and correct them.

Developing Your Audio

It's important to be entirely satisfied with the audio content before spending time adjusting the levels and adding filters to help audio quality. If you review your rough cut and find that your content feels flat or unrealistic, there are a few things you can do to liven it up and round it out that relate strictly to the content, not the levels and quality. Following are some common problems and solutions:

▶ Natural audio from wedding footage can tend to feel a bit messy, as it's often in small, spaced-out bites instead of continuous dialogue. If this is the case, try filling the spaces between the bits of audio with music or with room tone. This will help create a more continuous and encompassing sound. Having a separate audio recording of the wedding band from an MP3 recorder is one way to get continuous sound that can help smooth these sections.

▶ Sometimes, a video montage doesn't seem to fit well with the music underneath it. Indeed, a frequent complaint about wedding videos is that they are "images thrown on music." But montage sections might be important to your style or to your client—they show off the details that the client has worked hard on—so putting images to music is necessary. To liven up montages, first make sure you have picked music that fits the images. Using the right song will make a difference. Then, try to make all your cuts land on the beats of the music; this will go a long way to more intimately tying together audio and video that aren't naturally connected. Finally, consider adding natural sound clips. Did the bride say something about dress shopping in her interview? That might work very well with a montage of her preparation. Are there sound bites of the groomsmen giving the groom a hard time? That could be very funny placed over some playful couple shots, or poignant if placed over shots of the group of guys all together. Audio effects such as Champagne corks popping, cars driving up, and applause can be used the same way. Adding sound bites certainly won't work in every style or situation, however. Don't stretch too hard make sound bites fit; that can create discord or a lack of warmth in your audio.

▶ When possible, use natural audio for the first dances. The band version of the first dance will tend to be warmer than a studio recording of the same. If the band version is too hard to cut to or doesn't sound good, try incorporating the opening and closing applause and the crowd reaction during the dance. It may not be possible to separate out these sounds, but if you can, it will boost the realism and accessibility of your soundtrack immensely.

▶ Try adding a low-level track of the natural audio or room tone, even in places where no sound bites are used. The low-level buzz of the bridesmaids getting ready together or the clinks and murmurs of dinner in addition to music will add depth to these scenes. If there isn't enough room tone to cover the time you need filled, try duplicating the amount you have and adding more of the same. At low enough volume levels, you might be able to get away with it.

Live Level Adjustments

Once you have the audio you will be using on the timeline, it's time to work with the audio levels. All editing programs have a meter that shows output levels of all your tracks; many also have a tool that shows each track output individually (see Figure 9.24). In digital audio, the combined output of all the audio tracks should never exceed 0 decibels (dB), or there will be clipping and distortion.

Figure 9.24
In this elegant audio mix tool, each track of audio on the timeline gets its own volume slider. A combined output is shown by the master control on the right. Icons enable you to live mix, *solo track* (listen to the tracks individually), and change the pan, or direction, of the sound.

To keep audio levels even without going above a combined level of 0, each track should be well below that level. A general guideline is to set dialogue and natural audio to between −12dB and −6dB, and music to between −18dB and −12dB. (You'll learn how to set levels in the tutorial at the end of this chapter.) These levels, in combination, will tend to peak around −6dB to −3dB below the maximum level, but will still have to be checked throughout to ensure levels are correct. Minute adjustments may have to be made to accommodate particularly loud points, such as applause and laughter.

Some programs have a function that scans your sequence for audio levels that are higher than 0dB, leaving markers when levels are too high. This allows easy navigation right to the trouble spots on the timeline for readjustment.

Most programs allow audio adjustment right on the timeline. Just as the video tracks have a line through them indicating opacity, audio tracks have a line through them indicating sound levels. Unlike video, however, audio levels do not default to the highest point, but to a midpoint. Dragging them up or down will raise or lower the audio output. Keyframing audio is also regularly used, allowing gradual changes in sound. Audio keyframing can usually be "written" right onto the timeline with a Pen tool. This is an intuitive process; using two points to drag the audio line up will make levels louder, while using two points to drag the audio line down will fade the sound (see Figure 9.25).

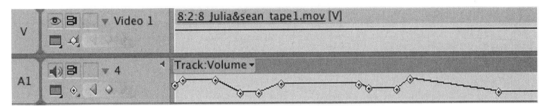

Figure 9.25
This figure shows keyframes applied to the audio line level on the timeline. When the keyframes go up, so does the volume. This example shows a slow fadeout at the end. Keyframes are particularly important, as they enable you to bring the volume of music up and down to accommodate other audio, such as dialogue.

Using the Mix Tool

Some editing programs come with a built-in sound mixer, which enables you to mix audio on the fly. The display, which looks like a studio sound board, has a graphical slider for each track of audio. While listening to the audio, drag the audio levers up or down to adjust the volume on each track individually. Each movement of a slider will keyframe the corresponding audio track so that the changes are dynamic over time. When you are finishing listening and adjusting the track levers, the tracks on your timeline will be keyframed to match the audio levels you selected. The keyframes can be further adjusted on the timeline, if need be.

Transitions

Adding transitions between audio tracks often helps smooth out dramatic changes between types of audio by mixing some frames of audio from the outgoing clip with some frames of audio from the incoming clip. This can also be a gentle way to introduce audio from silence. Audio transitions are applied the same way as video transitions: by dragging a transition onto the track at the edit point. Double-click the transition to its adjust parameters. Don't be lulled into applying transitions out of habit, though; clean audio should transition itself. Besides, a dramatic audio change is sometimes effective for storytelling.

Correcting Audio Problems

Some sound problems can be eliminated or covered. Sound problems that can be eliminated include clicks, pops, and any incidental noise that doesn't occur at the same time as important dialogue or other important sounds. To eliminate them, simply cut them out of the timeline. It might help to enlarge the timeline and toggle on the waveform overlays so that you can see where the noise you are cutting is located (see Figure 9.26). When you cut the sound out, avoid using a ripple delete or closing the gap where the sound was located. This will pull all the audio after that point out of sync. Instead, fill the space with room tone. (You'll learn how to do this in the tutorial at the end of this chapter.)

Although detailed coverage of this is beyond the scope of this book, note that you can send your audio to Adobe Soundbooth, a program in Adobe's CS4 suite that provides tools for working with audio. To send your audio from Adobe Premiere Pro to Adobe Soundbooth, right-click the file in Premiere and choose Edit in Adobe Soundbooth > Render and Replace from the menu that appears. To locate a powerful tool for cleaning up your audio, search Soundbooth's help information for "Remove a Sound."

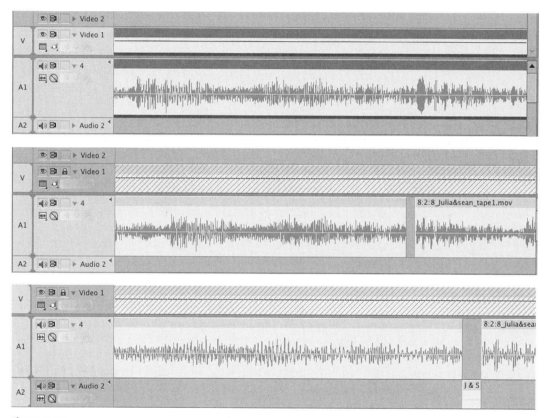

Figure 9.26
This figure shows keyframes applied to the audio line level on the timeline. When the keyframes go up, so does the volume. This example shows a slow fadeout at the end. Keyframes are particularly important, as they enable you to bring the volume of music up and down to accommodate other audio, such as dialogue.

Sounds that can be covered are of the same nature—clicks, pops, and hisses—but they tend to occur in places where eliminating them would interfere with dialogue or other necessary sound. In this case, the best you can do is use music or other effects to cover the extraneous noise. As with video, the listener's experience of audio can be guided; a well-placed clink of glassware, a limousine door closing, a child laughing, or a music cue can do wonders to divert ears from a small sound error.

Systemic sound errors—such as persistent hums, hisses, and buzzes, or the wind blowing—are harder to correct. To fix these troubled tracks, look to your software's equalizer, or EQ, and then to other specific filters.

EQ

Different parts of the sound spectrum have different frequencies. As shown in Figure 9.27, an *equalizer* lets you adjust the frequencies individually using graphical knobs or sliders that represent the volume of each piece, measured in Hertz (Hz) or kilohertz (kHz). Instead of changing the volume of an entire sound, the sliders adjust the sound in sections.

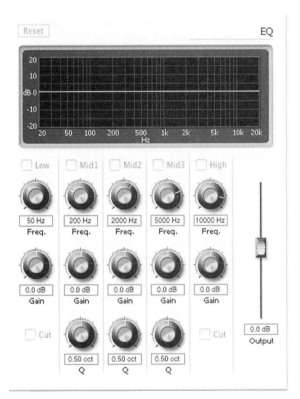

Figure 9.27
Every editing program should have a version of an EQ filter. It's a basic tool for audio adjustment.

The best way to get skilled with EQ sliders is to experiment with them, but here are some tips for using EQ in specific situations that may arise as you edit the audio in a wedding video.

▶ You can reduce wind and microphone noise by minimizing low frequencies (60–120Hz).

▶ You can reduce hisses and other high-frequency noises by minimizing high frequencies (5,000Hz, or 5kHz).

▶ You can make muffled dialogue more intelligible by raising the mid-range frequencies (2,000Hz, or 2kHz).

Other Filters

Although EQ is the most common fix for audio problems—and the effect most likely to be included with your software—there are other filters that can help you adjust your audio to make it clean and well balanced. These include the following:

▶ **Noise reduction.** This is an Adobe Soundbooth feature that enables you to identify and remove background noises, which is very effective for regular noises like microphone hum or air-conditioning whine. Typically, noise reduction won't work with irregular noise like crowd or traffic noise.

▶ **Compression.** A compression filter limits the dynamic range of a piece of audio—that is, the distance between the softest and the loudest points. For example, if a song contains some parts that are so quiet they must be turned up and some parts so loud they must be turned down, the range should be compressed.

▶ **Reverb.** A reverb filter matches the audio from your lavaliere microphone to the microphone on your camera by adding a short room reflection, or *ambience*, to the lavaliere audio. This makes it seem like it was shot with more background warmth than it actually was.

▶ **Shelf.** High and low shelf filters cut off high and low frequencies within an audio track, respectively. This can be useful for eliminating hisses (high frequency), equipment hums (low frequencies), and other persistent background sounds.

▶ **Gate.** Gate filters automatically drop the volume when a certain minimum audio level, or *threshold*, is met. If the background noise during wedding vows is high, you can't really turn it down; doing so will also lower the sound of the bride and groom speaking their piece. In the spaces between their vows, however, the audio will be lower, meeting the gate filter threshold. In those spaces, the gate filter will automatically lower the audio, keeping the ambient noise from being a distraction.

Sound editing will go more quickly if you familiarize yourself with your program's tools for listening to soloed tracks and combined audio. Make sure you know how to both single out, or *solo*, a track and then listen to the same track with all the others turned on.

External Plug-ins and Programs

Occasionally, you will find that your editing program is not robust enough in a particular area to achieve the look or sound you are after. In that case, you will want to find an external application or plug-in that can handle the task for you. A plug-in typically handles a small task, such as providing unique audio or video filters. Once installed, they work within your own editing software. Internet searches will easily lead you to plug-ins on an as-needed basis. It's also a good idea to keep an eye on what is available before you need it, especially with filters that provide unique looks and styles rather than just corrective tools. This will help you keep your ideas and videos new and inspired.

As discussed in Chapter 4, "Post-Production Gear," most editing software comes bundled with additional programs that can handle effects, titling, sound editing, and color correction. While these additional applications are useful—and may be a good reason to select a given package—most editing can be done from your primary application. Before attempting to become an expert in five or six programs at once, learn your primary editing application well. After you discover its limitations with respect to the style you want to achieve, you can focus your attention on determining which specialized programs will allow for the best use of your time and energy.

Following are features available through external programs that are not typically offered in primary editing software:

> ▶ **Sound programs.** These offer an interface designed specifically for audio editing, more tools for sound correction, specialized tools for certain types of audio (e.g., music or dialogue), royalty-free music tracks and sound effects, and surround sound support.

> ▶ **Effects programs.** These offer an interface designed specifically for effects, more specialized filters, comprehensive layering and masking tools, 3D graphics options, and customizable design templates.

> ▶ **Color-correction programs.** These offer an interface designed specifically for color correction, built-in color effects and looks, and specialized tools for particular tasks.

> ▶ **Titling programs.** These offer an interface designed for titles, the ability to adjust by character and word, and customizable design templates.

Summary

Moving your project from a rough cut to a polished final version takes an eye for detail and a tremendous amount of patience. It is also one important factor in separating the professional wedding videographers from their amateur counterparts. The ability to use the more advanced parts of your software program—such as audio editing, color correction, and compositing—with an eye (and ear!) for quality and aesthetics will make your product a standout. This chapter familiarizes you with methods and tools to bring your video up to a level where you can proudly show it off, knowing you have done everything you can to make each shot as good as possible.

What's Next

Really? We're not done yet? Well...not quite—but very close! Chapter 10 will help you take your finished edited sequence from your editing application to the final form in which you present it to the client. It also discusses archiving and backing up your files, which you must do to ensure that you can easily retrieve data if need be.

Chapter 9 Tutorial: Refine the Rough Cut

This tutorial teaches you more advanced editing skills to refine the rough cut of a wedding video. To complete this tutorial, you will need a copy of Adobe Premiere Pro. You will also need to copy the files from the DVD accompanying this book to your computer hard drive. Instructions to download a trial version of Premiere Pro and to copy the DVD are found in the Chapter 4 tutorial.

To begin this tutorial, navigate to Wedding Video_Start to Finish > Chapter 9 and launch Adobe Premiere by double-clicking the Refining a Rough Cut project file in the Chapter 9 folder. Allow the scratch disks to be set to your Documents folder at the dialog box prompt. Open the Sequences bin in your Project panel and notice that it has two finished sequences (M&J_Refining_Finished and Color Correction_Finished) and two started sequences (M&J_Refining_Start and Color Correction_Start). In this tutorial, we will use the started sequences to build to the finished ones, which you can review as reference.

Adding Video Effects

Start by double-clicking the M&J_Refining_Start icon in the Project panel to open it. Our first step to dressing up this sequence will be to add some effects. We will apply a basic black-and-white effect to four clips. To add the black-and-white effect, follow these steps:

1. Choose Windows > Effects or press Shift+7 to open the Effects tab.
2. In the Effects tab, navigate to Effects > Video Effects > Image Control > Black & White.
3. Drag the icon for the Black & White effect to the dress clip in the Timeline panel, which starts at time code 20:00. Drag the playhead over the clip; notice that the clip now appears in black and white in the Program panel.
4. Double-click the dress clip in the Timeline panel to open it in the Source panel.
5. Click the Effect Controls tab in the Source panel.
6. To see the difference between the clip with and without the effect in the Program panel, click the *fx* icon to the left of the Black and White effect to toggle the effect on and off.

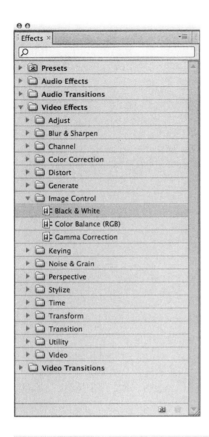

Apply all effects using the method described here: by dragging an effect's icon onto the clip in the timeline. To delete an effect, select the effect by clicking its name in the Effect Controls panel of any given clip and press the Del key on your keyboard.

You can paste effects from one clip to another; that way, you don't have to reapply the effects by hand. To do so, follow these steps:

1. In the timeline, select the clip whose effects you want to copy (in this case, the dress clip with the Black & White effect applied).

2. Select Edit > Copy or press Command+C (Mac) or Ctrl+C (PC) to copy the clip.

3. Select a clip to which you want to apply the same effects. (In this case, select the three clips that follow the dress clip on the timeline—shoes, zip dress, and garter—by using the default Selection tool to draw a marquee around them.)

4. Select Edit > Paste Attributes or press Option+Command+C (Mac) or Option+Ctrl+C (PC). This pastes the effects of the copied clip but not the clip's contents. Now the four clips should all appear black and white.

Compositing Effects

In this exercise, we will layer tracks of video to create a slightly more complicated vignette effect. Remember: In default compositing modes, only the top layer of video shows if layers are at full opacity, so we will create duplicate layers and change opacity levels to look at multiple layers and more complicated effects.

To create a duplicate set of clips, follow these steps:

1. On the timeline, select the following clips, starting at time code 40:05. (To select the clips, draw a marquee around the clips on the timeline using the default Selection tool.)

   ▶ M&J_couple_1

   ▶ M&J_couple_2

   ▶ M&J_couple_3

   ▶ first kiss

   ▶ recessional

2. Select Edit > Copy or press Command+C (Mac) or Ctrl+C (PC) to copy the clips.

3. At the end of the timeline, paste the five clips anywhere after the end of the sequence by dragging the playhead beyond 1:12 or so on the timeline and selecting Edit > Paste or pressing Command+V (Mac) or Ctrl+V (PC).

4. Select the newly pasted clips and drag them directly above the original clips (the ones you selected in step 1), on Video Track 3.

You can enable Premiere's Snap feature to give clips a magnetic-like property that attracts them to precise edit points on the timeline. This helps ensure that your two sets of five clips are perfectly aligned. To enable Snap, choose Sequence > Snap or toggle it on and off by pressing the S key on the keyboard.

5. Video Track 3 is currently at full opacity. As a result, the changes you make to Video Track 2 can't be seen as you look at the clips in the Program panel. To view Video Track 2, toggle off the track output of Video Track 3 by clicking the eye icon near the track name in the track header on the left.

6. Apply the following effects to the five original clips—the ones on Video Track 2—by selecting all the clips at once and then dragging each effect's icon from the Effects tab onto the clips on the timeline. (For the time being, ignore the video on Video Track 1, which has already been covered by the cutaways.)

   ▶ Video Effects > Blur & Sharpen > Gaussian Blur

   ▶ Video Effects > Image Control > Black & White

   ▶ Video Effects > Transform > Edge Feather

7. Double-click the first of the five original clips (on Video Track 2) and then click the Effects Control tab in the Source panel.

8. Click the Gaussian Blur triangle to view its parameters.

9. Change the Blurriness setting under Gaussian Blur to 12.0.

10. Click the Edge Feather triangle to view its parameters.

11. Change the Amount setting under Edge Feather to 100.

 The Black & White effect does not offer any customizable parameters.

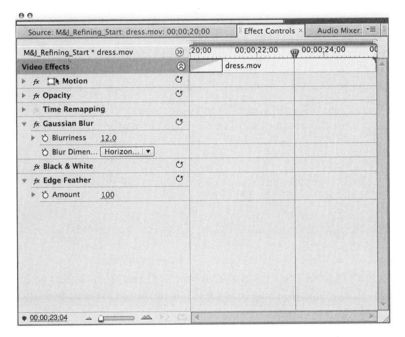

12. Repeat steps 7–11 for the remaining four original clips on Video Track 2.

 Another way to affect several clips would be to apply the effect to one clip only, change the parameters as needed, and then copy the clip attributes and paste them to the other clips, as described in the preceding section.

13. Now we will put effects on the duplicated clips on Video Track 3. To see your work, toggle back on the video output of Video Track 3; then select the five copied clips on Video Track 3.

14. Choose Effects > Video Effects > Transform > Edge Feather to apply an Edge Feather effect to the five clips.

15. Double-click the first of the five copied clips and click the Effects Control tab in the Source panel.

16. Click the Edge Feather triangle to view its parameters.

17. Change the Amount setting under Edge Feather to 85.

18. Click the Opacity triangle to view its parameters.

19. Change the Opacity setting to 60.0%.

20. Repeat steps 15–19 for the remaining four copied clips. Notice that these changes allow the edges of the vow clips on Video Track 1 to be seen, so we want to delete the video of the vow clips but leave the audio in, so that audio of the vows accompanies the effected clips.

21. Unlink the audio and video of the vow clips (M&J_vows_2 though M&J_vows_6) by selecting each clip and choosing Clip > Unlink.

22. Select the video of the five vow clips in Video Track 1 under the newly composited clips (M&J_vows_2 through M&J_vows_6) and delete them by pressing the Delete key on your keyboard. The audio should stay in place.

We have now created a soft, vignetted look with some of the color saturation removed. For additional practice, play around with the parameters of these effects or use other effects on either track of video.

 Animating effects is another advanced editing method to enhance your sequence. The tutorial for Chapter 11 contains exercises for animating.

Audio Editing

Before you begin editing the audio in your piece, it is a good idea to listen to the whole sequence, noting any problems such as audio levels that are off, unwanted noises or jagged transitions.

Adjusting Levels

Audio levels are *additive*, meaning they combine to produce the master output. At no point should audio on the master output be more than 0dB, which we took care of by lowering some of the interview audio in our rough cut. Now it is time to adjust levels so that spoken audio can be easily heard above the music, especially in the vows section where it is very low. From our work on the rough cut, our audio levels are currently at −10dB for the music track and +6dB for the vows clips.

1. If necessary, click the triangle next to Audio Track 1 in the timeline to fully expose the audio track and reveal the volume line.

2. Hover your mouse over the volume line of Matt_interview_1.mov until the cursor changes to the volume adjustment cursor; then click and drag the volume line for all the Matt interview clips down to approximately −3dB. This will ensure that at no point does Matt's speech go above 0.0 decibels, the limit for digital audio.

3. To more precisely change audio, double-click the audio clip so that it shows up in the Source panel; then click the Effects Control tab, click the Volume effect's triangle to open the effect, and enter the value in decibels that you want (using a minus sign if necessary) for the Level parameter.

The audio for the vows is still too quiet, but we can't take it above 6.0dB on the timeline. To add more volume, we will duplicate the whole track:

1. Unlink the audio and video in M&J_vows_1. To do so, select the clip on the timeline and choose Clip > Unlink.

2. Lock all the tracks except Audio Track 1.

3. Select all the audio for the six M&J_vows clips that begin at time code 37;05.

4. Select Edit > Copy or press Command+C (Mac) or Ctrl+C (PC) to copy the clips.

5. Click at the end of the timeline (after all the other clips) and select Edit > Paste or press Command+V (Mac) or Ctrl+V (PC) to paste the clips.

6. Unlock Audio Track 2 and click the track header to enable it. The track header will appear highlighted.

7. With the Snap feature enabled (press the S key on your keyboard or choose Sequence > Snap to toggle it on), drag all the copied clips to Audio Track 2 to sit beneath the original ones.

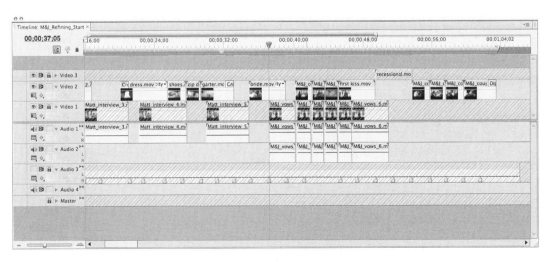

Although the audio is still a bit quiet, it is much better level now.

Add Room Tone

Currently, the dialogue audio is choppy, moving from talking and associated background noises to just music. To smooth it out, we will add a low-level background track and some transitions. We will start by adding room tone to the interview clips, placing the new audio on Audio Track 4 at the same point as the second interview clip begins. Follow these steps:

1. In the Project panel, open the Audio bin and double-click the m&J_roomtone.aif sound clip to open it in the Source panel.

2 Perform an overlay edit to place the entire m&J_roomtone clip on the timeline. To do so, select Audio Track 4 as the destination track. (Drag the A1 box to the left of Audio 4, click the A4 track header to make sure the track is active [the header will appear highlighted], and click the Audio 1, Audio 2, and Audio 3 track headers to make sure that they are not active.) Then place the playhead at the beginning of the second clip at time code 07;00, and choose Clip > Overlay or press the . (period) key on your keyboard.

While I generally encourage the use of keystroke commands, in this instance, an easier way to get the audio track in place is to simply drag the track from the Project panel to the spot on the timeline where you want it to appear (starting at time code 07;00). Remember to drag by clicking the icon associated with the file, not the filename.

3. Activate the Razor tool by pressing the C key on your keyboard or clicking the Razor icon in the toolbox.

4. Drag the playhead to the start of the M&J_Vows_1 at time code 37;05; then click the m&J_roomtone.aif clip at the playhead to cut the clip.

5. Press the V key on the keyboard or click the Selection icon in the toolbox to switch from the Razor tool to the default Selection tool. (This will prevent you from making accidental cuts with stray clicks while the Razor tool is activated.)

6. Delete the portion of the m&J_roomtone clip that is after time code 37;05 by selecting it with the default Selection tool and pressing the Delete key on your keyboard.

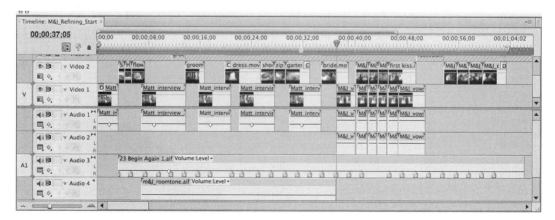

7. Bring the audio level of the room-tone clip down to about −16dB by either dragging the volume line down on the clip in the timeline or double-clicking the room-tone clip and changing the Volume Level parameter in the Effects tab in the Source panel, as described previously.

Add Audio Transitions

Audio transitions will help smooth out some of the places where the audio clips sound a bit jarring. To add audio transitions, follow these steps:

1. In the Effects tab, choose Audio Transitions > Crossfade > Exponential Fade.

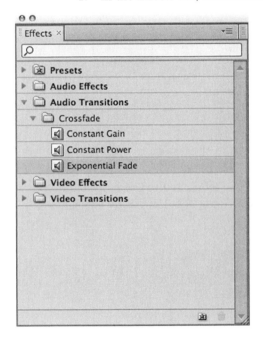

2. Drag the Exponential Fade icon to the beginning of the first audio clip of the timeline, Matt_interview_1, and release it. Notice that when you release the icon, purple lining represents the transition effect at the start of the audio clip in the timeline.

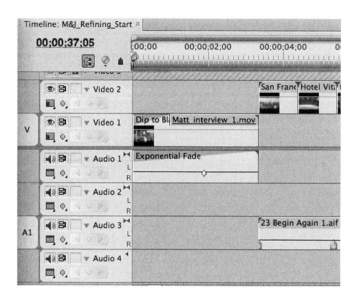

3. Double-click the purple lining for this transition effect to open it in the Source panel.

4. Change the Duration setting to 20 frames. (Click in the Duration field, type 20, and press Enter on your keyboard.) Notice that the purple lining gets shorter in the timeline.

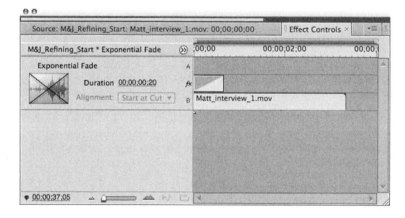

5. Drag another exponential fade to the end of the Matt_interview_1 audio clip in the timeline.

6. Double-click the purple lining for this transition effect to open it in the Source panel.

7. Change the Duration setting to 4 frames; notice that the purple lining becomes shorter in the timeline.

8. Select the four-frame transition you just applied and copy it by choosing Edit > Copy or pressing Command+C (Mac) or Ctrl+C (PC).

You might have to increase the viewing area of the timeline to select the transition. To do so, click the timeline. Then press the + key on your keyboard, press the Z key on your keyboard to use the Zoom tool, or move the timeline scale in the bottom-left corner of the timeline. (If you use the Zoom tool, make sure to return to the default Selection tool when you are finished.)

Now we will paste the four-frame transition at the beginning and ending of every Matt_interview clip:

1. Place the playhead at the beginning of the Matt_interview_2 clip (time code 07;00) and choose Edit > Paste or press Command+V (Mac) or Ctrl+V (PC) to paste in the four-frame transition.

2. Place the playhead at the end of the Matt_interview_2 clip (time code 13;27) and choose Edit > Paste or press Command+V (Mac) or Ctrl+V (PC) to paste in the four-frame transition.

3. Repeat steps 1 and 2 to paste the transition at the beginning and end of the three remaining interview clips.

For additional practice, use the clip called m&j_roomtone2, apply 20 frame transitions and perform volume adjustments to improve the evenness of sound in the vows section of the sequence.

Pressing the Page Down and Page Up keys moves you to the next or previous edit point on the timeline. These are convenient keys to use when applying transitions to the start of multiple clips on the timeline.

Adding Titles

In this exercise, we will use the Adobe Premiere Titler to add two titles to the sequence.

In addition to including native tools for creating titles, your editing software may provide access to additional programs for titling that offer more advanced capabilities and a smoother interface. That being said, you can create excellent titles using just those tools available within your primary editing application.

Add a Title Screen

The first title we will create will open the sequence, with a plain black background featuring our couple's names: Matt & Jyovanne. Click the Timeline panel to activate it; then click the Home key on your keyboard to move the playhead to the start of the sequence. Your Program window should be black. To build a title, start by doing the following:

1. Select Title > New Title > Default Still to launch the Titler.

2. Verify the following settings in the New Title dialog box that appears.

   ▶ Width: 720.

   ▶ Height:480.

   ▶ Timebase: 29.97 Drop Frame.

   ▶ Pixel Aspect Ratio: D1/DV NTSC Widescreen 16:9.

3. In the Name field, type **M&J Opening Title**.

4. Click OK; the Titler opens. Notice that it has several panels: Title Tools, Title Properties, Title Styles, Title Actions, and Main. We will mainly be concerned with the Main, Title Tools, and Title Properties panels.

5. To begin typing a title, activate the Type tool by pressing the T key on your keyboard or clicking the T button in the Title Tool panel.

6. Place the Type tool in the Titler's Main panel, type **Matt**, press **Enter**, and type **Jyovanne**. Pressing Enter between their names creates a line break.

7. With the text selected, click the Font Family down arrow in the Title Properties panel and choose #GungSeo from the list that appears. If you don't have this font, try Adobe Caslon Pro.

8. Ensure that the value in the Font Size field is 100.

9. Under the Fill checkbox, click the Color field to open the Color Picker, type DBD8D8 in the text field in the bottom-right corner of the Color Picker, and click OK.

10. Select the Shadow checkbox to generate a drop shadow. Then click the Color field, enter the color value 610C0C, and click OK.

11. Click the Opacity field under the Shadow checkbox, type 80, and press Enter.

12. Click the Distance field under the Shadow checkbox, type 5.0, and press Enter.

13. Click the Center Alignment icon in the Main panel to center your title. Then right-click the Matt Jyovanne text box in the Main panel, choose Position > Horizontal Center, and then right-click and choose Position > Vertical Center.

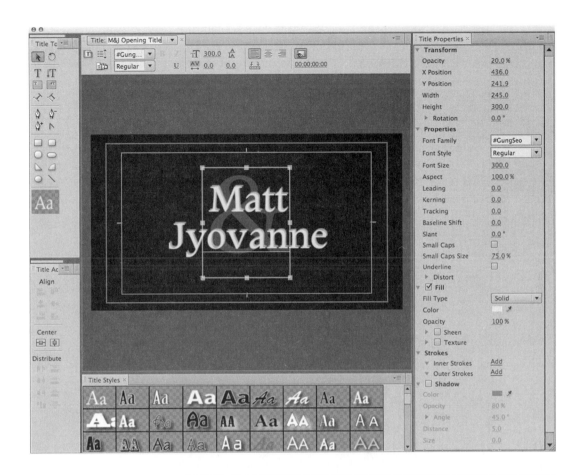

 To move a block of text around the frame in the Main panel, activate the Selection tool by pressing the V key on your keyboard or clicking the Selection tool in the Title Tool panel; then use the tool to drag text around.

14. Create a new text block by returning to the type tool and typing the ampersand (&) character onto the Titler's Main panel.

15. With the ampersand selected, adjust the parameters in the Title Properties panel to get a look you like. Here, we changed the following settings:

   ▶ Font Family: #GungSeo (If you don't have this font, try Adobe Caslon Pro.)

   ▶ Size: 300

   ▶ Color: 817272

   ▶ Opacity: 20

   ▶ Shadow: Deselected

16. As described previously, use the Selection tool in the Tool panel to move the ampersand to the middle of the existing text or right-click and choose Position > Horizontal Center, and then right-click and choose Position > Vertical Center.

17. If you are layering text, as shown in this example, you may have to specify which text blocks are on top and which are below. To do so, click a text block, right click it, and choose Select > Arrange > Bring to… to appropriately layer your title in front of or behind other pieces of text.

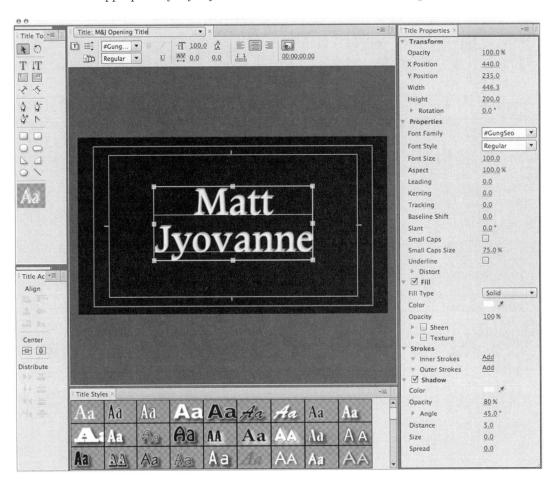

 As mentioned in this chapter, there are two white line boxes in the Titler's Main panel. These indicate title-safe and action-safe areas on the frame. To ensure that your titles are legible on all monitors, make sure your titles fall within the borders of the smaller box.

18. When you finish creating the title, click the Close button in the Titler's top-left corner (Macintosh) or top-right corner (Windows) to close it. Notice that the title now appears as a clip in the Project panel.

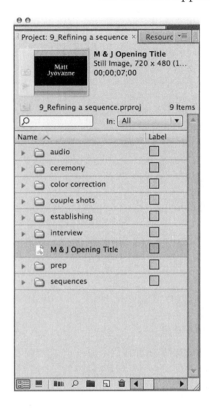

Now that the title is in the Project panel, it can be edited into the sequence like any other piece of video footage.

1. In the Project panel, click the title clip's icon and drag the clip to the Source panel. (If you double-click a title in the Project panel, the Titler, not the clip in the Source panel, will open.) With the title now open in the Source panel, it will operate the same way a piece of footage would.

2. In the Source panel, set an in point and an out point for the title clip, making the clip five seconds long.

3. Designate Video Track 4 as the destination track in the timeline by dragging the V text to the left of the Video 4 track, and make sure no tracks are locked.

4. If necessary, click the Home key to move the playhead to the start of the sequence.

5. Insert the title clip by clicking the Insert icon under the Source window or pressing the comma (,) key on your keyboard. Because your tracks are unlocked, all content should move backward (to the right) in the timeline to accommodate the new title, which should now be in the Video 4 track.

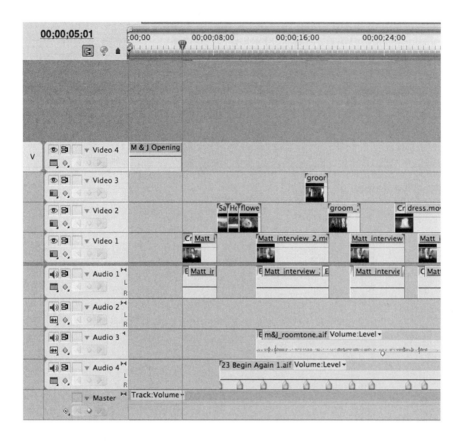

Add a Superimposed Title

Now we will create another title for our sequence, both to practice using the Titler and to learn about superimposed titles (that is, titles that appear over another piece of video). Our second title will be superimposed over the Matt's first interview clip. To begin, follow these steps:

1. On the timeline, place the playhead at time code 08;10, the last frame of the first interview clip. Make sure the groom is visible in the Program panel.

2. Select Title > New Title > Default Still to launch the Titler.

3. Verify the following settings in the New Title dialog box that appears:

    ▶ Width: 720

    ▶ Height: 480

    ▶ Timebase: 29.97 Drop Frame

    ▶ Pixel Aspect Ratio: D1/DV NTSC Widescreen 16:9

4. In the Name field, type **M&J Date**.

5. Click OK; the Titler opens.

6. Press the T key on your keyboard or click the T button in the Tools panel to activate the Type tool.

7. Place the Type tool in the Main panel and type **October 4, 2009**.

8. Play with the parameters on the Title Properties panel to get a look you like. Here, we changed the following settings:

    ▶ Font Family: #GungSeo (If you don't have this font, try Adobe Caslon Pro.)

    ▶ Size: 70

    ▶ Color: 181111

    ▶ Shadow Color: 610C0C

    ▶ Drop Shadow Opacity: 70

    ▶ Drop Shadow Distance: 3.0

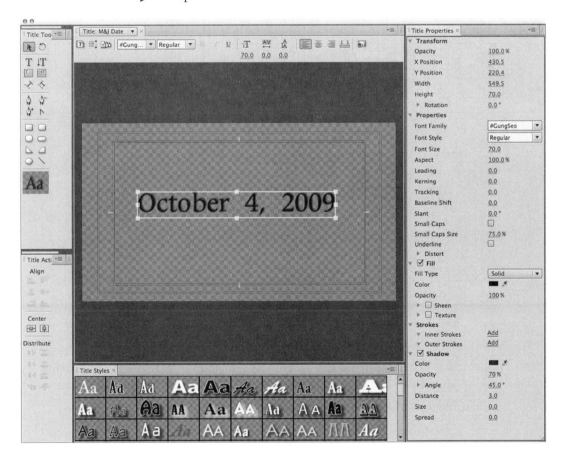

9. To determine where to place the text on the screen, it is helpful to look at the video over which the text will be superimposed. If the background video isn't showing in your title, choose Title > View > Show Video or toggle the Show Background Video button in the top-right corner of the Title Design panel.

Notice that the time-code indicator next to the Show Background Video button shows that the video is at frame 08;10, as we specified earlier with the timeline playhead.

10. To move the date text to a more appropriate place on the frame, activate the Selection tool by pressing the V key on your keyboard or clicking the Selection tool in the Title Tools panel; then use the tool to drag text around the Main panel, which now shows the video image as a guideline. In this case, drag the title until it appears on the bottom right, just inside the title safe zone.

11. When you finish creating the title, close the Titler. Notice that the title appears as a clip in the Project panel.

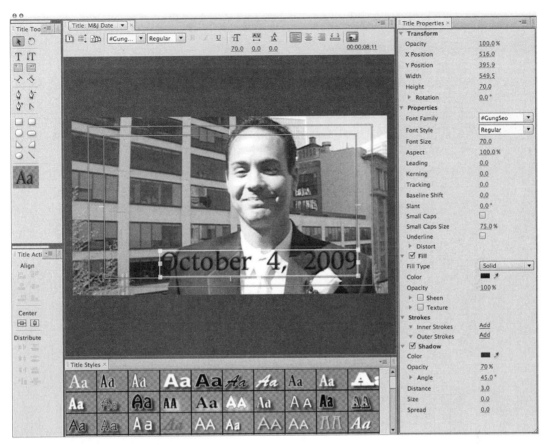

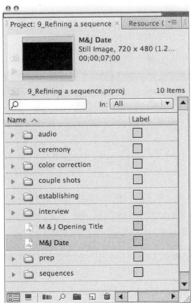

12. To keep your audio intact as you perform an overlay edit, deselect all the audio tracks by clicking their track headers. The audio track headers will no longer be highlighted.

13. In the Project panel, click the title clip's icon and drag the clip to the Source panel. (As with any title, if you double-click the title in the Project panel, the Titler, not the clip in the Source panel, will open.) With the title now open in the Source panel, it will operate the same way a piece of footage would.

14. In the Source panel, set an in point and an out point for the title clip, making the clip two seconds and ten frames (02:10) long.

15. Designate Video Track 4 as the destination track in the timeline and make sure all other tracks are locked.

16. With the playhead at the end of the first Matt interview clip (time code 8:10), click the O key on your keyboard to mark an out point on the timeline.

17. Overlay the title clip by clicking the Overlay icon on the bottom of the Source panel or pressing the period key (.).

Selecting the end point of a three-point edit instead of the in point is called *backtiming* a clip. Notice that the clip falls with its last frame on time code 08:11.

If you want to adjust the look of the title after it is on the timeline, double-click the title clip on the timeline to launch the Titler.

Color Correction

In this exercise, we will learn some basic skills to improve the color of your video footage. We'll go over some techniques for white balancing and changing contrast, two skills that can clean up a large number of problems (and as such are good starting points for more intricate color-correction skills you might later develop).

White Balancing

To begin white balancing, we will look at some footage that has an obvious color cast and attempt to fix it. Follow these steps:

1. Open the Color Correction_Start sequence in the Project panel's Sequences bin.

2. Choose Window > Workspace > Color Correction. Notice that the layout of your workspace changes, giving more room to the Effect Controls panel and adding a Reference monitor, where you can look at scopes, different scales, and comparison images.

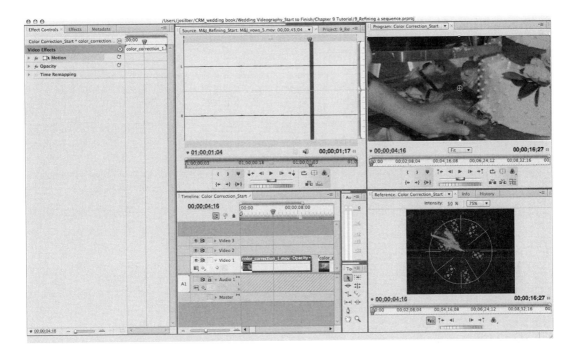

3. Notice that the first clip of the sequence has a yellow cast. To correct for that, we will apply the Fast Color Correction effect. In the Effects tab, navigate to Video Effects > Color Correction > Fast Color Corrector.

4. Drag the icon for the effect onto the first clip in the sequence (called color_correction_1).

5. Double-click the clip in the timeline to open it in the Source panel.

6. In the Effect Controls panel, now in the upper-left corner of the interface, click the Fast Color Corrector triangle to view its parameters. Notice the circle in the center of the color wheel; we are going to reset the image's white balance, which will change the circle's position.

7. Click the White Balance eyedropper, click and hold the Command key (Macintosh) or Ctrl key (Windows), drag it to the clip image in the Program panel, and click something in the image that *should* be white. Here, the cake is the most obvious choice; in less-obvious cases, you may have to enlarge the view in the program file to locate a good white-balance reference point. Notice that the image loses most of its yellow cast and that the circle in the color wheel is now away from the center and closer to a blue edge. (This reflects the blue that needed to be added to counteract the yellow already present; notice that these colors are directly opposite in the color wheel.)

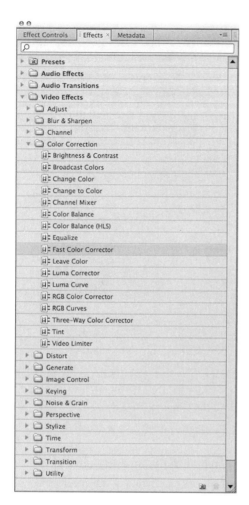

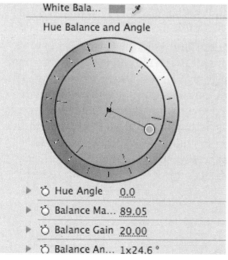

8. Click the circle in the color wheel and drag it around; notice that the image's color changes as you do so. You can use this method to add a tint of color to an image or to make additional white-balance changes. The vector direction indicates the color you are adding and the distance from the center of the circle reflects *saturation*, or how much of that color you are adding.

The Fast Color Corrector changes the white balance of all of the colors in the image systemically. For additional practice, apply the Three-Way Color-Corrector effect, which allows you to manipulate the color balance of the white tones, black tones, and midtones of any given image for more nuanced correction.

Changing Contrast

Contrast is the difference between the whites and black in an image. Typically, an appealing image will have high contrast, with dark blacks and bright whites. When there is low contrast, images tend to look muddy and dull. Editing applications have numerous ways to adjust contrast to make more compelling images. That being said, it is easy to overdo the contrast, which—unless for an artistic effect—should remain realistic and within broadcast-safe guidelines. In this tutorial, we will boost the contrast of a single clip. Follow these steps:

1. If you are not already in the color-correction workspace, choose Window > Workspace > Color Correction.

2. Drag the timeline playhead over the second clip in the color_correction_1 sequence to around 14;01.

3. Click the menu in the upper-right corner of the Reference monitor (visible in the bottom-right corner of your screen in the Color Correction workspace) and select YC Waveform. A waveform meter that enables you to assess the contrast of an image appears. Ideally, your image will include both high whites (toward the 100 setting) and low darks (toward the 7.5 setting); an image that is stuck in the mids, like the second clip in the sequence, will be muddy and not visually appealing.

 Although it's important that your image include high whites and low darks, keep in mind that whites should not be *too* high or they will burn out. Likewise, darks can't be too low, or detail will be lost.

4. In the Effects tab, select Effects > Video Effects > Color Correction > Fast Color Corrector.

5. Click the effect's icon and drag it onto the second clip in the sequence, color_correction_2.mov.

6. In the Effects tab, select Effects > Video Effects > Color Correction > Luma Corrector.

7. Click the effect's icon and drag it onto the second clip in the sequence.

8. Double-click the second clip in the timeline to open it in the Source panel.

9. In the Effect Controls tab, which is in the upper-left corner of the Premiere Pro interface in the Color Correction Workspace, click the Fast Color Corrector triangle to see its parameters.

10. Click the White Balance eyedropper, drag it to the clip image in the Program panel, press and hold the Command key (Macintosh) or Ctrl key (Windows), and click something in the image that *should* be white. In this case, the dress is the most obvious choice. Notice when you click the dress to color-correct the image, the change in color is not nearly as large as in the previous example; this image had better white balance than the prior clip.

11. In the Effect Controls tab, click the Luma Correct triangle to expose its parameters. Take note of the highs and lows in the Waveform monitor before we make any changes.

12. Change the Contrast setting from the default 0 to 10; note the changes in the image and on the Waveform monitor—specifically, how the values in the waveform seem to spread out, indicating an increase in contrast.

13. Boost the Contrast setting to 20, and then to 30. Notice that at a contrast of 30, the lines in the Waveform monitor are above 100 (whites too high) and below 7.5 (blacks too low).

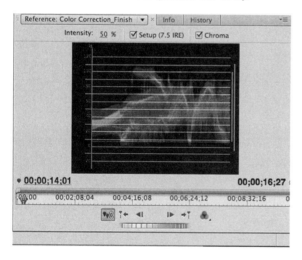

14. Change the Contrast setting to 16. Note that the image is visually compelling, but the Waveform monitor shows that there are still some errors to correct.

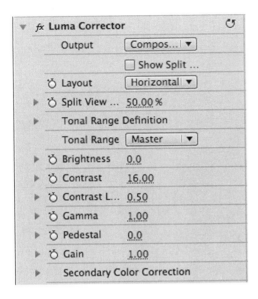

15. In the Effects tab, select Effects > Video Effects > Color Correction > Broadcast Colors. This effect alters pixel color to keep signal amplitudes within an allowable range for broadcast television.

16. Click the effect's icon and drag it onto the clip in the timeline.

17. In the Effect Controls panel, toggle the Broadcast Colors effect on and off by clicking the *fx* icon. Notice the clipping that occurs at the top of the Waveform monitor as you do so.

18. Leave the Broadcast Colors effect on so you can effectively maximize color contrast without having whites that are too high.

In order to watch a sequence with effects, animation, or generated video, it is often necessary to *render* the files, or allow the computer the opportunity to build images of the video that you have specified. That's because the frames of footage fading out, footage dissolving, or footage that is bluer than the original are not files that exist as yet; they must be built, or rendered. Once they are rendered, you can still make changes, but you must render again before you do a final output. Some systems won't play footage unless it has already been rendered. To render this section, select Sequence > Render Entire Work Area. Then save your work.

There are many more advanced editing tools at your disposal to help build the video piece you are imagining. These basic exercises should give you enough familiarity to practice, to play, and to develop further skills on your own.

Chapter 10
Output and Delivery

In this chapter:

▶ Outputting to DVD
▶ Outputting to other formats
▶ Archiving your project

You have a completed piece on the timeline in your editing software. Congratulations! All those days—maybe even weeks—of work were worth it. Your bride looks gorgeous in every shot; she'll never have to know how much footage wound up on the proverbial cutting-room floor, and how many shots were color-corrected or otherwise effected to make her appear so. You finally mastered compositing to create effects that are certain to impress the couple (not to mention yourself). In short, you have a piece to be very proud of.

And yet, you aren't quite finished. You can't just give your clients a data file containing the project you built, saved in the format used by your editing software. Not only would your client need a copy of the editing software you used in order to watch the video, they would also need all the raw footage and media; otherwise, the software pointers you've carefully placed on the timeline would point to nothing. So the last step in producing your wedding video is to provide your clients with a copy of your work in a format that they can watch. You also need to archive the project for your own purposes.

Outputting to DVD

The most common way to present a wedding video to your clients is as an authored DVD. An *authored DVD* is a DVD that can be played back on a DVD player. Authored DVDs can range from extremely simple to very elaborate. At its most basic, an authored DVD will automatically begin playing when placed in a DVD player. A more elaborate DVD might start by displaying a menu that lets the viewer choose which footage to watch. In the case of wedding videos, this might include the main video, a highlights video, a photo montage, an engagement video, a bridal video, and so on (see Figure 10.1).

Figure 10.1
This DVD menu shows buttons for viewing two different video pieces created for the couple (Wedding Video and Highlights), as well as a Scene Selection button, which leads to a submenu with links to the individual scenes.

For longer pieces—namely, the full wedding video—submenus that enable viewers to select a specific scene for viewing are not uncommon (see Figure 10.2). In addition to containing buttons to material on the DVD, the DVD menu itself might be very highly produced—for example, using motion menus and background audio, like you would see and hear in a DVD released by a Hollywood studio.

Figure 10.2
This submenu shows sections, or chapters, of the main wedding video, enabling the viewer to skip to a specific section. Make sure any submenus in your DVD contain a path (button) to return to the main menu.

There are dozens of programs—consumer level and prosumer/professional level—that you can use to author a DVD. Although even the simplest DVD-authoring program will enable you to get a project out the door, the more advanced applications allow you to customize your interface, use a simulation DVD player, and choose from more design and menu options (among other benefits), making them much more pleasant to work with.

Deciding which program to use is relatively simple: the one that most likely came bundled with the editing application you purchased. For example, Final Cut Studio contains DVD Studio Pro; Sony Vegas Pro contains DVD Architect Pro; and Adobe Creative Suite contains Adobe Encore. If you bought a standalone non-linear editing application, consider purchasing the authoring software that is compatible with it.

Because I discussed Adobe's Premiere Pro in the editing sections of this book, I will primarily use terms and examples from Adobe's authoring program, Encore, in discussing DVD output. Keep in mind, however, that these terms and examples are really meant as general ideas, which will be relevant regardless of which application you are working with.

Compressing Your Video for Output to DVD

Regardless of how elaborate your final DVD will be or what authoring program you use, you must compress your video to ensure that they will fit on the DVD. When applying compression, you must constantly balance video duration with video quality. That is, the longer the videos you want to include on the DVD, the more compression you have to apply to make them fit on the DVD. However, the more compression you apply, the lower the image quality. Ideally, you want to compress as little as possible while still creating files small enough to fit on the DVD you are sending out.

There are numerous DVD formats, each one capable of storing different amounts of data. (You'll learn about these various formats in a moment.) Typically, for a single-sided DVD with a 4.7GB capacity, you can include about 90 minutes of video without degrading quality. Go too far beyond that, however, and you'll have to apply more and more compression, which ultimately will degrade video quality.

Compression works by eliminating the spatial and/or temporal redundancy in the pixels that create video images. Different compression schemes take advantage of both spatial and temporal image redundancy. *Spatial redundancy* refers to blocks of color within a single image. If the pixel colors are identical—or similar enough—a block of color can be reduced to one piece of data through compression. For example, instead of storing data for each white pixel in the bride's gown, the compression operation will label small blocks of pixels with the same white color—an average of the white colors of the pixels in question. Although some detail may be lost, the human eye is not nearly as adept at discerning color, or *hue*, as it is brightness; with small enough blocks of pixels being averaged, spatial compression is often unnoticeable. *Temporal redundancy* refers to pixel changes—or lack thereof—over time. For example, if a bride stays in the same position for two seconds, moving only her head, all the visual information pertaining to her dress—60 frames' worth—can be compressed into a smaller piece of data. With high levels of temporal compression, a piece of video will look jumpy and jarring, but there can often be quite a bit of temporal compression before that happens.

Video Compression

Before you can produce an authored DVD, you must compress your video footage by exporting it into a standard compressed video format, called MPEG-2. Normally, this will be a simple matter of selecting a preset compression standard as you output the sequence from your editing software. For example, some external programs, such as Final Cut Studio's Compressor, suggest settings for various lengths of video to ensure that your footage will fit on the DVD.

How long it takes to export your video into the desired compression format depends on how much compression is required, the length of the piece, and the speed of the computer system. In general, though, this may be a long process; make sure you build it into the schedule of your workday!

Occasionally, however, you will still have to give some thought to—and most likely experiment with—your compression settings. These include the following:

You'll learn more about compression settings a bit later in this chapter, in the section "Outputting to Other Formats."

▶ **Data rate.** Also called the bit rate, the *data rate* is the amount of information that can be transmitted during each second of playback. The maximum data rate for the DVD standard is 9.8 megabits per second (Mbps), but to be safe, you generally want your combined audio/video data rate to be 8Mbps or lower when producing on recordable media. Lowering the data rate increases compression.

▶ **Size.** This determines the output screen size, measured in pixels. When compressing video for DVD, you typically use a resolution of 720×480. When compressing video for playback on the Internet or for backup reference, however, you might opt to decrease the video size.

▶ **Keyframes.** When compressing a video file, certain frames spaced at regular intervals are compressed with spatial techniques (like JPEG), not temporal ones. These frames are called *keyframes*. Compression utilities use keyframes as image-data benchmarks, extracting spatial and temporal data from the frames between, or intermediate frames. The spacing of keyframes is a big determinant in how much the piece is compressed; more keyframes, or frames with more image data, mean less compression.

Most applications allow for *batch encoding*—that is, queuing up several different files to be compressed in one go.

Audio Compression

Typically, when you compress video, you have to compress your audio as well. This is almost always handled at the same time by your editor or encoding tool. Depending on your software and your target output format, however, you may have a couple of choices when it comes to compression formats. These could include the following:

▶ **AC3.** This compressed audio format supports both stereo and surround sound. It maintains excellent quality despite high compression, and is typically the recommended format for DVD audio.

▶ **PCM.** PCM is an uncompressed format that stores as much audio information as is available. WAV and AIFF files are often used in the editing software, as well as in external audio editing tools such as Pro-tools or Soundtrack are versions of PCM files. These files have excellent quality, but are generally too big for DVDs or for streaming on the Internet.

▶ **MP3.** MP3 is a very popular audio-compression format used when producing Flash FLV files with the VP6 codec.

▶ **AAC.** AAC stands for Advanced Audio Coding, and is used when producing H.264 files for Blu-ray or Internet streaming.

DVD Formats

The object of compressing your video is to allow it to fit on one of several DVD formats (see Table 10.1).

TABLE 10.1 DVD FORMATS AND CAPACITIES

Name	Type	Capacity
DVD-5	Single sided, single layer	4.7GB
DVD-9	Single sided, dual layer	8.54GB
DVD-10	Dual sided, both sides single layer	9.4GB
DVD-14	Dual sided, one side dual layer	13.24GB
DVD-18	Dual sided, both sides dual layer	17.08GB
Blu-ray	Single layer	25GB
Blu-ray	Dual layer	50GB

All computer DVD burners can write the DVD-5 format; this format easily fits 90 minutes of compressed SD video, or about 40 minutes of HD video. Although the blank media is more expensive, most computer DVD burners can also write the DVD-9 format; this allows more room for longer projects, projects that contain lots of different sequences, or HD footage. DVD-10, DVD-14, and DVD-18 are rarely used; most home computer systems don't support these formats, and they require that the user flip the disc during the copy. The logical jump is from DVD-9 to Blu-ray.

Burning to Blu-ray

Blu-ray, which stores up to 25GB of data per single-layer disc and 50GB of media per dual-layer disc, derives its name from the blue-violet laser that is used to read the disc—a relevant point because said laser is not present in regular DVD players and HD DVD players, rendering Blu-ray discs incompatible with them. To watch a Blu-Ray disc, a Blu-ray player is required.

That being said, all the higher-end editing and authoring applications discussed in this book allow for Blu-ray disc authoring. Indeed, creating these types of discs is generally not much more difficult than changing a setting or two, as indicated in Figure 10.3. Just to state the obvious, since Blu-ray is a high definition format, you'll get the best results if you shoot in an HD video format. If you're shooting in SD, you're better off producing a standard DVD.

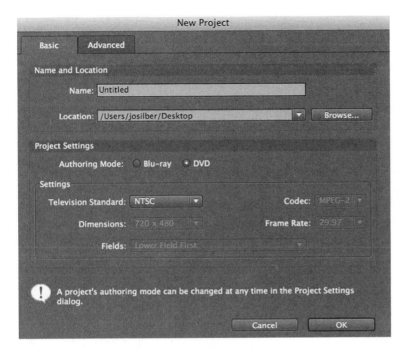

Figure 10.3
A mere click of a button will change this DVD authoring mode format from standard DVD to Blu-Ray.

Although authoring a Blu-Ray disc is simple, it's important to note that Blu-ray discs cannot be written by standard DVD burners; you need a Blu-ray recorder. At the time of this writing, external Blu-ray drives cost approximately $200–$350, and internal ones are slightly less—although prices are dropping. Blank Blu-ray media range in price depending on the face, quantity purchased, and vendor from about $2 to $4 per disc.

Although this format is gaining tremendous momentum in the feature-film DVD market, it has gained only a small toehold in the wedding-video market. For this reason, most wedding videographers are not yet offering Blu-ray at the time of this writing. Those that do often charge an additional fee to create a Blu-ray disc; others simply include a Blu-ray disc as part of their standard package, the assumption being that the couple will use it someday. Track your own local market to determine if and when you should expand your offerings to include Blu-ray discs. Being ahead of the curve might win you business, but prices will continue to drop and hardware will continue to improve, meaning it might be wiser to wait to invest in Blu-ray equipment.

Authoring Your DVD

After you finish editing all of your video, you're ready to begin the architecture and design of your DVD. While the workflow will vary among authoring programs and suites, generally there are two initial steps: setting up your project and importing your content. In the setup step, you ensure your DVD-authoring application is set up correctly for your project. This may include specifying the DVD standard (DVD or Blu-ray), resolution (SD or HD), and display mode. Display mode is especially relevant if trying to view footage with an aspect ratio of 4:3 in a widescreen, or 16:9, mode.

Also, if your authoring program features a simulator or DVD preview function, set its output settings to match the size and aspect ratio of the screen on which you expect the video to be viewed. A *simulator* is an extremely handy tool for previewing and error-checking your DVD; it enables you to preview without first writing the DVD, which can be time consuming and expensive. (You'll learn more about writing your DVD in a moment.)

After creating your new project, import the video (or videos) that you want to include on the DVD, as well as any additional music, graphics or still pictures that you might be using on the DVD menus. Some programs, such as Adobe Premiere Pro, let you export a sequence directly to Adobe Encore, its companion DVD authoring application, as shown in Figure 10.4. Otherwise, you must compress your sequences in your video-editing program, launch the DVD-authoring software, and import the compressed sequences. As with any type of project, you should immediately save your DVD-authoring project and continue to do so throughout the authoring process.

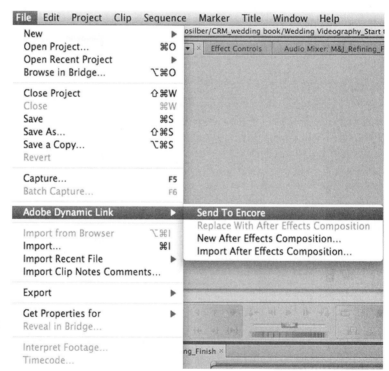

Figure 10.4
Adobe Premiere Pro enables you to export a sequence directly to Encore (the suite's dedicated authoring program) in a usable form, delaying compression until you actually burn the DVD.

Planning the Structure of Your DVD

Some authored DVDs are interactive, letting the user choose which content to view. The choices might be different videos, such as a full wedding video, a wedding highlights video, or a *montage*, or scenes within a video. Regardless of the options provided, your DVD must contain an obvious navigational structure that gives viewers the ability both to jump to various features on the DVD and to easily return to a starting point, or menu.

Consider the video you have available and how many choices you want to offer your viewer. For example, suppose you have just one video track—the main wedding video—which is one hour long. You could create a DVD that immediately launches the video and plays it straight through when it is inserted in a player. Alternatively, you could create a DVD that features a Welcome menu with one option: Play Video. Yet another option would be to create a DVD that features a Welcome menu from which you can either play the whole video or choose to view different scenes in the video. If the scene selection option is chosen, a second menu—called a *submenu*—will appear, enabling the viewer to start the DVD from various points, such as the scene containing the toasts or the scene containing the couple's first dance.

The very simplest DVD structure is to have a video that immediately starts playing upon insertion (without a menu) and *loops*, or plays again, on completion. But even those two basic directions must be specified in the authoring process.

To keep the DVD interactive, you have to plan what happens after the viewer finishes watching a video or stops playback in the middle. Typically, the DVD author will specify that a menu be shown when a video sequence is complete or stopped, allowing the viewer to continue with his or her viewing experience.

The more pieces of video you include, the more extensive your menu options and end destinations may become. Fortunately, your DVD-authoring program will likely offer a few different ways to keep track of your architecture, either in outline form or in graphical form, as shown in Figure 10.5.

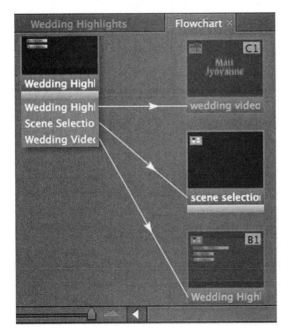

Figure 10.5
This is a very simple DVD, with two tracks and two menus, as represented here in the Adobe Encore Flowchart view. As the DVD authoring gets more complicated, these methods of tracing the connections between DVD elements are very helpful.

Make sure you have an understanding of what the DVD's overall structure will be before you start creating menus and buttons. In complicated scenarios, this may involve scratching diagrams or flow charts on the back of an envelope to ensure that the viewer has access to every video, and to make sure you know what happens when the viewer finishes watching or interrupts playback at any point.

Designing Menus and Buttons

DVD menus enable viewers to navigate your DVD. In order to be functional, a menu must have buttons that the viewer can select that force the DVD player to play back a different piece of video on the DVD, or jump to a different menu. Both the menu and the buttons are highly customizable. You can start from scratch using all your own elements or use one of the built-in templates that many authoring programs offer. Some programs even have wedding-specific templates.

 You should use built-in menu templates carefully, as some of the options will undoubtedly be tacky. I often find that starting with a template, but then toning it down by removing various elements or changing the color scheme and fonts, is an excellent way to save time on design work without subjecting your clients to the overdone design schemes that are often provided.

In my view, the best way to go about menu design is to spend a lot of time up front building your own design template that you can use over and over, for every wedding video you create. (This template will contain basic elements like your logo, your fonts, and your layout, ensuring that you don't have to rebuild these for every wedding.) By the time you include pictures of the couple, their location, their cake, etc., you will have sufficiently personalized the menu for them. Of course, you may wind up having clients who want more video elements than are in your template, meaning you may have to build more menus during post-production, but at least the basic design elements will be established.

Get to know your software's menu-creation options. Menus can be quite elaborate affairs, with music, picture slideshows, and video elements. While I highly recommend using various features to create a menu that is both technically advanced and personalized for the couple, as with effects, I strongly caution you to use these menu features sparingly. You want to create a menu that welcomes viewers in, not one that scares them off.

Button Design

To aid viewer navigation, buttons often change their appearance depending upon their state. For example, buttons often appear highlighted when touched, or selected. When the button is chosen, it is *activated*. If a button is neither selected nor activated, it is normal. By applying different colors or other looks to buttons for each these states, you help the viewer navigate through the buttons on the menu.

Button Navigation

To navigate the menu, viewers typically use the arrow keys on their remote control, which let them move up or down, or to the right or left. While creating your menu, you'll assign each button a destination for each navigation option; usually, the targets will be the buttons that, according to your design configuration, most closely match the direction selected. For example, if your buttons are in a vertical list, selecting down or right should take the viewer to the button below, while choosing up or left should take the viewer to the button above. Some programs let you set button navigation individually. For example, Adobe Encore provides several button-routing schemes, as shown in Figure 10.6. If your button configuration doesn't fit any of the available options, you can assign button routing manually for each button.

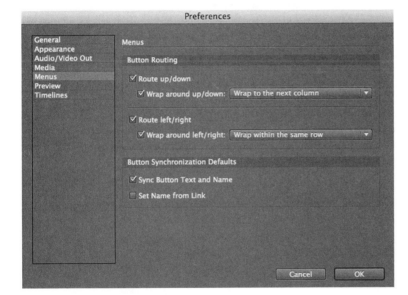

Figure 10.6
Set the navigation for your buttons logically for easy user navigation within your menu design.

Button Destination

Clicking a button has to lead somewhere. Make sure each button has a destination. The destination can be a new menu, the start of a video track, or a chapter of a video track (starting at a particular section of the video, somewhere in the middle). If you use chapters as destinations, they must be designated on the timeline.

It's a good idea to designate your chapter markers in your editing software *before* you export the sequence. After the video file is compressed for DVD, you are limited to adding chapter markers on keyframes; you cannot place a chapter marker on an intermediate frame. Chapter markers added during the editing process are automatically converted to keyframes when you export the video, appearing in the imported sequence both on the timeline and in your destination menu options.

If a button's destination is a video (as opposed to a submenu), make sure you provide direction on what to do after the section of video is over—that is, an end destination, or jump or action. Choices could include returning to one of the menus, replaying, or playing a different piece of video. Encore calls this an end action; if you don't set an end action for each piece of content in Encore, the program will let you know when you check the project before burning.

If you create chapters within a given video sequence and then navigate to one, the DVD will play from the chapter marker until the end of the video track, passing through all the other chapters. If instead you want the DVD to play the chapter and return to the Chapter Selection menu, your editing application may give you a workaround for this. In Encore, they're called *playlists*. Although coverage of playlists is beyond the scope of this tutorial, you can read about them in Encore's help system.

Checking for Errors

If your authoring software offers a simulation function, use it to play back your DVD and check it for errors before you finalize the disc (see Figure 10.7). In addition to making sure that the design elements look as expected and are appealing, ensure that there are no authoring errors. Specifically, ensure the following:

▶ When the DVD is inserted, something happens.

▶ Every button on the menu(s) can be navigated to logically using the arrow keys on a remote control.

▶ It is clear when every button on the menu(s) is normal, selected, and activated.

▶ Every button links to the intended destination.

▶ The video tracks appear in the right video format and don't look squeezed or extended.

▶ Every video track has the correct end action.

▶ All menu and button text is spelled correctly and capitalization rules are uniformly applied.

If you do not have the option of simulating playback with your authoring software, you must still go through this checklist. Unfortunately, you must build and possibly burn the DVD first, which takes time (as well as the cost of the media, should there be errors).

Fortunately, all prosumer authoring programs, such as Encore and Apple's DVD Studio Pro, as well as most consumer programs, now offer a preview/simulation function.

Figure 10.7
This image shows the DVD video sequence being played in a simulation window. This enables the DVD author to experience the DVD as a user would—useful for checking for errors and illogical navigation.

Adobe Encore offers an excellent project-checking function, which you can access from the Build menu (choose Check Project). This function checks for a number of common errors, such as errors related to disc capacity, overlapping buttons, end actions and the like. In fact, if you attempt to burn the DVD and errors exist, Encore will advise you of this before burning the DVD. Most programs have a similar function, which you should always use before burning your DVD.

Building the DVD

When authoring and error-checking is complete, you're ready to build and burn the DVD. Put a blank disc in your DVD recorder and click Build or Burn to record the DVD. Your authoring program will go on its merry way, taking all the steps necessary to produce the DVD with minimal interaction on your part. As you would suspect, the process is pretty technical, but happily, you don't need to know the details.

In case you're curious, though, here's what's going on: Building the DVD is the process of mixing the assets and creating code for the navigational instructions you have created. This process is called *multiplexing*, or *muxing* for short. The end result is two folders called Video_TS and Audio_TS (which may be empty), which are needed for the DVD.

With some authoring programs, a log will indicate whether any errors occur in the muxing process; these commonly include encoding errors and broken links, but can be any number of issues that you will have to go back and correct. But if you're using Encore, and you've cleared all the errors detected by the Check Project function, the disc will record successfully.

Despite all of your pre-burn error checking, you should definitely check out the DVD before sending it to your client. Make sure all the links work, the videos play smoothly, there are no editing glitches, and the like. Assuming the disc is error free, you have a deliverable. Hooray!

 It is likely that as well as well as an authored DVD, you will want to provide your client with self-contained data files on a DVD. These files can be used to play back your edited sequence on various media players, and are formatted to be more flexible than an authored DVD; your clients will be able to post and share them more easily, whether on the Internet, on iTunes, or on their phone. The process of creating these files is similar to compressing for an authored DVD, and luckily, your software often will supply the specific settings you need for any given file format. You'll learn how to prep your files for this type of distribution in the next section.

Packaging Your DVD

You should consider the packaging in which you present your finished DVDs to clients. Having spent months—possibly even years—working out the visual details for their wedding, clients will view your carefully thought through, personalized presentation as the mark of a professional, creative, and fun vendor. Additionally, your product packaging can serve as marketing for your own company, bearing your logo for all to see every time your bride shows her wedding video to a friend!

 Although the cost of blank media and packaging is relatively low, don't forget to factor it into your overall cost of the project. You'll find that by the time you include the price of cases and printed artwork, not to mention time it takes to create several copies of the DVD, it all adds up!

There are several ways to personalize the packaging for a DVD. One obvious step is to personalize the appearance of the disc itself, creating a customized design for each couple. You can then print that design on the face of each DVD you burn for them. To do this, you will need printable DVDs and an inkjet printer that accommodates DVDs. While this does enable you to personalize each DVD, note that doing so can be time consuming and can be expensive. Even if you find a cheap printer that can get the job done, the cost of ink cartridges can add up! By the way, when it comes to buying a printer for this purpose, avoid going too low quality wise. Otherwise, you will wind up with printed discs with poor color quality and smeared ink. Instead of enhancing your product, it may well detract from it!

Another way to personalize the disc is to print a label for it. Although this offers the advantage of easier (and cheaper) printing, labels tend to look less professional than direct printing. More importantly, they can impede the DVD player's ability to play back the disc. For these reasons, I do not recommend using printed labels, despite the advantages.

Another option is to have all your blank media printed by a company that specializes in bulk orders. This can be a very inexpensive way to produce a very professional-looking DVD without having to hand-feed each disc into a printer and check it for ink smears. The disadvantage of this method, of course, is the lack of personalization; the DVD will have your company information or logo, not information about the client's wedding.

Your DVD should also have a case, which could be a regular jewel box, a slim line jewel box, or a taller case, like you find with DVDs containing feature films. All these options offer room for customized artwork: front and back covers for jewel boxes or wrap-around covers for taller cases. As with DVD printing, you can choose to pre-print cover art that has your company name or you can customize covers for each couple, using a template.

Screening Your DVD

Although most wedding videographers simply send their clients the finished project, some prefer to set up a screening (assuming time and space allow it). This offers several advantages. For one, as most videographers will attest, one of the great pleasures of being a wedding videographer is getting to know your clients during a happy time in their lives—and their joyful reaction to their video can be very gratifying. Being with the client when you present the edited version can be a wonderful way to validate your own work and to extract some joy of your own out of it.

Besides the pleasure you will get from seeing your couple reduced to tears of happiness as they watch their video, there are also some practical reasons to set up a screening:

> ▶ Screening your video presents an opportunity to immediately determine what, if any, changes the couple wants to make to the video. This can be a relief when it comes to getting projects out the door and off the docket. You might even screen the video on a TV screen that is connected to a computer running your editing software. That way, if there are changes to be made, you can make them before you compress the sequence and burn the DVD made. Note that if take this approach, your clients will be able to see the video, but they won't be able to leave with a copy of it in their hands, which they may find frustrating. Moreover, using this approach may create extra work for you. That is, it may have the unfortunate consequence of inviting the couple to make changes that they might not have requested had you handed them a finished DVD.

A WORD ON CHANGES

The bane to every video editor's existence is the bride who wants her video changed...seven times. (Yes, that happens.) To avoid having to redo your piece multiple times, make sure your policy with regard to making changes is clearly and firmly stated in your contract. Are you willing to make changes at the client's request? How many times? At what point will you charge extra to make changes? How long do clients have to request these changes? This last bit is extremely important because at some point, you will archive the media (discussed later in this chapter, in the section titled "Archiving"). After you do, making changes becomes quite a bit more difficult—especially if you are working with tape media, which must be captured in real time.

▶ Screening your video enables you to develop material to help your own marketing and sales. The first time your couple sees your video, they will likely become quite emotional. If you want to collect material for the testimonial or references page on your Web site, that's the perfect time to make the request. One videographer I know even films his clients watching their videos for the first time to get good testimonial footage for his demo DVD and Web site. Moreover, having clients in your office who are thrilled with your product gives you the perfect opportunity to garner additional sales, be it more copies of the DVD, a standalone bridal piece, a photo montage of the wedding pictures, or even an edit of any honeymoon footage that they shot themselves.

Outputting to Other Formats

In addition to authoring DVDs for your client, you will want to output your wedding videos to other formats to enable your clients to view them on portable devices such as iPods or cell phones or online.

Compressing Your Video for Output to Other Media

As with authoring a DVD, the first step in outputting to other formats is to compress your video in order to reduce the file size. As mentioned, compression—which works by eliminating the spatial and/or temporal redundancy in the pixels that create video images—is all about balancing file size with file quality; the more compression, the lower the quality. But the smaller the file size, the more ways the file can be distributed.

To simplify matters, most image-editing and compression applications have preset formats with designated settings for various common output formats, such as YouTube and iPhone. That means compressing a file for any such format is as easy as specifying an output for the batch of files you are compressing. For example, in Adobe Premiere Pro, you can choose File > Export > Media and select one of the preset options, as shown in Figure 10.8.

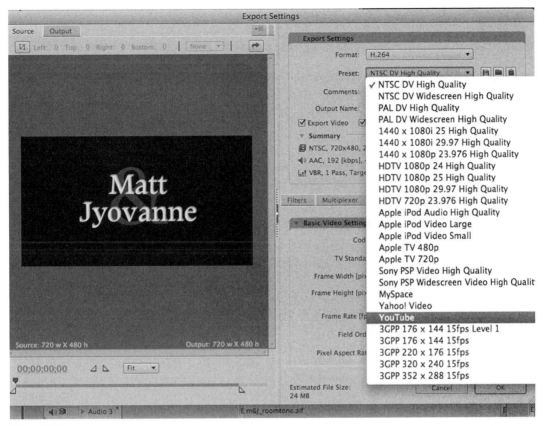

Figure 10.8
Higher-end editing programs have taken much of the mystery out of compression by including a number of presets that will enable you to easily make files of the right size and format for various uses, as shown in this example.

As mentioned earlier, how long it takes to export your video into the desired compression format depends on how much compression is required, the length of the piece, and the speed of the computer system.

Sometimes, however, you will want to experiment with the standard compression options to come up with the best possible video quality for the smallest file size. Here are the major factors to consider when experimenting with compression:

▶ **Size.** Reducing image size is a great way to cut file size. If you are outputting to a format for a portable device or for online use, the video's native image size will almost certainly be too big; you want an image size that maintains the aspect ratio but appears much smaller on the screen. For example, footage shot at 1280×720, which has an aspect ratio of 16:9, will maintain the same proportions if cut to 320×180; likewise, 720×540, which has an aspect ratio of 4:3, will maintain the same proportions if cut to 320×240. These are two standard sizes for video compressed for the Internet.

A good rule of thumb is to leave both the length and width as numbers divisible by 4.

▶ **Format.** The drop-down menu for format, or compression type, will give an intimidating list of options. Most often, you will be using H.264 or MPEG-4, both of which are compression standards that allow great flexibility for Internet delivery as well as for watching on your own computer system. There is a lot of overlap in these compression codecs; H.264 is based on MPEG-4 and they are jointly maintained. It is generally thought that H.264 provides a clearer image for HD footage, and it is becoming the more flexible and widely used option.

▶ **Frames per second.** The frames per second, or *frame rate*, is the number of images shown per second. Most likely, your footage was shot in NTSC standard, which means there will be 29.97 frames per second. Some producers drop to 15 frames per second for Web distribution; this can help to reduce the data rate without noticeable quality loss during scenes with minimal motion, but can cause sections with more motion to look choppy. Because you must pick one frame rate for the whole compressed sequence, take special care to monitor the video quality in the fastest-moving scenes if you lower the frame rate.

▶ **Keyframes.** As mentioned, *keyframes* are frames of video that are compressed using spatial but not temporal techniques. Keyframes are the highest quality frames but are the least efficient compression-wise, so if you're trying for top quality at a small file size, you're better off with fewer keyframes. For most Web delivery, one keyframe every five seconds is a good starting point, while some producers use one keyframe every 10 seconds.

▶ **Data rate.** The most important encoding parameter is data rate because that controls how much compression is applied to the file. The higher the data rate, the better the quality—but the harder the file is to stream, e-mail, or download. So what's the right data rate? Well, that depends upon resolution, format, frame rate, and the amount of motion in your source footage. You'll have to experiment using a short section of your video. Encode that until you find a data rate that looks stunning, and keep dropping it in 50Kbps increments until the video quality is unacceptable. Then choose an intermediate data rate that provides the best mix of quality and transportability.

▶ **Audio.** Although audio files are very small compared to video files, they can still make a difference in compression, when every megabyte counts. Most editors let you choose the target data rate for your audio files; usually 128Kbps will be just fine. Not surprisingly, different audio tracks will respond differently to these adjustments, so you will need to listen to different parts of the compressed piece to determine what works.

This balance often requires quite a bit of experimentation; indeed, many people, myself included, refer to compression as a black art. The rules that define it appear mysterious, as different sequences require different combinations to achieve the best results.

As you learned earlier, most applications allow for *batch encoding*—that is, queuing up several different files to be compressed in one go.

Posting Your Video Online

As mentioned in Chapter 2, "The Business of Weddings," an important part of your business is your Web site. You can use your Web site—as well as a blog—to share videos you have created with current and prospective clients. You have a few options when it comes to posting your videos online (after compressing them for the Internet, of course). One option is to post the video on a video-sharing site, such as YouTube, and then embed the video in your own site or blog.

Posting your video on YouTube is simple. First, you prepare your video for YouTube by choosing YouTube from your editing program's list of export options (refer to Figure 10.8). If your editing program doesn't enable you to automatically compress your video for use on YouTube, you can apply the necessary compression manually; the specs at the time of this writing are shown in Figure 10.9.

After your file has been prepared for upload, you simply direct your Web browser to YouTube (www.youtube.com), log on to your YouTube account, click the Upload Video button, and locate and select the video file you want to upload from the dialog box that appears.

In order to upload a video to YouTube, you must create an account with the site; doing so is free. For details, see YouTube's help information.

Once you have uploaded your video to YouTube (or some other video-sharing site), you simply send viewers to the site itself by distributing the URL. Alternatively, you can embed the video in your own Web site or blog (see Figure 10.10) by copying the embedding information from the video-sharing site and pasting it into your site.

Getting Started: Optimizing your video uploads

Summary

Here's a summary of the audio and video specifications you need for the best results on YouTube. For further details, please read the information listed directly below this summary.

Video	
Resolution	**Recommended: Original resolution of your video - for HD it is 1920x1080 (1080p) or 1280 x 720.**
Bit rate	Because bit-rate is highly dependent on codec there is no recommended or minimum value. Videos should be optimized for resolution, aspect ratio and frame rate rather than bit rate.
Frame rate	The frame rate of the original video should be maintained without re-sampling. In particular pulldown and other frame rate re-sampling techniques are strongly discouraged.
Codec	H.264 or MPEG-2 preferred.
Preferred containers	FLV, MPEG-2, and MPEG-4
Audio	
Codec	MP3 or AAC preferred
Preferred containers	FLV, MPEG-2, and MPEG-4
Sampling rate	44.1kHz
Channels	2 (stereo)

Figure 10.9
YouTube's current specs.

Figure 10.10
You can easily embed a YouTube video in your own Web site or blog simply by cutting and pasting the URL provided by YouTube. Notice that when you take this approach, the YouTube logo appears on the video.

Posted: 06 Feb, 2010 | No Comments
Categories: Uncategorized | Tags: | By: josilber. (edit this)

Another option is to post the video directly on your own site or blog. If you host the video on your own site, the video will not have any third-party logos attached to it, as will be the case if you post the video on a site hosted by someone else—but you will have to pay for the space required to store it. If you choose this route, the method you use to post your video will differ depending on how your site is set up and on your Internet service provider (ISP). Typically, however, it's an easy process that involves uploading a file on your own hard drive to the server run by your ISP on which your Web site lives (see Figure 10.11). Most blogging software also makes inserting video very simple. For more details, contact your ISP or view your blog provider's help information.

Figure 10.11
This wedding Web site hosts its own videos. A pop-up window appears to allow video screening when selected. Different Web designers and ISPs will provide different video-posting options, all of which should make posting your videos quite simple.

Archiving Your Project

You are so close to being finished! But before you wrap things up, while everything is still fresh in your mind, consider any use you might have for this footage beyond the video you just created for your client. Do you want to use it to create any still images for use on your Web site? Should you create any sequences or pull any shots from it for your demo? Are there generic shots—establishing or otherwise—of the city, the ceremony site, or the reception locale that you might be able to use in wedding videos for other clients? If so, create sequences or pull clips and save them somewhere that will make it easy for you to pull the footage into other projects as needed.

Once that is done, you are finally ready to *archive* your project—that is, move it from your computer to some other storage device. That way, you free up space on your computer to work on other projects. Your workflow here will depend on your computer's operating system and your storage device, but is generally a matter of dragging files to a new location (such as an external hard drive connected to your computer) to copy them. You might also create data DVDs (that is, unauthored DVDs) of archived media by dragging footage onto a blank DVD and burning it.

Ideally, you would store every piece of every project on an external hard drive, which is itself then backed up by *another* external hard drive. This approach is cumbersome, however, and will unnecessarily clog up your drives. Typically, the final project and your various output sequences will be pretty small; it's the raw footage that becomes a problem in terms of storage space. Depending on how many weddings you do and your storage capacity, creating tape backups of raw footage might be a better idea.

Whatever storage medium you choose, here's what you want to do to close out the project:

> ▶ Keep one copy of the finished product you gave to your client for yourself, including the authored DVD and any data files.

> ▶ Create a folder on your external hard drive or burn a DVD to include all the media collateral—besides the actual raw footage—that you used in the project. This includes the music, photos, graphics, images used in the DVD packaging, scans of the wedding invitation, menu, and program, etc.

> ▶ Save a copy of the project file from your editing software.

> ▶ Create and archive a full-quality video file, both for reference and to make easy changes should they be required after the media is offline.

> ▶ Create and archive any additional cuts you might need for your own marketing purposes—for example, a highlights version without the titles that the couple requested or a demo of a three-camera wedding shoot pulled from a longer piece. Store these pieces as both full-quality QuickTime files and in whatever compressed form you might need.

> ▶ Save the raw project footage. If you shot on tape, this is easy: Just save the tape. If you started with digital files, this can be more complicated. Although you can store the files digitally, this can consume quite a bit of drive space, especially when you consider backups. That being said, drive space has become significantly less expensive, meaning that this option is not entirely

outlandish. You can also make tape backups of your digital files by printing them to tape. To do this, you will need a camera that uses tape or a deck. You can inexpensively purchase a camera exclusively for printing tape; this might save some money in drive room in the long run.

 In addition to providing clients with an edited wedding video, some videographers also give the raw footage to the client. If you decide to provide your clients with your raw footage, be aware that clients will be able to see all the times you accidentally left the camera on and will be able to hear all your audio—including that stream of swear words you let fly under your breath when you tripped over your tripod. Be careful!

Summary

This chapter discusses ways to deliver your product to your client and to archive it for yourself. The specifics of this part of the workflow will vary significantly between vendors, as they depend on the software used, the product promised, the level of client contact feasible and desired, and of course the vendor's own artistic style. Use this chapter as a guideline for building your own system to finish up and close out your projects. However you set up your workflow, don't scrimp on these last steps; they're an important part of staying organized and conveying professionalism.

Next Up

Hooray! With your video finished and out the door, you're ready to tackle the next one! I promise: They only get easier. The time you spent this time around figuring out how to make the product actually happen will soon be spent learning how to make it look better and happen more easily—which is infinitely more fun.

You are on the way up! In fact, now that this wedding-videography business is practically old hat, you're ready spend some time looking at ways to grow your business in new directions. Chapter 11, "Add-On Business Ideas," will give you some ideas on how to develop your business to make it more fun...and more lucrative.

Chapter 10 Tutorial: Preparing a Sequence for Output

This tutorial teaches you specific editing skills to output the wedding video you have built. To complete this tutorial, you will need a copy of Adobe Premiere Pro and to copy the files from the DVD accompanying this book to your computer hard drive. Instructions for downloading a trial version of Adobe Premiere Pro and copying files to the DVD are found in the tutorial for Chapter 4.

To begin this tutorial, navigate to Wedding Video_Start to Finish > Chapter 10 Tutorial and launch Adobe Premiere by double-clicking the 10_Exporting a Sequence project file in the Chapter 10 folder. When prompted, allow the scratch disks to be set to your Documents folder.

Open the Sequence bin in your Project panel and notice that it has a bin of clips and one finished sequence: M&J_Refining_Finish. This is the same sequence we completed in the Chapter 9 tutorial. In this tutorial, we will output this sequence into three different formats: for an authored DVD, for specific media players, and for your archives.

Exporting a File for an Authored DVD

The most common way to output your work for a client is on an authored DVD, which can be viewed on a computer or using a DVD player. DVDs can be of the SD, HD, or Blu-ray variety. In this exercise, we will use Adobe Premiere Pro to export a sequence for an SD DVD.

If you are using a DVD-authoring program other than Adobe Encore (which is included in the Adobe CS4 suite), follow these steps to export your project file from Adobe Premiere Pro:

1. In Adobe Premiere Pro, double-click the M&J_Refining_Finish sequence in the Project panel to open it in the timeline.

2. In the timeline, move the playhead to time code 34;27.

3. Choose Marker > Set Encore Chapter Marker to add a chapter marker. Type Garter in the Name field and click OK to create the marker. As you read in the chapter, markers serve as chapter points when you open the file in the DVD-authoring program. By setting chapter markers, you enable the person viewing your DVD to skip to different sections of the video. (Although this short sequence does not require chapter markers, it is helpful to look at the process of adding them.)

 Although you can add chapter markers within Encore and other authoring programs, you can do so only at keyframes. That means if you want to place a chapter marker with accuracy, you must do so in the editing application—*before* DVD compression. The marker you add in the editing software will appear when the compressed file is placed on the timeline of DVD-authoring software.

4. With the Timeline panel activated, choose File > Export > Media to open the Export Settings window. Notice that on the left side of the window, there is a Source tab and an Output tab. The Source tab shows the video as it exists on the timeline, while the Output tab previews how the video will look after exporting. The right side of the window features an Export Settings panel.

The viewing monitor in the Output tab is a very handy tool; it enables you to see the changes that occur when you choose various settings. Although it doesn't preview the affects of compression, it does preview resolution and pixel aspect ratio, which can help you catch a lot of errors before actually compressing the file.

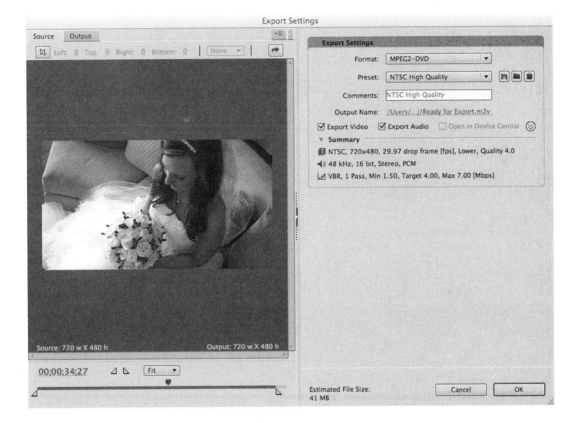

5. In the Export Settings panel, change the Format setting to MPEG2-DVD.

6. Click the Output tab; then change the Preset setting in the Export Settings panel to NTSC High Quality. Notice the letterboxing that appears in the Output tab as a result. Now choose the NTSC Progressive Widescreen High Quality preset, which is the setting we actually want to use; the letterboxing disappears. Typically, letterboxing indicates a mismatch between the source aspect ratio and the target aspect ratio, which is rarely the desired result. Always check the Output tab before exporting your video; it makes mistakes like these very obvious.

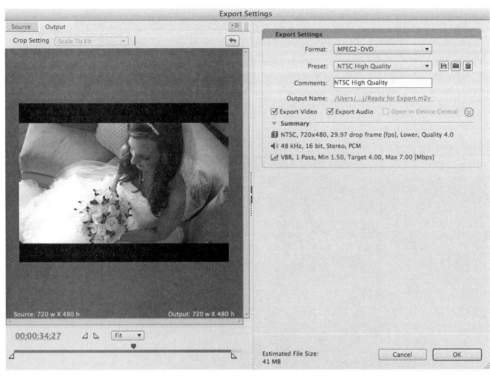

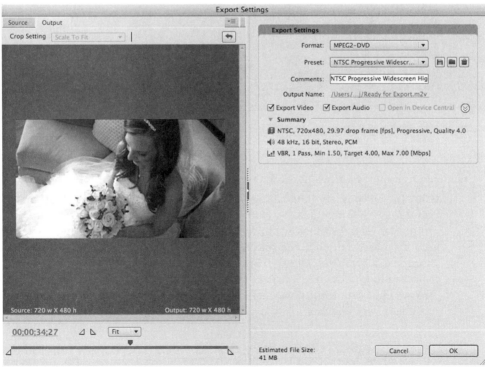

7. Click the Output Name link to open a Save dialog box, where you can name your file and specify where it should be saved. After you do, click Save.

Be sure to name the sequence something you will recognize. The name should include the name of the couple or the date as well as the format (since you will likely make many versions), such as M & J_MPEG2_DVD.

8. Make sure the Export Audio and Export Video checkboxes in the Export Settings panel are checked.

9. On the right side of the Export Settings panel, click the Simple/Advanced Mode button (the small round button with arrows on the right, just below the Name field) to toggle between simple and advanced modes to see the available options. (We will remain in simple mode.)

The DVD authoring program you use might require your audio files to be formatted a specific way. If you aren't using Encore, check your program documentation to ascertain the required audio format.

10. Click OK to launch the Adobe Media Encoder. Your file appears in the export queue. Double-check that you have appropriately named the file and placed it in the desired location. You can make changes to the file format, presets, output name, and location by clicking in the Encoder window.

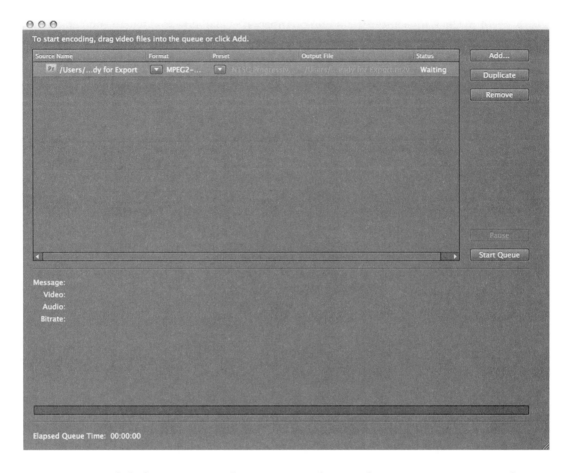

11. Click the Start Queue button to start the encoding process. A status update appears along the bottom of the Encoder window. When the encoding process is complete, two files—one audio and one video—will appear in the location you specified in step 7. These files are ready to be imported into your DVD-authoring software.

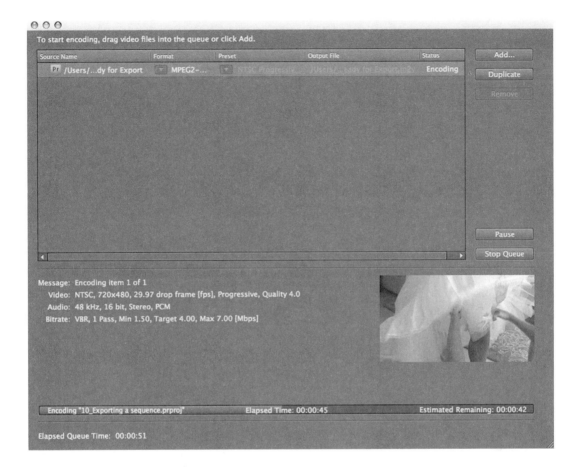

If you are using Adobe Encore as your DVD-authoring program, you can export your project file directly from Adobe Premiere Pro to Adobe Encore by following these steps:

1. In Adobe Premiere Pro, double-click the M&J_Refining_Finish sequence in the Project panel to open it in the timeline.

2. In the timeline, move the playhead to time code 34;27.

3. Choose Marker > Set Encore Chapter Marker to add a chapter marker. Type **Garter** in the Name field and click OK to create the marker.

4. With the Timeline panel activated, choose File > Adobe Dynamic Link > Send to Encore.

5. Adobe Encore launches. Name your new Encore file and specify where it should be saved.

6. In the Project Settings area, choose DVD Authoring Mode, and choose NTSC as the television standard in the Settings box. Then click OK.

7. Like the Premiere interface, the Encore interface includes a Project panel, a Monitor, and a Timeline panel. Your file is ready and waiting in the Project panel; click it to open it in the timeline. Notice the markers that come with it—one at the beginning of the timeline and one at 34 seconds, inserted during this exercise.

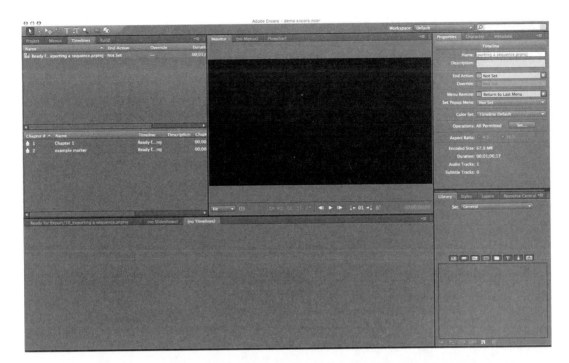

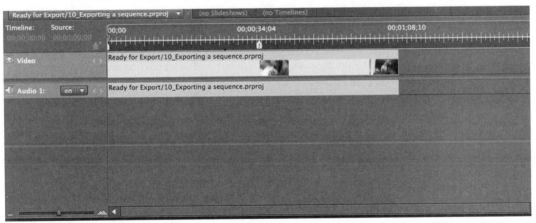

For further instructions on DVD authoring with Adobe Encore, see the Adobe Web site, various software tutorials on the Web, or the author's Web site at www.taketwodv.com.

Exporting for Specific Media Formats

In addition to an authored DVD, your clients will probably want a version of the video that they can post online or play back on an iPod or other portable device. There are many factors that go into exporting files for these types of formats, the most important of which is length of the piece itself. That is, the longer the video, the larger the file will be, regardless of the compression settings.

 Typically, you will export highlight videos rather than full wedding videos for use with portable devices or online, although that is certainly not always the case.

1. In Adobe Premiere Pro, with the same M&J_Refining_Sequence open in the timeline, choose File > Export > Media. The Export Settings window appears. Notice that on the left side of the window, there is a Source tab and an Output tab. The Source tab shows the video as it exists on the timeline, while the Output tab previews how the video will look after exporting. The right side of the window features an Export Settings panel.

2. In the Export Settings panel, select the following settings:

   ▶ Format: H.264

   ▶ Preset: iPod Video Small

3. Click the Output Name link to open a Save dialog box, where you can name your file and specify where it should be saved. After you do, click Save.

4. Make sure the Export Audio and Export Video checkboxes in the Export Settings panel are checked.

5. Click OK to launch Adobe Media Encoder. Your file appears in the export queue. Double-check that you have appropriately named the file and placed it in the desired location.

 One of the benefits of an export queue is that it permits a *batch export.* That is, you can specify all the files that need to be encoded and then encode them all at the same time with one command. Working in batches leaves you free to do something else while your computer churns files for you; you need not monitor the operation, issue commands, or save files between sequence compressions.

6. To add another file to the queue, return to Premiere, open the file you want to export in the timeline, and repeat steps 1–5, this time specifying the following settings

   ▶ Format: H.264

   ▶ Preset: YouTube

7. Your second file will appear in the export queue below the first. Double-check that you have appropriately named the file and placed it in the desired location.

8. After you are finished adding all the files you want to export, click the Start Queue button.

Typically, Adobe Premiere Pro's presets will include all the formats you might need to use for output. If, however, you need to customize the compression operation to tweak the quality or size of a given file, you can click the Simple/Advanced Mode button beneath the Name field to toggle into advanced mode and access additional compression settings for audio and video.

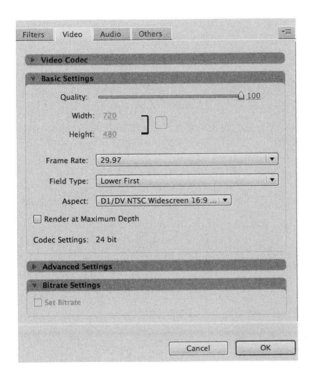

Exporting for Archives

It's critical that you export a full-size, high-quality version of your wedding video for your own archives (and possibly for the client). In addition to serving as a reference, this version can also be re-imported into an editing application for quick fixes if need be. You can include this export with the others in a batch export.

It is worth noting that this is not an ideal way to archive because when you import the exported file back into your editing software, it will be one long clip. Your tracks, edits, and keyframes will no longer be visible. Still, using this version can be very handy in a pinch for making simple changes, such as adding a title to the beginning or end, without reloading all your media.

In this example, we will export to QuickTime. QuickTime videos can be played back using the QuickTime player, which, in addition to coming bundled with iTunes, is distributed with all Macs and is available as a free software download for all PCs. It's safe to say that most of your clients will have access to a QuickTime player.

 Instructions for downloading a QuickTime player are included in the Chapter 5 tutorial.

1. In Adobe Premiere Pro, with the Timeline panel activated, choose File > Export > Media. The Export Settings window appears. Notice that on the left side of the window, there is a Source tab and an Output tab. The Source tab shows the video as it exists on the timeline, while the Output tab previews how the video will look after exporting. The right side of the window features an Export Settings panel.

2. In the Export Settings panel, select the following settings:
   ▶ Format: QuickTime
   ▶ Preset: NTSC DV Widescreen

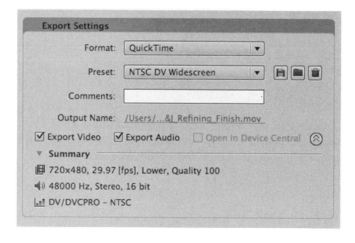

3. Click the Output Name link to open a Save dialog box, where you can name your file and specify where it should be saved. After you do, click Save.

4. Make sure the Export Audio and Export Video checkboxes in the Export Settings panel are checked.

Some applications, such as Final Cut Pro, ask you to specify whether the movie should be self contained. A *self-contained* movie includes all the necessary media, meaning that it can be viewed on any system. Movies that are not self contained include pointers to media, but not the media itself—meaning that if the media files are not available, the movie file will not "point" to anything, and the movie cannot be viewed. Accordingly, when archiving, if given the choice, always opt for a self-contained movie. Note that with Adobe Premiere Pro, movie files are always self contained.

5. Click OK to launch Adobe Media Encoder. Your file appears in the export queue. Double-check that you have appropriately named the file and placed it in the desired location.

6. Click the Start Queue button.

Be warned: Exporting a self-contained file can take quite a bit of time. Just how long depends on your hardware, the length of movie, and the settings you chose.

Part IV

The Marriage

Chapter 11
Add-On Business Ideas

In this chapter:

- ▶ Photo montage
- ▶ Same-day edit
- ▶ Engagement video
- ▶ Concept video
- ▶ Personalized Web page
- ▶ Other ideas

It's a huge accomplishment to finish and deliver your first wedding video. From there, your work should get easier. The nuts and bolts of the production and post-production process will become smooth, leaving you more time to devote to the art and craft of your videography. With that in mind, this chapter provides some details, techniques, and instructions for products and services beyond a basic wedding video that you can offer your clients. Aside from generating additional revenue, these products can help you think and work creatively, keeping your wedding work fresh and personalized for every client.

Photo Montage

A *photo montage*—a video composed of moving pictures set to music—is an easy way to supplement the services you provide as a wedding videographer. Indeed, photo montages are tremendously popular. Couples often commission them for their engagement party, the rehearsal dinner, the wedding itself, or after the event.

 Many venues have equipment for screening videos such as photo montages, but offering to set up your own audio/visual equipment may set you apart as a vendor.

Building the Montage

You build a montage using photographs that your clients supply to you. When conferring with your clients about the montage, specify to them the format in which these photos should be supplied. Ideally, you will receive high-resolution digital files, preferably in TIFF format; that said, editing applications accept a variety of image formats. In addition, make sure to clarify the following with your clients:

▶ What type(s) of music do your clients want to feature in the montage?

 The same issues of copyright law that are relevant to weddings are relevant to montages. A discussion of these copyright issues can be found in Chapter 8, "Basic Editing."

▶ Do your clients want the montage to include opening and closing titles?

▶ Should the images appear in a specific order? Perhaps they want them to appear chronologically, or all groom photos followed by all bride photos, or intertwined specifically.

▶ Do they want superimposed titles to appear on any of the images? If so, the text should be included with the photos they provide.

▶ Are you expected to color-correct or improve the photos in any way? If so, make sure to include this service in your fees; it can be quite time consuming!

▶ Do you have creative license to remove pictures from the sequence that don't look good? Or does the client want to include all the pictures, regardless of the image quality? Often, the content of the photos or the storyline to which they relate is more important to clients than a shot's lack of resolution or some other problem with the image. Be sure to find out in advance whether out-of-place shots should make the final cut or can be tossed guilt-free!

If you request digital files, be sure that they are scanned (dust-free!) at the highest resolution possible. It's likely that your video will be screened at 720×480; you want to make sure that your original images are larger than that so that you have some wiggle room for panning and zooming and filling the screen (since the images are unlikely to be correctly sized). If you scan the images yourself, aim for 1,500×1,000 pixels.

Prepping the Images

Most likely, many of the images will need to be resized in image-editing software such as Adobe Photoshop or Apple's Lightroom or Aperture. The images will likely be shown in a 720×480 frame, although as mentioned, you might choose to size the image slightly larger (see Figure 11.1) so that any movement or zooms that you incorporate into the montage will not result in the display of a black background.

A   **B**

Figure 11.1
This photo is larger than the 720×480 frame, which allows it to fill the entire frame as it slides across the viewer from left (image A) to right (image B).

If an image is smaller than your sequence frame size, a black background will be around the image (see Figure 11.2). Although zooming the image in your video editor can eliminate this black space, doing so is likely to result in a grainy or washed-out image. To preserve data on your image, you can *upsample* it in an image editor; this creates pixels through interpolation, increasing the pixel resolution and yielding a clearer image. Be careful of too much upsampling, however, as it can result in artifacts. Use artistic judgment to determine how much enlarging, upsampling, or black space to use.

Figure 11.2
Images that are too small often do not work well in photo montages; they're hard to see and too much black space makes the image visually unappealing. Use an image-editing program to resize your images, being careful to preserve the image quality if needed.

To resize images, it's often necessary to adjust both the image size and the canvas size. That way, you correctly size and proportion the image, which was most likely not shot in the correct ratio for video. Follow these steps to resize an image (assuming it was too big to start with):

1. Import the image into your image-editing software.

2. Select the Image Size (or similarly named) option.

3. Make sure the proportions are constrained so you don't distort the aspect ratio of the image when you resample it.

4. Change either the width or the height of the image, making sure that both the width and height end up larger than the height and width of your video sequence. For example, if working with DV, make sure the width is greater than 720 and height greater than 480; otherwise, you'll end up with black bars somewhere.

5. If there's a Resample Image or similar checkbox (see Figure 11.3), make sure it's checked. Otherwise, the image editor will simply duplicate pixels in the image to make it larger, creating a jaggy, ugly look.

6. Select the Canvas Size (or similarly named) option.

7. Change the dimension that is too big to the size that you need and press Enter. The image will now have the correct dimensions, which may be exactly the same as your sequence presets, slightly smaller (meaning there will be some space around the image), or slightly larger (giving you some room to incorporate motion). Note that a bit of cropping is likely to occur; your program should allow you to specify which portion of the image should be cropped (see Figure 11.4). Figure 11.5 shows the resulting image.

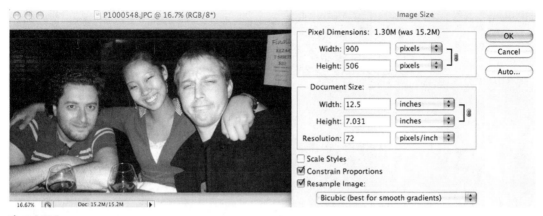

Figure 11.3
When changing a photo's image size, constrain the properties to keep the proportions of the horizontal and vertical dimensions intact (that's the Constrain Proportions checkbox). To avoid winding up with an image that is too small, change the dimension that will leave both horizontal and vertical sizes larger or equal to the needed frame size. In this example, resizing the horizontal dimension to 900 pixels leaves the vertical dimension at 506 pixels, well within the 720×480 pixel size of the sequence.

Figure 11.4
Changing the canvas size will crop the image, which is why both dimensions should be larger than needed. In this example, the photo is cropped vertically from 506 pixels to 590 pixels. Because the canvas resize is anchored at the bottom center, the cropped pixels will be the ones along the top of the image.

Figure 11.5
This image was resized to 800×540 pixels, larger than the 720×480 pixel sequence it will be used in, as indicated by the white box. This allows for some animation of the sequence while still using the image to cover the entire viewer.

8. Save the image in a file format that your editing software will accept, such as a JPG or TIFF.

Building the Sequence

The default length of a still clip that is imported into video-editing software is usually customizable. Although you will likely make adjustments on the timeline to match the music, you should select a default duration that will be easy to work with, such as seven or 10 seconds or the length of time between measured beats of the music. Sometimes, marking the music can help you determine how long you want the clips to be.

When you mark music, you put a visible arrow, or icon, on the timeline to serve as a visual reminder of a point you need to remember. Using markers is a lot like using Post-It notes. While some people write detailed memos on their Post-Its, for others, the mere presence of a Post-It is reminder enough. Markers in video operate the same way, offering you the option of including detailed descriptions or simply using them as a visual cue (see Figure 11.6).

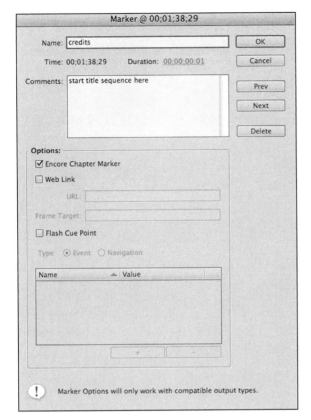

Figure 11.6
When a marker is inserted, you have the option to add a marker name and notes. Detailed information about your marker may be unnecessary, but can serve as a helpful reminder, such as this one used to indicate where titles will go. As you can see by the eponymous checkbox, this particular marker also does double duty as an Encore chapter marker.

 Markers can also be used to indicate chapter points, as discussed in Chapter 10, "Output and Delivery."

To use markers to mark the beat in Adobe Premiere, open the audio in the Source panel and play it. On the beats, click the Set Unnumbered Marker button in the navigation panel beneath the monitor. (It looks like a little home plate just to the right of the Set Out Point icon.) Notice that markers appear on the clip in the Source panel; they will remain there when the images are brought to the timeline, as shown in Figure 11.7.

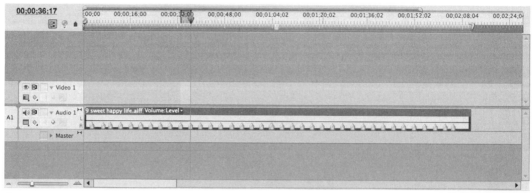

Figure 11.7
This piece of music has been marked on the beat, to indicate where edits between pictures should occur. By selecting sequential markers for an in point and an out point on the timeline, determine the duration of time with which you would like your still images to be imported.

Some programs allow you to mark music that is on the timeline. In that case, make sure to select the audio clip before you begin marking. If the audio clip is not first selected, or highlighted, the markers will show up on the timeline instead of the audio clip. These will work—unless the clip is moved, in which case the markers will be left behind. By marking the audio clip, not the sequence, you have more flexibility.

The duration between an in and an out point on the timeline appears in the bottom-right corner of the Program window. Use this duration to set the default length of imported images, which can be further fine-tuned later (see Figure 11.8).

Once you've marked your audio file and set your default duration, import all the images. It's not necessary to import them individually; you can import them in a batch or import a folder containing images. Once they are in your browser, the images behave in the same way as video clips; they can be opened and viewed in the Source panel, and then inserted into and edited in the timeline.

If your images are listed in the order they will be used, many programs will allow you to drag the entire batch onto the timeline at once. They will fall on the timeline at their default length. (This is called a *storyboard edit*.)

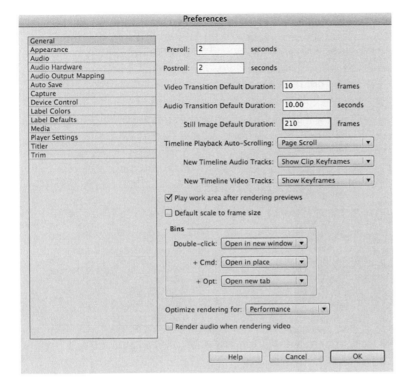

Figure 11.8
The duration assigned to imported images can be specified in user preferences. To expedite your montage-editing process, determine the length of time you want to display the majority of your images so that you can customize this setting, shown in this example as 210 frames in the Still Image Default Duration option.

Animating and Effecting the Sequence

Once images are on the timeline, they can be edited and refined just as if they were video clips. Start by making sure that the images are the right length, with the edits falling in the right places. In Premiere Pro, as with most editors, you can simply click and drag either edge inward or outward to make the image longer or shorter on the timeline. Having accomplished that, you will have the equivalent of your montage rough cut. At that point, you can consider the following:

▶ **Image effects.** Before adding motion or transitions, add desired filters to your images. These might include image-altering effects such as vignettes, hues, or desaturations, or corrective effects such as color adjustments.

▶ **Edit transitions.** Applying transitions between photos can add fun and continuity to the montage. Be warned, though: This is an area where a video editor can easily go overboard. Stick to transitions that highlight the style and mood of your montage, not ones that will define it or take away from the content. Likely candidates are cross dissolves and fades, although there are dozens more worth considering.

▶ **Clip animation.** Use changes in image size, position, and rotation to add visual interest to the photos (see Figure 11.9). You do this by applying keyframes to the images, a process described in the tutorial at the end of this chapter. Be careful of going overboard here, too; although small movements will highlight the image content, too many or overly exaggerated motions will detract from what is being shown. Also, be careful of too much black space. As you move a clip's position or change its size, do so without allowing too much background in. (This is a main reason for using images that are slightly oversized.)

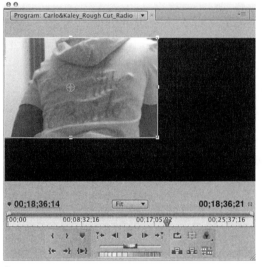
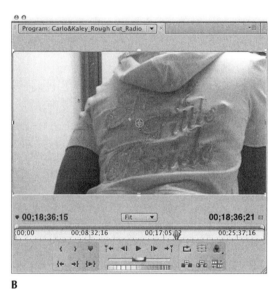

A   B

Figure 11.9
Animating an image provides visual interest. The first image shows the starting point of the animation, as indicated by a smaller image positioned in the top-left corner. The second image shows the ending point of the animation, which has been animated to "grow" and move to a centered position. Though not shown in the figure, the change in the image's size and position can be seen numerically in the Effect Controls tab in the Position and Scale settings and visually in the Program panel, where a dotted line indicates the path of motion.

▶ **Titles.** Most likely, you will use opening and closing titles. In addition, superimposed or crawl titles are a great way to personalize the montage, making it more informative or funny by way of descriptions and editorial comments provided by your clients or their family and friends.

Outputting the Montage

Once the images are on the video timeline and the sequence is built to completion, it needs to be output to the proper format. As with the video itself, the format you choose will depend on the montage's intended use. Since the montage will likely be screened at an event, find out from the couple or the venue how the video will be shown. If the montage will be screened using a DVD player, you will need to compress it to MPEG-2 format to build the DVD. If the montage will be screened from a computer, you will need to format it as a QuickTime or AVI file. More information about sequence output can be found in Chapter 10.

If you are creating an authored DVD of the wedding event, it's easy to include the montage as an item on the menu.

Screening the Montage

Often, the venue or wedding coordinator will take care of screening logistics. In some situations, however, it may be advantageous to offer audio and video screening as a part of your services. To provide screening, you must have an overhead projector that can be connected to your own laptop computer, external speakers, and a collapsible screen on which to show the video in case the room in which the viewing will occur does not have an appropriate wall space. Make sure that you have the right connection cables for your laptop to the projector and from your laptop to the speakers; you must test this prior to the event date!

If you are in charge of setup, make sure your kit includes multiple extension cords, electrical tape (to safely secure any cords and cables), and the battery charger for your laptop computer.

Carrying and setting up this equipment is not terribly difficult, although it may interfere with the timing of your regular day shooting. Most likely, you will set up the montage at the rehearsal dinner or at the reception, either as an event of the evening or to be shown on a loop throughout the night.

This is a simple, one-person job for a rehearsal dinner. The same is true if the montage is to be screened once during the reception—for example, as after-dinner entertainment. You will likely have plenty of time to move gear and set up as the guests are eating (traditionally a bad time to shoot video). If your clients want the montage to be shown on a loop as guests arrive, however, this may become more difficult. Chances are, shooting demands—such as the cocktail hour, shots of the couple, or shots of first dances—will interfere with your ability to set up and run the necessary equipment. If this is the case, look carefully at the timeline of the day's events to determine when you can gain access to the room in which the photo montage will be screened, and consider whether your equipment will be safe if left unattended. If you can't gain access to the reception site or, more likely, you don't have a safe place to store your equipment, it may be advantageous to secure an assistant to help the screening setup so that you are free to attend to your shooting responsibilities.

You may be able to get setup help from the wedding coordinator, but you shouldn't count on this unless you've made prior arrangements. Similarly, with prior arrangements, the DJ may be able to help with projection.

Same-Day Edit

With a same-day edit (often called a *shotgun video* or *mad-scramble edit*), a video of the ceremony is shown at the reception, usually later that day. That means if there is shooting to be done between the ceremony and the reception, a same-day edit is going to involve at least two people on your team. Same-day edits can be very fun—and incredibly impressive when pulled off well—but of course come with some level of risk. Software bugs, equipment failure, or forgetting even one small item, suddenly becomes a significant roadblock to getting the task done. The ability to work well under pressure is a necessary skill if you plan on offering this service.

Some things to note about a same-day editing before you commit to providing this service:

▶ It's important to feel confident in your shooting skills before taking on a same-day edit. Time will not allow for many of compensatory tricks available in a longer post-production time frame.

▶ Prep as much of the edit ahead of time as possible. Titles, graphics, and music can be selected and imported into a project before the event begins. If you have shot other weddings at the ceremony venue, pull any B-roll or cut-away footage you have of the location—for example, establishing shots of the building, signage, or room details—and have it ready to go in a saved project that includes music and titles, as shown in Figure 11.10. (Of course, this footage should not include guests or participants from the previous project!)

▶ If you plan to do the edit on a laptop away from your home studio, make sure you have a place with plenty of electrical outlets where you will be able to work uninterrupted. Also be sure to bring all the equipment, cords, and blank media you will need. (More on this in the coming sections.)

▶ Clarify with your client whether you will be in charge of screening the video or you will be turning it over to someone else, such as the event coordinator, a venue representative, or the DJ. If you are in charge of the screening, make sure to review the instructions in the previous section. If you will be handing off a file or DVD to someone else, make sure you know exactly what you need to provide and to whom and by when. Have their contact information immediately available in case you run into a problem.

▶ As with all your video services, ensure that a contract with your client allows for errors. A same-day edit is stressful enough without worrying about the legal issues surrounding the accidental breaking of a contract.

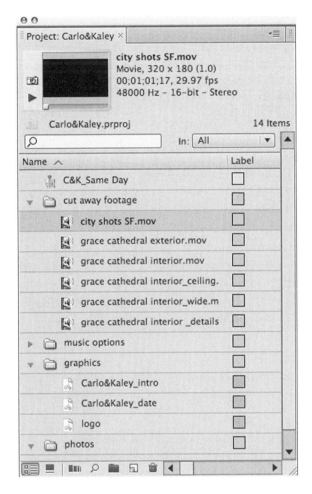

Figure 11.10
There is much work that can be done before the footage is shot. In this example of a same-day edit project, the browser files contain the music, graphics and some establishing and B-roll footage so that the rough cut can begin as soon as the footage is captured.

Building the Sequence

The steps to building the ceremony sequence in a same-day edit are not particularly different from those for constructing a full video. You will need to log and capture your footage, build a rough cut, refine it, and output it. That being said, there are certainly places where your editing decisions will be different in a same-day edit than when editing the full piece. For starters, it's unlikely you will spend as long logging the footage (though some editors are devoted to that practice and would argue that doing so actually saves time). Second, you simply won't have time to include shots that require too much post-production experimental tweaking. Finally, your same-day sequence should be on the shorter side. The saying "Keep your audience wanting more" is particularly applicable to reception guests!

Although the steps to building the same-day edit are basically the same as constructing a full video, the *purpose* of a same-day edit is very different. In the full video, the couple is likely to want most of the footage so they can re-hash every moment and make sure that the whole thing is recorded for the sake of history. A same-day edit, however, is designed merely to provide wedding guests and participants a flavor of the ceremony, not a repeat performance. After all, many of them were present at the ceremony itself and aren't interested in watching the whole thing twice. Just offer a few minutes of artistically rendered imagery using only the best shots. Often, the vows are a key component to a same-day edit. It is very likely that your camera, lavaliere microphone, and MP3 recorders captured better audio than the guests were able to hear in the first place!

Logistics

Depending on the location of the wedding events, it's unlikely that you will be able to get to your editing studio to provide a same-day edit. Even it is possible, you'll probably lose a lot of time in transit. Ideally, you should be set up for a portable edit. The bare minimum needed for a portable edit includes the following:

> ▶ A camera from which to import footage and its power supply
>
> ▶ A laptop loaded with editing software, sufficient drive space for the video files you'll be capturing (or an external drive), and the laptop's (and external drive's) power supply
>
> ▶ A cable to connect the camera to the laptop or, if you're shooting AVCHD or other card-based format, an SD card reader or the equivalent
>
> ▶ A mouse and mouse pad
>
> ▶ Headphones for laptop audio
>
> ▶ A DVD burner and blank media (if the output is to DVD)
>
> ▶ Power cords for the camera and the computer—don't count on the batteries lasting

Most likely, you will not use an external video monitor in a same-day edit. (Some videographers shoot with a field monitor that could be used, but the size and weight of these monitors make them rare on wedding shoots.) Because you won't be able to use a video monitor for reference when editing, be sure to get good color during the shoot by performing frequent white-balance operations. Also, use your video scopes frequently in post-production; they will serve as a decent guide (although they are certainly no replacement for watching an external monitor). Ideally, project titles will have already been created using an external video monitor and imported into the project.

Before the day of the event, scout out a location where you can settle down to edit the piece. Make sure the location has power outlets, will not be in the way of reception setup, and is relatively quiet. Although I don't particularly recommend it, if you have enough battery life, it's actually possible to perform the entire edit in your car—an unimaginable feat 15 years ago!

Engagement Video

Engagement videos tell the couple's courtship story. This can be achieved in lots of ways; a standard method is to interview the couple, either separately or together, and then shoot footage of their lives together in their home(s) or at a place that has meaning to them.

Engagement videos are a blast to create, offering loads of room for creativity and fun with your clients. Like a photo montage, they are often screened at the rehearsal dinner or the ceremony, but might also be created as a standalone video and presented as a menu item of the main wedding video.

Shooting an engagement video is helpful to you, the videographer, because it affords you an intimate view of your clients before the wedding. This knowledge of your clients will increase the odds of having an easy and comfortable wedding shoot, which will inevitably improve the quality of the footage. Similarly, establishing the main video's editing and style will be much easier when you have the chance to discover your client's humor, preferences, and boundaries.

Engagement videos are powerful marketing tools, showcasing your skills as a filmmaker. They give potential customers a chance to look at something besides the various wedding photos and videos with which they are inundated while selecting wedding vendors. Be sure to create versions for your own marketing purposes that can be posted online. (Get permission from the participants before putting any videos on your Web site.)

Shooting an Engagement-Video Interview

Although styles differ, I prefer shooting interviews of the couple individually. I find that the similarities and differences in the stories they tell can add humor to the final edit. Then, I shoot an interview with both the bride and the groom together. This additional footage showcases their style and manner as a couple, before the pressure and performance of the wedding day is at hand.

Unlike when you shoot the wedding day, you often have time to set up a flattering shot when shooting an engagement video. Consider using studio lights if available (as described in Chapter 7, "The Big Day") and arranging for a naturally well lit and quiet place. Set up lavaliere microphones so that interview dialogue is captured at the highest quality possible.

When you are interviewing the couple, ask questions that will lead them to tell you stories about themselves and their courtship. These might include the following:

- ▶ How did you meet?
- ▶ When did you know you wanted to get married?
- ▶ How did you propose?

Make sure to get answers that are complete sentences so that editing is easier. For example, if the question is "Where did you get engaged?" the answer "We got engaged at the beach" is more usable as a standalone sound bite than "At the beach." By carefully phrasing your questions, you can get more in-depth answers that are likely to come in complete sentences. For example, saying "Talk about your first date," or "Describe your engagement," will likely result in your getting a good story, not just a dangling clause. Ask the bride and the groom some of the same starting questions for good editing options, but allow their answers to guide the interview conversation.

One important trick to interviewing on camera is to allow the speaker to continue until they are completely finished before speaking again. This will introduce a pause between the interviewee's last thought and your next question. While awkward, this pause is necessary and serves two purposes. First, it makes for easier editing, because the speakers won't overlap each other and you will have a few seconds of room tone to play with. Second, interviewees will often continue storytelling to cover the awkwardness of the pause—and quite regularly, the funniest, best, and most engaging material comes from these afterthought sound bites.

Shooting Additional Engagement-Video Footage

There may be a particular event that the bride and groom want you to capture, such as an engagement party. If not, create an event so that you can obtain footage of them together: walking the dog at the park, going to a quiet beach or lake, or drinking wine on the porch. Use their interests and personalities to dictate what footage you might obtain.

If budget and time allow, it can be highly amusing to obtain additional footage of the couple interacting with their friends and family. Like the wedding itself, these people's comments will add warmth, personality, and depth to the video—even if the comments are off the cuff or said in jest.

Putting the Engagement Video Together

While engagement videos tend to be short and sweet, there are no specific guidelines for creating them—which is why they can be such fun. You can get some input from your clients about length and music preferences, but for the most part, putting the video together in a way that introduces the couple effectively and with visual appeal is a creative exercise for you. Use titles, photos, and music to enhance your storytelling. Like the final video, your client should specify the format in which they want the engagement video to be given to them.

Concept Video

More expensive and time consuming, concept videos are often a harder sell. As well as the expense, they tend to require more active participation on the part of the clients and potentially the involvement of their friends and family. If you can show potential clients how unusual your product is and what fun they can have in its creation, however, concept videos can be a creative outlet and a lucrative niche for your business.

Concept videos are usually outside the regular wedding budget. Such services are often purchased by friends or family as a gift to the couple or by one half of the couple for the other—which is important to consider if you are marketing these videos.

Concept videos are typically very short—aim for five minutes or less to make it a feasible job, a realistic price, and a video that is brief and fun enough that the couple will want to show it off to their friends and family. Concept videos could be used on the couple's wedding Web site, be loaded on a phone, be screened at the couple's reception, or open their wedding video.

While concept videos differ from each other tremendously—indeed, that's the whole point—here are some ideas to get you started:

- ▶ An advertisement for the couple's wedding to put on their wedding Web site
- ▶ A staged newscast with stunning headlines about the couple being engaged
- ▶ An investigative news report about the mysterious symptoms that afflicted the groom when he met and fell in love with the bride
- ▶ A *Sliding Doors*-style movie about what would have happened if circumstances changed slightly and the couple never met
- ▶ A humorous re-enactment of the couple meeting and courting
- ▶ A typical date night of the couple—with or without some hijinks thrown in
- ▶ A series of interviews of friends and family about the couple
- ▶ A documentary, or mockumentary, about the planning of the couple's wedding

Although they can turn into elaborate affairs, a concept video can also be a quick and inexpensive adventure. For example, you might follow the bride and groom to their favorite restaurant or shoot one of them talking to the other on camera. Have smaller concept-video ideas on hand for couples who might be intrigued by the idea but put off by what might feel like a large production or unrealistic expense.

Putting a concept video together is much more like creating a narrative or feature film than a wedding video, which relies on documentary-style shooting. Concept videos tend to be somewhat scripted and staged, offering the opportunity to shoot and reshoot, getting multiple takes from which to edit.

Pre-Production

A video that involves a storyline will need to be scripted. Your script might be very loose and require improvisation on the part of some of your "actors," or may be very detailed and require memorization. In addition, you may need to storyboard your video. A storyboard uses a series of images to graphically represent a movie sequence to help you visualize the end result. Storyboards can be simplistic indicators of a storyline and scenes, drawn in pencil on the back of a napkin (see Figure 11.11), or they can be meticulously crafted using dedicated software, showing every camera angle and movement. Either way, the point of a storyboard is to allow you, the director, to organize your shoot, determining what types of shots and angles you will need to obtain at each location. This can be very useful for planning an efficient shoot; in fact, some directors would say they are shooting in the dark without it. Make sure you have a basic script and/or storyboard well before the shoot begins so that you can figure out the best location(s) for the shoot.

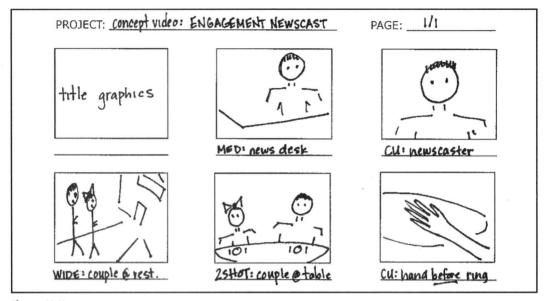

Figure 11.11
Notice that a storyboard doesn't need to be well-rendered or pretty to be useful—even just the beginning of this crudely drawn storyboard offers a lot of information about the shoot locations and angles.

 A three-minute video might have four scenes with three different locations. Having a storyboard will help you plan the best order to shoot those locations, which might be different from the chronological order in which they appear in the video. Similarly, your storyboard will help you choose angles from which to shoot. For example, if you know you will shoot a wide establishing shot and then move to a close-up for the first scene, you will want to open the second scene with, say, a mid-range shot for visual variance.

Concept videos require the active participation and enthusiasm of your clients. Because the details about your couple is what will make this video unique and funny, it's important that at least the bride or the groom—or perhaps close friends and family—are in on the creative brainstorming as you do the pre-production.

While you will rely on content input from your clients, make sure to guide the scriptwriting process yourself since you are the one with filmmaking experience. Weigh in on script decisions that involve locations, effects, and angles, as you will be the one running the shoot. Stick to simple locations, and avoid having too many of them. Define a time limit to the shoot, such as a half-day, and make sure the script is of a manageable length to shoot in that time.

Typically, the more detailed your script and storyboard, the faster your shooting will go. But if you have a couple who is dynamic, funny, and not afraid of the camera, you might want to forego a traditional script and let them play on camera. As a director, use your judgment about how much pre-production preparation will be needed.

Shooting

With some experience behind you shooting weddings, you will most likely find that a staged shoot feels easy. All of a sudden, the light is more controllable, and you can capture multiple takes in case an airplane flies overhead, ruining your audio. With that in mind, aim for simple and well executed instead of fanciful and unrealistic.

On the day of the shoot, bring everything you would normally bring to a wedding shoot, as well as a simple light kit and microphone stand. Remember that your clients are paying for the experience of making a movie as well as the final product, and it's unlikely that they are professional actors. Get the best footage you can, but remember to have a fun time while you do.

Editing

The process of editing a scripted piece is the same as editing a wedding video: Log, capture, rough cut, refine, and output. When editing a piece that has a script and multiple takes, however, the goal is to collect the best version of every shot as opposed to finding good shots and creating a story around them. The logging process is especially important when you are looking at multiple takes of the same shot; analyzing and labeling different takes will save time as you place the shots in the sequence. With a detailed script, a rough cut can come together quickly; find the best takes from your logging efforts and put them together in the order of your piece.

A concept piece is more likely to be dialogue driven than most wedding videos. Consider this in your editing style; it might be a good idea to use a radio edit for your rough cut, locking the audio down first. With your rough cut on the timeline, spend some time massaging the edit points. You will find that how the dialogue is spaced and where you put the pauses can dramatically change the humor or tone of a scene. Use filters as described in Chapter 9, "Advanced Editing," to smooth out the discrepancies between audio takes.

After the rough cut is complete, you can massage timing, transitions, and cutaways. The information in Chapter 9 should help guide the refinement of your rough cut into a fun, unique, and professionally crafted piece that will highlight your clients' personalities—and showcase your skills.

Personalized Web Page

Offering clients a customized Web page to host their highlights video can be an excellent way to both develop a revenue stream and market your own services. Clients are thrilled to have the opportunity to easily show their friends and guests their wedding. In turn, your work gets lots of exposure—much of which will be aimed at the couple's friends, who are likely to be planning weddings of their own.

There are several ways to host a Web page for your clients. One is to build a customized page on your own Web site; another is to set up a whole new site with a new domain for them. Your decision may be based on how your own site is built and how Web savvy you are. If you make a new site for every client, you will have to control a large number of domains; however, you will have a very easy time building customized pages on simplistic Web-development programs (such as iWeb or the Web-based weebly.com) that often come with free or cheap hosting. If you make your client pages part of your own site, you might have some added design and architecture issues to contend with; on the other hand, domains and hosting will already be taken care of.

Regardless of the architecture you use to put up Web pages for your clients, make sure your client pages include the following:

- The highlights video from the wedding
- Any text content that the clients want, such as thank yous or a copy of their vows
- Design elements that showcase both the wedding and your skills as a visual artist
- A link back to your own site (Don't lose this golden marketing opportunity!)

Like your videos, your Web pages can be as elaborate as your imagination and skills, and will serve as a fun way to make additional income from your customers.

Other Ideas

As you consider ways to expand your services, the ideas presented in this chapter are a good place to start; it has been shown that there is a market for these products. Don't feel limited, however, to using ideas that are already in the marketplace. In fact, what will make your business stand out will likely be innovative ideas that are fresh takes on what is already out there.

Consider both your skills as a videographer and your clients' requests when you think about expanding services. For example, if you have a bride who is worried about getting enough of her friends talking on camera, offer to bring a second camera to the reception and set up a dedicated interview area. Provide the bride a compilation of everything her guests said to her on a separate interview sequence. Or if you prefer editing to shooting, offer to edit the rehearsal dinner footage shot by the groom's dad. Thinking creatively about the features your clients want and the services you especially enjoy delivering will enable you to build a line of customized products and services to further define your wedding-videography business.

Summary

Often, offering services that go beyond basic wedding coverage will make you the wedding videographer that stands out. There is tremendous room to showcase your creativity, film-making skills, and business savvy in add-on services. In this chapter, you learned about some areas into which wedding videographers have successfully expanded their traditional services: photo montages, engagement videos, same-day edits, concept videos, and video hosting. Let this list be a starting place for your own ideas about where to take your business. Remember: Add-on services are a place to capitalize on your own interests and talents!

Next Up

It's true! You've made it! You've built a business, obtained some clients, shot, edited, and output some videos, and developed your business! Congratulations. As any business owner will tell you, though, the work is never done. In the next chapter, you'll learn some strategies for keeping your business running smoothly so that you can focus as much of your energy as possible on the video aspect of your work.

Chapter 11 Tutorial: Making a Photo Montage

This tutorial teaches you to build a photo montage using the editing skills you developed in Chapters 8 and 9. To complete this tutorial, you will need a copy of Adobe Premiere Pro, and you will need to copy the files from the DVD accompanying this book to your computer hard drive. Instructions for downloading a trial version of Adobe Premiere Pro and copying the files on the DVD to your hard drive are found in the Chapter 4 tutorial.

To begin this tutorial, navigate to Wedding Video_Start to Finish > Chapter 11 and launch Adobe Premiere by double-clicking the 11_Engagement Montage project file in the Chapter 11 folder. Allow the scratch disks to be set to your Documents folder at the dialog box prompt.

Open the Sequences bin in your Project panel and notice that it has five starting sequences and one final one. In this tutorial, each step will build upon the next. You can build one sequence, start to finish, or use the starter sequences to perform individual tutorials. The finished sequence can be used as a reference.

Mark the Music

Our first step of the montage is to mark the music over which we will be adding photographs. To begin this exercise, double-click the (empty) sequence titled Mark the Music_start in the Sequences bin to open it in the Timeline panel and Program panel. Then follow these steps:

1. Open the Music bin in the Project panel and double-click the icon for the Build It for Me track to open it in the Source panel.

2. In the Source panel, play the music from the beginning. At each downbeat, click the Unnumbered Marker button along the bottom of the Source panel or press the asterisk key above the numerical keypad on the right of your keyboard to add an unnumbered marker. Alternatively, instead of playing the music and noting the beat, you can navigate to each of the following time codes and add a marker using the same method.

02:05	04:15	06:24	09:01	11:10	13:20
16:00	18:12	20:21	23:01	25:09	27:20
30:00	32:14	34:20	37:03	39:18	41:23
44:03	46:09	48:19	50:25	53:04	55:16

If you add a marker by mistake and you notice it right away, select Edit > Undo or press Command+Z (Mac) or Ctrl+Z (PC). If you need to remove a marker later, after having performed other editing steps that you don't want to undo, navigate to the marker by selecting Marker > Go to Clip Marker > Next or Previous and delete it by selecting Marker > Clear Clip Marker.

3. Click the speaker icon at the bottom of the Source panel and drag the music track to the beginning of the timeline to add it to your sequence.

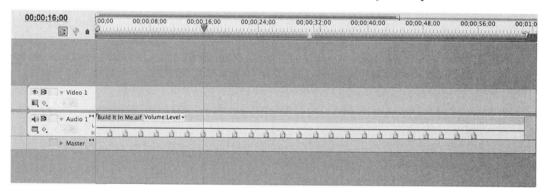

4. Save your work.

Build a Rough Cut

Our next step will be to bring all our photos onto the timeline. Continue with the sequence you built in the preceding section or open the Build a Rough Cut_start sequence in the Project panel's Sequences bin. Then follow these steps:

1. In the Project panel, display the contents of the Photos bin by clicking its triangle.

2. Bring all the photos to the timeline, placing the first photo at time code 09:01 (the fourth marker). You can do this in a number of ways, starting by dragging your playhead to 9:01:

> ▶ In the Project panel, double-click the photo you want to add to display it in the Source panel. With the playhead positioned at 9:01 (or with an in point selected at that location), press the comma (,) key to insert the photo using an overlay edit.

> ▶ Use your mouse to drag a photo from the Project panel to the timeline, releasing the mouse button when the photo is aligned with the playhead.

> ▶ Select all the photos in the Project panel, drag them to the timeline, and release them when the first photo is aligned at 9:01. Dragging all the clips to the sequence at once is called a *storyboard edit*.

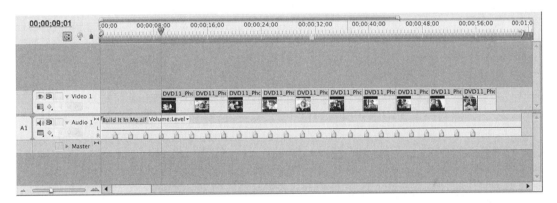

If you add the photos all at once, they will appear in the timeline in the order they are listed in the Project panel. In some cases, you may need to do some rearranging to place them in the correct order. Do this by dragging the photos around in the timeline with your mouse.

STORYBOARD EDITING WITH ADOBE PREMIERE PRO'S AUTOMATE TO SEQUENCE FUNCTION

Premiere Pro has further streamlined the storyboard edit process with the Automate to Sequence function. This function not only enables you to bring all the clips onto the timeline at the same time (as described in the preceding section) but refines the process by allowing you to specify certain parameters such as the order and placement of the clips, the type of edit, transitions, and whether to ignore either audio or video. To use this function, select the photos (or clips) to be put on the timeline in the Project panel; then choose Project > Automate to Sequence. A dialog box opens, where you can customize the aforementioned parameters. This can be a very quick, handy method to use in simple photo montages in which each photo is shown with identical parameters, but it isn't as flexible if you want to use different transitions and durations. For more on the Automate to Sequence function, check Adobe's help file or see the excellent tutorial at www.adobetutorialz.com/articles/1680/1/Edit-storyboard-style.

3. Now we are going to change the duration of each clip slightly so that the edit points are on the markers we noted, synchronizing the photos changing with the musical beats. With the exception of photos 7 and 10, each photo should last the duration of two markers, or approximately five seconds.

4. The Rolling Edit tool will lengthen and shorten two clips simultaneously such that the duration of both together remains constant. This is handy to make the edit points between photos land exactly on music markers. To select the Rolling Edit tool, press the N key on your keyboard or click its icon in the Toolbox (the pointer with two arrows on each side, and the fourth icon from the top).

5. To use the Rolling Edit tool, place the tool over an edit point in the timeline (between two images) and click to drag the edit point right or left. In this case, roll each edit point such that

▶ The first photo starts at time code 09:01.

▶ All the photos last for two markers (approximately five seconds) except photos 7 and 10.

▶ Photo 7 extends the duration of one marker (approximately two seconds and 15 frames) from time code 37:03 to time code 39:18.

▶ Photo 10 extends to time code 58:00, a duration of nine seconds and 11 frames.

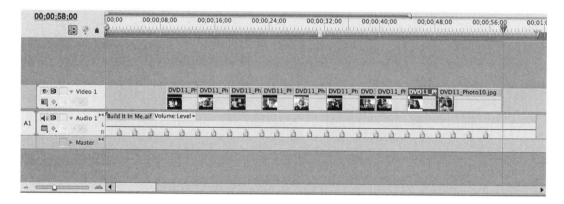

 To determine how long a clip on the timeline (in this case a photo) is, click the clip in the timeline to select it and then press Command+R (Mac) or Ctrl+R (PC) to open a dialog box that displays clip durations. You can also change clip durations in this dialog box.

6. Review your work by playing it back in the Timeline and Program panels.

7. Save your work.

Add Transitions

We will now add transitions at the edit points of the sequence. Continue with the sequence you built in the preceding section or open the sequence titled Add Transitions_Start in the Project panel's Sequences bin. Then follow these steps to add a 10-frame cross-dissolve transition at every edit point (except between photos 2 and 3 and 3 and 4):

1. Click the Effects tab, which is behind the Media Browser (the fifth panel that we have not used much). Alternatively, open the Effects tab separately by navigating to Window > Effects.

2. In the Effects tab, select Video Transitions > Dissolve > Cross Dissolve.

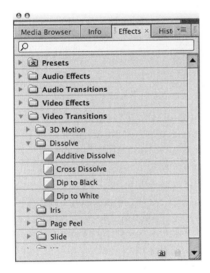

3. Click the Cross Dissolve icon and drag it to the timeline, letting go of the mouse button when the pointer is over the edit point between photo 1 and photo 2. Play the section of video to see the transition effect.

4. To change the length of the transition, begin by double-clicking the transition in the timeline. You might have to enlarge your view of the timeline to click on the transition; to do so, use the Scale slider in the bottom-left portion of the Timeline panel.

5. The transition appears in the Effect Controls tab located in the Source panel. Change the Duration setting to 10 frames by clicking the Duration text field to make it active, typing **10**, and pressing the Enter key on your keyboard.

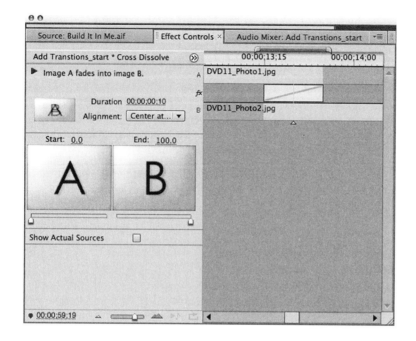

6. Instead of applying a transition in each point, we will take a shortcut, copying and pasting the first transitions onto the other edit transition locations. Press the V key on your keyboard to return the pointer to the Selection tool. Then select the transition in the timeline and choose Edit > Copy or press Command+C (Mac) or Ctrl+C (PC) to copy it.

7. Paste the transition to every edit point on the timeline (except between photo 2 and photo 3 and between photo 3 and photo 4) by placing the playhead on the appropriate edit point and selecting Edit > Paste or pressing Command+V (Mac) or Ctrl+V (PC). Note that instead of dragging the playhead, you can use the Page Down key to easily jump to the next edit point.

Next, we will add a 30-frame fade-in to the beginning of the clip and a 30-frame fade-out to the end. Follow these steps:

1. Click the Effects tab, which is behind the Media Browser (the fifth panel that we have not used much). Alternatively, open the Effects tab separately by navigating to Window > Effects.

2. In the Effects tab, choose Video Transitions > Dissolve > Dip to Black.

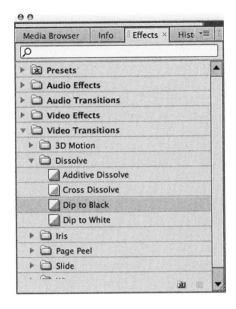

3. Click the Dip to Black icon and drag it to the timeline, letting go of the mouse button when the pointer is over the beginning of Photo 1. Play the first photo to see the transition effect.

4. Assuming you haven't changed Premiere Pro's default transition duration, the length of the transition should be one second, or 30 frames, which is what you want. If you need to adjust the length of the transition, begin by double-clicking the transition in the timeline. You might have to enlarge your view of the timeline to click on the transition; to do so, use the Scale slider in the bottom-left portion of the Timeline panel.

5. The transition appears in the Effect Controls tab, located in the Source panel. Change the Duration setting to 30 frames, or 1 second.

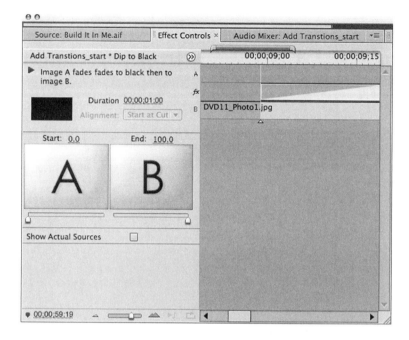

6. Now we will copy and paste the same transition to the end of the piece. To begin, select the opening Dip to Black transition in the timeline and copy it by selecting Edit > Copy or pressing Command+C (Mac) or Ctrl+C (PC).

7. Put the playhead at the end of last photo and paste the transition to the end of the sequence by selecting Edit > Paste or pressing Command+V (Mac) or Ctrl+V (PC). Rather than dragging the playhead to the last clip, you can simply press the End key on your keyboard, which will move the playhead to the end of the sequence.

Note that you can add your default transition to multiple edit points by selecting the target clips and choosing Sequence > Apply Default Transitions to Selection. You can specify the default transition by right-clicking any transition in the Effects pane and choosing Set Selected as Default Transition (the cross dissolve is the initial default transition). If you want to change the transition duration before applying the default transition, use the Video Transition Default Duration setting in the Preferences window shown in Figure 11.8.

Finally, we will cut photos 3 and 4 into three shorter clips each so that we can later change their size. Follow these steps:

1. Select the Razor tool by pressing the C key on your keyboard or by clicking its button in the Toolbox (the fifth button from the top).

2. Make two cuts in photo 3 and two cuts in photo 4 by clicking with the Razor tool at the following points on the timeline:

   ▶ Photo 3: 19:18 and 20:21

   ▶ Photo 4: 24:02 and 25:10

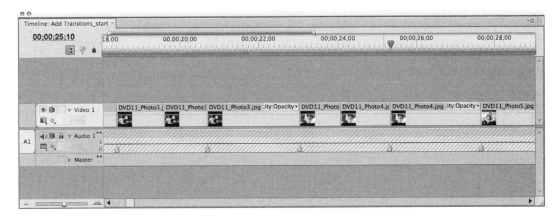

The new clips formed are referred to as photo 3a, photo 3b, photo 3c, photo 4a, photo 4b, and photo 4c, respectively, throughout this tutorial.

3. To avoid accidentally making more cuts, return to the default Selection tool by pressing the V key on your keyboard or clicking the arrow button in the toolbox.

4. Preview your work. Notice that you can't tell that photos 3 and 4 have been cut into three sections each. That will become obvious when you make the changes detailed over the next two sections of this tutorial.

5. Save your work.

Change Basic Motion Parameters and Add Filters

We will now change some basic motion parameters and add filters. Continue with the sequence you built in the preceding section or open the sequence titled Change Motion Add Filters_start in the Project panel's Sequences bin. Then follow these steps to change the starting size of each photo (we will add animation, or shrinking and growing, in the next tutorial):

1. Double-click photo 1 in the timeline to open it in the Source panel.

2. Click the Effects Control tab in the Source panel.

3. Click the Motion triangle to reveal the basic motion parameters.

4. To change the scale (or size) of the first photo, enter a new number for the Scale setting. In this case, change the scale to 55.

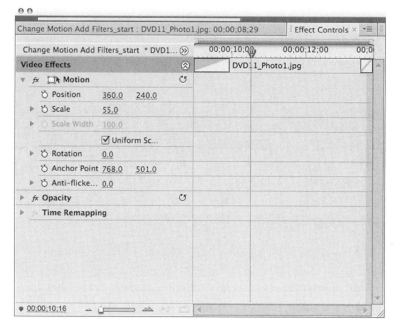

5. Review the change of scale by looking at the photo in the Program panel.

6. Repeat steps 1–5 to change the size of the remaining photos. Use the following values as input for the scale parameter:

   ▶ Photo 1: 55

   ▶ Photo 2: 60

   ▶ Photo 3a: 40

   ▶ Photo 3b: 50

   ▶ Photo 3c: 60

   ▶ Photo 4a: 40

   ▶ Photo 4b: 50

- ▶ Photo 4c: 60
- ▶ Photo 5: 70
- ▶ Photo 6: 65
- ▶ Photo 7: 60
- ▶ Photo 8: 70
- ▶ Photo 9: 70
- ▶ Photo 10: 60

Now that the clips are scaled correctly, we will add a Black & White filter to photos 3a, 3b, 3c, 4a, 4b, and 4c by following these steps:

1. Click the Effects tab, which is behind the Media Browser (the fifth panel that we have not used much). Alternatively, open the Effects tab separately by selecting Window > Effects.

2. In the Effects tab, choose Video Effects > Image Control > Black & White.

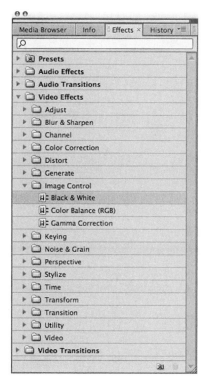

3. In the timeline, use the default Selection tool to draw a marquee around photos 3a, 3b, 3c, 4a, 4b, and 4c.

4. In the Effects tab, click the Black & White icon, drag it to the selected clips in the timeline, and release. Play the clips to see the Black & White effect.

Add a Gaussian Blur filter to photos 3a, 3b, 4a, and 4b by following these steps:

1. Click the Effects tab, which is behind the Media Browser (the fifth panel that we have not used much). Alternatively, open the Effects tab separately by choosing Window > Effects.

2. In the Effects tab, choose Video Effects > Blur & Sharpen > Gaussian Blur.

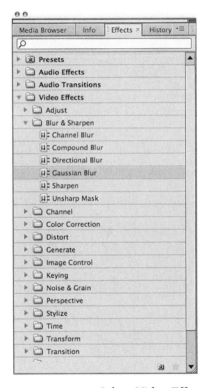

3. Select Video Effects > Blur Effects > Gaussian Blur.

4. In the timeline, press and hold the Shift key on your keyboard and click photos 3a, 3b, 4a, and 4b.

5. In the Effects tab, click the Gaussian Blur effect icon, drag it to the selected clips in the timeline, and release.

Finally, adjust the Gaussian blur amounts:

1. Double-click photo 3a to open it in the Source panel.

2. Click the Effect Controls tab in the Source panel.

3. Click the Gaussian Blur triangle to display the effect parameters.

4. Change the Blurriness setting to 30.0 by clicking the Blurriness text field to make it active, typing **30**, and pressing Enter.

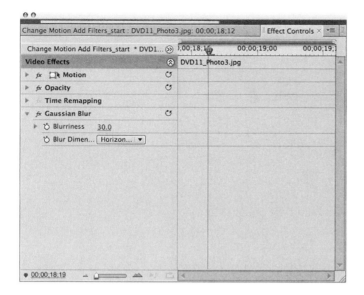

5. Repeat steps 1–4 for photo 3b (Blurriness = 15), photo 4a (Blurriness = 30), and photo 4b (Blurriness = 15).

6. Preview the clips to see the Gaussian Blur effect.

7. Save your work.

Animate Motion

We will now animate the motion of some of the photos. Continue with the sequence you built in the preceding section or open the sequence titled Animate Motion_start in the Project panel's Sequences bin. Then follow the steps in this section to make the photos move slightly across the screen. We will start by animating the scale—that is, changing the size of the photos as the sequence plays. Note that we will animate the scale of photos 1, 5, 8, 9, and 10.

1. In the Timeline panel, put the playhead on the first frame of the first photo. (Note that it is black; this is because we reduced the opacity by adding a Dip to Black transition earlier in this tutorial.)

2. Double-click the first photo to open it in the Source panel.

3. Click the Effect Controls tab in the Source panel.

4. If you don't see the timeline area to the right of the effects, open it by clicking the Show/Hide Timeline View button, which is a circle with two arrows pointing to the left on the upper-right corner of the Effect Controls panel.

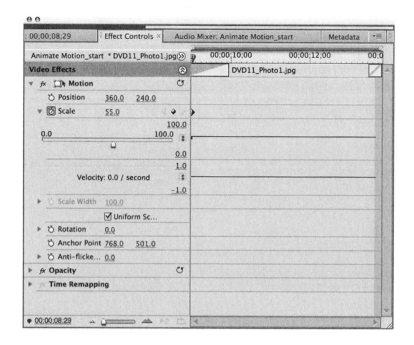

5. If necessary, click the Motion triangle to reveal the parameters. Notice that the scale is 55, as designated in the preceding exercise.

6. If necessary, click the Scale triangle to reveal options for the Scale parameter.

7. Click the toggle animation button to the left of the Scale effect to activate keyframing options.

8. Add a keyframe to the first frame of the clip by clicking the Add/Remove Keyframe button (the diamond-shaped button to the right of the Scale setting, which has the value 55). This effectively tells the program that at this frame, the scale of the image should be 55, and it will change (increase or decrease) from here. We will set another keyframe at the end of the clip, and the motion will be built, or interpolated, between the two points that we have designated.

You remove a keyframe the same way you add one: by clicking the Add/Remove Keyframe button to the right of the Scale setting. Don't do it now, though, because we need that initial keyframe.

9. On the timeline, navigate to the last frame of the photo 1's ending transition. It should be five frames past the last image of the clip before the transition begins. An easy way to get there is to press the Page Down key on your keyboard, which takes you to the first frame of the next clip, and then press the left arrow key on your keyboard to move back one frame to the last frame of the previous clip.

10. In Effect Controls panel, change the Scale setting to 65. (Click in the Scale field, type **65**, and press Enter.) Note that Adobe Premiere Pro creates a keyframe at that location. When keyframes are enabled for a specific effect, Premiere Pro creates a keyframe anytime you move the playhead to a new location and adjust any parameter for that effect.

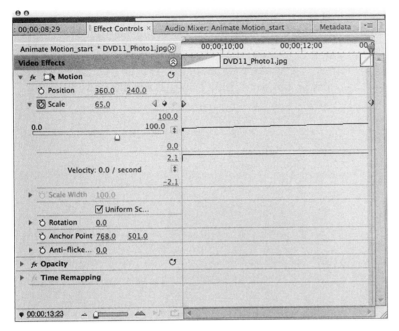

11. Click the small left arrow next to the diamond-shaped keyframe marker in the Scale parameters of the Effects Control tab to navigate back to the first keyframe.

12. Play the clip and watch the photo grow in scale.

 In this exercise, we keyframed the motion through the transition to create more smoothness between photos. You can end animation at any point on a clip, however; it does not need to be the end of the clip or the clip's transition.

13. Repeat steps 1–12 for clips 5, 8, 9, and 10 using the following scales:

   ▶ Photo 5: Start 70, end 60

   ▶ Photo 8: Start 70, end 55

   ▶ Photo 9: Start 70, end 60

   ▶ Photo 10: Start 60, end 70

14. Preview the sequence to see your scale animation at work.

Next, we will animate the motion—that is, change the position of the photos as the sequence plays. Note that the motion of photos 2, 5, 6, 9, and 10 will change.

1. In the timeline, put the playhead on the first frame of the fifth photo's transition.

2. Double-click photo 5 to open it in the Source panel.

3. Click the Effect Controls tab in the Source panel and open the Motion disclosure triangle if necessary. Notice that the rotation is at a default setting of 0.0.

4. Click the toggle animation button to the left of the Rotation effect to enable keyframes for that effect. If necessary, click the triangle next to the Rotation setting to reveal keyframing options for the Rotation parameter.

5. Change the Rotation setting to −5.0.

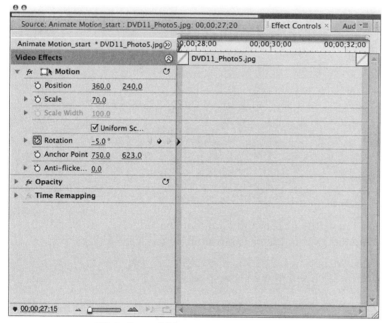

6. Click the Add/Remove Keyframe diamond to add the first keyframe.

7. On the timeline, navigate to the last frame of photo 5's ending transition. It should be five frames past the last image of the clip before the transition.

8. Change the Rotation setting to 5.0.

9. Click the small left arrow next to the diamond-shaped keyframe marker in the Scale parameters of the Effects Control tab to navigate back to the first keyframe.

10. Play the clip and watch the photo rotate.

Let's try that again for photo 6, but this time we will change the center of the image instead of the rotation:

1. In the timeline, put the playhead on the first frame of the transition leading into photo 6.

2. Double-click photo 6 to open it in the Source panel.

3. Click the Effects Control tab in the Source panel and click the Motion triangle to view the parameters if necessary. Notice that the Position setting is in the default 360 (x axis), 240 (y axis).

4. Click the toggle animation button to the left of the Position effect to enable keyframes for that effect. If necessary, click the triangle next to the Position setting to reveal keyframing options for the Position parameter.

5. Change the value for the Position setting's x axis to 300. (Click in the first text field to the right of the Position effect, type **300**, and press Enter.) Leave the y axis set to 240.

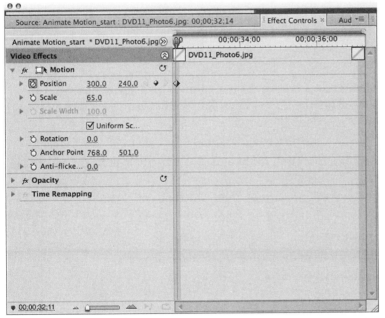

6. Navigate to the last frame of photo 6's outgoing transition in the timeline.

7. In the Position parameters of the Effect Controls tab, change the Position setting's x axis to 410; leave the y axis set to 240.

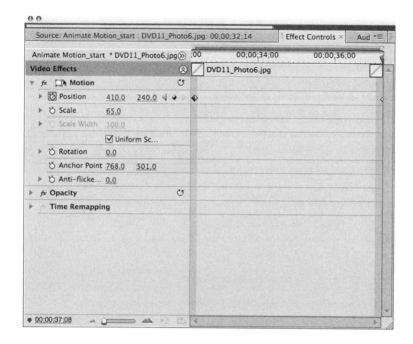

8. Click the small left arrow next to the diamond-shaped keyframe marker in the Scale parameters of the Effects Control tab to navigate back to the first keyframe.

9. Play the clip to watch the photo move across the screen.

10. Repeat the steps in this section for photos 2, 9, and 10, making the following changes:

   ▶ Photo 2: Position starts at (340, 180), ends at (340, 290)

   ▶ Photo 9: Position starts at (325, 145), ends at (340,180)

   ▶ Photo 10: Rotation starts at −5, ends at 5

11. Review the sequence from the beginning to see your work.

12. Save your work.

 If you want to add titles to your photo montage, see the tutorial in Chapter 9 for instruction. There's space for titles at both the beginning and the end of the sequence.

Chapter 12
Maintaining Your Business

In this chapter:

▶ Equipment maintenance
▶ Client maintenance
▶ Business trends

Even the most talented videographer can't run a busy, lucrative, and competitive business without regular attention to everyday operational efforts. Like most things, an ounce of prevention is worth a pound of cure: A busy post-production can't preclude marketing for the upcoming year; likewise, regular use of your equipment requires regular maintenance to avoid malfunctions. This chapter provides some techniques and information for keeping your business running smoothly so you can spend the majority of your time and effort on the art of videography.

Equipment Maintenance

The major start-up costs involved in wedding videography are those associated with your equipment. For that reason, it's of particular importance that you keep your equipment in the best condition possible—both to ensure working gear when you need it and to prolong the life of your equipment.

Camera Maintenance

The environmental hazards most likely to affect your camcorder are moisture, dirt, and temperature. Your camcorder's function depends on the complex movement of delicate parts; particles of dirt and moisture can interrupt smooth usage. And temperature changes can expand, contract, freeze, or melt the internal pieces. For these reasons, it's imperative that you store your camcorder in a dry place, at room temperature, at all times.

Unfortunately, you will likely have to shoot in environments that are bad for your camera on occasion: at the beach, in the rain, under the baking-hot sun. In any adverse condition, the most important thing to remember is to avoid opening the cassette-tape door or the card slot; both cover the delicate sensors on the equipment. Load fresh, empty media to begin the shoot, and go indoors when you need to change it out. If contaminants do make it inside the camcorder casing, do your best to clean them off as soon as possible to avoid a buildup. Use compressed air or cloth wipes to deal with particulates, or use a blow dryer on a low setting to handle moisture. As tempting as it may be, do not dismantle any part of your camcorder to better access the dirt and grime. Doing so will invalidate any warranty you have on the camera, and a deep cleaning is best left to the experts anyway.

 A detailed sidebar on shooting in the rain can be found in Chapter 7, "The Big Day."

For regular maintenance, you'll want to do the following on a regular basis:

> ▶ **Clean your camera lens.** Use soft tissue or specially made lens wipes. Your fingers have oils on them that can be damaging, and regular cloth may scratch your lens.

> ▶ **Clean the cassette heads.** If your camcorder uses cassette tapes, make sure to clean the cassette heads on a regular basis (a good rule of thumb is every three months or so). This requires a head-cleaning cassette tape, which literally wipes dirt off the heads with a mildly abrasive cleaning ribbon. Insert the cleaning tape into your camcorder (or deck) and press Play; allow the cleaning tape to play for about 15 to 30 seconds before ejecting.

If you notice that you camera is having problems that extend beyond regular maintenance such as incorrect color or trouble with the LCD (to name a few of the more common ones), you may have to send it to the dealer or manufacturer for repairs. Ask them to send you a temporary replacement if this occurs during wedding season so you don't have to pay for a rental.

Computer Maintenance

Like your production gear, your post-production gear will need a bit of love and consideration. That includes your computer, your monitor, and your software, all of which should run smoothly with just a wee bit of regular attention.

Drives

Drives used to be a major line item in the wedding-videography–business budget. With storage space becoming cheaper and cheaper, however, drives are less of a financial burden. But just because they have become easier to obtain doesn't lessen the video editor's dependence on them; data drives hold your entire business in their delicate arms, so it's important to keep your computer and its drives (internal and external) in the best condition possible.

Virus Protection

When it comes to your computer, a primary maintenance task is protecting it from viruses. A virus is a program that can copy itself and infect a computer by harming its data or functional performance. A true virus must be self-replicating, but other types of malware, or malicious software, can affect your computer. Virus protection is a significantly bigger issue for PC users than for Mac users; although both types of computers can become infected, the vast majority of viruses are aimed at PCs.

Virus protection comes in several forms, all of which should be diligently applied:

> ▶ Make sure to only open e-mail attachments if you know and trust the sender, as that is the primary transmission method of malware.

> ▶ As discussed in Chapter 10, "Output and Delivery," regularly back up all your drives. That way, in the event your computer becomes infected by a virus, your system can more easily be recovered.

> ▶ Invest in good anti-virus software, which will detect known viruses, and update it regularly to combat new viruses.

Even if you run anti-virus software, it's imperative that you use caution with attachments and regularly back up your data. That's because there are viruses from which anti-virus software can't protect you.

Defragmentation and Cleanup

In addition to protecting against viruses, you should also defragment drives on a regular basis to keep them running efficiently and to prevent crashes. (Note that this is required on Windows systems; on Macs running OS 10.2 or higher, defragmentation is unnecessary, as the operating system doesn't allow fragmentation of files in the first place.)

When your system saves files, Windows stores the information files in an empty space on the hard drive, called a sector. If the sector is too small to hold the whole file, the bits that don't fit are saved in the next available sector. When you open the file, Windows must access all its various bits from the sectors in which they were saved to reconstruct it, which can be time-consuming. Defragmenting your system puts these files back together, storing them in contiguous sectors. This enables the drive to access information more easily, thus improving drive speed and reducing the likelihood of problems or crashes.

Windows computers also include a utility called Disk Cleanup. This utility determines which files on the computer may no longer be needed and deletes them (after giving you the option to review the files to ensure that they are indeed unneeded) in order to free up space on the drive. Although user input in the cleanup process is minimal, it is worth noting that the analysis process can take awhile, especially for very full drives.

Backing Up and Archiving

As discussed in Chapter 10, backing up and archiving your projects is a crucial step in the video-production process. If you tend to be lazy about performing these tasks during the post-production phase of work (and you certainly wouldn't be alone), be sure to schedule regular backup sessions to ensure that you have an additional copy of everything you have created in case your computer or drive crashes.

With or without regular post-production backups, scheduling regular archiving sessions is smart, since it's important that you also duplicate your administrative files such as accounting data, client lists, and calendars. In the event of a computer malfunction, your business could grind to a halt without this crucial data! There are software programs available to help you easily create backup systems, complete with regularly scheduled reminders.

Monitor

Not all monitors display color in the same way. To produce the best images possible, you must calibrate your monitors so that the colors you see are true to the colors that will appear when you play back your video on a TV monitor or another—hopefully calibrated—computer monitor.

Various applications are available that enable you to easily calibrate your computer monitor. Some of the better color calibration applications come with a colorimeter, a mouse-like device that is attached to or dangles in front of the monitor to read colors sent from calibration software and determine their accuracy—that is, whether the color being sent as "red" is really red. If the monitor is off, the calibration software will create a compensatory scale, or matrix, called an ICC (International Color Consortium) profile.

It's also important to calibrate your external video monitor—a slightly more complicated process. While you should follow the specific instructions for your monitor's make and model, the basic steps for calibrating any NTSC monitor are as follows:

1. Turn your monitor on and let it warm up for approximately 30 minutes.

2. Make sure the monitor is not receiving any glare and that room lights are low.

3. Use your image-editing program to run NTSC SMPTE color bars (you can usually find them in the Generated Video pop-up menu). These consist of seven tall vertical bars, seven short bars lined up directly underneath, and six wider bars lining the bottom (see Figure 12.1).

Figure 12.1
NTSC SMPTE color bars.

4. Engage your monitor's Blue Only function, which will make the top seven bars appear as three dark bars and three light bars.

5. Adjust the hue so that the three dark bars are the same color. Adjust the saturation so that the short color bar is as close as possible in color to the tall color bar above it. Hue and saturation affect each other, so there will be a dance between these two calibrations.

6. Underneath the sixth bar of seven (the red one) is the fifth bar of six of the bottom row, which is divided into three narrow columns that should be grey. Adjust the brightness so that the leftmost of the three bars is black, blending in with the fourth, wide black bar to its left; the middle bar is as close to that black as possible; and the rightmost bar is dark grey.

Color calibration should be done before you use your equipment for the first time, and then several times per year as maintenance.

Software

Most likely, your image-editing software will have regular downloadable updates. Stay abreast of these updates by running online update checks, reading the software publisher's Web site or e-mails, or from user groups of which you may be a part. Keep in mind, however, that just because the software has an update does not mean you want to immediately install the new version. For starters, upgrades often have bugs. You might want to wait for other users to demo the software upgrades and read any reviews online before you dive in. This is particularly true if the updated software doesn't contain new features that you need right away.

When considering whether to upgrade your software, remember that projects saved in an earlier version will open in a later version, but the opposite is not always true. That is, programs saved in a later version often will not open in an earlier version. To avoid compatibility issues, make sure you won't want to revert to an earlier version of the software when you do decide to upgrade. Maintaining software version compatibility is crucially important if you have multiple systems or work with other editors on the same projects.

Similarly, when considering upgrading operating-system software, make sure you know for sure that your editing application (and any other post-production peripheral applications you use) will still run, and run smoothly. Reading online forums, reviews and your own software manufacturer's Web site will help you determine whether upgrading is a good idea. Although it's true that in general, updating is useful and can improve how your system runs, there is no reason to fix something that isn't broken—or worse, break something that isn't broken. Proceed with updates only after you have done the appropriate research, *not* the minute an upgrade becomes available.

Client Maintenance

Wedding vendors are often careless with their clients, viewing them as one-time customers as opposed to an ongoing clientele. This attitude can be costly in terms of opportunities lost. Just as your equipment requires ongoing care, your client base does, too. Although it's unlikely that you will shoot a second wedding for a single customer (though it has certainly happened!), your previous clients represent the best pathway to new ones. Their siblings, cousins, and friends are reason enough to keep in touch with them. Furthermore, satisfied customers might be a source of additional videography jobs if you are inclined to move your business in new directions. The marketing avenues you'll take with former clients are slightly different from those taken with new wedding clients (discussed in Chapter 2, "The Business of Weddings"), but they are arguably much easier because they already know—and presumably like—you.

Here Comes Your Guide

Your former clients represent your best opportunity to obtain feedback about your business. After all, well before you hand over your final video, they will have become experts in wedding vendors. Find out from them what aspects of your product and services they appreciated most and what they would change. This input could be extremely valuable information when it comes to developing and structuring your business. Don't shy away from negative feedback; only those vendors who are willing to learn and grow in the industry will have a long future in it.

Ask satisfied clients with whom you enjoyed working to provide testimonials for your Web site and to write positive reviews of your services for Web sites such as www.weddingwire.com, www.yelp.com, and www.citysearch.com. If you are conscientious about treating your couples well both throughout and after their event, they will surely return the favor. But no matter how much they liked you and your services, don't expect that kind of support without prompting; it simply won't be on your clients' minds, even if they are happy to do the favor.

There are many ways to go about soliciting this information. One is to simply casually ask your clients. Depending on the personalities involved, you may be able to set up an informal discussion on this topic with your clients after you have submitted your work, but this is both hard to arrange and likely to be sugar-coated. One alternative is to send them a formal survey to fill out via e-mail. Chances are if you use this approach, your clients will answer your questions more candidly, increasing the odds that you'll get the information you need. Structure your survey carefully using categories such as filming style, editing style, business relationship, day-of professionalism, etc.

Various Web sites enable you to create your own Web-based survey. Two examples of such Web sites are www.surveymonkey.com and www.polldaddy.com, both of which allow you to customize the look and feel of your survey to match your company branding. As you start gathering more and more data, you will be able to see trends in the responses and address the ones that seem to be problems across the board.

As an example, I know one videographer whose brides repeatedly reported frustration that his product took so long to get into their hands, even though it was well within the time frame he had specified in their contract. These brides wanted to show off their wedding while they were still in the afterglow from the event and while it was still fresh in their guests' minds. To address this, he started churning out highlights videos first—within two weeks—so his clients would have something to enjoy immediately (almost). This tactic bought him more time to finish the final product, without having to change his contracted finish date and risk missing deadlines. Getting the highlights out so quickly was no small feat; he was forced to hire an assistant to help with the logging and capturing process, which represented a significant business change. But having a delighted bride proudly show a highlights video to all her girlfriends is about the best marketing a videographer could hope for. It's safe to guess that the assistant he hired to make it happen more than likely paid for himself—and then some.

Often, what someone likes best about your product or service is the same thing someone else likes the least. For example, one bride might provide feedback that you "put everyone at ease with [your] irreverent humor," while another might describe you as "crass and rude." One bride might describe your video piece as "romantic and beautiful," while another might call it "cheesy and drawn out." The point of using surveys is to look at trends, not to take any one piece of criticism (or praise) too seriously.

Marketing to Former Customers

The key to marketing to your former clients is staying in touch. That way, when their friend needs a videographer—or you need a reference—the connection is already in place. As mentioned, conducting a survey is an excellent way to start that post-wedding communication. Moving forward, consider sending a regular e-mail newsletter to your clients to let them know what is new and exciting in your company. You can personalize your communications by sending anniversary cards or small gifts (you do, after all, know their wedding date!) or sending a note after shooting at the venues they used. A quick e-mail to a particular bride to say you were thinking of her as you shot at her wedding venue might be the warm reminder she needs to pass along your phone number to her recently engaged girlfriend.

Social marketing tools, discussed in Chapter 2, are another easy way to maintain connections with your customers. Make sure to include them on all your social networks. Whether for posting a project of which you are particularly proud or asking a question about a specific venue, using your network will deliver fast answers and enable you to maintain easy, informal contact with your clients—which will undoubtedly lead to jobs, either directly and indirectly.

Other Event Videography

Maintaining relations with your former clients is critical if you decide to expand your business. As a wedding videographer, you have the skills and equipment to handle lots of event videography—baptisms, bar and bat mitzvahs, graduations, corporate parties, awards ceremonies, retirement parties, sports events, and concerts or recitals. Although wedding videography is by far the biggest of these markets, opening yourself up to other work will diversify your skills and could increase your business revenue. This is especially relevant if you are concerned about surviving the off-season for weddings. Former wedding clients may provide you the opportunity to determine whether you want to work in these markets—or just provide a bit of additional income—without requiring you to engage in a large marketing effort or expense.

Business Trends

In a business like videography, which is based on rapidly changing technology, it's crucially important that you stay up on the latest trends. As discussed in Chapter 1, "The World of Wedding Videography," client expectations have changed enormously as technology in the world of video and video delivery has changed. Making your business flexible enough to adapt to—or, ideally, anticipate—these changes will give you a competitive edge in your market.

Watch Video

It's important to watch other wedding videos, both for inspiration and to pinpoint where your work falls in the spectrum of what is available. Understanding your niche in the market is invaluable for marketing efforts. Furthermore, if you are looking to make changes in your business, an understanding of the local wedding video industry and its different players will help you determine the demands and elasticity of the market in which you are operating.

Every wedding videographer worth his or her salt will have a Web site with demos. Wedding videos can also be found on YouTube and on the WEVA site (www.weva.com). Chances are, the wedding videographers you like the most are the ones most likely to post new work often; visit their sites regularly to see what they're up to. As mentioned earlier, one of the biggest challenges of wedding videography is keeping your videos looking fresh and new in the face of an unchanging storyline, and exclusively watching your own work will dig you deeper into a rut. Watching videos by other videographers will help lift you out; use their work as inspiration to experiment with new shots, effects, music styles, and themes.

Take inspiration from everything you watch, not just weddings. As you learn the art of editing, it will be hard—for a while at least—to watch any video without carefully considering the cuts, transitions, effects, and soundtrack. Although this can be somewhat annoying, try to use your new editing-sensitive eyes to look for styles and effects that you can incorporate into your work. Using techniques from music videos, documentaries, feature films, and even commercials will prevent your videos from getting weighed down by wedding-video clichés and conventions; try ideas you've never seen in wedding videos and see if they work. One of my favorite effects is to use a wide shot cropped and broken into duplicated vertical stripes— an effect I borrowed from a British television program about a mentalist.

Use Your Outreach as Input

Chapter 2 discussed a lot of marketing methods and how to get your name out there as a wedding vendor. It's also important to use these methods, such as bridal fairs, magazines, and online outlets to stay current on what's going on in the wedding industry. Like every other industry, the wedding industry experiences trends, which, among other things, are reflected in the styles of dresses, photography, cakes, and colors that couples choose.

While wedding videography is arguably more affected by video trends than by wedding trends, staying on top of your industry and knowing what couples are looking for is integral to maintaining your business. Marketing materials must showcase a look and style that potential clients want to emulate, not remember with a grimace. The videos you show must reflect new looks and current styles; otherwise, prospective clients will assume that your video skills are old and stale, too. Keeping on top—or even ahead—of the latest styles, fads, and trends will help you showcase the pieces that will be appealing to your clients. Having said that, you must avoid falling victim to gimmicky trends. Your own style must prevail; it is what you are selling. Finding a balance between staying true to your instincts and keeping an eye on current styles is a challenge of the job, but hopefully one of the more fun ones to tackle!

Thinking about what couples are looking for will also help shape your marketing efforts. For example, when a particular venue gains popularity for staying open until the wee hours, you'll want to try to get on their preferred vendor list by providing demos with flashy and fun dance sequences instead of slow and dreamy romantic sequences.

Technology Trends

As mentioned in Chapter 1, technology trends dictate changes in wedding videography more dramatically than wedding trends do. In just a few decades, wedding videos have evolved from two-hour, single-take affairs, to condensed, stylized, and highly edited HD pieces. But the changes won't stop there; wedding videographers are increasingly incorporating stylized shooting methods, elaborate effects, and advanced output into their work. Staying on top of these trends could make you the videographer in your market that stands out. Whether it's a film-look effect, a steadicam, or your output to Blu-ray, knowing what the options are ahead of the curve will help you to invest your resources correctly.

One problem for videographers is that they work in a void. In charge of the whole production, they lack exposure to other people in the video-production field, which can stunt the development of skills. It's important to connect with other shooters and editors to learn (and teach!) new skills and emerging technologies. Joining a local professional association can be valuable for building professional connections that will help you stay on top of your field. Similarly, reading online forums, product reviews and industry news will keep you on top of technologies and trends with which to experiment.

Summary

Wedding videography is not for the faint of heart. It's hard work, both on a day-to-day basis and over the long haul. This chapter includes lots of techniques, tips, and ideas to keep your business growing. You don't want to work for just a season or two; instead, you want to build the foundation for a steady, lucrative, and long-term business that will grow and evolve with you and with the industry.

In Conclusion

In Chapter 1, I warned that wedding videography is not an easy business. Presumably, having gotten through this last chapter and having gained some practical experience along the way, you agree. But having been in the industry for more than 10 years, I also know that with this line of work comes tremendous joy—in the independence that comes with running your own business, in the excitement of production, in the creative expression of post-production, and in the industry's continual innovation, exploration, and evolution. The wedding industry is never stagnant—and you can't be either!

Wedding videography is unique in that it requires so many different skills—which can seem daunting at times! Just accept that you like some aspects of the job better than others. You are certain to find aspects of wedding videography that you love, in which you shine, and on which you can focus lots of your time and energy.

I hope this guide has given you some practical skills for the creation of both your business and your products, but also some inspiration to build a business that can grow, flourish, and be a source of joy to you and your clients.

Glossary

A

activated: Also called selected. Describes the state of a button on an authored DVD that has been selected by the user.

anamorphic: A technique of squeezing a widescreen image into a standard 4:3 aspect ratio.

animation: An illusion of continuous motion created by the careful placement of discrete keyframes.

aperture: The opening through which light is passed to the camera lens. The amount an aperture is opened determines the amount of light allowed in and contributes to the exposure of the image.

aspect ratio: The ratio of width to height in a video or film image. Typical aspect ratios include 4:3 (standard definition) and 16:9 (high definition).

authored DVD: A DVD that contains files that will play in a DVD player, and is likely to contain options for user interaction.

AVCHD (Advanced Video Codec High Definition): A type of video compression that allows high-definition video images to be stored on camcorder hard drives or flash drives.

B

backlight: A light used to illuminate the subject from behind.

backtiming: An editing method that uses the last frame of a clip as the determining factor of the length and/or placement of the clip.

bird's eye angle: A camera angle obtained by placing the camera above the scene and shooting down.

bit rate: Also called *data rate*. The rate at which data is transferred from one point to another. In audio and video compression, bit rate is used as a measure of quality. The more data per second of playback, the higher the quality of the compressed file.

Blu-ray: An optical disc medium offering high-density storage to accommodate high-definition video files.

bridal video: A type of wedding video that highlights the bride only. It may singularly focus on her preparations for the wedding or can include other footage showcasing the day and her personality.

C

camcorder: A portable, single device that contains both a camera and a video recorder.

capturing: The process of transferring video from a camcorder to a computer.

CCD (charged coupled device): A chip found in digital camcorders that converts light to electronic signals that can be stored on tape or drive memory.

chrominance: The portion of a video signal that defines color.

cinematic: A wedding video style that incorporates heavy dramatization and stylization, made possible through a variety of production and/or post-production techniques.

CMOS (complementary metal-oxide semiconductor): An alternative to CCD sensors, CMOS sensors are smaller, use less power, and generate less noise and heat. Their conversion of light to electronic signal, however, is considered to be less refined than that of the CCD sensors.

compositing: The combination of multiple visual elements.

composition: The placement or arrangement of visual elements within the video field.

concept video: A type of wedding video that incorporates a story or narrative, as opposed to a straightforward documentary.

CPU (central processing unit): A hardware component of a computer that interprets instructions and processes data in order to run software.

cut-away: An image that is inserted into a sequence of continuous footage.

D

data rate: *See* bit rate.

depth of field: A measure of the depth, or distance, at which an image comes into focus.

digital zoom: An enlargement of an image that occurs through the enlargement of each pixel in the image. This can severely degrade image quality.

diversity: The incorporation of two antennae on the receiver portion of a wireless microphone. True diversity implies the incorporation of two radio receivers as well as two antennae.

documentary: A wedding video style that involves a straightforward rendition of the wedding events, usually in chronological order.

dolly: An advanced camera technique that involves placing the camera on a cart (or other moving vehicle) to enable smooth movement of the camera in relation to the subject.

dolly zoom: An advanced camera technique that combines the smooth physical movement of the entire camera in relation to the subject with a zoom of the camera lens.

drag-and-drop: An non-linear editing function that allows clips to be dragged onto the timeline using the mouse. Often, though not always, drag-and-drop is a crude editing method used for a rough cut.

drop-frame time code: A type of time code that allows a specified amount of NTSC footage to match the same amount of time on a clock by dropping a few time code labels while leaving all the frames of footage intact.

Dutch tilt: A camera angle obtained by tilting the camera to one side so that the horizon is on an angle.

E

EIS (electronic image stabilization): A method to reduce the shake or motion in a camera by electronically shifting the image.

engagement video: A type of wedding video that highlights the story of the bridal couple's relationship.

equalizer (EQ): A tool to alter audio frequencies in order to change sound levels and properties.

exposure: The process of allowing light into the camera to produce a recorded image.

extreme close-up: A type of shot that encompasses the subject across the whole frame, often so close that the entire subject will not fit.

extreme wide shot: A type of shot that is so wide it may not have an obvious subject. Often used to establish context.

eye-level angle: A camera angle that is generally neutral, appearing to the viewer as a real-world or expected perspective.

F

fill light: A light used to illuminate the areas of a scene that might otherwise be in shadow.

filter: An effect that can be applied to a piece of footage to change its properties.

finalization: A process that closes the recording state of a DVD so that it can be read in other devices.

FireWire: Apple's name for the IEEE-1394 specification, which is a high-speed serial interface that attaches DV cameras and storage devices to a computer.

fit-to-fill edit: *See* four-point edit.

flash memory: A type of rewriteable memory storage that has no movable parts, found in computer peripherals and camcorders.

focal length: A measurement (in millimeters) expressing the distance between a camera lens and the focal point, or the point at which an image comes into focus on the camera sensor.

follow: A camera move that has the camera following the subject at a roughly constant distance.

four-point edit: A non-linear edit function that places a clip in the timeline by specifying in and out points in the clip and on the timeline, even if the durations aren't equal. Also called *fit-to-fill*.

frame accurate: Describes a device, usually a camera deck, that can accurately perform an edit on a specific frame as opposed to being off by a few frames.

frame rate: The number of video frames, or discrete images, shown per second.

G

gain: The amplification of a signal.

gamma point: A luminance measure that represents the midpoint between an image's black and white levels.

H

handle: Frames left at the beginning and end of a selected clip to allow room to edit the footage later, if need be.

hard drive: Hardware that holds and spins a magnetic or optical disk and reads and writes digital information on it, used for both internal and external computer data storage and on some camcorders.

HDMI (high definition multimedia interface): An audio/video interface for transmitting uncompressed digital data.

HDV (high-definition video): A video format that can record high-definition video on standard DV tapes, using MPEG-2 compression.

headroom: The visual space between the top of a subject and the top of the video frame.

Hertz: A unit measuring frequency in cycles per second.

high angle: A camera angle that shows the subject from above, with the camera pointed down.

high definition (HD): A general term for a video signal with increased resolution, which provides greater detail and clarity to the image. This typically refers to video shot or delivered at a resolution higher than 720×480.

highlighted: Describes the state of a button on an authored DVD that the user's cursor or remote control selector is pointing to.

highlights: A wedding video style that incorporates only a fraction of the images shot, resulting in a short piece that showcases the most interesting and memorable portions of the wedding day.

histogram: A bar graph used to represent the tones of an image.

hot shoe: An accessory holder on the top of a camcorder that allows a flash or other accessory to be stably mounted.

I

image sensor: A device inside a digital camera that, through different mechanisms, will convert an optical image to an electric image.

insert edit: A type of edit that allows a piece of footage to be added to a sequence without losing or covering anything already in the sequence, instead moving existing media forwards or backwards to accommodate the new addition.

interlaced: A process of scanning video whereby one frame of video containing half the horizontal lines (e.g., even-numbered lines) is scanned followed by a frame of video containing the other half of the horizontal lines (e.g., the odd-numbered lines), adding up to a complete video frame.

interpolated: The construction of data points, or video images, between keyframed parameters, as performed by editing or animation software.

J–K

jump cut: An edit in which two different views of a similar subject are placed next to each other, interrupting visual continuity. Can also refer to any visually jarring edit.

keyframes: In an editing program, keyframes are frames with defined parameters; animation can then be interpolated across the intervals between. In a compressed file, keyframes are frames encoded using spatial, but not temporal, techniques.

key light: The primary light source used to illuminate a subject.

L

lavaliere microphone: Also called a *lav* or *lapel microphone*, this small microphone is attached to the subject's clothing with a clip so it can be used hands free.

LCD (liquid crystal display): A flat panel used to display electronic information with a relatively low power requirement. Most camcorders have an LCD screen to enable you to view the image being captured.

LED (light emitting diode): Electronic lights known for low power consumption, small size, and durability.

lens: An optical device that transmits and bends light rays to converge on a certain point or, in the case of a digital camcorder, on a sensor.

letterbox: A method to show widescreen images in standard video formats while preserving the original aspect ratio.

line-level audio: A term used to describe the strength of an audio signal.

logging: The process of making identifying notes about video clips in preparation for capturing or editing.

low angle: A camera angle that shows the subject from below, with the camera pointed up.

luminance: A measure of the brightness of an image in terms of black and white.

M

master shot: Also called a *safety shot*, a type of shot that is wide and static.

master shot–style coverage: An editorial style of developing a rough cut that builds one primary view of the subject.

matte: A tool used to composite, or combine, images.

medium close-up: A type of shot that shows a person from about the shoulders up.

medium shot: A type of shot that shows a person from about the waist up.

MiniDV: A videocassette format compatible with DV and HDV cameras.

mini jack: A common audio connector and port, cylindrical in shape.

monopod: A single pole or stick used to support a video camera and prevent movement in the vertical plane.

MPEG-2: A standard compression format for DVDs.

MPEG-4: A video standard that includes the H.264 codec, which is used for Blu-ray discs and many different streaming formats.

multi-camera editing: A technique that synchronizes several angles of the same scene, while allowing the editor to choose the view actually shown in an edited sequence.

multiclip: A video clip that contains the data from several synced camera angles.

multiplexing: Also called *muxing*. The joining of several files into one, an integral part of building authored DVDs.

N

neutral-density filter: A camera filter that reduces the amount of light striking the sensor by nearly uniformly absorbing light.

noise: An undesirable feature of some image capture, characterized by unusual variance in luminance and chrominance data.

non-linear editing: A type of video editing that permits random access to any given piece of footage.

normal: Describes the state of a button on an authored DVD that the user's cursor or remote control selector is not pointing to.

normalize: To increase the volume of an audio file uniformly to the maximum level possible without distorting any audio in the file.

O

OIS (optical image stabilization): A mechanism used in a video camera to reduce the shakiness or motion of the camera by moving the camera lens in direct response to the camera motion.

optical zoom: An enlargement of an image that occurs by zooming in with the camera lens, as opposed to simply enlarging the image electronically during or after capture.

overlapping edit: Also called an *L-cut*, an overlapping edit is one in which the audio moves at a different point than the video.

overlay edit: A type of edit that places one piece of footage over another, essentially deleting the first.

P

pan: A basic camera technique that refers to horizontal movement, either left or right.

PCMCIA (Personal Computer Memory Card International Association): An international standards body that developed and promoted the PC card, a computer peripheral designed for storage but used for other devices.

pedestal: A basic camera technique that refers to the movement of the whole camera vertically with respect to the subject while maintaining a constant angle.

photo montage: A type of wedding video that shows a series of still images set to music, often shown at the rehearsal dinner or wedding reception.

pixel: A dot that represents the smallest element of data contributing to a digital image.

point of view: A type of shot that shows the view from the subject's perspective.

progressive: A method for displaying video in which the entire frame is shown at one time, with no fields (in contrast to interlacing).

R

rack focus: A camera technique that involves shifting the focus of an image from one subject to another or from the foreground to the background in order to direct the viewer's attention.

radio edit: An editorial style of developing a rough cut that builds the piece around an audio track.

RAID (redundant array of independent disks): Multiple hard drives that are banded together to build a faster and more secure drive through data replication and sharing.

RAM (random access memory): A type of temporary computer memory that allows the computer to perform tasks. The amount of system RAM is a primary determinant in computer speed with respect to data processing

receiver: The portion of a wireless microphone that picks up the signal transmitted from the subject. The receiver must be connected to the camcorder or other recording device in order to record the audio.

rendering: While editing, the process of putting into effect any edits made to a particular clip or region of a clip so the editor can preview the edits more precisely. At the end of the project, the process of creating an output file from the sequence edited on the timeline.

resolution: A measure of the amount of detail, or data, that an image holds.

RGB parade: A scope that displays the red, green, and blue color data in an image.

ripple: An advanced editing tool that extends or shortens a clip, moving all other footage on the timeline backward or forward, respectively, to accommodate the change.

ripple delete: An edit function that both removes a clip and closes the gap created by removing the footage behind the deleted footage.

roll: An advanced editing tool that changes the edit point between two clips so that the first clip will get longer or shorter and the second clip will do the opposite to preserve the combined length of the two clips.

rough cut: A first, or preliminary, draft of a video piece.

S

same-day edit: A type of wedding video in which the ceremony is quickly edited to be shown at the reception, on the same day. Providing a same-day edit requires editing expertise as well as highly detailed logistical planning.

scrubbing: Dragging the playhead through a source clip or timeline to quickly preview the audiovisual elements of the clip or timeline.

shoot-only: A type of wedding video in which the raw footage is provided to the clients, with no editing performed.

shutter speed: The length of time that the shutter is open, allowing light exposure to a camera sensor.

simulator: Also called a *previewer.* A tool used in DVD authoring programs to allow review of the DVD as it would be seen on a DVD player, before the DVD is multiplexed.

slide: An advanced editing tool that moves the middle clip of three forward or backward, adjusting the first and last clips to accommodate the change while preserving the combined length of the three clips.

slip: An advanced editing tool that moves the start and end point of any one clip without changing the length of the clip itself.

snap: A tool in image or video-editing software that gives a magnetic property to image components or clips, facilitating precise alignment.

spatial redundancy: A type of video compression that groups blocks of similarly colored pixels together within an image in order conserve data storage space.

standard definition (SD): Video that is 720×480 resolution or smaller.

steadistick: A mechanism that allows a camera to be supported by the user's body, providing a steadier image during shots that involve motion.

storytelling: A type of wedding video style whose storyline is driven by an audio narrative. A storytelling-style wedding video is similar to a documentary-style video in its straightforward nature.

subclips: Clips that are sections of a larger clip, created so the editor can work with them separately from the larger master clip.

superimpose edit: A type of edit in which a piece of footage being placed on the timeline automatically occupies the next available track above the current edit and at the same length.

S-video (super video or separate video): An analog video transmission standard that separates luminance and chrominance signals.

T

tally light: A small light that indicates when a camera is recording.

telephoto lens: A camera lens that magnifies the subject, with a longer focal length and narrower field of view. The opposite of a wide-angle lens.

temporal redundancy: A type of video compression that groups similar pixels together over a sequence of frames in order to conserve data storage space.

three-point edit: A type of edit that involves adding a clip to the timeline by specifying in and out points in either the source clip or the timeline and then specifying a start or end point (in or out) in the other.

tilt: A basic camera technique in which the camera angle changes in the vertical plane (i.e., up and down).

time code: A numeric sequence used to label frames of video.

time-lapse video: A video technique that captures frames of video at designated intervals so that in playback, the events captured appear accelerated in time.

timeline: A graphical representation of a video sequence, shown chronologically.

track: A camera technique in which the camera moves while maintaining a constant distance from the subject.

transferring: The process of bringing logged, digital files into a non-linear editing system.

transmitter: The portion of a wireless microphone, whether the microphone is worn or held by the subject, that sends a signal to the receiver for recording.

turnkey system: A combined hardware and software editing system that is ready to go out of the box.

two-shot: A type of shot that includes two people as the subject—usually, though not always, from the torso up.

U

UHF (ultra high frequency): A spectrum of audio signals from 300–3,000MHz.

USB (universal serial bus) 2.0: A standard that allows data transfer and communication between a computer and peripherals, often used as a video interface for delivering camcorder images to a computer drive.

V

vectorscope: A graph that provides chrominance image data.

VHF (very high frequency): A spectrum of audio signals from 30–300MHz.

video card: A card typically inserted into a computer that enables the display on a monitor.

W

waveform monitor: A graph that provides luminance image data.

white balance: A color-calibration method for a camcorder. When you define "white," systemic changes can be made to display other colors accordingly.

wide-angle lens: A camera lens that diminishes the subject, with a shorter focal length and wider field of view. The opposite of a telephoto lens.

wide shot: A type of shot that encompasses enough scenery that it could show a person from head to toe.

X–Z

XLR: A generic term for a 3-pin audio connecter, often used to connect external microphones to camcorders.

Zebra stripes: Stripes shown on an image in either a camera or image-editing software that indicate when specified luminance levels are met or exceeded.

Index

3190105053017l